A Brighter Future

A Brighter Future

Improving the Standard of Living Now and for the Next Generation

Richard P.F. Holt and Daphne T. Greenwood, Editors

With a Foreword by Robert H. Frank

M.E.Sharpe
Armonk, New York
London, England

The EuroSlavic fonts used to create this work are © 1986–2014 Payne Loving Trust.
EuroSlavic is available from Linguist's Software, Inc.,
www.linguistsoftware.com, P.O. Box 580, Edmonds, WA 98020-0580 USA
tel (425) 775-1130.

Library of Congress Cataloging-in-Publication Data

A brighter future : improving the standard of living now and for the next generation / edited by Richard P.F. Holt and
Daphne T. Greenwood ; foreword by Robert H. Frank.
    pages cm
  Includes index.
  ISBN 978-0-7656-3488-7 (hardcover : alk. paper)—ISBN 978-0-7656-3489-4 (pbk. : alk. paper)
  1. Cost and standard of living—United States. 2. Income distribution—United States. 3. United States—Economic
conditions. I. Holt, Richard P.F., 1953– II. Greenwood, Daphne T., 1949–

  HD6983.B775 2014
  339.4′70973—dc23   2013046490

Printed in the United States of America

The paper used in this publication meets the minimum requirements of
American National Standard for Information Sciences
Permanence of Paper for Printed Library Materials,
ANSI Z 39.48-1984.

∞

GP (c) 10   9   8   7   6   5   4   3   2   1
GP (p) 10   9   8   7   6   5   4   3   2   1

To the memory of
Nelson Mandela

If you wish to achieve the impossible, you must attempt the absurd
—Miguel de Unamuno

and

To my students
Who bring me hope for a Brighter Future

—RH—

****

To the memory and inspiration of my grandmother, Tirzah Roberts McCandliss

and

My son, Scott David Magee

—DG—

Contents

Foreword

ROBERT H. FRANK

People have always had a tendency to long wistfully for the "good old days." Yet for most of the past two centuries, each generation's standard of living was unambiguously better than their parents'. Life spans were increasing steadily, as were real wages. Education levels were rising sharply. Dramatic progress was occurring in racial and gender equality. Similar advances were taking place in public sanitation and infrastructure. And although the early days of industrialization often brought increases in air and water pollution, the last 100 years have seen striking improvements on that front as well.

There were good reasons, in short, for believing that people's nostalgia for better days gone by was largely misdirected. No longer. GDP per capita is still growing, but much more slowly and unevenly than in the past. CEOs of large US corporations, for example, saw their pay increase tenfold over the past three decades, while the inflation-adjusted hourly wages of their workers actually fell during the same period. Savings rates have declined significantly, and the middle class is awash in debt.

American infrastructure is also crumbling. Roads are often riddled with potholes, and engineers rate tens of thousands of bridges as structurally unsound. Water supply and sewage systems fail frequently. Countless schools are in serious disrepair. Many Americans live downstream from poorly maintained dams that could collapse at any moment. Funding has been cut for programs to lock down poorly guarded nuclear materials in the former Soviet Union. Proposals to build new infrastructure, such as high-speed rail systems or a smart electric grid, consistently fail in Congress. On these and countless other urgent problems, our political system seems almost completely paralyzed.

In this pathbreaking volume, Ric Holt and Daphne Greenwood have enlisted an extremely talented group of scholars to share their thinking about how we might turn things around. Readers who study the chapters carefully will come away with a renewed sense of optimism. Collectively, their authors make a compelling case that we can well afford what needs to be done. And they will persuade you that continued growth is fully consistent with environmental sustainability.

An important first step, according to Holt and Greenwood, is to think about our standard of living in terms far broader than traditional measures like per-capita income (the annual market value of all final goods and services produced within a country divided by its total population). For the United States, that was just under $30,000 in 1980 and just over $48,000 in 2011 (both figures in 2011 dollars). The real value of goods and services bought by Americans in 2011 was thus more than 50 percent higher than in 1980. But that does not mean we were roughly 50 percent better off in 2011.

One obvious problem, for example, is that many expenditures included in GDP reflect reductions, not increases, in our standard of living. When crime rates increase, people spend more on burglar alarms, purchases that clearly do not signal improved living standards. A similar objection applies when tasks once performed at home are now more often bought in the marketplace—as when time-pressed parents substitute meals at fast-food restaurants for home-cooked meals.

The bias that results from the inclusion of such expenditures in GDP works in the opposite direction from other known biases, such as one caused by inaccurate inflation adjustment. For all anyone knows, such distortions may roughly offset each other.

But as the chapters in this volume make clear, there are vastly bigger problems—ones that challenge the very foundation of the presumed link between per-capita GDP and well-being. Most important among them is the fact that GDP takes no account of how economic activity threatens environmental sustainability. And here by far the most worrisome problem is climate change.

Each new estimate from the scientific community is more pessimistic than the last. According to one highly respected global simulation model, there is a roughly one in ten chance that the average surface temperature of the earth will rise by more than 12 degrees Fahrenheit by the end of this century.

A temperature rise that great would melt the permafrost, releasing vast quantities of methane gas into the atmosphere. And since methane is some fifty times more potent a greenhouse gas than carbon dioxide, that would launch a cascade of events making wholesale destruction of life all but certain. Average temperatures will probably rise by some amount less than 12 degrees by the end of the century. But even the low end of the range of consensus estimates would entail astronomical losses to life and property.

A second major shortcoming of the traditional per-capita-GDP measure of our standard of living is the assumption of standard economic models that absolute income levels are the primary determinant of individual well-being. This assumption is contradicted by compelling evidence that context also matters. How much house do you need to be middle class? To demonstrate greater success? These questions simply cannot be answered without a suitably chosen frame of reference.

Surveys consistently reveal that when everyone's income grows at about the same rate, average happiness remains essentially the same. Yet at any given moment, wealthy people in any country are happier, on average, than poor people. Together, these findings suggest that relative income is a much better predictor of well-being than absolute income. Context REALLY matters.

In the three decades after World War II, the relationship between well-being and income distribution was not a big issue, because incomes were growing at about the same rate for all income groups. Since the mid-1970s, however, income growth has been confined almost entirely to top earners. Changes in per-capita GDP, which track only changes in average income, are completely silent about the effects of this shift.

When measuring the economic welfare of the typical family, the natural focus is on median, or 50th percentile, family income. But while per-capita GDP has grown by more than 85 percent since 1973, median family income has grown by less than one-fifth that amount. Changing patterns of income growth have thus caused per-capita GDP growth to vastly overstate the increase in the typical family's standard of living during the past four decades.

Some economists have advanced an even stronger claim—that there is no link, at least in developed countries, between absolute spending and well-being. Recent work suggests that this is especially true for spending categories in which the link between well-being and relative consumption is strongest. For instance, when the rich spend more on larger mansions or more elaborate coming-of-age parties for their children, the apparent effect is merely to redefine what counts as adequate.

Evidence also suggests that higher spending at the top instigates expenditure cascades that pressure middle-income families to spend in mutually offsetting ways. Thus, when all spend more on interview suits, the same jobs go to the same applicants as before. The average wedding in the United States now costs almost three times as much as in 1980, yet surely no one believes that today's marrying couples are substantially happier than their earlier counterparts because of that.

Those observations, however, do not imply that economic growth is irrelevant. On the contrary, greater levels of absolute income have been shown to promote many outcomes people value, even in the richest societies. The economist Benjamin Friedman argues that higher rates of GDP growth are associated with increased levels of social tolerance and public support for the economically disadvantaged. Richer countries also typically have cleaner environments and healthier populations than their poorer counterparts. Nonetheless, as many economists represented here show, many nonmarket aspects for a better standard of living such as public safety and climate stability do not necessarily improve with just market income.

That per-capita GDP is an imperfect index of economic welfare is of course not news. However, the authors in this volume will persuade you that its weaknesses are far more serious than most of us previously realized. They will also persuade you that a more comprehensive measure of our standard of living must take explicit account of how childhood poverty affects intergenerational mobility, and how our methods of production will be affected not only by growth in the stock of traditional capital, but also by growth in social and other less tangible forms of capital.

During a time of chronic budget deficits, readers might be forgiven for wanting to steer clear of a volume outlining a laundry list of expensive new problems that must be tackled. But while many of the steps we will need to take will indeed be costly, the best solutions in many cases generate external benefits that partly or wholly offset their costs.

Consider climate change. The simple reason that we spew too many greenhouse gases into the atmosphere is that nonpolluting alternatives are so costly. The most straightforward solution to this problem is to charge people in proportion to their emissions of such gases.

As we discovered from our experience with acid rain, wholesale cutbacks in pollution occur with surprising speed and efficiency whenever firms and individuals are forced to take external costs into account. Power companies in the Midwest were discharging large quantities of sulfur dioxide into the air during the 1960s and 1970s, which was precipitating out as sulfuric acid in rains over the Eastern states, causing large-sale destruction of forests and fisheries. More than twenty-five years elapsed between the time economists first recommended the establishment of a market for tradable SO_2 permits and the actual launch of such a market through amendments to the Clean Air Act in 1995. Following that step, air quality targets were achieved in a small fraction of the time and at a small fraction of the cost of achieving similar reductions through traditional regulatory means.

Similar policy measures promise to be similarly effective in the case of greenhouse gases. According to earlier estimates by the Intergovernmental Panel on Climate Change, a tax of $80 a metric ton on carbon dioxide would stabilize global temperatures by midcentury. But since more recent climate estimates have been more pessimistic, suppose we assume that a tax as high as $300 a ton might be required. Such a tax would cause the prices of goods to rise in proportion to their carbon footprints—in the case of gasoline, for example, by roughly $3 a gallon.

If phased in gradually, a tax of that magnitude would cause relatively little harm. Given sufficient lead time, manufacturers would develop substantially more efficient vehicles. But even from the existing menu of offerings, a motorist could trade in a 15-mpg Ford Explorer for a 32-mpg Ford Focus wagon, in the process completely escaping the effect of higher gasoline prices, even with no reduction in miles driven. Europeans, many of whom already pay $5 a gallon more than Americans do for gasoline, spend less per capita on gasoline than we do.

In short, the cost of preventing catastrophic climate change would actually be very small and would involve just a few simple changes in behavior. And the tax incentive required to induce those changes would generate much of the revenue needed to address many of the other problems discussed in this volume.

In the domain of infrastructure as well, the cost of moving forward is substantially smaller than portrayed by many pessimists. Austerity advocates are wont to say that we cannot fix our roads and bridges right now, because doing so would require government going deeper into debt. Just as a family must balance its budget, they say, governments must also ensure that current expenditures do not exceed current tax revenues.

But that advice makes no sense at all when applied to capital investment. Consider an indebted family faced with a decision to borrow $5,000 to pay a contractor to add additional insulation to its attic in the wake of an energy price increase. Austerity advocates would counsel against the move, noting that it would add to the family's indebtedness. But to know whether the move makes sense requires knowledge about how the family's energy costs would decline with the added insulation. If its monthly loan repayments to the insulation contractor were $50 for the next five years, for example, and if the resulting decline in its monthly utility bill would be larger than $50, then the investment makes compelling sense, no matter how much the family currently owes. Making the investment would improve the family's financial position in both the short run and the long run.

The same logic governs government spending to refurbish infrastructure. The question in almost every case is not whether to fix a road or bridge, but rather whether to fix it now or later. Each year road resurfacing is postponed, the cracks in the roadbed go deeper, causing significant increases in the cost of the job. Long-term interest rates are now still near record lows. If we wait, they will be higher. Many of the workers and machines required for infrastructure work remain idle as the economy continues to struggle to recover from the 2008 financial crisis. We will have to bid them away from other useful tasks if we wait. Materials prices are also near record lows in world markets, and they too will rise with further delay. In short, the case for an immediate, full-bore attack on our infrastructure repair backlog is completely compelling. The question is not, how can we afford to do it? Rather, we must ask, how can we afford not to?

There are still further grounds for hope. As I have argued in *The Darwin Economy* and elsewhere, one simple bit of fiscal alchemy could balance government budgets without requiring painful sacrifices from anyone. Countries should scrap their progressive income taxes in favor of much more steeply progressive taxes on consumption.

Families would report not only their income but also their annual savings, as many now do for tax-exempt retirement accounts. The difference—income minus savings—is the household's annual consumption. That amount less a large standard deduction—say, $30,000 for a family of four—is taxable consumption. Rates would start low, and most families would pay no more than before. But once consumption exceeds a certain threshold, rates on additional consumption would begin to rise sharply, topping out at much higher levels than under current income taxes.

The fiscal alchemy implicit in this tax is illustrated by the way it would change the incentives confronting a wealthy family that was considering a $2 million addition to its mansion. If this family faced the top marginal consumption tax rate of, say, 100 percent, its project would now require a $4 million outlay—$2 million for the project itself and $2 million for the additional tax. Like everyone else, the rich respond to price incentives (that is why they live in much smaller homes in Manhattan than in Dallas). If the tax led them and other wealthy families to scale back their additions by half, each family's total outlay would be no higher than before, and the government would collect $1 million from each project. And because it is only relative mansion size that matters, beyond some point, no rich family would be any less happy than it would have been.

Yet government would now have additional revenue to restore crumbling infrastructure. Can anyone doubt that driving a luxury sedan on well-maintained roads is a more satisfying experience than driving a slightly more expensive sedan on pothole-ridden ones? So even the very rich, who might imagine they would be harmed by a progressive consumption tax, would likely find the resulting package of private and public goods more satisfying than their current one.

It is an exciting time in economics and in the social sciences more broadly. Models that incorporate a greater range of human concerns are at long last receiving serious attention. And as the authors in this volume vividly demonstrate, these models open up promising new ways to think about the pressing policy problems that confront us.

It is tempting to dismiss the kinds of proposals they have put forward on the grounds that they may sound good in principle, but stand little chance of being adopted in our current political climate. Maybe so. But one thing that social scientists have learned is that changes in the political climate are extremely difficult to predict. Virtually no experts predicted the fall of the governments in the former Soviet Socialist Republics, nor did any predict the violent upheavals of the Arab Spring. And who would have predicted four years ago that public opinion would have shifted so rapidly in favor of permitting same-sex marriage?

Once substantive conversations about an issue begin, at least some individual opinions change. And because opinions are far more interdependent than most of us realize, the resulting feedback loops can induce explosively rapid swings. Read this volume carefully, and be stimulated to launch some intelligent discussions of your own. From there, what happens is anyone's guess.

Acknowledgments

First, we are especially grateful for Elizabeth Cushman's generous gift to the Public Policy Research Fund at the University of Colorado. It made possible the 2011 Conference, "A Brighter Future: Improving the Standard of Living Now and for the Next Generation," which became the basis of this book. We also appreciate the support of the College of Letters, Arts, and Sciences and the very able Margie Oldham, as well as of the Economics Department and the Economics Club at the University of Colorado at Colorado Springs.

We thank all who attended the conference, particularly the presenters, and especially Robert Frank for his keynote address. It has been a pleasure working with all the authors. We thank them for their responsiveness to our many requests and deadlines as well as their insightful discussions of each other's papers at the conference.

Ric would like to thank the students in his Environment and Local Economy class at Southern Oregon University during the spring of 2013 for their helpful comments on several chapters in this book. Their insights will make the book more accessible and enjoyable for others. He also wants to thank many members of the Ashland, Oregon, community for listening and giving him feedback on many of the ideas and policy recommendations in this book.

Daphne appreciates the help of members of the Advisory Board of the Colorado Center for Policy Studies, especially Paul Kozlowski and Dean Tom Christensen; the staff at the Kraemer Family Library, particularly Carla Myers, for assistance in locating references; the research assistance of Sarah Switzer on Chapter 7; and the editorial work of Cynthia Jones and Carole Denise Ellsworth.

Introduction

RICHARD P.F. HOLT AND DAPHNE T. GREENWOOD

For most of the twentieth century, the American standard of living was the envy of the world. Workers saw steady increases in their wages. Higher education in the United States was known worldwide for its quality and accessibility. Our national parks were the first to protect special places. Progress in public health improved living conditions in cities. The American dream of economic mobility became very real as more and more families joined the middle class.

During the 1960s economic opportunities expanded for women, African Americans, and other minority groups and poverty rates fell. Income inequality was quite stable, so growth benefited all income groups. As President John F. Kennedy famously noted: "a rising tide would lift all boats." But it took more than high rates of economic growth to improve the standard of living. Government programs such as Social Security were expanded and civil rights legislation was enacted.

Starting in the late 1970s, however, this began to change. The rate of economic growth slowed and the benefits went increasingly to those at the top rather than trickling down. Over the last decade, surveys have shown less satisfaction with quality of life and less confidence about opportunity. Many doubt that the standard of living will improve for future generations.[1] While belief in the American dream continues, too many people feel left on the sidelines even during economic booms.

This volume addresses concerns about the standard of living in the United States today as well as policies that could lead to improvement. It is based on a conference we organized through the Colorado Center for Policy Studies at the University of Colorado in Colorado Springs in 2011. Our interest in putting the conference together developed from a book we had just published on local economic development that focused on achieving broadly based and sustainable increases in the standard of living. We used a richer definition of the standard of living than is found in most economic writing and argued that economic development is much more than just income growth. It must also consider quality of life and sustainability, since they do not automatically follow from economic growth. This led to new prescriptions for local economic development beyond the familiar "create more jobs" slogan.

To move these ideas beyond the local level and explore them in greater depth, we invited a group of distinguished scholars from across the country. Their task was to explore particular aspects of the standard of living and policy changes that could lead to improvement. We challenged them to consider whether a single-minded focus on economic growth from past policies contributed to the financial crisis of 2008, the Great Recession, and the slow recovery. While other books have focused on reforms in banking or the financial system—both very important —the papers at this conference dealt with underlying causes. That includes greater inequality of income and wealth, stagnant wages, environmental degradation, and changing institutional arrangements. In sum, given rising concerns with inequality, sustainability and quality of life in the United States today, it was an opportune time for a conference (and a book) that focused on a broader understanding of the standard of living.

RETHINKING THE DEFINITION OF THE STANDARD OF LIVING

Although economists realize that most people place high value on many noneconomic aspects of life, the traditional definition of the standard of living equates it with income. There is an assumption that more income (or economic growth) will lead to improvements in nonmarket aspects of quality of life. Increased production of more goods and services (gross domestic product, or GDP) has therefore been widely used as the primary indicator of improvements in individual and social welfare.

But that is starting to change. Concerns with how economic growth impacts nonrenewable resources, future productive capacity, and quality of life are behind some new methods for tracking social welfare. The United Nations Human Development Index averages per capita GDP with measures of life expectancy, adult literacy, and school enrollment. The Genuine Progress Index subtracts some environmental and social costs from GDP and adds some nonmarket activities. In addition, many communities have developed locally based indicators of sustainability or quality of life to supplement more traditional measurements of growth. The Levy Institute Measure of Economic Well-Being (LIMEW) used in this book is another measure that goes beyond income. Development of these alternatives reflects an awareness that well-being requires more than income growth.

It is important to note that many aspects of quality of life are not purchased in a market. Clean air and water, access to parks and schools, time with friends and family are also important in the standard of living. And for future generations to be able to live at least as well as we do today, the standard of living must be sustainable. That requires focusing on all the capital stocks necessary for producing what humans need for a good standard of living, which we discuss in Chapter 1. Sustainability does not require continuing to produce the same goods in the same way as we do today. It does mean serious planning for a transition in how to use resources for production and consumption. For more people around the world to have a good standard of living, finite and nonrenewable resources like fossil fuels and land must be used differently. We hope that moving the focus from GDP to a multifaceted standard of living will inspire more careful thinking about complementarities and trade-offs.

PLURALIST THEMES IN THIS BOOK

We believe the best way to increase a multifaceted standard of living is to take a pluralist approach. Pluralism means moving beyond neoclassical economics to the rich literature of institutionalist, ecological, social, behavioral, feminist, and complexity schools of thought. A pluralist approach sees production as the joint result of many types of capital rather than attributing it primarily to private capital. It recognizes that individual choices and public decisions are greatly influenced by institutions and culture. It treats justice, equality, and opportunity as important ends, not just means to support the primary goal of economic growth.

One of this book's central themes is that people and their standard of living should be at the center of the economy. This has been well articulated by Amartya Sen (1999), as well as institutional economists such as Thorstein Veblen (1973 [1899]) and John Kenneth Galbraith (1969 [1958]).[*] They took issue with the neoclassical assumption that private accumulation of capital is the primary force behind improvements in the standard of living. Instead, Veblen and Galbraith saw economic development as an evolutionary process created by changing knowledge and its implementation through technology—that may or may not be embodied in capital equipment.

Technologies, which hold both promise for and threats to the standard of living, have their origin in human creativity. Families and family networks are where people first develop the social and human capital to make this creativity possible—the first institutions of an economy. It is only as societies become more developed that institutions expand to include laws facilitating market exchange. This makes the economy a subset of the larger society. Human society, in turn, exists as a subset of the environment, which leads to our next theme.

A second theme comes from ecological economists—both the economy and society are subsumed by the environment. Kenneth Boulding's "The Economics of the Coming Spaceship Earth" (1993 [1966]) was an early and important influence. Economic growth creates waste that threatens the natural environment. When there are no substitutes available for something essential to human life, such as the natural waste absorption capacity of the environment, preserving natural capital must take priority over development (Holt 2005). Ecological economists have two major reservations about growth. The first is whether continued economic growth is environmentally and socially sustainable. The second is whether economic growth is likely to cause improvements in overall well-being and happiness.

A third theme is the cost of increasing inequality. Inequality affects consumer behavior, public support for investments in the future (such as children's education) and economic mobility. Inequality also creates pressures to consume "positional" goods (Frank 2005) that distract from long-term investments in health, education, and environmental sustainability. And because ownership is power, more highly concentrated income and wealth shape economic and political decisions in ways that can limit opportunity and sustainability. Piketty's *Capital in the Twenty-First Century*

---

[*]We will now refer to John Kenneth Galbraith simply by his last name, since we do not reference here the important economic work in other areas by his son, James K. Galbraith.

explains why this is likely to be an ongoing problem. Top earners in America exert unprecedented control over capital—including "intellectual property rights" undreamed of in the past. Without actions to counterbalance, this could lead to concentrations of wealth surpassing those in nineteenth-century Europe.

A fourth theme is attention to nonmarket aspects of the standard of living. Three examples are self-provisioning, human capabilities, and aesthetic values. If the central problem in economies is provisioning (Gruchy 1972), some of that will be accomplished outside of markets. Attention to self-provisioning alters the primacy neoclassical economics has placed on market values. It also puts social relationships in the middle of the economic equation. The human capabilities approach to provisioning (Sen 1999) has influenced social and feminist economists as well as development policies at the United Nations, and many authors in this book. Another aspect of nonmarket qualities has been emphasized by Thomas Power (1996), who argues that humans at virtually all levels of affluence value the aesthetic, whether within or outside markets.

A fifth theme is that the institutional arrangements of a society matter greatly. Market forces operate within a structure shaped by people—some of it formal and some of it informal. Improvements in the standard of living depend at least as much on the composition of output (*how* resources are used) as on increases in the quantity of capital. So attributing too much to "market forces" is dangerous when it sidesteps the possible effects of different laws, public institutions, and social values on the standard of living.

A sixth theme is that time and history matter (Holt and Setterfield 1999). Several chapters illustrate the importance of path dependence on human development, economic mobility, and the use of renewable energy. By path dependence we mean that current choices are constrained by what has happened in the past and that time is irreversible. It follows that future options will be shaped by today's choices. Almost all pluralist approaches emphasize path dependence, complexity, and change through time, whereas neoclassical economics centers on equilibrium, and abstracts from time and history. Path dependence is particularly important in complexity, post-Keynesian, and institutionalist approaches to economic policy.

A seventh and final theme is the pragmatic approach to problem solving in pluralist economics. Learning by doing means that we do not have to reinvent the wheel or start from scratch on each problem. Throughout the book there are calls for policy that is evidence based rather than ideologically based. Many of the authors compare the United States to other affluent countries that have similar problems but choose different policy solutions. This shows habits and institutional constraints can be difficult to overcome, even when there are "win-win" opportunities for growth that are compatible with environmentally and socially sustainable goals. It is time to use the emerging findings of complexity, experimental, and behavioral economics where rational choice models fall short. That requires a pluralistic approach.

A SUMMARY OF THE CHAPTERS

The book has three sections. Part I—Recent History and Prospects for the American Standard of Living—explores what is meant by the standard of living (or economic well-being) and how it can be measured. The section also includes comparisons of the US standard of living to the recent past and to other affluent countries. In Part II—Lagging Incomes and the Middle-Class Dream—several chapters address how macroeconomic, labor-related, and family oriented policies have affected Americans. One chapter looks at changes in opportunity and mobility across the income distribution and how to improve them. Finally, Part III—Policies to Improve Quality of Life and Sustainability—is focused on specific aspects of quality of life and sustainability. Many of the chapters provide cross-national or historical perspectives. All present policy implications and alternative solutions.

Part I begins with Daphne T. Greenwood and Richard P.F. Holt's discussion of the mainstream view of the standard of living and its roots in neoclassical economics. In the traditional view, a better standard of living means having more market goods and services to consume. This leaves out much that is important. Chapter 1 presents a new definition of the standard of living that encompasses nonmarket aspects of quality of life, including the degree of income and wealth inequality and long-term sustainability. The authors contrast their definition with other measures of well-being, including the Levy Institute Measure of Economic Well-Being (Zacharias et al. 2014), and discuss its policy implications.

Greenwood and Holt focus on all the capital stocks that underlie the standard of living. These include privately and publicly owned manufactured natural, human, and social capitals. Their suggestions for improving the standard of living contrast with current policies that give primacy to private business capital. For example, they emphasize that education must foster creativity and flexibility, not just prepare people for the workplace. Infrastructure must be designed for environmental sustainability and social interaction.

In Chapter 2, Ajit Zacharias, Edward N. Wolff, Thomas Masterson, and Selçuk Eren present detailed comparisons of current economic well-being in the United States and in several other countries, as well as trends in the United States since 1959. Their expanded measure of economic well-being, the LIMEW, takes into account how households provision from the private market, government, and their own nonmarket production.

The authors find that median living standards between Canada, Great Britain, and the United States are converging. The United States still has the highest standard of living but also more inequality. The gap in inequality rose over time relative to Great Britain and France. Looking at changes within the United States, the authors focus on the middle quintile, or 20 percent of households. Well-being grew sluggishly and came primarily from public sector programs, with private sector rewards largely bypassing this group.

In Chapter 3, Thomas Michael Power demonstrates that amenities, particularly natural ones, have been primary reasons for migration within the United States during recent decades. Population growth led economic activity in Florida, much of the rural western United States, and other parts of nonmetropolitan America. Many people left high-income areas to go where incomes were lower—showing the high value people put on quality of life. Formerly depressed areas experienced some economic vitality from these moves, but also incurred some economic, social, and environmental costs from the rapid in-migration.

Power argues we need to end the "Daniel Boone syndrome of fleeing social problems rather than confronting and resolving them." For too long, the pattern has been to leave a place where quality of life has fallen for another where it seems higher, only to eventually abandon the new place after "fouling it up." This phenomenon affects urban as well as rural areas across the country. Power emphasizes that quality of life cannot be sustainable if this pattern continues.

David Colander's provocative Chapter 4 begins with a spirited defense of classical liberalism. Observing that it is often difficult to get broad agreement on what outcomes to pursue, he defines a brighter future in terms of structure and process. Colander sees the primary role of government as establishing an "ecostructure" to facilitate social goals. But he argues that it will work better from the bottom up rather than from the top down. Colander sees social entrepreneurship as an alternative to relying on government programs or nonprofit organizations.

Capitalism's early focus on material welfare led to organizational forms such as for-profit corporations, which were highly conducive to increasing material goods. But it left social welfare to government, which has often done the job poorly, according to Colander. The gap has not been adequately filled by nonprofit organizations. Colander outlines a new and interesting way adopted by many states of establishing "for-benefit" corporations that legally are able to pursue social goals and profitability at the same time. (We note that the focus on maximizing shareholder value—which came out of neoclassical economic and finance theory in the 1970s—made it increasingly difficult for traditional corporations to pursue both profits and social goals.)

The second section begins with two chapters on workers and their pay. In Chapter 5, Paul J. Kozlowski and Steven Spirn look at the past and future of middle-class jobs in the United States. From the 1950s through the late 1970s, unions and macroeconomic policies contributed to their prosperity. Since then, changes in both, along with globalization of production and changing business models, have contributed to a decline in labor's share of national income. A section of the chapter reviews how declines in unionization accelerated during the Great Recession with attempts at the state level to weaken public sector unions. The authors propose rethinking the move toward "privatization" or contracting out public services, along with some innovative tax and training policies that would affect private sector workers.

Kozlowski and Spirn also emphasize the importance of macroeconomic policies for wages and employment. Since 1980 there has been an emphasis on fighting inflation or reducing federal deficits, even during the most serious recession since the Great Depression. Failure to adequately use fiscal policy during the Great Recession left the task entirely to monetary policy. The authors call for restoring job creation as a macroeconomic priority, with active use of fiscal policy to stimulate demand.

Chapter 6 by David R. Howell, Bert M. Azizoglu, and Anna Okatenko addresses why the United States—alone among affluent countries—has 25 percent of its workforce making less than two-thirds of the median wage. The authors conclude that labor market institutions, particularly minimum wage policies, are the primary explanation. Their detailed comparison of policies in the United States and France shows that the French Salaire Minimum Interprofessionnel de Croissance (SMIC) has been far higher than the US minimum wage for decades. But the gap has grown dramatically since the late 1990s.

The conventional wisdom is that large numbers of young and less skilled French workers have been priced out of the labor market, leading to "catastrophic" unemployment. Howell and colleagues show little difference between the United States and France on several key employment indicators, substantial convergence on others, and unequivocally superior performance based on job quality. The authors conclude that it is possible to reduce the number of workers with really low wages to one-fifth the current level in the United States without notably worse employment outcomes.

Not only is there a much larger share of low-paid workers in the United States, their children have a more difficult time moving up the income ladder than in many other countries. In Chapter 7, Daphne T. Greenwood and Richard P.F. Holt look at intergenerational mobility in the United States today and what it reveals about the structure of opportunity. Mobility and opportunity are important to the standard of living not just for improving economic circumstances and reducing inequality. It is also widely acknowledged that a merit-based society has more economic vitality. Opportunity to achieve the American dream of mobility is an integral aspect of our quality of life.

Chapter 7 contrasts recent mobility with earlier generations and with several affluent countries. Greenwood and Holt explore how changes in institutional arrangements have shifted costs for college education and vocational training directly onto students. This has made upward mobility more difficult, while creating large profits for private technical schools and lenders. They address the disproportionate effect on minority students and its contribution to persistent gaps in mobility between whites and blacks. Greenwood and Holt close with suggestions for improving opportunities for workers already in the labor market, as well as ways to help education and training programs best serve the people who need them.

In Chapter 8, Steven Pressman and Robert Scott III begin with the high poverty rate for children in the United States compared to other affluent countries. They focus on a "root cause of the problem"—the lack of paid parental leave in the United States. Along with significant medical expenses from a birth, there are financial opportunity costs from time off during pregnancy or after the birth of a child. Young families often cope by taking on consumer debt. An interesting section shows how many more children live in poverty once these interest payments are subtracted from their parents' income. In addition to the financial burdens caused by losing one parent's income—or paying costly child care—quality of life for both infants and parents is damaged by the lack of paid parental leave.

Pressman and Scott observe stark differences between the many countries that have universal paid parental leave and the United States. Roughly two-thirds of divorces in the United States are because of financial problems, and that often leaves children in newly poor households. Without parental leave policies, other affluent countries would also have much higher child poverty rates. Pressman and Scott outline how to fully cover the costs of paid parental leave through the Social Security system. This would entail either slightly higher premiums or slightly longer working lives for parents. They conclude that a paid parental leave system would be self-financing over the long run, due to its positive effects in the future.

Part III includes several chapters focused on particular aspects of quality of life or sustainability that are important to the standard of living. The first two deal with natural capital and how its use affects human well-being. Chapter 9, by Robert Pollin, puts specific numbers and economic consequences on what it would take for the United States to lessen its heavy contributions to climate change. He finds that achieving the Obama administration's intermediate goal for reducing greenhouse gas emissions will require a full-scale transformation in the US's energy use.

Pollin concludes that there must be significant improvements in how efficiently energy is used. In addition, there must be much more reliance on renewable sources, especially wind and solar power, that deliver energy without generating any greenhouse emissions. To the extent that fossil fuels continue as an energy source, it makes sense to shift away from coal and petroleum to natural gas. The chapter contains detailed costs and benefits for an economically realistic plan to reduce greenhouse gas emissions and examines the investments and financing needed. Adopting policies for greater efficiency and more renewables actually *expands* employment opportunities because it raises the labor intensity and the domestic content of energy production and consumption from what it is today, according to Pollin. He outlines why the changes will not have significant negative effects on GDP growth.

Chapter 10, by Emily Northrop, looks at how food is produced, distributed, and consumed in the United States and the effects on economic, environmental, and social well-being. Along with energy use, the food system is also closely intertwined with the standard of living and its sustainability. But it is often overlooked by economists. The author first reviews how industrial agriculture depletes natural resources through contamination of potable water and effects on climate. She goes on to summarize the growing body of evidence that food engineering and food marketing promote unhealthful diets and obesity. These in turn affect health, health care costs, quality of life, and even life expectancy.

Shortcomings in today's food system impact the standard of living now and for future generations. Northrop suggests major changes at the national level to encourage private sector innovations in agriculture and food processing. Rather than relying solely on educating consumers to make more informed decisions (the neoclassical approach), she points out the complex influences on what people buy and eat and the power of large corporations to use this knowledge for their own profitability. That brings us to the last chapter, which explores the importance of intangible capital in many aspects of human well-being.

Chapter 11, by John Tomer, explains the importance of intangible capital and how it affects two social problems: chronic health issues and persistent poverty and inequality. He defines *intangible capital* as an umbrella term that includes all the capacities embodied in individuals or human relationships. These can be cognitive or noncognitive and within or outside organizations. Tomer argues that insufficient attention to the role of intangible capital is behind a widespread inability to solve many social and economic problems.

Tomer focuses first on how the level and quality of intangible capital contributes to chronic disease and obesity. Then, in a section on poverty and inequality, he examines how investments in early childhood education can fundamentally change lives and contribute to the overall standard of living through better economic performance, lower crime rates, and healthier lives. This final chapter addresses some very specific components of human capital and social capital that are often neglected by economists and that interact with the more concrete capital stocks—manufactured and natural—for both economic and noneconomic production.

CONCLUSION

As concerns about economic mobility, quality of life, and sustainability mount in the sluggish aftermath of the Great Recession, it is time to explore new ways of thinking about improving the standard of living. Some of the ideas presented by the authors in this volume might be dismissed as costing too much. But one of every five dollars in US GDP has been estimated to be "uneconomic growth," such as spending for environmental cleanup, highway accidents, substance abuse, lawsuits, and unnecessary health care and administrative overhead in the US health care system (Lovins, Lovins, and Hawken 1999). While this spending does create income and jobs, much of it contributes little to quality of life or to sustaining the environment. A brighter future requires rethinking how the money and resources we have are used. We hope that the chapters in this book—read cover to cover or sampled—will also inspire action.

NOTE

1. "Forty-three percent of those in the middle class expect that their children's standard of living will be better than their own, while 26 percent think it will be worse and 21 percent think it will be about the same. Four years ago, in response to the same question, the middle class had higher hopes for their offspring, with 51 percent predicting they would have a better standard of living and 19 percent thinking it would be worse. As for the nation as a whole, the verdict from the middle class is likewise muted. Only about one-in-ten (11 percent) say they are very optimistic about the country's long-term economic future, 44 percent are somewhat optimistic and 41 percent are somewhat or very pessimistic" (Pew Research Center 2012, 6).

BIBLIOGRAPHY

Boulding, K. 1993 [1966]. "The Economics of the Coming Spaceship Earth." In *Valuing the Earth: Economics, Ecology, and Ethics*, ed. H.E. Daly and K.N. Townsend, 311–313. Cambridge, MA: MIT Press.

Frank, R.H. 2005. "Positional Externalities Cause Large and Preventable Welfare Losses." *American Economic Review* 95, no. 2: 137–141.

———. 2007. *Falling Behind: How Rising Inequality Harms the Middle Class*. Berkeley: University of California Press.

Frank, R.H., A.S. Levine, and O. Dijk. 2005. "Expenditure Cascades." Cornell University Working Paper.

Galbraith, J.K. 1969 [1958]. *The Affluent Society*. 2nd ed. Boston: Houghton Mifflin.

Greenwood, D.T., and R.P.F. Holt. 2010. *Local Economic Development in the 21st Century: Quality of Life and Sustainability*. Armonk, NY: M.E. Sharpe.

Gruchy, A.G. 1972. *Contemporary Economic Thought: The Contribution of Neo-Institutional Economics*. Clifton, NJ: Augustus M. Kelley.

Holt, R.P.F. 2005. "Post-Keynesian Economics and Sustainable Development." *International Journal of Environment, Workplace and Employment* 1, no. 2: 174–186.

Holt, R.P.F., and M. Setterfield. 1999. "Time." In *Encyclopedia of Political Economy*, ed. P. O'Hara, 1158–1161. London: Routledge.

Lovins, A.B., L.H. Lovins, and P. Hawken. 1999. "A Road Map for Natural Capitalism." *Harvard Business Review* May–June: 145–158.

Pew Research Center. 2012. *The Lost Decade of the Middle Class.* www.pewsocialtrends. org/2012/08/22/the-lost-decade-of-the-middle-class/.

Piketty, T. 2014. *Capital in the Twenty-First Century.* Cambridge: Harvard University Press.

Power, T. 1996. *Environmental Protection and Economic Well-Being: The Pursuit of Quality.* 2nd ed. Armonk, NY: M.E. Sharpe.

Sen, A. 1999. *Development as Freedom.* New York: Knopf.

Veblen, T. 1973 [1899]. *The Theory of the Leisure Class: An Economic Study in the Evolution of Institutions.* New York: Macmillan.

Recent History and Prospects for the American Standard of Living

Improving the Standard of Living

Income, Quality of Life, and Sustainability

DAPHNE T. GREENWOOD AND RICHARD P.F. HOLT

The focus of this chapter is twofold: first, to develop a better understanding of the term *standard of living*, and second, to explore new ways to improve the standard of living now and for future generations. We use the term *standard of living* rather than *well-being*, *happiness*, or *life satisfaction*, in part because the term is more familiar to policy makers and citizens. While there is a rich academic literature on well-being, happiness, and social welfare, it has been far removed from public policy debates until quite recently.[1] Some of the authors in this volume use the term *well-being*, and we have also when it seemed appropriate. Policy makers often speak of maintaining or improving the standard of living, and general public discussion and polling questions also use this terminology.

Public familiarity and acceptance of the term *standard of living* was a key reason that we specified it as a primary goal in our book *Local Economic Development in the 21st Century* (Greenwood and Holt 2010b). We went beyond the traditional focus on income to add many nonmarket quality-of-life factors: publicly produced goods and services, freely available environmental goods and services, and production of goods and services outside the market. And since the majority of people express concern about the world in which their grandchildren will live, sustaining the standard of living for future generations is also part of our definition.

We define the standard of living more broadly than most economists do because we believe improving it now and for future generations requires more than simply increasing total output or income. When policy focuses primarily on the level of income, quality of life and sustainability are considered separate issues. It is often assumed that economic growth will take care of them. Throughout this chapter, as well as others in this book, evidence is presented that this approach does not work very well. For example, if average income increases slightly but there is much more crime and congestion, then the *overall* standard of living may fall. And protecting the environment might limit the rate of economic growth, but do more to increase the standard of living.

In today's world, it is increasingly important to understand the impact of economic choices on social and ecological systems. Economic growth can contribute to the standard of living, but also it can *subtract* from it. This leads us to question the economic assumption that more is always better, particularly when it comes to the standard of living. Does increasing the square footage of homes, the number of medical tests and treatments, or the size of fast-food meals make people better off? The world's population and consumption levels are growing exponentially while environmental and natural resources are becoming more fragile. It is ever more useful to think of our planet as a closed system—"spaceship Earth," in the words of Kenneth Boulding (1993). To do this, we need a multidimensional approach to improving living standards rather than the one-dimensional approach of using gross domestic product (GDP) as the primary measure of well-being.

The structure of this chapter is the following: first, we begin with a brief discussion of the popular view of the standard of living and discuss its shortcomings. Second, we outline a new definition of the standard of living that is (1) based on multiple methods of provisioning, and (2) includes nonmarket aspects of quality of life. Third, we emphasize the importance of investing in a variety of different capital stocks to sustain the standard of living over time. Fourth, we compare our definition of the standard of living to several other measures of well-being, including the Levy Institute's Measure of Economic Well-Being (Wolff and Zacharias 2007; Zacharias et al. 2014) and various subjective measures. And fifth, we discuss new policy directions consistent with this new and broader definition of the standard of living.

SHORTCOMINGS OF THE TRADITIONAL VIEW OF THE STANDARD OF LIVING

Improving human well-being has been the central focus of economics since the time of Adam Smith and as far back as Aristotle's coining of the word *economics*. The dominant view of both economists and policy makers throughout the twentieth century was that income levels are the basis of most other important aspects of human well-being. For example, Michael Spence, a Nobel Prize winner in economics, stated in his role as chair of the Commission on Growth and Development:

> We chose to focus on growth because we think that it is a necessary condition for the achievement of a wide range of objectives that people and societies care about. One of them is obviously poverty reduction, but there are even deeper ones. Health, productive employment, the opportunity to be creative, all kinds of things that really matter to people seem to depend heavily on the availability of resources and income, so that they don't spend most of their time desperately trying to keep their families alive. (2008)

Benjamin Friedman has even argued that economic growth has intrinsic moral value, since with increases in income people show more empathy and become willing to support programs and policies to help the poor and increase opportunity. He writes that "economic growth—meaning a rising standard of living for the clear majority of citizens—more often than not fosters greater opportunity, tolerance of diversity, social mobility, commitment to fairness, and dedication to democracy. . . . When living standards stagnate, or decline, most societies make little if any progress toward any of these goals" (2005, 4).

Underlying these widely held views are the following assumptions:

- The costs of providing environmental quality and other public goods will fall as an economy becomes more affluent and its technologies and institutions become more sophisticated. Hence, more income and output contributes to achieving environmental and social sustainability.
- In addition, people are naturally more willing to pay for environmental protection and to help their fellow human beings as they become more affluent, further contributing to long-term environmental and social sustainability.
- Most nonmarket aspects of quality of life (such as good health, strong family and community relationships, and civic participation) are positively correlated with income, so more income will improve each of them.
- Economic growth tends to be a rising tide that lifts all boats, increasing incomes throughout the population and raising the overall standard of living.

However, these assumptions do not hold in all times and places, and they do not seem to have been true in the United States during the last few decades. In addition, the world is changing, and the expectations that people have are changing along with it. That leads us to propose a broader measure of the standard of living. This is not because we minimize the importance of economic growth for improving well-being. Not only does it bring vitality and innovation; in general, people are better off with higher incomes because they can buy more or better quality goods and services. More spending can create job opportunities and provide higher tax revenues to support needed public goods.

Nevertheless, it is important to point out that many nonmarket aspects of the standard of living (good health, improved public safety, climate stability) do not necessarily move in tandem with market income and output. And growth in average GDP over the last decades has not trickled down to provide more well-being for all of the population in the United States (Zacharias et al. 2014). And greater concentration of income at the top has not caused an outpouring of generosity toward the less fortunate (Hacker and Pierson 2010; Reich 2010).

In fact, there is increasing evidence that higher incomes can subtract from the standard of living by lowering various aspects of quality of life (Greenwood and Holt 2010a, 2010b, 2010c). In addition, economic growth can be volatile and temporary, setting the economy on a path that is economically, environmentally, and socially unsustainable, and therefore does not provide long-term improvements (Holt 2005, 2010). Finally, for income growth to increase the *overall* standard of living, the benefits of that growth must flow to the great majority of the population. For at least the last thirty years, this has not been the case in the United States (Jones and Weinberg 2000; Piketty and Saez 2003; Saez 2006; Weinberg 1996).

Yet income growth continues to be the central focus of policy decisions and the default yardstick for well-being.[2] The primary goal of economists and policy makers since the Great Recession seems to have been to restore the indiscriminate growth of the old economy, instead of focusing on growth that would better protect environmental quality, economic opportunity, and social equity. But there are some encouraging signs of change. New measurements are being developed that capture improvements in the standard of living beyond income growth (McGillivray 2007), such as the United Nations Human Development Index, the Genuine Progress Index (Kubiszewski et al. 2013; Talberth, Cobb, and Slattery 2007), and the European Commission (2013).[3] Many communities in industrialized countries are also developing locally based indicators of sustainability or quality of life to supplement traditional economic measures (Greenwood 2004; Greenwood and Holt 2010b; Wismer 1999).

The development of new measures to supplement the use of GDP reflects increased awareness that improving people's lives depends on more than raising income.[4] We believe this recognition stems primarily from two factors. The first is a desire to *balance* income growth with other aspects of human welfare such as health, aesthetics, human relationships, democratic principles, and the environment. The second is a growing realization that economic prosperity *depends* on environmental and social sustainability. In the next section, we discuss how a broader definition of the standard of living better reflects this dependence.

WHAT IS THE STANDARD OF LIVING AND WHAT DOES IMPROVING IT MEAN?

We recognize that coming up with a workable and measurable definition of the standard of living is difficult. That explains, in part, why economists have focused primarily on measurements of income or wealth. But another part of the story may also be methodological and ideological. Neoclassical economics is based on a particular view of individuals and their relationship to society and the environment. This view affects judgments about what comprises the standard of living and about how to improve it. Questioning these assumptions leads to different definitions and measurements of the standard of living, not to mention policy recommendations that may be antithetical to certain powerful interests. Reexamining what is meant by the standard of living is likely to influence the policy choices we make. That is the point, of course, but those who are happy with present policies and a narrower and more easily measured goal will disagree.

To be clear about our meaning of the standard of living, we begin by making a distinction between different elements of well-being that are individual as compared to social. In Figure 1.1, we separate these elements into factors that are primarily individual (the smaller box on the left) and factors that are social, economic, and environmental and therefore more likely to be directly affected by public policy (the larger box on the right). Happiness, life satisfaction, and individual well-being are all greatly affected by factors in the left-hand box such as personality, inherited abilities and life outlook, physical and mental health, and expectations of the larger culture (Diener and Suh 1999; Kahneman and Tversky 1996; Kiron 1997; Lane 1997; Myers and Diener 1995). Elements that are more directly influenced by public policy, in the economic, social, and environmental spheres, are in the right-hand box.

Of course, there is not an impermeable wall between these boxes, as the arrows in the chart show. Individual choices affect environment, social, and economic spheres, as indicated by the rightward pointing arrow. And economic, social, and environmental

Figure 1.1 **Contributors to Human Well-Being**

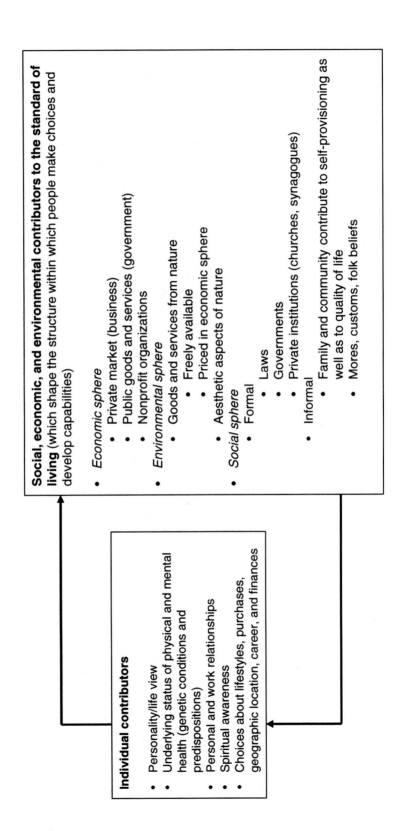

Social, economic, and environmental contributors to the standard of living (which shape the structure within which people make choices and develop capabilities)

- *Economic sphere*
  - Private market (business)
  - Public goods and services (government)
  - Nonprofit organizations
- *Environmental sphere*
  - Goods and services from nature
    - Freely available
    - Priced in economic sphere
  - Aesthetic aspects of nature
- *Social sphere*
  - Formal
    - Laws
    - Governments
    - Private institutions (churches, synagogues)
  - Informal
    - Family and community contribute to self-provisioning as well as to quality of life
    - Mores, customs, folk beliefs

Individual contributors

- Personality/life view
- Underlying status of physical and mental health (genetic conditions and predispositions)
- Personal and work relationships
- Spiritual awareness
- Choices about lifestyles, purchases, geographic location, career, and finances

factors affect individual behavior and choices, as indicated by the arrow pointing to the left. For example, many consumer choices are heavily influenced by social pressures derived from external economic and social factors (Frank 1999, 2007) as well as from advertising (Galbraith 1969). This new definition of the standard of living is focused primarily on what public policy can influence: the external economic, social, and environmental factors and investments in the different capital stocks, which contribute to them (discussed in a later section of this chapter).

Public policy must focus not only on improving *outcomes*, but also on the appropriate *process* for change. Increasing access to education and health insurance, establishing a floor for retirement income through Social Security, and reducing unemployment have all been shown to reduce economic anxieties and improve well-being and the standard of living (Easterlin 2013; Moss 2004; Rose and Gallup 2007). But *how* a society achieves those goals is also important. The *process* matters a great deal to many people and is therefore part of their quality of life. That is why there are such contentious debates about means, even when people are in general agreement about the end goals. We turn now to the building blocks that are the foundation of the standard of living in any society.

THE STANDARD OF LIVING: OPPORTUNITIES FOR PROVISIONING

Our broader definition of the standard of living is based on the ability of individuals, families, and the larger society to provide for needs and wants. People can satisfy these through a combination of private market, public sector, and self-provisioning.[5] (The term *provisioning* is used to emphasize that since people are at the center of any economy, its purpose is to fulfill their needs and wants). In modern economies, the purchase of goods and services for money in the market is a major component of provisioning, so having sufficient income is important to being able to provide for oneself. This leads many to use income to measure the standard of living and to define human capital as the skills that are likely to increase an individual's income.

Even in the modern economy, it is impossible to provide all the goods and services needed for a good standard of living through the market. There are no humanly produced substitutes for many freely available services of nature (Holt 2005). Some provisioning is more efficient through the public sector (building infrastructure and providing public safety). Household production, or what Juliet Schor (2010) calls self-provisioning, provides some unique services. It also substitutes for many items that could be purchased with income, such as vegetables, child care, or musical entertainment. Other provisioning comes from nonprofit organizations or family, friends, and neighbors. Some publicly or socially provided services are impossible to purchase in the market (love and concern), while others (publicly provided health insurance or education) are substitutes for market purchases. But they all contribute to the standard of living.

Traditional measurements based on income alone do not capture all of this. Provisioning through the public sector or nonprofit organizations is counted in GDP although it is valued only at the cost of inputs. But human needs or wants are also met through free environmental services (clean air, protection from the sun, beautiful views, and the songs of birds). Self-provisioning (household production) and informal social networks are also not measured in national economic output. In addition, income is presumably always beneficial to the recipient. But it may be earned in a way that causes negative externalities. For all these reasons, income never fully measures the standard of living of a nation or an individual. And as we see in the next section, the way income and wealth are distributed is also important to opportunities for provisioning and improving quality of life. Traditional measures miss that completely.

ECONOMIC INEQUALITY AND THE STANDARD OF LIVING

The neoclassical assumption that inequality is necessary to provide incentives to stimulate economic activity has been tempered by studies showing mixed effects of rising inequality on negative growth (Panizza 2002; Voitchovsky 2005) as well as other studies showing *negative* effects on economic growth (Aghion, Caroli, and Garcia-Penalosa 1999; Persson and Tabellini 1994). With more evenly distributed resources more participants in society are likely to care about outcomes. This may lead to a higher level of effort and output (Aghion and Bolton 1997; Quintin and Saving 2008). Rising inequality can also affect economic mobility, as we show in Chapter 7 of this volume. So a broader view of the standard of living must focus not only on the growth rate of income, but on the distribution of that income and whether there is enough trickle down to ensure that "a rising tide lifts all the boats."[6]

There is always a degree of inequality in any dynamic economy. But from the 1950s to the 1970s, people at all levels benefitted from economic growth due to a relatively stable distribution of income. This trickle down disappeared, beginning in the 1980s, and measures of inequality have steadily increased. Even *within* the highest income quintile, economic gains have been concentrated in the top 1 percent (Piketty and Saez 2003). In 2005, all of the economic gains went to an even smaller group, the top *one-tenth of 1 percent* (Saez 2006). Without getting the benefits of economy-wide productivity growth, other households lost ground.

Increased inequality has reversed what was a *positive* trickle down that benefited all income groups to what we call a *negative* trickle down (Greenwood and Holt 2010c). When most of the increase in income goes to households at the top, there are negative externalities that affect the well-being of other households. This was manifested in three ways during the last few decades in the United States:

1. decreased availability of moderately priced houses
2. less access to high-quality local public goods
3. a change in accepted consumption standards

First, inequality can drive prices up where supply is relatively inelastic. For example, with limited space at Ivy League schools, when more students want to attend tuition skyrockets. But many more people are affected when the demand for certain kinds of housing grows much more rapidly than the supply. With more purchasing power at the top, the demand for luxury condos and trophy homes grew rapidly. In areas where land, building permits, and materials were limited this drove prices up for everyone (Matlack and Vigdor 2008). An economy with more equality will build more moderately sized and affordably priced housing units than another economy with the same per capita income but more income concentration.

Developers and builders built fewer small homes with low profit margins and instead focused on larger, more expensive trophy homes and "McMansions," leading to a shortage of affordable homes (Gyourko and Linneman 1993, 41). Many households had to pay higher rent or take out a bigger mortgage even though their income was not rising. Powerful interest groups in the banking and housing sectors accommodated this strategy.

Second, rapidly rising income and wealth at the top led to economic segregation and increased variation in local public goods such as schools, clean air, and public safety. This set in motion more competition for areas with quality public goods and services—further driving prices up—rather than a move to establish good schools and safe neighborhoods everywhere (Greenwood and Holt 2010c).

Third, higher levels of discretionary income and consumer spending at the top created "expenditure cascades" (Levine, Frank, and Djik 2010). These trickled down from the very highest earners in the top 1 percent to those at the bottom of that group, then to the rest of the top 5 percent, and the rest of the top 10 percent, and so on. The farther down the chain, the greater the decline in well-being. Some who complained of an inability to keep up with the new rich were labeled envious and even accused of class warfare. Not so, writes Frank (1999). When conspicuous consumption by those who can afford it ratchets up middle-class standards, it may be necessary to spend more to get or keep the right job or to be successful in business.

In *Falling Behind* (2007) and *Luxury Fever* (1999), Frank explored many aspects of this phenomenon. For homes, cars, gifts, wedding receptions, clothing, and a host of other goods and services, the price of what is considered "adequate" has been rising (Frank 2007, Chapter 5). Frank coined the term *positional goods* to describe consumption whose utility is largely derived from the message it sends about the individual (Frank 1991). For example, people may cut corners on the quality of the food they eat at home because it is a private matter. But since the car they drive signals success, they may drive a new or more expensive model. This is not just for status, but in the belief that "success breeds more success."

In addition to economic inefficiencies and negative externalities, greater inequality has a negative impact on many aspects of quality of life, such as crime rates and health, which are part of the standard of living (Marmot, Banks, and Oldfield 2006; Morris and Tweeten 1971; Rodriguez 2000). It negatively affects the social capital needed for cohesion and stability (Glaeser, Scheinkman, and Schleifer 2003, You and Khagram 2005). In *The Spirit Level: Why Greater Equality Makes Societies Stronger* (2009), Richard Wilkinson and Kate Pickett examined the relationship between inequality and social problems like teen pregnancy, poor health, and lack of community life. These affect not only the poor, but also the standard of living for everyone.

This brings us to the influence of inequality on attitudes toward the less fortunate. We earlier cited Benjamin Friedman's argument that affluence increases generosity. This does not appear to hold true, at least when accompanied by rising inequality. As income has become more concentrated at the top over the last decades, rates of taxation have become *less* progressive, not more (Davis et al. 2009)—further concentrating the after-tax distribution of income. Public support for social spending has weakened among the affluent and across society in general. Support for workers' rights through competitive bargaining and minimum wage increases has also fallen as the distribution of income has become more unequal. Inequality appears to have shaped public policies in the direction of less concern for the well-being of others, not more. That affects elements of quality of life like individual freedom and justice.

FREEDOMS, JUSTICE, AND CAPABILITIES: PART OF QUALITY OF LIFE

Throughout history, once people have met their most basic needs, they have expressed a desire for civic, social, and spiritual freedom and for what Amartya Sen calls "agency" (1993, 1999). That means making one's own decisions about how to live and how to act. Along with Martha Nussbaum, Sen argues that the freedom and opportunities to fully develop human capabilities (artistic, intellectual, physical, spiritual, etc.) and interact with others in a fair and just way are all integral parts of quality of life (Nussbaum and Sen 1997). "Unfettered inquiry" and free exchange of ideas are also integral to a good standard of living and do not need to be justified by positive contributions to economic growth (Klein and Miller 1996). That means that policies which trade cherished freedoms for more economic production may lower the standard of living, and vice versa (Colander 2014). The "good society" is one where social and economic institutions embody equality, justice, and fairness, according to John Kenneth Galbraith (1997, 159). We turn now to quality.

QUALITY AND THE STANDARD OF LIVING

Amenities have real economic value—whether they are provided by the private or public sectors. Thomas Power writes that income growth is often treated as objective and practical and is

> pitted against the largely "social" or "aesthetic" concerns of those who would pursue their vague notions about the "quality of life," the suggestion being that subjective judgments about quality are somehow noneconomic . . . [but] economic activity is now and always has been centered on the pursuit of qualities we judge to be attractive and, therefore, important. . . . The pursuit of quality, as guided by our individual aesthetic judgments and the larger society's cultural values, clearly dominates the commercial economy. (Power 1996, 11–12)

One of the first economists to use the term *quality of life* was Galbraith, who observed how odd it would be to pursue economic growth "in order to make our surroundings more hideous and our culture more meretricious" (1971, 24). He noted that life experiences, including work, are important to quality of life. Galbraith suggested that an affluent society use labor productivity growth to provide safer and more satisfying work environments, rather than directing it solely to lower prices or higher incomes. This would be a major re-ordering of priorities for modern American society, given its focus on GDP. If those priorities change, so will "investment" strategies.

CAPITAL STOCKS AND THE ABILITY TO HAVE
A GOOD STANDARD OF LIVING

To improve future living standards, there must be investment in *all* the capital stocks used for producing income and quality of life (Goodwin 2003). The linkage between each capital stock (manufactured, natural, and human) and each kind of provisioning (private, public, and self-provisioning) is shown in Figure 1.2. The ability to invest in each depends on the state of knowledge, which depends in turn on human and social capital. It is also influenced by how well formal and informal institutions facilitate creative change. We turn now to a discussion of the capital stocks.

In neoclassical economics, capital originally meant only private business equipment, but it has been expanded by modern economists to include manufactured public capital (infrastructure) and the skills of human capital. We extend the capital concept further to include natural capital and social capital—also stocks that must be maintained in order to have a good standard of living. In Figure 1.2, solid arrows show a direct relationship of a capital stock to one or more ways of provisioning. Some parts of each type of capital are owned privately and others are owned publicly.[7] For example, some manufactured capital is private (I-A), while other portions (infrastructure) are publicly owned (I–B). Natural capital, such as water and forests, can be owned privately (II-A) or publicly (II-B). A third category of natural capital—such as the sky and the atmosphere—consists of common resources available to all (II-C).

Individual skills and talents can also be privately or publicly held. Skills and innovations that earn money income or contribute to self-provisioning are called human capital (III–A) and are privately owned by individuals. But there are also skills and talents that contribute primarily to the well-being of others and fall under the category of what is often called social capital (III–B). They affect parenting, community participation, and commitments to justice, fairness, and equality of opportunity discussed earlier.

The laws that govern civil society and the customs and traditions that prevail informally are also part of the jointly owned social capital of any community. Individual opportunities to develop and profit (financially or otherwise) from capabilities cannot operate in a vacuum. They depend on how these formal and informal institutions shape the structure of a society and economy as much as on physical infrastructure. But all of these types of capital must be maintained and invested in for the standard of living to be sustainable over time.

SUSTAINABILITY AND THE STANDARD OF LIVING

Provisioning includes planning for the future, since most people are concerned not only about their own lifetime, but about the world their children and grandchildren will inhabit. More recently, the awareness of human impacts on environmental services and resources as well as on social capital has led to increased interest in growth that is sustainable—economically, socially, and environmentally (Greenwood and Holt 2010a, 2010b; Norgaard 1988). Since the standard of living depends on more than income, improving the life of future generations—or at least sustaining what we

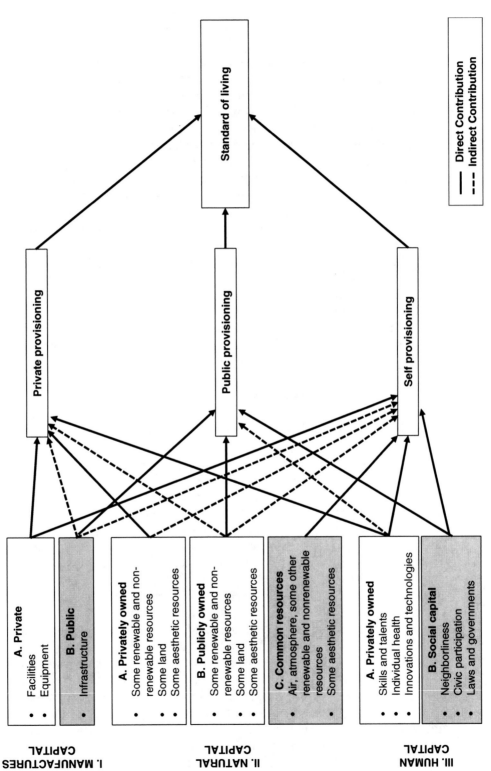

Figure 1.2 **Capital Stocks and Contributions to Provisioning**

13

have now—requires valuing *all* the capital stocks used in producing and sustaining income and quality of life. Not only must there be investments in private and public manufactured capital, but in natural, human, and social capitals.

However, both time and resources are limited. So trade-offs between the different types of capital stocks must be well understood when setting investment priorities. Depleting natural or human capital in order to support investments in manufactured capital does not always make sense. Natural capital that provides services freely or inexpensively may become scarce due to economic growth. Urbanization or geographic mobility can deplete social capital, making help from neighbors or extended families less available. These negative effects on other capital stocks must be weighed against the positive aspects of more income and output in order to evaluate the net effect on the standard of living.

To do that, any community or society needs indicators that track changes in each of the capital stocks. Only then can the relationship of capital stocks to current income and quality of life be clearly seen. And even though the goal of achieving a higher standard of living is universal, the specific indicators will necessarily vary over time and place. For example, public infrastructure in Venice includes canals, whereas in the Netherlands it includes a complex set of dykes. When it comes to natural capital, some areas are most worried about their supply of water, while others are most concerned about the viability of their forests. We look now at several other measures of well-being and their usefulness in setting public policy.

THE STANDARD OF LIVING AND MEASURES OF WELL-BEING

OBJECTIVE MEASURES OF WELL-BEING

The Levy Institute's Measure of Economic Well-Being (LIMEW) provides a far superior measure than current income alone (Wolff and Zacharias 2007; Zacharias et al. 2014). For example, it includes public spending on education and transportation as well as the value of time spent in household production. The LIMEW encompasses many nonmarket aspects that we have included in quality of life. However, important parts of the standard of living such as environmental services or years of healthy life expectancy are impossible to capture in a measure like this. In addition, public goods and services are measured in the LIMEW in terms of expenditures on inputs rather than in terms of how they affect outcomes in health, mobility, or educational achievement. In Figure 1.3, the inner rectangle illustrates the overlap between the LIMEW and our broader concept of standard of living. The outer rectangle includes several examples that the LIMEW does not capture.

The LIMEW is an impressive expansion of what can be measured beyond current income and provides far superior comparisons between countries and across time. But like income, it is a flow measure that does not include the capital stocks used to produce well-being. It needs to be supplemented with measures that do, as well as with outcome-based measures of health status, life expectancy, educational attainment, public safety, and environmental quality. Community indicators of quality of life (Greenwood 2004; Greenwood and Holt 2010b), the Index of Social Health

Figure 1.3 **The LIMEW and Examples of Other Aspects of the Standard of Living**

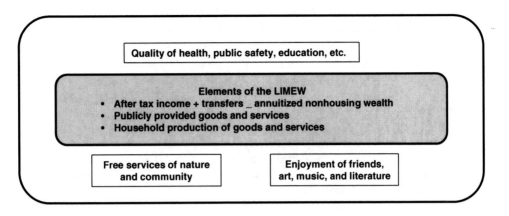

(Miringoff and Opdycke 2007), and the Genuine Progress Index (Kubiszewski et al. 2013; Talberth, Cobb, and Slattery 2007) have all integrated some of these elements at either the macroeconomic or the community level. Another approach is to use a more narrow measure but fill in the gaps with subjective measures of well-being.

SUBJECTIVE MEASURES OF WELL-BEING: HAPPINESS, LIFE SATISFACTION

An alternative way to measure well-being is to ask people to evaluate their own, including elements such as health, economic security, ability to maintain a middle-class lifestyle, opportunities for upward mobility, educational resources, access to nature, and safety. People can also be asked to evaluate outcomes in general and for the next generation. The Pew surveys (2006) are one example, but there are many other surveys that focus on health, crime, and other topics. One strength of subjective measures is that people are likely to incorporate process as well as outcome if they see both as important to their standard of living.

According to numerous surveys on happiness, the rise in average income over the past forty years in the United States and Western Europe has led to only slight increases in happiness (Easterlin 1974, 1995, 2003; Slottje 1991). It appears that at very low levels of income where subsistence is in question, income growth clearly makes people permanently happier. However, at moderate and high levels of income, increased income causes only temporary improvements in reported happiness that fade as people become used to the higher income level (Deaton 2008; Easterlin 2003, 2013). This may be because higher income is less valuable in both psychological and economic terms when many others are also better off (Duesenberry 1949) and the frame of reference has changed (Frank 1999, 2007).

This "Easterlin paradox" has been challenged with separate empirical studies showing that increased income produces more happiness regardless of income level (Stevenson and Wolfers 2008; Sacks, Stevenson, and Wolfers 2012). Easterlin (2013) counters that their results were dependent on several outlier observations of countries in transition from communism, such as the German Democratic Republic (the former East Germany), as well as the analysis of change over shorter time periods than he used. Easterlin continues to find a weak relationship between more income and more happiness at higher income levels. But he does find strong correlations between happiness and greater stability (derived from full employment or public safety net policies), using data from countries that have both increased and decreased these stabilizers. Easterlin observes that

> life satisfaction in China over the last two decades remained constant or perhaps even declined, despite a more than fourfold multiplication of output and incomes. It seems reasonable to infer that with the emergence and rise of unemployment and breakdown of the social safety net, new concerns arose among workers about such things as jobs and income security, the availability of health care and pensions, and provision for care of children and the elderly. Rapid economic growth may have partially alleviated these concerns by providing increased employment opportunities, but the net effect was no gain in happiness. (2013, 11)

There are still many questions about the value of subjective data on happiness for making general policy decisions.[8] Happiness is highly influenced by the internal factors outlined on the left in Figure 1.1, such as personal relationships and temperament (Diener and Suh 1999). Personal depression is caused by family problems more often than by housing or job problems (Lane 1999). Of course, policies that affect the external factors and thereby reduce the incidence or severity of job and housing problems can also have an indirect effect on depression and happiness.

The role of expectations in perceptions of happiness is also significant. If personal income rises less than was expected or less than a co-worker's, then happiness might not increase with more income. In the same way, perceptions of a person's health are influenced not only by objective health conditions but by expectations of what one's health should be at a particular age or life situation, which is influenced by the health of friends, family members, and the community at large (Di Tella and MacCulloch 2006; Diener and Seligman 2004; Kahneman and Krueger 2006).

A *combination* of subjective and objective data on the various components of the standard of living appears to be the most useful way to assess the past and the present, as well as what a brighter future for the next generation might be. We turn finally to what kinds of policies are needed to improve a broadly defined standard of living and how they contrast with common practices today.

POLICY DIRECTIONS

If improvements in the standard of living come from factors besides income and must be sustainable over time, this points to the need for new kinds of policies. First, the policies of the past have focused on short-term economic growth, assuming that improvements in environmental protection, health, and education will be a by-product. They have also been oriented toward the needs of private capital and investment, with public spending on infrastructure and education often tailored to support those same needs. And policies that result in the highest increase in per capita income may not increase incomes for the greatest number of people. For example, more focus on full employment could increase happiness and the standard of living by more than maximizing GDP growth.

Second, particularly when quality of life is recognized as part of the standard of living, it becomes clear that investments in many forms of capital are needed. And it is not enough to spend more on education; it must be spent on the *right kind* of education. That means education to develop critical thinking skills and flexibility for a rapidly changing world. These skills are needed not only for success in the workforce, but for participating in the decision making process in a democracy and navigating the perilous new world of personal finances.

Third, measurements matter to improving the standard of living. For example, if policy makers looked at progress in the LIMEW rather than GDP they would be more likely to value public goods and activities (such as parenting) that are part of household production. Valuing public goods should bring more attention to investing in capital stocks such as infrastructure. And for the twenty-first century, the *right kind* of infrastructure contributes to clean air, transportation alternatives, and water conservation.

Fourth, policies focused on sustainability of capital stocks, as well as on income, include more than investments in infrastructure and human capital. They will also protect nonrenewable natural capital that provides environmental services with no known substitute. This means moving beyond the idea that because some resources were initially "free" they have no economic value. For example, emphasis on capital stocks and sustainability is required to address intergenerational mobility as well as climate change, just to name two concerns.

Does more attention to sustainability undermine the need to create jobs and income now? Not at all. There are ways to invest in each of the capital stocks that will improve other aspects of the standard of living while raising incomes and creating jobs. But this requires moving beyond a focus on private capital as the "goose that lays the golden egg" to recognizing the importance of other capital and other forms of provisioning.

Historically, sustained economic growth has been driven by major technological changes, such as the railroads in the 1870s, the auto industry in the early twentieth century, and computer and communication technology in the 1990s. One likely candidate on the horizon is "green growth." Robert Pollin catalogs renewable energy needs later in this volume, while Emily Northrop addresses changes in the food system. Both would require major technological and even cultural changes along with changes in how goods are produced, distributed, and consumed. The social and economic power behind "green growth" could equal other major industrial changes from the past and would require new investments in all the capital stocks. This is only one example of new directions for the economy that would be compatible with environmental and social well-being.

In contrast, for the last thirty years spending on housing and finance has been the driving force behind growth in the US economy. This did little to establish a foundation for future productivity growth or better quality of life. Instead, housing and stock market bubbles built and then burst, leading to the deepest recession since the Great Depression of the 1930s. The kinds of change suggested in this chapter, as well as others in this volume, can be the engines for economic prosperity for the twenty-first century. But they will also support a better quality of life that is sustainable.

NOTES

1. See, for example, the works of Derek Bok, *The Politics of Happiness* (2010), and Sissela Bok, *Exploring Happiness* (2010). Bruno Frey and Alois Stutzer (2000), *The Gross National Happiness Index of Bhutan*, and the *New Economics Foundation's Happy Planet Index* are other examples of how happiness has been used in recent policy discussions. We note, however, that there is a complex relationship between happiness and the objective aspects of the standard of living with which economists are generally concerned. Opium addicts with a ready supply may be happy even if they have very poor health and economic prospects, for example.

2. As we pointed out in our book on local economic development and quality of life (Greenwood and Holt 2010b), communities regularly turn to economic indicators to show their viability. But none of these, including income, are adequate measures of the standard of living. Overreliance on them can distort policy choices.

3. *The Measurement of Economic Performance and Social Progress Revisited* (Stiglitz, Sen, and Fitoussi 2008) considers the limits of GDP as an indicator and its inability to capture all dimensions of the standard of living.

4. Although a Pew survey (2006) shows a much higher percentage of people with over $100,000 in income reporting happiness with their life than those with income under $30,000, this is consistent with relative income effects (Duesenberry 1949) rather than absolute income levels.

5. Provisioning was first defined as the various ways of acquiring goods and services by Allen Gruchy (1972) but has come to have a broader connotation that includes all that contributes to the life process.

6. This phrase comes from President John F. Kennedy's 1962 speech in Pueblo, Colorado: "What I preach is the interdependence of the United States. We are not 50 countries—we are one country of 50 States and one people. And I believe that those programs which make life better for some of our people will make life better for all of our people. A rising tide lifts all the boats." A copy of the full speech is at www.presidency.ucsb.edu/ws/?pid=8821.

7. This section draws from a more extensive discussion in Greenwood and Holt (2010a).

8. See D. Bok, *The Politics of Happiness* (2010, 60–62).

BIBLIOGRAPHY

Aghion, P., and P. Bolton. 1997. "A Theory of Trickle-Down Growth and Development." *Review of Economic Studies* 64, no. 2: 151–172.

Aghion, P., E. Caroli, and C. Garcia-Penalosa. 1999. "Inequality and Economic Growth: The Perspective of the New Growth Theories." *Journal of Economic Literature* 37, no. 4: 1615–1660.

Berg, A.G., and J.D. Ostry. 2011. "Equality and Efficiency." *Finance and Development* 48, no. 3: 12–15.

Bok, D. 2010. *The Politics of Happiness: What Government Can Learn from the New Research on Well-Being*. Princeton, NJ: Princeton University.

Bok, S. 2010. *Exploring Happiness: From Aristotle to Brain Science*. New Haven, CT: Yale University Press.

Boulding, K. 1993. "The Economics of the Coming Spaceship Earth." In *Valuing the Earth: Economics, Ecology, and Ethics*, ed. H.E. Daly and K.N. Townsend, 311–313. Cambridge, MA: MIT Press.

Croker, D. 1997. "Functioning and Capability: The Foundation of Sen's and Nussbaum's Development Ethic, Parts 1 and 2." In *Human Well-Being and Economic Goals*, ed. F. Ackerman, D. Kiron, N. Goodwin, J.M. Harris, and K. Gallagher, 301–307. Washington, DC: Island Press.

Davis, C., K. Davis, M. Gardner, R.S. McIntyre, J. McLynch, and A. Sapozhnikova. 2009. *A Distributional Analysis of the Tax Systems in All 50 States*. 3rd ed. Washington, DC: Institute on Taxation and Economic Policy.

Deaton, A. 2008. "Income, Health and Well-Being Around the World: Evidence from the Gallup World Poll." *Journal of Economic Perspectives* 22, no. 2: 53–72.

Diener, E. 1999. "National Differences in Subjective Well-Being." In *Well-Being: The Foundation of a Hedonic Psychology*, ed. D. Kahneman, E. Diener, and N. Schwarz, 434–450. New York: Russell Sage.

Diener, E., and M.E.P. Seligman. 2004. "Beyond Money: Toward an Economy of Well-Being." *Psychological Science in the Public Interest* 5, no. 1: 1–31.

Diener E., and E. Suh. 1999. "Personality and Subjective Well-Being." In *Well-Being: The Foundations of a Hedonic Psychology*, ed. D. Kahneman and N. Schwarz, 434–450. New York: Russell Sage.

Di Tella, R., and R. MacCulloch. 2006. "Some Uses of Happiness Data in Economics." *Journal of Economic Perspectives* 20, no. 1: 25–46.

Duesenberry, J.S. 1949. *Income, Saving and the Theory of Consumer Behaviors*. Cambridge, MA: Harvard University Press.

Dugger, W., and J. Peach. 2010. *Economic Abundance*. Armonk, NY: M.E. Sharpe.

Easterlin, R.A. 1974. "Does Economic Growth Improve the Human Lot?" In *Nations and Households in Economic Growth: Essays in Honor of Moses Abramovitz*, ed. P.A. David and M.W. Reder, 89–125. New York: Academic Press.

———. 1995. "Will Raising the Incomes of All Increase the Happiness of All?" *Journal of Economic Behavior and Organization* 27, no. 1: 35–48.

———. 2003. "Explaining Happiness." *Proceedings of the National Academy of Sciences* 100, no. 473: 465–484.

———. 2013. "Happiness, Growth, and Public Policy." *Economic Inquiry* 51, no. 1: 1–15.

European Commission. 2013. "The Standard Eurobarometer: Public Opinion Analysis." www.ec.europa.eu/public_opinion/index_en.htm.

Frank, R.H. 1989. "Frames of Reference and the Quality of Life." *American Economic Review* 79, no. 2: 80–85.

———. 1991. "Positional Externalities." In Strategies and Choice: Essays in Honor of Thomas C. Schelling, edited by Richard Zeckhauser, pp. 25–47. Cambridge: MIT Press.

———. 1999. *Luxury Fever: Money and Happiness in an Age of Excess*. New York: Free Press.

———. 2007. *Falling Behind: How Rising Inequality Harms the Middle Class*. Berkeley: University of California Press.

Friedman, B. 2005. *The Moral Consequences of Economic Growth*. New York: Alfred A. Knopf.

Frey, B.S., and A. Stutzer. 2000. "Happiness Prospers in Democracy." *Journal of Happiness Studies* 1, no. 1: 79–102.

———. 2006. "Political Participation and Procedural Utility." *European Journal of Political Research* 45, no. 3: 391–418.

Galbraith, J.K. 1964. "Economics and the Quality of Life." *Science* 145, no. 3628: 52–56.

———. 1969 [1958]. *The Affluent Society*. 2nd ed. Boston: Houghton Mifflin.

———. 1971. "Economics and the Quality of Life." In *A Contemporary Guide to Economics, Peace, and Laughter: Essays of John Kenneth Galbraith*, ed. A.D. Williams. Boston: Houghton Mifflin.

———. 1997. *The Good Society: The Human Agenda*. Boston: Houghton Mifflin.

Glaeser, E., J. Scheinkman, and A. Schleifer. 2003. "The Injustice of Inequality." *Journal of Monetary Economics* 50: 199–222.

Goodwin, N.T. 2003. "Five Kinds of Capital: Useful Concepts for Sustainable

Global Development and Environment Institute, Tufts University, Working Paper 7, no. 03.

Greenwood, D. 2004. "Measuring Quality of Life with Local Indicators." In *What Has Happened to the Quality of Life in the Advanced Industrialized Nations?* ed. E.N. Wolff, 334–374. Cheltenham, UK: Edward Elgar Press.

Greenwood, D., and R.P.F. Holt. 2007. "Quality of Life and Conventional Wisdom: John Kenneth Galbraith and Economic Development." Working Paper.

———. 2010a. "Growth, Development, and Quality of Life: A Pluralist Approach." In *Economic Pluralism*, ed. R. Garnett, E. Olsen, and M. Starr, 169–175. London, UK: Routledge.

———. 2010b. *Local Economic Development in the 21st Century: Quality of Life and Sustainability.* Armonk, NY: M.E. Sharpe.

———. 2010c. "Growth, Inequality and Negative Trickle-Down." *Journal of Economic Issues* 44, no. 2: 403–411.

———. 2014. "Opportunity and Mobility: The American Dream and the Standard of Living." In *A Brighter Future: Improving the Standard of Living Now and for the Next Generation*, ed. R.P.F. Holt and D.T. Greenwood, 140–164. Armonk, NY: M.E. Sharpe.

Gruchy, A.G. 1972. "John Kenneth Galbraith and the Economics of Affluence." *Contemporary Economic Thought: The Contribution of Neo-Institutional Economics.* Clifton, NJ: Augustus M. Kelley.

Gyourko J., and P. Linneman. 1993. "The Affordability of the American Dream: An Examination of the Last 30 Years." *Journal of Housing Research* 4, no. 1: 39–72.

Hacker, J.S., and P. Pierson. 2010. *Winner-Take-All Politics.* New York: Simon & Schuster.

Holt, R.P.F. 2005. "Post-Keynesian Economics and Sustainable Development." *International Journal of Environment, Workplace and Employment* 1, no. 2: 174–186.

———. 2010. "Traditional Economic Development Versus Sustainable Economic Development." In *Introducing Microeconomic Analysis*, ed. H. Bougrine, I. Parker, and M. Seccareccia, 248–262. Toronto: Edmond Montgomery Publications.

Jones, A.F., Jr., and D.H. Weinberg. 2000. "The Changing Shape of the Nation's Income Distribution, 1947–1998." *U.S. Bureau of the Census: Current Population Reports P60-204.* I-11, June.

Kahneman D., and A. Krueger. 2006. "Developments in the Measurement of Subjective Well-Being." *Journal of Economic Perspectives* 20, no. 1: 3–24.

Kahneman, D., and A. Tversky. 1996. "On the Reality of Cognitive Illusions." *Psychological Review* 103, no. 3: 582–591.

Kennedy, J.F. 1962. "Remarks in Pueblo, Colorado Following Approval of the Frying Pan-Arkansas Project." In Gerhard Peters and John T. Woolley, *The American Presidency Project*. www.presidency.ucsb.edu/ws/?pid=8821.

Kiron, D. 1997. "Amartya Sen's Contributions to Understanding Personal Welfare." In *Human Well-Being and Economic Goals*, ed. F. Ackerman, D. Kiron, N. Goodwin, J.M. Harris, and K. Gallagher, 197–202. Washington, DC: Island Press.

Klein, P.A. 1979. "Economics: Allocation or Valuation?" In *The Economy as a System of Power*, vol. 1, ed. W. Samuels, 7–33. Piscataway, NJ: Transactions Books.

Klein, P.A., and E.S. Miller. 1996. "Concepts of Value, Efficiency, and Democracy in Institutional Economics." *Journal of Economic Issues* 30, no. 1: 267–277.

Kubiszewski, I., R. Costanza, C. Franco, P. Lawn, J. Talberth, T. Jackson, and C. Aylmer. 2013. "Beyond GDP: Measuring and Achieving Global Genuine Progress." *Ecological Economics* 93: 57–68.

Lane, R.E. 1999. "The Joyless Market Economy." In *Well-Being: The Foundation of a Hedonic Psychology*, ed. D. Kahneman, E. Diener, and N. Schwarz, 29–32. New York: Russell Sage.

Levine, A.S., R.H. Frank, and O. Dijk. 2010. "Expenditure Cascades." Working Paper, September 13. Available at SSRN 1690612 (2010).

Marmot, M., J. Banks, and Z. Oldfield. 2006. "Disease and Disadvantage in the United States and in England." *Journal of the American Medical Association* 295, no. 17: 2037–2045.

Massey, D.S., and M.J. Fisher. 2003. "The Geography of Inequality in the United States, 1950–2000." *Brookings-Wharton Papers on Urban Affairs*, 1–40.

Matlack, J.L., and J.L. Vigdor. 2008. "Income Inequality and Housing Affordability." *Journal of Housing Economics* 17, no. 3: 212–224.

McGillivray, M. 2007. *Human Well-Being: Concept and Measurement.* New York: Palgrave Macmillan.

Miringoff, M.L., and S. Opdycke. 2008. *Putting Social Issues Back in the Public Agenda.* Armonk, NY: M.E. Sharpe.

Morris, D., and L. Tweeten. 1971. "The Cost of Controlling Crime: A Study in the Economics of City Life." *Annals of Regional Science* 5, no. 1: 33–49.

Moss, D.A. 2004. *When All Else Fails: Government as the Ultimate Risk Manager*. Cambridge, MA: Harvard University Press.

Myers, D.G., and E. Diener. 1997. "Who Is Happy?" In *Human Well-Being and Economic Goals*, ed. F. Ackerman, D. Kiron, N. Goodwin, J.M. Harris, and K. Gallagher, 174–176. Washington, DC: Island Press.

Norgaard, R. 1988. "Sustainable Development: A Co-evolutionary View." *Futures* 20, no. 6: 606–620.

Nussbaum, M.C., and A. Sen, eds. 1997. *The Quality of Life*. Oxford, UK: Clarendon Press.

Panizza, U. 2002. "Income Inequality and Economic Growth: Evidence from American Data." *Journal of Economic Growth* 7, no. 1: 25–41.

Persson, T., and G. Tabellini. 1994. "Is Inequality Harmful for Growth?" *American Economic Review* 84, no. 3: 600–621.

Pew Research Center. 2006. "Are We Happy Yet?" www.pewsocialtrends.org/files/2010/10/AreWe-HappyYet.pdf.

———. 2008. "Inside the Middle Class: Bad Times Hit the Good Life." www.pewsocialtrends.org/2008/04/09/inside . . . middle-class . . . /555–2/.

Piketty, T., and E. Saez. 2003. "Income Inequality in the United States 1913–1998." *Quarterly Journal of Economics* 18, no. 1: 1–39.

———. 2006. "The Evolution of Top Incomes: A Historical and International Perspective." *American Economic Review* 96, no. 2: 200–205.

Power, T. 1996. *Environmental Protection and Economic Well-Being: The Pursuit of Quality*. 2nd ed. Armonk, NY: M.E. Sharpe.

Quintin, Erwan, and Jason L. Saving. 2008. "Inequality and Growth: Challenges to the Old Orthodoxy." Economic Letter–Insights from the Federal Reserve Bank of Dallas 3, no. 1.

Reich, R.B. 2010. *After-Shock: The Next Economy and America's Future*. New York: Alfred A. Knopf.

Rodriguez, C.B. 2000. "An Empirical Test on the Institutionalist View on Income Inequality: Economic Growth Within the United States." *American Journal of Economics and Sociology* 59, no. 2: 303–313.

Rose, L.C., and A.M. Gallup. 2007. "The 39th Annual Phi Delta Kappa/Gallup Poll on the Public's Attitudes Toward the Public Schools." *Phi Delta Kappan* 89, no. 1: 33–48.

Sacks, D.W., B. Stevenson, and J. Wolfers. 2012. "The New Stylized Facts About Income and Subjective Well-Being." *Emotion* 12, no. 6: 1181. psycnet.apa.org. Abstract 1.

Saez, E. 2006. "Income Concentration in a Historical and International Perspective." In *Public Policy and Income Distribution*, ed. A. Auerbach, D. Card, and J. Quigley, 221–258. New York: Russell Sage.

Schor, J. 2010. *Plenitude*. New York: Penguin Press.

Sen, A. 1993. "Capability and Well-Being." In *The Quality of Life*, ed. M. Nussbaum and A. Sen, 30–53. Oxford, UK: Clarendon Press.

———. 1999. *Development as Freedom*. New York: Alfred A. Knopf.

Slottje, D. 1991. "Measuring the Quality of Life Across Countries." *Review of Economics and Statistics* 73, no. 4: 684–693.

Solow, R. 1994. "Perspectives on Growth Theory." *Journal of Economic Perspectives* 8, no. 1: 45–54.

Spence, M. 2008. Report, Commission on Growth and Development. www.growthcommission.org/index.

Stevenson, B., and J. Wolfers. 2008. "Economic Growth and Subjective Well-Being: Reassessing the Easterlin Paradox." *Brookings Papers on Economic Activity*, 1–87.

Stiglitz, J., A. Sen, and J. Fitoussi. 2008. *The Measurement of Economic Performance and Social Progress Revisited*. Paris: Commission on the Measurement of Economic Performance and Social Progress.

Talberth, J., C. Cobb., and N. Slattery. 2007. "The Genuine Progress Indicator 2006: Executive Summary: Redefining Progress." *The Nature of Economics*. www.rprogress.org/publications/2007/GPI2006_ExecSumm.pdf#search=%221950–2004%22/.

Veblen, T. 1899. *The Theory of the Leisure Class: An Economic Study in the Evolution of Institutions*. New York: Macmillan.

———. 2006 [1908]. "On the Nature of Capital." *Quarterly Journal of Economics* 22, no. 1. Reprinted in *The Place of Science in Modern Civilization*, 324–386. New Brunswick, NJ: Transaction.

———. 2006 [1919]. "Industrial and Pecuniary Employments." Reprinted in *The Place of Science in Modern Civilization*, 279–323. New Brunswick, NJ: Transaction.

Voitchovsky, S. 2005. "Does the Profile of Income Inequality Matter for Economic Growth? Distinguishing Between the Effects of Inequality in Different Parts of the Income Distribution." *Journal of Economic Growth* 10, no. 3: 273–296.

Weinberg, D.H. 1996. "A Brief Look at Postwar U.S. Income Inequality." *U.S. Bureau of the Census: Current Population Reports, P60-191*. June.

Wilkinson, R., and K. Pickett. 2009. *The Spirit World: Why Greater Equality Makes Societies Stronger*. New York: Bloomsbury Press.

Wismer, S. 1999. "From the Ground Up: Quality of Life Indicators and Sustainable Community Development." *Feminist Economics* 5, no. 2: 109–114.

Wolff, E.N. 2013. "The Asset Price Meltdown, Rising Leverage, and the Wealth of the Middle Class." *Journal of Economic Issues* 47, no. 2: 333–342.

Wolff, E.N., and A. Zacharias. 2007. "The Levy Institute Measure of Economic Well-Being United States, 1989–2001." *Eastern Economic Journal* 33, no. 4: 443–470.

You, J., and S. Khagram. 2005. "A Comparative Study of Inequality and Corruption." *American Sociological Review* 70, no. 1: 136–157.

Zacharias, A., E. Wolff, T. Masterson, and S. Eren. 2014. "Economic Well-Being in the United States: a Historical and Comparative Perspective." In *A Brighter Future: Improving the Standard of Living Now and for the Next Generation*, ed. R.P.F. Holt and D.T. Greenwood, 23–52. Armonk, NY: M.E. Sharpe.

2 Economic Well-Being in the United States

A Historical and Comparative Perspective

Ajit Zacharias, Edward N. Wolff, Thomas Masterson, and Selçuk Eren

In our parlance, *economic well-being* refers to the household's command over goods and services produced during a given period of time. We will focus here on modern capitalist economies, but the notion applies equally to other types of economies as well. The Levy Institute Measure of Economic Well-Being (LIMEW) is premised on the view that the command exercised by the households is mediated by three key institutions: the market, state, and household. The magnitude of the command is approximated by a measure that reflects the resources available to the household for facilitating current consumption or acquiring physical or financial assets. The three institutions form interdependent parts of an organic entity, and household economic well-being is fundamentally shaped by the complex functioning of this entity.

In this chapter, we compare economic well-being in Canada, France, Great Britain, and the United States using our expanded measure, the LIMEW. We will use the terms *LIMEW* and *economic well-being* interchangeably in the chapter. An ongoing research project at the Levy Institute has developed long-term estimates of LIMEW for the United States for a set of benchmark years dating from 1959 to 2007[1] and collaborated with an international team of scholars to produce estimates for Canada, France, and Great Britain. Our hope is that the new metric will contribute to a better understanding of the structure and dynamics of economic well-being in advanced industrialized countries.

We also look at long-term trends in economic well-being in the United States, from 1959 to 2007. As shown here, changes in economic well-being in the United States over the last half-century or so can be better understood by considering what has been stable over this period and what attributes have changed. Further insights can be gained by considering similarities and differences between the United States and other affluent countries during the last decade of the twentieth century and first decade of the twenty-first century. In this chapter, we focus on the middle class in particular and document the importance of public spending to improvements in the economic well-being of the middle class.

An important finding we discuss here is the convergence in median economic well-being between the United States and the other three countries over time. The convergence with Britain was the most dramatic: the average household in the United States was only 5 percent better off than its British counterpart by about 2005 as against 28 percent in the mid-1990s. The level of inequality was considerably higher in the United States than in the other three countries. Moreover, the inequality gap between the United States and Britain widened from 5.6 to 8.8 Gini points in the decade after the mid-1990s and that between the United States and France from 8.2 to 12.9 Gini points. In contrast, the difference narrowed between the United States and Canada.

We also find that median economic well-being in the United States grew sluggishly between 1959 and 2007 (0.67 percent per year), particularly when compared to the annual growth in GDP per capita (2.3 percent). Increases in well-being for this middle-income group came primarily from the public sector rather than from private sector rewards. The effect of net government expenditures in sustaining middle-class living standards was particularly strong between 1959 and 1982 and between 2000 and 2007. Indeed, between 2000 and 2007, the increase in net government expenditures accounted for *134 percent* of the growth of well-being, as base income and income from wealth both contracted in absolute terms. This increase in net government expenditures benefiting the middle quintile was mainly due to increased transfers and only secondarily to increases in publicly produced goods and services.

There was also a substantial growth in the inequality of economic well-being in the United States over the years from 1959 to 2007. Decomposition analysis shows that income from nonhome wealth made by far the largest contribution to the increase in inequality recorded for well-being between 1959 and 2007. This was somewhat moderated by the rise in net government expenditures during this period.

The next section of the chapter provides a brief outline of the LIMEW measure. We then present our most important comparative results in a series of bilateral comparisons between the United States and each individual country.[2] Next, we present the main results on long-term trends in the LIMEW for the United States and compare to trends in gross money income (MI or census income), the most common measure of economic well-being. Last, we summarize our findings and provide some brief policy recommendations.

The Structure and Logic of LIMEW

Historical Background

A household's command over the goods and services produced during a given period of time is normally calibrated by an income measure. The logic behind this is that household income is a good reflection of the resources available to the household over a given period of time (typically, a year) for facilitating current consumption or acquiring assets. MI is the standard measure used for this purpose in the United States.[3]

However, census income is known to have many shortcomings. The landmark report by the Canberra Group (2001), a group of international experts on household income statistics, highlighted many of these deficiencies. In particular, census income does not include an estimate of in-kind benefit transfers, no valuation is included for household production or consumption of public goods and services, property income is a limited indicator of the benefits from wealth holdings, and taxes are not netted out of the measure. As a result, census income gives a somewhat distorted picture of actual economic well-being.

The LIMEW overcomes many of the shortcomings of census income and disposable (i.e., after-tax) money income.[4] Since the state plays a crucial role in the direct provisioning of many "necessaries and conveniences of life" (to use Adam Smith's famous expression), such as public education and highways, we include estimates of publicly provided goods and services in our measure. Since nonmarket household work—such as child care, cooking, and cleaning—also provides many necessaries and conveniences, we include household production in LIMEW. We also include estimates of long-run benefits from the ownership of wealth (other than homes) in the form of an imputed lifetime annuity. This procedure, in our view, is superior to considering current property income from assets. Services derived from owner-occupied housing are valued by means of imputed rent in our measure.

The LIMEW is best thought of as a measure of resource availability that provides both actual and potential consumption from market, private (household), and public sources. It begins with money income and adds (imputed) income from nonhome wealth. These both constitute resource availability that is largely determined by market forces, although underpinned by historical and institutional factors. Imputed values of benefits from owner-occupied housing, noncash government transfers, and household production account for these market substitutes. Imputed rent to owner-occupied housing is a substitute for the payment of actual rent for a similar dwelling (this, in fact, is the definition of imputed rent in national accounts). Noncash government benefits such as food stamps, Medicare, and Medicaid provide payment for market services. Our definition of household production is also based on the provision of market substitutes by the household.

Publicly provided goods and services in the LIMEW consist of education, health, water and sanitation, and the like: services for which equivalents exist in the private market because they are rival and excludable in consumption. In fact, many of these services, such as water and sewage treatment, are "bought" by individuals through a user fee charged by the government—indicative of a market transaction. We exclude defense spending and government overhead costs because they do not provide any direct service to specific groups of households. The latter criterion (the provision of services directly usable by households) is the motivation behind including expenditures on some types of "partial" public goods such as highways or fire departments.

We believe that our measure of economic well-being is a better guide to actual trends in the standard of living than income alone because we account for nonmarket household labor, the security value of wealth, in-kind social benefits, and the consumption of public goods and services. Intergroup disparities in economic well-being can be understood in a more complete fashion with the aid of LIMEW than by focusing solely on pre- or post-tax money income. As a result, our measure of economic well-being provides a more comprehensive measure of economic inequality. As one might expect, household production and publicly provided goods and services are distributed much more equally than household incomes. On the other hand, inequality in wealth is generally much higher than that of income or earnings. LIMEW allows us to estimate the net effect of including all three components, as well as compare their impact on overall inequality with that of earnings, taxes, and the like.

Our measure is not the first attempt to construct an extended income concept. The Canberra Group (2001), mentioned above, proposed a measure of extended income, though it is in many ways narrower in scope than ours.[5] Smeeding and Weinberg (2001) also proposed a measure that is broader than, but similar to, the Canberra Group's measure. However, it is still narrower than ours.[6]

CONSTRUCTION OF THE LIMEW

Our measure of economic well-being is constructed as the sum of the following components: base income; income from wealth; net government expenditures (both cash and noncash transfers and consumption of public goods and services, net of taxes); and household production. The major components of the LIMEW for the United States between 1989 and 2007 are shown in Table 2.1.[7]

Base money income is defined as MI less the sum of property income (interest, dividends, and rents), private pension income,[8] and government cash transfers. Earnings make up the overwhelming portion of base money income. The remainder consists of interpersonal transfers, workers' compensation paid by the private sector, and other small items. Noncash remuneration provided by employers is added to base money income to derive base income. For example, employer contributions for health insurance premiums are added to base money income in the case of the United States, as they constitute the main form of noncash compensation for US employees.[9] The second component is imputed income from the household's wealth holdings. MI includes interest, dividends, and rent. From our perspective, property income is an incomplete measure of the economic well-being derived from the ownership of assets. Owner-occupied housing yields services to its owners over many years, thereby freeing up resources otherwise spent on housing. Financial assets can, under normal conditions, be a source of economic security in addition to property-type income.

We also distinguish between home wealth and other wealth. Housing is a universal need and home ownership frees the owner from the obligation of paying rent, leaving an equivalent amount of resources for consumption and asset accumulation. Hence, benefits from owner-occupied housing are reckoned in terms of the replacement cost of the services derived from it (i.e., a rental equivalent). We estimate the benefits from nonhome wealth (including private pension wealth[10]) with a lifetime annuity based on a given amount of wealth, an interest rate, and life expectancy.[11] The third component is net government expenditures—the difference between government expenditures incurred on behalf of households and taxes paid by households. This includes cash transfers, noncash transfers, and publicly provided goods and services.[12] Government cash transfers are treated as part of the money income of the recipients. In the case of government noncash transfers, our approach is to distribute the appropriate actual cost incurred by the government among recipients of the benefit.

The other type of government expenditure that we include in our measure of economic well-being is publicly provided goods and services that have direct benefit to

Table 2.1 **Construction of the LIMEW Files for the United States, 1989–2007**

Line no.	Component	Source
1	Earnings	
2	Money income other than earnings	
3	Property income	
4	Private pensions	ADS/ASEC
5	Government cash transfers	
6	Other money income	
7	Money income (MI): Sum of lines 1 and 2	
8	*Less:* Property income (line 3), private pensions (line 4), and government cash transfers (line 5)	
9	*Equals:* Base money income	
10	*Plus:* Employer contributions for health insurance	ADS/ASEC
11	*Equals:* Base income	
12	*Plus:* Income from wealth	Statistical matching of ADS/ASEC with SCF
13	Annuity from nonhome wealth	
14	Imputed rent on owner-occupied housing	
15	*Less:* Taxes	
16	Income taxes	
17	Payroll taxes	ADS/ASEC and NIPA
18	Property taxes	
19	Consumption taxes	ADS/ASEC and estimates from ITEP
20	*Plus:* Cash transfers	Same as line 5 above; and NIPA for relevant aggregates
21	*Plus:* Noncash transfers	ADS/ASEC, administrative data, and NIPA
22	*Plus:* Consumption of public goods and services	ADS/ASEC and others
23	*Plus:* Household production	Statistical matching of ADS/ASEC and AUTP/ATUS
24	*Equals:* LIMEW	

Notes: ADS = Annual Demographic Supplement; ASEC = Annual Social and Economic Supplement; SCF = Survey of Consumer Finances; NIPA = National Income and Product Accounts; ITEP = Institute for Taxation and Economic Policy; AUTP = Americans' Use of Time Project; ATUS = American Time Use Survey.

individuals. We begin with a detailed functional classification of government expenditures and exclude certain items because they fail to satisfy the general criterion of increasing the household's command over goods or services. These items generally form part of the social overhead (e.g., national defense) and do not substitute for market spending. Other expenditures, such as transportation, are allocated only in part to households because part of the expenditure is also incurred on behalf of the business sector. The household sector's share in such expenditures can be estimated on the basis of information regarding its utilization (e.g., miles driven by households and businesses). The remaining expenditures (such as health) are allocated fully to households.

In the second stage, the expenditures for each functional category are distributed among households. Some expenditures, such as education, highways, and water and sewage treatment, are distributed on the basis of estimated patterns of utilization or consumption, while others, such as public health, fire, and police, are distributed equally among the relevant population.

The third part of net government expenditures is taxes. We include payroll, income, and property taxes in our measure.[13]

The fourth component of LIMEW is the imputed value of household production. Three broad categories of unpaid activities are included in the definition of household production: (1) core production activities, such as cooking and cleaning; (2) procurement activities, such as shopping for groceries and for clothing; and (3) care activities, such as caring for babies and reading to children. These activities are considered as "production," since they can generally be assigned to third parties apart from the person who performs them, although third parties may not provide a close substitute, especially for care.

Our strategy for imputing the value of household production is to begin by valuing the amount of time spent by individuals on the basis of its replacement cost as indicated by the average earnings of domestic servants or household employees. However, since research suggests significant differences among households in the quality and composition of the "outputs" of household production, as well as the efficiency of housework, the differentials are correlated with household-level characteristics (such as wealth) and characteristics of household members (such as the influence of parental education on child-rearing practices). We then modify the replacement-cost procedure and apply to the average replacement cost a discount or premium that depends on how the individual whose time is being valued ranks in terms of a performance index. Ideally, the performance index should account for all the factors relevant in determining differentials in household production, and the weights of the factors should be derived from a full-fledged multivariate analysis. Given the absence of such research findings, we incorporated three key factors that affect efficiency and quality differentials—household income, educational attainment, and time availability—with equal weights attached to each.

As noted by Greenwood and Holt (Chapter 1 in this volume), the LIMEW lacks certain aspects of a broader notion of economic well-being or, more generally, the "quality of life." In particular, leisure, environmental services, and years of healthy life are not captured in the LIMEW measure. Moreover, public goods and services are measured in terms of government expenditures on input rather than in terms of how such spending affects health outcomes, the degree of public safety, mobility, educational achievement, and the like. In addition, such aspects of well-being as the free services provided by nature and the community or the enjoyment of friends, art, music, and literature are not depicted by the LIMEW index. Greenwood and Holt, for example, argue in favor of supplementing the elements of the LIMEW with objective outcome measures of health status, life expectancy, educational attainment, public safety, and environmental quality. However, our measure, while more narrowly defined than a true "standard of living" measure, is measurable in a way that the latter measures are not and does shed light on important trends in economic well-being and the impact of policy on it.

THE CHANGE IN ECONOMIC WELL-BEING IN THE UNITED STATES IN A COMPARATIVE LIGHT

ECONOMIC WELL-BEING OF THE AVERAGE HOUSEHOLD

The most widely used indicator for comparing economic performance across countries is per capita GDP.[14] According to this indicator, the United States had a solid lead over Britain, Canada, and France during the period studied here. US per capita GDP was 31 percent higher than Britain's around 2005 compared to 34 percent higher in the mid-1990s. The United States GDP was 23 percent higher than Canada's around 2005, only slightly lower than the 25 percent lead it had around 2000. In the case of France, the United States lead in per capita GDP actually widened from 32 percent in 1989 to 39 percent in 2000.

Unlike per capita GDP, which comes from a measure of aggregate economic performance, the LIMEW is a broad measure of household economic well-being. Using it, we find that the advantage of the average US household over the median household in Britain and Canada shrank noticeably during the 1990s and the first half of the 2000s (Figure 2.1). Convergence with Britain was the most dramatic: the average household in the United States was only 5 percent better off than its British counterpart in the mid-2000s as against 28 percent in the mid-1990s. The average Canadian household also narrowed its deficit vis-à-vis the United States from 12 percent around 2000 to only 8 percent around 2005. The comparison with France narrowed the least: the average US household was 27 percent better off than the average French household was in 1989 and 25 percent better off in 2000. The relative economic well-being of the average American household to Britain, Canada, and France is significantly overstated by looking only at per capita GDP comparisons.

MIDDLE-INCOME AMERICANS AND THEIR COUNTERPARTS IN BRITAIN, CANADA, AND FRANCE

To better understand the gap in the economic well-being between the average American household and its counterparts in the other countries, it is useful to take a closer look at the average well-being of the households in the middle fifth (quintile) of the distribution of household well-being.[15] Estimates of economic well-being and its components discussed in the subsequent bilateral comparisons of middle-income households are reported in Table 2.2.

Britain

Turning first to the most dramatic case of convergence observed above (Britain), we find that the American middle quintile lost some of its lead in base income over the period because the growth in base income was faster in Britain than in the United States (Table 2.2). However, the decline in the US lead in LIMEW was far higher than the decline in the US lead in base income ($13,000 versus $2,000 in 2000 purchasing power parity [PPP] adjusted dollars).[16]

Figure 2.1 **US Lead in Economic Performance as Measured by Alternative Indicators** (gap between the US value and the other country's value expressed as a percent of the other country's value)

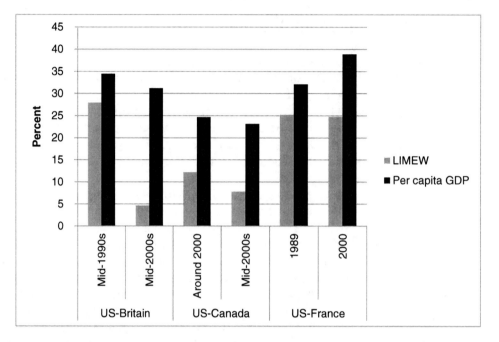

Notes:

(i) LIMEW: The values for LIMEW shown in the graph are based on the household median values of LIMEW in each country, adjusted by an equivalence scale. The equivalence scale used in the calculation was the three-parameter equivalence scale used in several studies by the US Bureau of Labor Statistics and Census Bureau (see, e.g., Short 2001). The equivalent median LIMEW for each country was adjusted for inflation using the implicit price deflator for actual individual consumption with the base year of 2000. The inflation-adjusted estimates were then converted into 2000 US dollars using the purchasing power parities (PPPs) for actual individual consumption. We obtained the implicit price deflators and the PPPs from the OECD website. OECD.Stat Extracts (http://stats.oecd.org).

(ii) Per capita GDP: The values for per capita GDP shown in the graph are based on real per capita GDP estimates in 2000 purchasing power parity US dollars. They were obtained from the OECD website. OECD.Stat Extracts (http://stats.oecd.org).

A much bigger shift than in base income took place in net government expenditures, where the US-British gap turned from $3,000 to *negative* $4,000. Government expenditures for households in the form of transfers and publicly provided goods and services increased *much faster* in Britain than in the United States, while the extent to which the US middle quintile enjoyed a lower tax liability narrowed.

Moreover, in a striking reversal of fortunes, the American middle quintile lost its lead in income from wealth almost completely over the period: from a level that was about 80 percent higher than the British in the mid-1990s, it became virtually on par with them in the mid-2000s. The convergence was apparently due to the disturbing immiseration of the American middle quintile in terms of wealth—reflected in the absolute decline in the amount of income from wealth in the United States—accompanied by a modest increase in the amount for the British.[17] It should be noted that this trend in the United States occurred even *before* the onset of the Great Recession of 2007 to 2009.

Table 2.2   **Economic Well-Being of the Middle Class** (middle quintile of equivalent LIMEW; average values in 2000 PPP US$, except for hours)

A. United States and Britain

	Mid-1990s		Mid-2000s		United States to Britain ratio	
	United States	Britain	United States	Britain	Mid-1990s	Mid-2000s
Base income	47,491	33,505	53,703	41,181	1.42	1.30
Income from wealth	5,623	3,148	4,106	3,987	1.79	1.03
Net government expenditures	9,600	6,611	10,539	14,595	1.45	0.72
Transfers	12,521	16,545	14,508	23,959	0.76	0.61
Consumption of public goods and services	9,258	5,031	11,204	8,095	1.84	1.38
Taxes	−12,179	−14,964	−15,174	−17,459	0.81	0.87
Household production	17,886	20,186	22,176	26,534	0.89	0.84
LIMEW	80,601	63,450	90,524	86,296	1.27	1.05
Hours of household production	2,420	2,339	2,538	2,569	1.03	0.99

B. United States and Canada

	Around 2000		Around 2005		United States to Canada ratio	
	United States	Canada	United States	Canada	Around 2000	Mid-2000s
Base income	54,165	40,377	51,150	44,549	1.34	1.15
Income from wealth	9,494	9,936	8,303	9,784	0.96	0.85
Net government expenditures	6,479	6,363	11,248	9,135	1.02	1.23
Transfers	12,110	15,249	15,071	17,017	0.79	0.89
Consumption of public goods and services	10,407	10,785	11,220	12,164	0.96	0.92
Taxes	−16,037	−19,671	−15,043	−20,046	0.82	0.75
Household production	22,041	25,300	23,793	23,955	0.87	0.99
LIMEW	92,179	81,978	94,495	87,424	1.12	1.08
Hours of household production	2,603	2,491	2,704	2,443	1.05	1.11

C. United States and France

	1989		2000		United States to France ratio	
	United States	France	United States	France	1989	2000
Base income	46,668	23,003	55,952	30,663	2.03	1.82
Income from wealth	6,043	6,358	7,114	8,349	0.95	0.85
Net government expenditures	6,546	11,689	6,524	11,784	0.56	0.55
Transfers	10,120	18,576	12,172	21,546	0.54	0.56
Consumption of public goods and services	8,554	6,833	10,384	8,155	1.25	1.27
Taxes	12,127	13,720	16,032	17,917	0.88	0.89
Household production	18,616	20,978	21,782	22,357	0.89	0.97
LIMEW	77,873	62,028	91,372	73,154	1.26	1.25
Hours of household production	2,483	2,315	2,581	2,073	1.07	1.24

Note: See note to Figure 2.1 for an explanation of the equivalence scale and PPP used in the estimates.

Canada

The gap in base income between the middle quintiles in Canada and the United States shrank between 2000 and 2005. While Canadians experienced an increase in base income, the American experience was the opposite. Unlike the case of Britain, the fall in the US lead in economic well-being was smaller than the decline in the US lead in base income ($3,000 vs. $7,000 in 2000 PPP US dollars). However, just as in the case of Britain, the income from wealth of the American middle quintile became smaller with respect to its Canadian counterpart over the period.[18] Income from wealth, which, around 2000, was only 4 percent lower in the United States than in Canada became 15 percent lower around 2005. In fact, income from wealth fell in both countries, but it fell by a much greater extent in the United States (13 vs. 2 percent).

Net government expenditures were, somewhat surprisingly, higher for the middle quintile in the United States than in Canada, because of the higher average tax liability in Canada. The US lead in net government expenditures became larger over the period, reflecting the sharp increase in transfers and decrease in taxes, thus ameliorating the extent to which the US middle quintile was losing ground in terms of LIMEW relative to Canada. The gap between the two countries would have narrowed more except for an increase in household production in the United States (13 percent lower for the middle quintile in the United States than in Canada), which raised the US LIMEW figures.[19]

France

In the case of France, the middle quintile's lower average economic well-being relative to its US counterpart was entirely due to its lower base income (reflecting primarily lower household earnings). However, the gap in base income was smaller in 2000 than 1989, as the United States-to-France ratio declined from 2.03 to 1.82. France had a lead over the United States in both years in terms of other components. Just as in the British and Canadian comparisons, the position of the US middle quintile relative to the French worsened in terms of income from wealth, falling from a level that was 5 percent lower than the French in 1989 to a level that was 15 percent lower in 2000.

The gap in net government expenditures, on the other hand, remained stable. The US middle quintile received 56 cents for every dollar received by its French counterparts. Most of the gap here can be accounted for by the much higher level of transfers received by the middle-quintile French households. Publicly provided goods and services were actually higher and taxes were only slightly lower in the United States. The average value of household production moved toward parity between 1989 and 2000, primarily due to increased hours of household production in the United States and a decline in France.

CHANGES IN WELL-BEING FOR THE RICHEST AND POOREST: HOW DO AMERICANS FARE COMPARED TO BRITONS, CANADIANS, AND THE FRENCH?

We now shift our focus from the middle of the LIMEW distribution to examine how American households in the different deciles of the LIMEW distribution have fared relative to their counterparts in the other countries. The comparison of the United States and Britain is shown in Figure 2.2, Panel A. The figure on the left side ("gap in well-being") shows the percentage by which the average LIMEW of each decile in the United States exceeded or fell short of its British counterpart. In the mid-1990s, the lead enjoyed by the US households was positively correlated with the position in the distribution. That is, the rich American households were richer than the rich British households by a greater extent than the poor American households were better-off than the poor British households.[20]

By the mid-2000s, American households throughout the distribution lost their lead in LIMEW over the British households. Most notably, the bottom 40 percent were now *below* their British counterparts. This is a sharp contrast from the mid-1990s, when they enjoyed a lead of 16 to 24 percent over their British counterparts. Those in the top 50 percent did maintain the lead over their British counterparts, but the extent of the lead increased with higher deciles, just as in the mid-1990s. In fact, the distribution of the gap has become even more "pro-rich," as shown by the steeper gradient of the curve in the later period.

The change in the distributional profile of the US-British gap is largely due to the difference in how growth in well-being was shared across the distribution in each country, as shown in the figure on the right side ("change in well-being"). "The rich got richer" in the United States, while growth benefited lower-income groups in Britain. In the United States, the households in the higher rungs of the distribution experienced faster growth than those in the lower rungs, while the opposite pattern prevailed in Britain.

A similar comparison of the United States with Canada revealed that, just as with Britain, the lead enjoyed by American households was heavily concentrated among the richest in both years (Figure 2.2, Panel B, "gap in well-being"). In particular, the lead was much larger for the top two deciles.[21] We can see that American households throughout the distribution lost their lead over Canadian households, similar to what we showed earlier with Britain. It appears that the relative reduction in the gap was higher for those in the upper portions of the distribution. This pattern is accounted for by the differences in income growth rates across the deciles, shown on the right-side figure ("change in well-being"). Growth in well-being favored the higher-income groups more than the lower-income groups in Canada as well as in the United States, in contrast to what we observed for Britain from the mid-1990s to the mid-2000s. However, the Canadian pattern was actually more pro-rich than that in the United States, as shown by the steeper gradient of the Canadian curve. One reason why the US pattern appears less pro-rich is that the top decile in the United States suffered a notable absolute decline in its LIMEW over the period.

Comparing households in the United States to their French counterparts shows that the higher the relative position in the LIMEW distribution (Figure 2.2, Panel C, "gap in well-being"), the stronger the US advantage over a French household. However, the meager advantage that the bottom 10 percent of households in the United States had over their French counterparts in 1989 appears to have almost vanished by 2000. In contrast to this convergence at the bottom, the gaps between the other portions of the distribution, except at the top two deciles, remained stable across the two years.

Figure 2.2   **Economic Well-Being by Deciles of Equivalent LIMEW: Bilateral Comparisons of (A) United States and Great Britain; (B) United States and Canada; and (C) United States and France**

A. United States and Great Britain

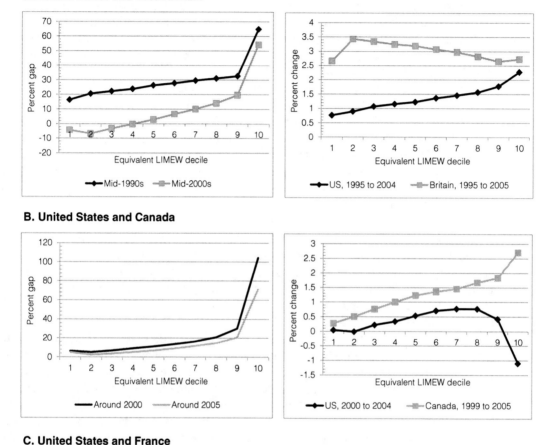

B. United States and Canada

C. United States and France

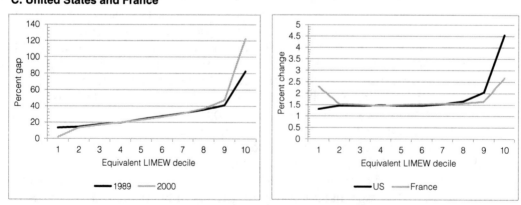

1. Gap in average equivalent LIMEW by decile (gap between the US value and the other country's value expressed as a percent of the other country's value).

2. Average annual percent change in average equivalent LIMEW by decile.

Note: See note to Figure 2.1 for an explanation of the equivalence scale and PPP used in the estimates.

This reflected comparatively similar rates of income growth for households in these portions of the distribution in the two countries (figure on the right, "change in well-being"). Notably, the gap between the top deciles in the two countries widened greatly over the period, with the American top decile's average LIMEW exceeding its French counterpart by 123 percent in 2000, compared to "only" 83 percent in 1989.

EXPLORING THE STRUCTURE OF INEQUALITY IN THE UNITED STATES AND COMPARISON COUNTRIES

The distribution of LIMEW by decile offers a visual and intuitive picture of inequality. But such a picture is not altogether helpful in understanding the differences in the overall level of inequality and its structure across countries or across time. In order to further explore the nature of inequality in the four countries, it is useful to have a summary measure of inequality that can be decomposed by individual component. We now turn to this task using the Gini coefficient—the most widely used summary measure of inequality—and its decomposition by the major components of LIMEW across countries.[22]

Our results so far suggest that overall inequality would have declined in Britain (because the lower rungs of the distribution gained more from overall growth than the higher rungs) and increased in the United States (because the higher rungs of the distribution gained more from overall growth than the lower rungs).[23] This expectation is borne out by the Gini ratios of the two countries, and the fact that the gap in the inequality of LIMEW between the two countries widened between the mid-1990s and around 2005 from 5.6 to 8.8 Gini points (Table 2.3, Panel A). The relatively high level of inequality in the United States compared to Britain is mainly accounted for by the higher disequalizing effect of base income and income from wealth, the two components of LIMEW that are most susceptible to the functioning of markets (labor and capital markets).

The redistributive effect of taxes and government spending accounted only for a very small part of the difference in the inequality between the two countries. Out of the 8.8-point gap in the Gini between the two countries in the mid-2000s, base income contributed 3.9 points, income from wealth contributed 6.1 points, and household production made a negative (offsetting) contribution of 2.9 points. The contribution of net government expenditures to the difference in inequality was only 0.7 and 0.4 Gini points in the mid-1990s and mid-2000s, respectively.

Our comparison of growth across deciles in Canada and the United States indicates that we should expect overall inequality to decline in the latter (recall the drop in the average LIMEW for the top decile) and rise in the former (because the top parts of the distribution gained more from the growth in well-being). The estimates of the Gini ratio (Table 2.3, Panel B) confirm this. The gap in Gini ratios between the two countries fell from 12 to 9.2 Gini points during the first half of the 2000s. Similar to our findings from the British comparison, the results indicate that the much higher level of inequality in the United States is principally accounted for by the disequalizing effect of market forces. Out of the 9.2-point gap between the two countries around 2000, base income contributed 3.8 points, while income from wealth contributed 8.3

Table 2.3   **Decomposition of Economic Inequality Gini Points** (Gini decomposition of equivalent LIMEW)

A. United States and Britain

	United States		Britain		United States *minus* Britain	
	Mid-1990s	Mid-2000s	Mid-1990s	Mid-2000s	Mid-1990s	Mid-2000s
Gini	31.7	34.0	26.2	25.2	5.6	8.8
Base income	21.3	21.1	18.4	17.2	2.8	3.9
Income from wealth	9.8	11.0	4.2	4.9	5.6	6.1
Net government expenditures	−5.7	−4.6	−6.5	−4.9	0.7	0.4
Household production	6.4	6.5	10.0	8.0	−3.5	−1.5

B. United States and Canada

	United States		Canada		United States *minus* Canada	
	Around 2000	Mid-2000s	Around 2000	Mid-2000s	Around 2000	Mid-2000s
Gini	38.6	37.6	26.6	28.5	12.0	9.2
Base income	18.0	18.1	13.5	14.3	4.5	3.8
Income from wealth	20.3	18.2	8.0	9.9	12.4	8.3
Net government expenditures	−5.6	−4.2	−4.4	−4.2	−1.2	−0.1
Household production	5.9	5.6	9.6	8.5	−3.7	−2.9

C. United States and France

	United States		France		United States *minus* France	
	1989	2000	1989	2000	1989	2000
Gini	32.0	38.2	23.7	25.3	8.2	12.9
Base income	18.9	19.0	9.2	6.9	9.6	12.1
Income from wealth	12.4	18.8	5.3	9.5	7.1	9.3
Net government expenditures	−6.0	−5.8	0.9	1.6	−6.9	−7.4
Household production	6.7	6.3	8.3	7.3	−1.6	−1.1

points. In contrast, household production made a negative contribution of 1.5 points. Analogous to the British comparison, net government expenditures, often taken as an index of the redistributive effect of government expenditures and taxation, contributed very little to the difference in inequality between the United States and Canada.

Turning next to the French-US comparison, we find that the level of overall inequality in France rose modestly by 1.6 Gini points from 1989 to reach a level of 25.3 in 2000 (Table 2.3, Panel C). This is consistent with the pattern of income growth across deciles that we observed earlier, which showed almost identical income growth for the second through ninth deciles and higher growth rates for the top and bottom deciles. Because the Gini coefficient is sensitive to changes in the middle of the distribution (in this case, loss in income shares), it showed a modest increase. In contrast, the increase in economic inequality in the US was far from modest: the Gini ratio increased by 6.2 Gini points from 1989 to attain a level of 38.3 in 2000. The increase is consistent with the pro-rich pattern of income growth that we saw across the deciles, which led to an increase in the share of aggregate LIMEW going to the higher rungs of the distribution and a decrease in the share of the lower rungs of the distribution.

As a result of the greater increase in the United States, the gap in the inequality of economic well-being between the United States and France widened from 8.2 Gini points in 1989 to 12.9 in 2000. The results from the decomposition analysis suggest, just as in the case of the other two comparisons, to the much larger disequalizing effects of markets in the United States. Base income and income from wealth contributed, respectively, 12.1 and 9.3 Gini points to the inequality gap between the two countries in 2000. However, unlike in the comparisons of the United States with Canada and Britain, net government expenditures actually contributed substantially toward narrowing the inequality divide.

Somewhat surprisingly, this was entirely due to the inequality reducing effects of net government expenditures in the United States rather than in France, where net government expenditures had a minor inequality enhancing effect in both years. In the case of France, this appears to be due to a relatively high tax burden on the lower and middle classes. We next turn to trends in economic well-being in the United States from 1959 to 2007.

LONG-TERM TRENDS IN ECONOMIC WELL-BEING IN THE UNITED STATES

TRENDS IN THE LEVEL OF ECONOMIC WELL-BEING, CENSUS INCOME, AND HOURS WORKED

Over the entire 1959–2007 period, median economic well-being in the United States grew at an annual rate of 0.67 percent (Figure 2.3, Panel A). However, there was considerable variation by subperiods. Trends also differ substantially between economic well-being and census income.

From 1959 to 1972, median LIMEW gained only 0.4 percent per year, while from 1972 to 1982 median economic well-being suffered an absolute decline. This was followed by a growth burst from 1982 to 1989 of 2.8 percent per year. But when growth slowed from 1989 to 2004, median economic well-being could muster only a 0.9 percent advance per year, and it collapsed to a snail's pace of 0.2 percent per year between 2004 and 2007.

How do these growth rates compare to the conventional measure of income? Over the entire 1959–2007 period, median census income grew at almost the same rate as median economic well-being, 0.63 per year compared to 0.67 percent per year. There are much larger differences by subperiods. Between 1959 and 1972, median census income grew at an annual rate *four* times higher than that of median economic well-being. The so-called golden age of income growth does not appear so golden when a broader measure of well-being is employed as the yardstick. From 1972 to 1982, both economic well-being and census income fell in absolute terms, with the former showing a rate of decline that was twice as high. As a result of these uneven trends, the level of economic well-being in 1982 was roughly 2 percent lower than in 1959 while the level of census income was approximately 16 percent *higher*.

Subsequently, in the years 1982 to 1989, both measures recorded very high growth rates, but economic well-being grew almost twice as fast.[24] The growth during this period appears to be spectacular partly because of the depression-like conditions of 1982.

Figure 2.3   Annual Rates of Change in Economic Well-Being, Census Income, and Hours Worked in the United States, 1959–2007

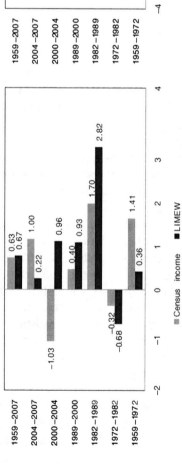

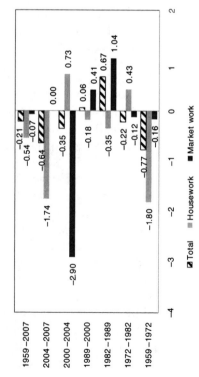

A. Economic well-being and census income

B. Hours worked

Similar to economic well-being, census income also registered a decline in the annual growth rate between 1989 and 2000, growing at only half the pace of the LIMEW. The two measures moved in different directions between 2000 and 2004—economic well-being rising and census income falling. In the succeeding years, 2004 to 2007, census income grew almost five times as fast as economic well-being, yet the level of census income in 2007 was lower than in 2000.[25] Our dissection of the growth rates by subperiods shows that the difference between the measures in the picture they convey regarding trends in well-being is, in fact, substantial. The underlying reason for the difference lies in the fact that while median census income is driven largely by movements in earnings, the LIMEW is subject to more complex influences (such as changing asset values or the time spent on household production).

However, the story is not complete without considering hours worked, since these subtract from leisure time. By our calculations, there was a noticeable decline in median annual hours worked from 1959 to 1982 (0.5 percent per year) that was almost entirely due to a large decline in housework (Figure 2.3, Panel B). In contrast, there was a marked rise in total hours worked from 1982 to 1989 (0.7 percent per year) that was entirely due to an increase in market work (i.e., the labor market).[26] There was little change from 1989 to 2000. But between 2000 and 2007, total hours fell at the annual rate of 0.5 percent, due mainly to the sharp decline in market work and secondarily to a more modest reduction in housework. During the 1959–2007 period, median hours worked fell by 9.6 percent overall, as median market work fell by 3.3 percent and housework fell by 23.0 percent. This contributes positively to average household well-being, *ceteris paribus*. But it is important to consider what happened to average Americans.

THE CHANGING FORTUNES OF MIDDLE-INCOME AMERICANS

We now turn to a closer examination of changes in the third quintile of the LIMEW distribution, where both mean and median economic well-being in 1982 was slightly lower than in 1959.[27] The decline in the mean was partially due to a fall in household production from 32 to 21 percent or by $7,000 in 2007 dollars (Table 2.4)[28] Decreases in housework hours and the unit value of housework represented 28 and 72 percent of the decline, respectively (estimates not shown). This decline was partially offset by robust growth in net government expenditures, from 3 to 12 percent of LIMEW, an increase of $5,300. Another reason for the sluggish growth in economic well-being over this period was the drop in base income between 1972 and 1982, (from 62 to 59 percent, or by $4,400), that wiped out the $4,400 gain in the 1959–1972 period.

The composition of LIMEW for the middle quintile remained relatively stable from 1982 to 1989, and the very high rate of growth of the mean LIMEW of the middle quintile (22 percent) was due to relatively balanced growth in all four components. In particular, average base income for the middle quintile rose by $6,600, and household production, which had fallen for this group in the earlier period, increased by $5,200. But in this case most of the gain (98 percent) in household production was due to a rise in the unit value of housework, not to more hours worked.

The growth of the mean LIMEW of the middle quintile slowed between 1989 and 2000. The composition of LIMEW of the middle quintile was also relatively stable

Table 2.4 Economic Well-Being of the Middle Quintile in the United States, 1959–2007

A. Average LIMEW of the middle quintile (in 2007 dollars) and its composition (in percent)

Year	Mean LIMEW (in 2007$)	Total	Base income	Income from wealth	Net government expenditures	Household production
1959	62,482	100	57.9	6.5	3.2	32.4
1972	65,701	100	61.8	8.4	7.0	22.7
1982	61,329	100	59.0	8.1	12.0	20.9
1989	74,507	100	57.4	8.2	10.2	24.2
2000	82,535	100	58.0	8.7	9.7	23.5
2004	85,769	100	53.0	7.4	15.1	24.5
2007	86,224	100	54.0	7.7	14.7	23.5

B. Contribution by component to the change in LIMEW and census income (MI) of the middle quintile

	1959–1972		1972–1982		1982–1989		1989–2000		2000–2004		2004–2007		1959–2007	
	LIMEW	MI	LIMEW	MI	LIMEW	MI	LIMEW	MI	LIMEW	MI	LIMEW	MI	LIMEW	MI
Base Income	7.1	10.5	-6.7	-7.0	10.7	12.4	6.9	6.0	-3.0	-3.6	1.3	2.5	16.6	23.4
Income from wealth	2.3	2.2	-0.9	2.2	1.9	0.6	1.5	-1.9	-1.1	-1.3	0.4	0.4	4.1	1.7
Home wealth	1.6		-0.5		0.5		-0.6		-0.6		-0.1		-0.3	
Nonhome wealth	0.7		-0.3		1.4		2.1		-0.4		0.5		4.4	
Net government expenditures	4.2	8.0	4.1	3.9	0.5	-0.3	0.6	3.1	6.0	3.3	-0.3	-2.2	17.1	18.0
Transfers	5.3	8.0	4.1	3.9	0.7	-0.3	2.0	3.1	2.7	3.3	1.3	-2.2	17.9	18.0
Consumption of public goods and services	4.5		-0.6		2.0		1.6		0.6		0.8		9.5	
Taxes	-5.6		0.6		-2.2		-3.0		2.7		-2.3		-10.3	
Household production	-8.5		-3.2		8.5		1.8		2.0		-0.9		0.1	
Total	5.2	20.7	-6.7	-0.9	21.5	12.7	10.8	7.2	3.9	-1.6	0.5	0.6	38.0	43.2

over this period, with reduced growth of all components. Just as all four components had contributed to a positive increase in the 1982–1989 period, all four grew more slowly from 1989 to 2000. However, between 2000 and 2004, the growth of mean LIMEW of the middle quintile slowed to a crawl, gaining only 3.9 percent. At the same time, the composition of LIMEW changed dramatically in favor of net government expenditures, which rose by $4,900, while base income and income from wealth declined by $2,500 and $900, respectively. A reversal of both trends from 2004 to 2007, with net government spending showing negative growth and base income and income from wealth showing positive gains, shows the importance of net government spending in cushioning cycles in the private economy. However, household production also declined over these years, and mean LIMEW grew by only 0.5 percent.

Both the mean and median LIMEW of the middle quintile grew by about 38 percent over the 1959–2007 period. Of this gain, 17.1 percentage points (or 45 percent) was due to the increase in net government expenditures (Table 2.5) in the form of an increase in transfers (18 percentage points) and consumption of public goods and services (10 percentage points), while an increase in the tax burden subtracted 10 percentage points. The increase in base income added another 17 percentage points to the growth in LIMEW of the middle class, while gains in income from wealth contributed only 4 percentage points. Household production barely made any contribution toward the growth of middle-class LIMEW over the period.[29]

The public sector was as important as income growth to increases in economic well-being of the middle class between 1959 and 2007. The share of net government expenditures in the LIMEW of the middle quintile rose dramatically from 3 to 15 percent between 1959 and 2007. As a percentage of LIMEW, expenditures rose by 17 percentage points from 12 to 29 percent between 1959 and 2007. Much of this increase was driven by more transfers, which, as a percentage of LIMEW, rose from 4 to 16 percent over the period, an increase of 12 percentage points. Two-thirds of the increase in the percentage share of transfers in LIMEW occurred as a result of the expansion of transfer programs which did not exist in 1959 (including Medicare, Medicaid, and the earned income tax credit). Publicly provided goods and services also increased much faster than LIMEW although more slowly than transfers, reflected in their percentage share of LIMEW, which rose from 8 to 13 percent between 1959 and 2007. The largest share (3 of 5 percentage points) in the increased consumption of public goods and services came from the increasing share of education expenditures in LIMEW.

Higher labor income contributed most of the growth in census income and was a close second to net government expenditures in contributing to higher economic well-being for the middle quintile between 1959 and 2007. Gains in income from wealth were a distant third, even with increases in housing wealth and more participation in the stock market. How has all this affected trends in inequality?

ECONOMIC INEQUALITY OVER TIME IN THE UNITED STATES

As the final part of our analysis, we turn to overall inequality trends in the United States over the last half century. It is striking that the shares of the middle three quintiles were *lower* in 2007 than in 1959 in the distributions of both economic well-being and

Table 2.5   **Share of Each Quintile and the Top 5 Percent in Aggregate Income in the United States, 1959–2007** (in percent)

	Quintiles					Top 5 percent
	1	2	3	4	5	
1959						
LIMEW	5.6	12.0	17.4	23.2	41.8	17.1
MI	3.4	10.9	17.3	24.3	44.0	17.3
1972						
LIMEW	5.7	11.7	17.1	23.5	41.9	16.8
MI	3.7	9.7	17.4	25.2	43.9	16.2
1982						
LIMEW	6.4	11.6	16.6	22.9	42.4	17.6
MI	4.0	10.1	16.6	24.7	44.7	16.4
1989						
LIMEW	6.3	11.6	16.6	22.9	42.6	17.5
MI	3.9	9.7	16.2	24.5	45.6	17.0
2000						
LIMEW	5.5	10.3	14.9	21.1	48.2	23.5
MI	3.6	8.9	14.8	23.1	49.7	21.8
2004						
LIMEW	5.6	10.5	15.4	21.7	46.8	22.6
MI	3.4	8.7	14.7	23.3	50.0	21.6
2007						
LIMEW	5.4	10.4	15.1	21.3	47.8	23.1
MI	3.4	8.7	14.8	23.5	49.6	21.0

census income (Table 2.5). A changing division of the economic pie favored the top quintile and the top 5 percent far more than the bottom quintile. The bottom quintile showed a slight drop in its share of total LIMEW but no change in its share of total census income, while the top quintile's share of aggregate LIMEW and census income went up by 6.0 and 5.6 percentage points, respectively.

From 1959 to 1989, the increase in the share of the top quintile and the top 5 percent was relatively moderate in terms of both aggregate LIMEW and census income. But that was followed by a big surge from 1989 to 2000 and then little change between 2000 and 2007. The bottom quintile also saw modest growth in its share until 1989, but lost ground thereafter. In all the years studied here, the top quintile fared better according to census income than LIMEW in terms of its share in the overall pie (50 vs. 48 percent in 2007), and the bottom quintile received a larger share in LIMEW than census income (5.4 vs. 3.4 percent in 2007). Conventional income actually overstates the gap between the bottom and top quintile in economic well-being because some key components of well-being are neglected in the conventional measure. For example, excluding income taxes can overstate the income share of the top quintile because the effective income tax rate of the top quintile is higher than that of the bottom quintile. Similarly, exclusion of means-tested noncash transfers can understate the income share of the bottom quintile because it receives a larger share of such benefits than the top quintile.

The decline in the income share of the middle class (the third quintile) between 1959 and 2007 was similar in LIMEW and census income (2.3 and 2.5 percentage points). The share of the second quintile fell by 1.6 percentage points in LIMEW and 2.2 percentage points in census income, while that of the fourth quintile fell by 1.9 and 0.8 percentage points in LIMEW and census income, respectively. The most pronounced declines in the shares of the middle three quintiles happened during the 1989–2000 period. Consistent with the data on quintile shares, census income shows a larger degree of inequality than LIMEW according to the Gini coefficient (Table 2.6).

Our finding of less inequality in economic well-being compared to census income is due to the inclusion of consumption of public goods and services, household production, and taxes. Consumption of public goods and services and household production are relatively large in size and distributed less unequally than earnings or income from wealth across the rungs of the distribution. Therefore, adding them to an income measure would result in an income measure with lower inequality. Inclusion of taxes tends to lower inequality because they constitute a larger fraction of the pre-tax income of households in the upper echelons of the distribution than of those in the bottom rungs. As a result, the inclusion of taxes generally leads to lowered measured inequality.

Equivalence-scale adjustment—that is, the adjustment of income for family size and composition—lowers measured inequality in both economic well-being and census income. This is not surprising in light of the well-known correlation that exists between household size and income. The bottom rungs of the income distribution tend to have more single-person households and smaller families than the higher rungs, so this adjustment lowers the measured inequality in both economic well-being and census income. Additionally, in the case of economic well-being, consumption of public goods and services and household production display strong positive correlation with household size.

Consider, for example, households with school-age children. The single largest component of consumption of public goods and services is public education, for which we have imputed per-pupil expenditures as a part of economic well-being. Households with more school-age children would, in general, have larger amounts of consumption of public goods and services allocated to them. Similarly, hours spent on household production also tend to increase with both the number of adults and the number of children at home, thus producing a positive correlation between household size and value of household production.

The Gini coefficients indicate a considerably higher level of inequality in 2007 than 1959 for both LIMEW and census income. This result is also consistent with the pattern of changes in quintile income shares discussed earlier. The increase was about the same for census income (5.8 Gini points) and LIMEW (5.9 Gini points).[30] Neither measure shows considerable change in inequality between 1959 and 1972. According to both census income and the LIMEW, almost all of the increase in inequality occurred from 1989 to 2000.[31]

The results from our decomposition analysis showed that the leading contributor to inequality in LIMEW and census income was base income (Table 2.7). However, the size of its contribution is notably different as base income accounts for almost all of the inequality in census income. The higher contribution is mainly because base income constitutes a larger share of census income than of LIMEW. Conversely, in-

Table 2.6   **Economic Inequality in the United States by Measure, 1959–2007**
(Gini coefficient x 100)

	1959	1972	1982	1989	2000	2004	2007
LIMEW	36.1	36.3	36.0	36.3	42.3	41.0	42.0
MI	40.3	40.7	40.9	41.8	46.0	46.5	46.2
Equivalence scale adjusted measures							
Equivalent LIMEW	32.8	31.7	30.8	31.9	38.2	36.5	37.8
Equivalent MI	40.1	38.9	39.1	40.0	44.1	44.5	44.3

come from wealth constituted a much larger share of LIMEW than census income and this accounts for the much higher contribution of income from wealth to inequality in LIMEW than census income.

The estimates suggest that although economic well-being and census income show comparable increases in inequality over the 1959–2007 period, the principal source of the increase is different in the two measures. Changes in the level and distribution of income from nonhome wealth account for the bulk of the growth in the inequality of economic well-being, while for census income, base income accounts for by far the largest part in the increase in MI inequality.

Net government expenditures ameliorated the increase in the inequality of economic well-being. Transfers served the same function for census income. The moderating effect of net government expenditures was stronger in economic well-being in comparison to transfers in census income between 1959 and 2000. However, when we also include the first years of the twenty-first century in our comparison, the position is reversed: net government expenditures accounted for a reduction of 0.4 Gini points between 1959 and 2007, compared to the contribution of transfers toward a reduction of 1.2 points in census income. The main reason behind this reversal appears to be the notable decline in the inequality reducing effect of taxes in economic well-being.

It is striking that household production was the largest single component restraining the growth of inequality of economic well-being between 1959 and 2007. The decline in its contribution (of 3.4 Gini points) stemmed entirely from the decline in its share of LIMEW. As noted before, there was a sizable decline in the overall hours spent on household production activities, which is mirrored in the fall in the share of household production in LIMEW.

CONCLUDING REMARKS

In this chapter, we compare economic well-being in Canada, France, Great Britain, and the United States during the 1990s and 2000s using an expanded measure of economic well-being called the Levy Institute Measure of Economic Well-Being (LIMEW). We find convergence in median living standards between the United States and the other three countries over time, meaning that the "US advantage" is shrinking. Convergence with Britain was the most dramatic: the average household in the United States was only 5 percent better off than its British counterpart in the

Table 2.7 **Decomposition of Inequality in the United States by Income Source and Income Measure** (Gini points x 100)

	1959	2000	2007	Change, 1959–2007
LIMEW				
Base money income	19.7	20.9	19.4	−0.4
Income from wealth	6.4	17.1	16.5	10.1
Imputed rent	1.2	1.8	1.5	0.4
Annuities	5.2	15.3	14.9	9.7
Net government expenditures	−1.4	−3.9	−1.8	−0.4
Transfers	0.8	1.0	1.4	0.6
Consumption of public goods and services	1.8	2.4	2.7	1.0
Taxes	−3.9	−7.3	−5.9	−2.0
Household production	11.4	8.2	8.0	−3.4
Total	36.1	42.3	42.0	5.9
Money Income				
Base money income	38.6	43.6	43.7	5.1
Property income	1.5	3.4	3.4	1.9
Transfers	0.2	−1.0	−0.9	−1.2
Total	40.3	46.0	46.2	5.8

Note: Contribution of each income source is expressed in Gini points multiplied by 100. The numbers shown in the row labeled "Total" refer to the Gini ratio of the income measure.

mid-2000s as against 28 percent in the mid-1990s. The average Canadian household also narrowed its gap vis-à-vis the United States: from 12 percent around 2000 to only 8 percent around 2005. However, in the case of France, the higher lead enjoyed by the average US household declined only slightly.

But when we look at relative well-being *within* the United States, we see that inequality was considerably higher than in the other three countries. Moreover, the inequality gap between the United States widened substantially relative to Britain and France, while narrowing relative to Canada.

We also find that median census income in the United States grew sluggishly over the 1959 to 2007 period, at .63 percent compared to the annual growth in GDP per capita of 2.3 percent. Growth in the LIMEW measure of well-being was slightly higher than census income at 0.67 percent. However, the relative congruence between LIMEW and the conventional measure, census income, in the rates of change in the median over the 1959–2007 period masks important differences by subperiod. Median economic well-being showed much slower growth from 1959 to 1982 than median census income. Subsequently, median economic well-being grew faster from 1982 to 2007. These differences indicate the importance of public expenditures and changes in hours of work, both in the household and the marketplace.

According to the LIMEW measure, the public sector was as important as labor income in its contribution to the growth in the economic well-being of the middle class between 1959 and 2007. The effect of net government expenditures in sustaining middle-class economic well-being was particularly strong between 1959 and 1982 and between 2000 and 2007. In the latter period, when median economic well-being grew by only 0.6 percent per year, the increase in net government expenditures accounted for *134 percent* of the growth of LIMEW, as base income and income from wealth both contracted in absolute terms. The increase in net government expenditures of the middle quintile, in turn, was mainly due to increased public transfers and only secondarily to increases in publicly provided goods and services.

There was also substantial growth of inequality in the United States over the years from 1959 to 2007 in both census income and LIMEW. Time trends were similar for the two measures, though for different reasons. Both show a modest rise in inequality from 1959 to 1989 and then a large spike from 1989 to 2000, followed by little change through 2007. Income from nonhome wealth made by far the largest contribution to the increase in inequality between 1959 and 2007 recorded for LIMEW. In contrast, in the case of census income, the principal factor behind the increase in inequality was the rising contribution from base income. These two factors were particularly important in explaining the inequality surge of their respective measures during the 1990s. Net government expenditures helped moderate the increase in inequality between 1959 and 2007 in the case of economic well-being.

POLICY RECOMMENDATIONS

The results of this chapter support arguments for enhanced public spending and transfers as important to the living standards of the middle class as well as to low-income households. As outlined above, net government expenditures made a contribution that was roughly as large as that of labor income to the growth of economic well-being of the middle class from 1959 to 2007. Moreover, the public sector was crucial in sustaining median economic well-being in the United States from 2000 to 2007 because labor income and income from wealth were lower in 2007 than in 2000.

What kinds of programs are best for helping the middle class? With regard to publicly produced goods and services, the single most important program is education. In this period of retrenchment of educational spending by state and local governments, we call instead for an enhancement of educational expenditures. This will lead to further improvements in the economic well-being of the middle class. Another important government program is spending on transportation—particularly roads and highways. Not only will such an effort improve the country's infrastructure, but also it will improve broadly based living standards.

With regard to transfer programs, the two most important ones for middle-class well-being are Social Security and Medicare. In contrast to recent calls for reduced spending on these two programs, we urge *enhanced* government-provided benefits for these programs. If there are to be spending reductions, these should be based on true efficiencies and reduced waste and fraud rather than on benefits cuts to recipients. They can ill afford these cuts given what is happening to base income in the middle of the distribution.

Reductions in taxes have also improved economic well-being among the middle class. The largest tax paid by the middle class is the payroll tax (mainly to finance Social Security), so the two-year reduction in rates from 2011 to 2012 had an enormous positive impact on middle-class well-being as well as on consumer spending. Rather than ending the rate reduction, as happened in January 2013, we recommend its reinstatement—at least in part or for some groups. We also propose permanent reductions in federal and state income tax rates for middle-income Americans that would be offset by higher tax rates for the rich. With decades of inequality in income and well-being likely to continue, a more progressive tax schedule is critical to reducing inequality in the United States.

NOTES

We are grateful to the Alfred P. Sloan Foundation for its generous financial support. Asena Caner, Hyunsub Kum, and Melissa Mahoney contributed to the creation of the LIMEW estimates for the United States. The LIMEW estimates for Canada were developed in collaboration with Andrew Sharpe, Alexander Murray, Benjamin Evans, and Elspeth Hazell. We are grateful for contributions by Ramzi Hadji and Georges Menahem toward the estimates of LIMEW for France. We have also benefited greatly from the comments and suggestions made by the editors and participants at the conference "A Brighter Future: Improving the Standard of Living Now and for the Next Generation" held at the Colorado Center for Policy Studies, October 20–22, 2011.

1. The choice of years was dictated by data availability. For Canada, the estimates are for 1999 and 2005 (Sharpe et al. 2011); for France, the estimates are for 1989 and 2000 (Masterson et al. 2011); and for Great Britain, the estimates are for 1995 and 2005 (Eren et al. 2011). The choice of benchmark years was guided by three considerations: they should not be earlier than the late 1980s; appropriate microdata on income, wealth, and time-use should be available; and comparable estimates for the United States should be possible.

2. Our goal was to develop for each country estimates that were as comprehensive as permitted by the data for comparison with the United States. As the quality and extent of data available varied across countries, we did not aim to produce multilateral comparisons because that would have meant compromising on the comprehensiveness of our measure for individual countries.

3. We describe MI as "census income" below because it is regularly measured in the United States by the Census Bureau via its Current Population Survey supplements.

4. Wolff and Zacharias (2007) provided an overview of the LIMEW and discussed results for the United States in the 1990s using census income, LIMEW, and the Census Bureau's broadest definition of disposable income.

5. In particular, they argued in favor of retaining property-type income as their nonhome wealth measure (identical to that of money income), whereas we use an imputed annuity to nonhome household wealth. Like us, they also propose using imputed rent on owner-occupied housing. While they net out only income taxes, payroll taxes, and property taxes to obtain their measure of adjustable disposable income, we also net out consumption taxes, whenever sufficient information is available to do so. Moreover, we include an imputed value to public expenditures allocated to households, while their proposed measure does not.

6. In particular, their "wealth" measure is property-type income plus net realized capital gains on wealth. This concept is narrower than ours since we implicitly include both realized and unrealized capital gains. Smeeding and Weinberg use the return on equity on owner-occupied housing to value home real estate, whereas we, like the Canberra Group, use imputed rent on housing. While the former subtract only income taxes, payroll taxes, and property taxes to obtain their measure of net total income, we also deduct consumption taxes, subject to availability of data. Finally, as noted above, we include consumption of public goods and services in our measure, whereas Smeeding and Weinberg do not. Also see Wolff and Zacharias (2003) for further comparisons with alternative approaches to the measurement of economic well-being. Another approach to measuring extended income is from Citro and Michael (1995) in the context of measuring poverty.

7. It should be noted that there are some differences depending on the years that are compared. There are also some differences in the construction of LIMEW across bilateral comparisons. These differences will be noted later during the course of our discussion. We now turn to a summary of the

procedures used to construct LIMEW. See Wolff, Zacharias, and Masterson (2009) for a discussion of the methodology used to construct the US historical estimates reported in this paper.

8. In general, we include under this heading only private pensions from defined-contribution plans because we impute income from wealth held in the form of defined-contribution pension plans. However, in the US-Canada comparison, we also included pensions from defined-benefit plans because we also imputed income from this form of wealth. See below.

9. We did not have enough information to impute the employer contributions for health insurance in the US LIMEW prior to 1982. Therefore, the historical estimates of LIMEW discussed later in this chapter do not include this component.

10. In the Canadian LIMEW, the estimated values of defined-benefit pension plans are included in pension assets, in addition to defined-contribution plans. For the purposes of comparison, we estimated the value of defined-benefit pension plans for the United States also.

11. The annuity is the same for the remaining life of the wealth holder and the terminal wealth is assumed to be zero (in the case of households with multiple adults, we use the maximum of the life expectancy of the head of household and spouse in the annuity formula). Moreover, in our method, we account for differences in portfolio composition across households. Instead of using a single interest rate for all assets, we use a weighted average of asset-specific and historic real rates of return, where the weights are the proportions of the different assets in a household's total wealth.

12. These expenditures, in general, are derived from the National Income and Product Accounts.

13. We align the aggregate payroll, income, and property taxes in the microdata with their NIPA counterparts, as we did for government expenditures. Estimates of consumption taxes are also included in the household tax burden. However, it is not aligned to a macroeconomic aggregate because national accounts do not report the household portion of consumption taxes separately. Detailed information required for the estimation of consumption taxes was not available for the United States prior to 1989. As a result, our historical estimates discussed later in the chapter do not include consumption taxes.

14. We used real per capita GDP estimates in 2000 PPP US dollars in the comparisons stated in this paragraph. The source of data is the OECD website: http://stats.oecd.org/Index.aspx?DatasetCode=SNA_ TABLE 1. (The series identifier is "GDPHVPVOB: GDP per capita, 2000 constant PPPs, U.S. dollars.")

15. In general, the change in the LIMEW of the average household is quite closely approximated by the change in the average LIMEW of the middle quintile. Unlike the former, the latter can be decomposed exactly into its constituent parts, and such a breakdown can offer some insights about the factors affecting the well-being of the average household (e.g., improved labor market conditions that might be reflected in higher earnings as distinct from increased government expenditures on public services that might be reflected in higher net government expenditures).

16. All the dollar values reported in this section are in 2000 PPP US dollars. See note to Figure 2.1 for details.

17. The relative position of the US middle quintile worsened with respect to household production also over the period, mainly because of the change in the gap in the hours spent on household production. From a level that was about 3 percent higher than the British, the US middle quintile came to a position of near parity with the British. Coupled with the relatively lower hourly wage of domestic workers in the United States, this resulted in the lower value of household production for the US middle class.

18. We included the estimated values of wealth associated with defined-benefit pension plans in our definition of household wealth for the United States in order to facilitate comparisons with Canada. In the public-use version of the Canadian wealth survey datafile, a single variable is provided for "pension wealth," and it is impossible to distinguish the wealth associated with defined-benefit versus defined-contribution pension plans.

19. Part of the reason behind this was that the higher hours of housework in the United States became still higher, while they fell in Canada. The other reason is the narrower gap in the implicit unit value of household production due to the decline in the Canadian unit value, which primarily reflects the decline in the hourly wage of domestic workers in Canada. The hourly wage of domestic workers

in Canada fell from $9.20 to $8.80, while it rose from $7.42 to $7.74 in the United States (all amounts are in 2000 PPP dollars).

20. Of course, the gap was the greatest for the top decile in the United States at 65 percent, which is almost double the gap enjoyed by the ninth decile.

21. The top decile in the United States had an average LIMEW that was double that of its Canadian counterpart in 2000 and about 75 percent higher in 2005. The relatively less "pro-very rich" pattern in the later year was probably a result of the losses suffered by the rich US households in their income from wealth and also because of the growth in income from wealth for the rich Canadian households.

22. Decomposition of inequality by income components is a standard technique used to assess the amount of inequality accounted for by individual components in the total amount of inequality (Lerman 1999). The decomposition results are not conclusive evidence on causality. However, they do identify the contribution of individual components to overall inequality. The degree of inequality accounted for by a component is the product of that component's concentration coefficient and its share in income (Kakwani 1977).

23. The evidence is from the pattern of growth in well-being across the deciles in the US-British comparison.

24. Note the fact that 1982 was the bottom of a deep recession, which increases the measured growth accordingly.

25. We also compared economic well-being and census income after adjusting both with the three-parameter equivalence scale used in the US Census Bureau's experimental poverty measures. The results regarding the comparisons of the trends in the two measures were identical to that obtained with unadjusted values and are hence not reported here.

26. Again, the increase in labor market hours is due in part to comparing a recession year to an expansion year.

27. See note 13.

28. All the dollar estimates in this section are in 2007 dollars.

29. Table 2.4 also presents a growth decomposition of the average census income for its middle quintile. For MI, 54 percent of its 43 percentage point gain was attributable to the growth of base income and 42 percent to increased cash transfers.

30. Time trends are quite similar for equivalence-scale adjusted measures.

31. The LIMEW measure shows almost no change in inequality from 1959 to 1982, a modest rise from 1982 to 1989 (0.2 point increase), and then a large spurt of 6.0 points from 1989 to 2000, followed by little change between 2000 and 2007.

BIBLIOGRAPHY

Canberra Group. 2001. *Expert Group on Household Income Statistics: Final Report and Recommendations.* Ottawa: Canberra Group.

Citro, C.F., and R.T. Michael, eds. 1995. *Measuring Poverty: A New Approach.* Washington, DC: National Academies Press.

Eren, S., T. Masterson, E.N. Wolff, and A. Zacharias. 2011. "The Levy Institute Measure of Economic Well-Being, Great Britain, 1995 and 2005." April. Working Paper No. 667. Annandale-on-Hudson, NY: Levy Economics Institute of Bard College. www.levyinstitute.org/publications/?docid=1375.

Kakwani, N.C. 1977. "Applications of Lorenz Curves in Economic Analysis." *Econometrica* 45, no. 3: 719–727.

Lerman, R.I. 1999. "How Do Income Sources Affect Income Inequality?" In *Handbook on Income Inequality Measurement*, ed. Jacques Silber, 341–362. Boston: Kluwer.

Masterson, T., A. Zacharias, S. Eren, and E.N. Wolff. 2011. "The Levy Institute Measure of Economic Well-Being, France, 1989 and 2000." April. Working Paper No. 679. Annandale-on-Hudson, NY: Levy Economics Institute of Bard College. www.levyinstitute.org/publications/?docid=1398.

Sharpe, A., A. Murray, B. Evans, and E. Hazell. 2011. "The Levy Institute Measure of Economic Well-Being: Estimates for Canada, 1999 and 2005." July. Working Paper No. 680. Annandale-on-Hudson, NY: Levy Economics Institute of Bard College. www.levyinstitute.org/publications/?docid=1399.

Short, K. 2001. *Experimental Poverty Measures: 1999.* U.S. Census Bureau, Current Population Reports, 60–216. Washington, DC: U.S. Government Printing Office. www.census.gov/prod/2001pubs/p60-216.pdf.

Smeeding, T.M., and D.H. Weinberg. 2001. "Toward a Uniform Definition of Household Income." *Review of Income and Wealth* 47, no. 1: 1–24.

Wolff, E.N., and A. Zacharias. 2003. "The Levy Institute Measure of Economic Well-Being." *Indicators: A Journal of Social Health* 2, no. 4: 44–73.

———. 2007. "The Levy Institute Measure of Economic Well-Being: United States, 1989 to 2001." *Eastern Economic Journal* 33, no. 4: 443–470.

Wolff, E.N., A. Zacharias, and T. Masterson. 2009. "Long-Term Trends in the Levy Institute Measure of Economic Well-Being (LIMEW), United States, 1959–2004." January. Working Paper No. 556. Annandale-on-Hudson, NY: Levy Economics Institute of Bard College. www.levyinstitute.org/publications/?docid=1115.

3 Measuring the Standard of Living

Quality of Life and Income Differences in the United States

Thomas Michael Power

The most widely used measure of the standard of living is per capita income, aggregate money income divided by the number of people sharing that income. Comparisons of the standard of living in one location to another are often based on this. Yet since the 1970s, people in the United States have been "voting with their feet" by moving away from many areas with high per capita income to others with much lower per capita income, indicating that they evaluate the relative standard of living quite differently.

In this chapter, this apparent economic anomaly is explained by analyzing the inadequacies of per capita income as a measure of the standard of living. In particular, we focus on the role that location-specific characteristics, such as the cost of living and the amenities and disamenities often called "quality of life," play in adding to the measure of per capita income or subtracting from it. The standard of living available at a particular location is tied to both income-earning potential in the area as well as to the net value of the mix of local amenities and disamenities found there and the higher or lower cost of living in that area. As a result, per capita income by itself can be expected to provide very misleading indications of the standard of living. It will be depressed in areas with an array of attractive characteristics and will be high in areas with negative characteristics. Basing public economic policy on such a misleading indicator has the potential to damage the standard of living rather than improving it, at least in areas where lower than average per capita income reflects a high level of net amenities or a low cost of living.

A significant part of our analysis will focus on the economic importance of the quality of life in any measure of the standard of living (see also Chapter 1 in this volume). Some noneconomists (as well as some economists who should know better) tend to dismiss concerns about quality of life as hopelessly subjective and beyond empirical measurement. Contemporary economics, however, is built around analyzing a consumer economy in which individuals pursue their subjective preferences by comparing a broad array of goods and services with various qualities that have the capacity of satisfying those preferences. In that sense, subjective qualities are at the heart of a market economy. Those qualities are what consumers seek to purchase and what firms seek to produce and sell. The billions of individual participants in our globalized economy, both producers and consumers, are not baffled or confounded by the dominance of subjective preferences and qualities.[1]

It is not the subjective and qualitative aspects of quality of life that are problematic for markets and economists. It is the "public goods" character of many aspects of quality of life that makes it difficult for those qualities to be provided or protected in an optimal way through commercial market transactions. Many of these qualities of life either have characteristics that make it difficult for private businesses to provide them (e.g., difficulty in excluding people from enjoying them without paying) or are considered by the general population to be things to which all citizens should have access regardless of their ability to pay ("equity goods"). When commercial businesses cannot provide many of these "qualities of life" or when people do not want them provided on a fee-for-service basis, they will not be priced by the market and their value may be ignored in evaluating local economic well-being.[2] One of our conclusions is that the wide geographic differences in economic well-being implied by the use of per capita income as a measure of standard of living are an exaggeration of reality. That conclusion might be interpreted as implying that differences in economic well-being and the existence of poverty are less important problems than we have been led to believe. That is not true. The accurate conclusion is that measures of economic well-being based solely on money income overstate both poverty and affluence in some areas and understate both in others. More importantly, there remain substantial differences in well-being within almost all communities regardless of the metric we use to measure the overall standard of living. There are households whose very low economic status excludes them from full participation in the economic and social life of the community and threatens the opportunities open to them and, especially, their children. There are also regions of the nation that face persistent poverty and ongoing decline, often trapping poor families in place. Improvements in the accuracy of our measure of the standard of living will give us a better indication of where differences in economic well-being are serious and where they are not.

This chapter is organized in the following manner: We first discuss the economic reality and importance of quality of life in measuring economic well-being and, therefore, the standard of living. We focus on the "place-based" or geographic characteristics of some of the most important qualities of life. We then discuss how the site-specific character of many qualities of life allows them to be pursued through residential location decisions. This affects the geographic distribution of economic activities and has implications for the measurement of the standard of living. We then turn to the evidence that per capita income alone is an inadequate measure, or even proxy, for the standard of living because it ignores geographic differences in the qualities of life and in the cost of living. Finally, we discuss the economic policy implications of our findings.

THE ECONOMIC IMPORTANCE OF THE "QUALITIES OF LIFE"

Economists have long recognized the fact that many of the important determinants of our well-being are noncommercial in character and cannot be appropriately provided by commercial businesses coordinated by markets. That is one of the reasons economics exists as a social science separate and apart from the study of commercial business. Site-specific characteristics of a particular locale that make it a more or less attractive place to live make up one important group of such noncommercial goods and services. These site-specific qualities have come to be labeled "quality of life" or "amenities" (Power 1996a and 1996b). Greenwood and Holt's definition of the standard of living includes such qualities of life (Chapter 1, Figure 1.3) along with income. As they point out, current and future qualities of life are tied to the size and health of capital stocks, such as common environmental resources and publicly owned infrastructure and resources, as well as social capital that supports the private, public, and self-provisioning that determines the standard of living (Chapter 1, Figure 1.2).

The range of potentially relevant local amenities potentially of significance in determining the local standard of living is quite broad. All of the following may be relevant:

1. Natural landscape features, including coastlines and lakeshores, varied topography and landscape characteristics, wildlife, rivers, and other unique natural characteristics.
2. Climate, including frequency of sunshine, temperature extremes, humidity, and average wind speed.
3. Social environment, including the quality of schools and other public services, the quality of community (neighborliness, civic engagement), crime rates, and levels of congestion.
4. Cultural environment, including local diversity or homogeneity, cultural richness and integrity, and the presence of higher educational and other cultural institutions.
5. Human-built environment, including air and water quality, population density, quality of homes and businesses, and basic public and commercial infrastructure.

Amenities, to economists, go beyond characteristics of the local market economy such as market size, job opportunities, and cost of living. They include all of those location-specific public good characteristics of a place that increase that place's attractiveness as a residential or business location and are valued and shared by a significant portion of the local population. Thus, we are not including valuable aspects of quality of life that are associated with individuals and households such as personality traits, family relationships, and so on.

Economists have been analyzing the economic importance of these site-specific amenities to both household well-being and to the location of population and economic activity for at least half a century. In the mid-1950s, economic geographer Edward Ullman (1955) used natural amenities to explain the growth of population in the desert Southwest, the Pacific Northwest, and Florida. About the same time, regional economist Charles Tiebout (1956) was describing how households could "vote with their feet" among different government jurisdictions to find the most attractive mix of government services and tax structures. By the mid-1960s, economists George Borts and Jerome Stein (1964) modeled entire national economies and concluded that in a mobile, open economy, it would be an area's ability to attract and hold a labor force without bidding up labor costs that would determine the geographic distribution of economic activity. Attractive local amenities could potentially play a role in attracting and holding a productive labor force at a somewhat lower cost and give a local area a competitive advantage for the location of economic activity because of the presence of those amenities or qualities of life.

Economists have also worked to develop the tools that allow the measurement of such noncommercial economic values so that in public policy decisions in which both commercial and noncommercial economic values are at stake, better, more fully informed decisions can be made. By studying the actual choices made by individuals in the pursuit of noncommercial economic values, economists have been able to measure those noncommercial economic values through the sacrifices people actually make. Analyses of travel costs, property value differentials, and wage differentials have revealed the economic value people place on nonmarketed goods and services. Where that type of hedonic analysis has not been possible, economists have developed survey techniques (e.g., contingent valuation and conjoint analysis) that allow people to express the strength of their preferences for nonmarketed goods and services in economic terms (Goodstein 2011).

A half century of such analyses has clearly documented the economic importance of these amenities to individual well-being. In some ways, this work has only documented what we already knew. Real estate professionals have always understood the role that the qualities associated with a particular site play in determining property values. As their cliché puts it, "Location, location, location."

THE IMPACT OF GEOGRAPHIC DIFFERENCES IN THE QUALITY OF LIFE ON THE OVERALL ECONOMY[3]

Each region and each locality has a unique set of conditions that affects both the attractiveness of living there and the cost of living and of doing business in that place. On the attractiveness side, we can include all of the diverse amenities listed above.[4] Where the costs of doing business are concerned, things that make living in a place attractive to individuals and families also implicitly reduce business costs, because workers as well as business owners are willing to accept lower incomes in order to enjoy the local amenities. Other features of a locality may affect business costs directly: proximity to markets, public infrastructure such as roads and communications facilities, research and development capabilities, tax rates, and so forth. Size of place and urban density may also increase business productivity by reducing transportation and communications costs. This, in turn, can allow a much broader variety of specialized businesses and workers to be located nearby and encourage the cross-fertilization of ideas and technologies. Economists have described these benefits of larger urban population and economic concentrations in terms of "agglomeration economies." All of these tend to lower firms' per unit production costs.

If higher population and economic densities brought only greater productivity, the more densely settled areas would become economic "black holes" drawing more and more economic activity to them. They could pay higher and higher wages, drawing more and more workers and families to those areas. There must be offsetting economic forces to explain why population and economic activity remain distributed across a wide variety of differently sized places from rural areas to small and large cities to sprawling "megalopolises."

One reason relates to the cost of living. Dense settlement increases the demand for land in the central core. This leads land costs to rise. The rising cost of land and the other cost increases that the rising cost of land triggers drive up both the cost of living and the cost of doing business. Those cost increases are part of the offsetting economic forces. Density not only provides economic benefits, but also it generates economic costs.

Those firms that do not particularly benefit from density's impact on productivity will find densely settled areas too costly and will locate somewhere else. In addition, workers who do not find enough compensating attractions in high-density urban areas will demand higher wages to compensate for the higher cost of living. If congestion, pollution, crime, commuting costs, and so on are sufficiently unattractive to outweigh the benefits of a wider array of economic opportunities, greater diversity, cosmopolitan atmosphere, and wider cultural opportunities, firms will also have to compensate workers. If the balance of amenities and disamenities is perceived by enough workers as negative, firms will have to raise pay even further to attract enough workers. This will raise costs even more to firms that choose to locate in those dense settings.

Firms will weigh the productivity advantages of locating in densely settled areas against the costs associated with them. Workers will do the same. They will compare the higher wages offered them to the higher costs they will face in terms of cost of living and their evaluation of the amenities and disamenities of living in more densely settled urban areas. Each firm and each individual or household will make different judgments depending on the mix of costs and benefits to them and their own personal preferences. That mix of judgments will lead to a particular geographic distribution of firms and workers because not all will be drawn to the same location. The result will also be geographic differences in pay. But those pay differences, as will be explained below, will not necessarily represent real differences in well-being for workers at different geographic locations or real differences in unit costs to firms.[5]

Differences in the costs of doing business and the value of local amenities from one place to another give rise to differences in incomes, through a process in which migration is the driving force. There are cultural and social amenities associated with large urban areas and cultural and social disamenities associated with small cities and rural areas. Preferences vary between people and sometimes over the life cycle. However, most survey data of the last several decades indicate that if employment and income opportunities were not an issue, more people would choose to live outside big cities than do now. They prefer small cities, suburban, or exurban settings, albeit with convenient travel distance to large urban areas with cultural and commercial opportunities. As in all market settings, unanimity of preferences among the population is not necessary. Even minority preferences create markets.

Suppose, for example, that workers in two localities—say, Los Angeles and Boise, Idaho—earned the same wages for equivalent qualifications and faced the same costs for equivalent housing. Suppose further that more workers value the amenity/disamenity mix in Boise than in Los Angeles. In that case, there will be a net migration of workers to Boise. As a result of the increasing supply of workers and increased demand for housing, there will be a tendency for wages to fall and housing costs to rise. Eventually, wages would fall, housing costs would rise, or both, enough to choke off migration to Boise.

The two cities would reach an equilibrium in which permanent differentials in wages and housing costs would prevail, reflecting differences in local quality of life. Most of the adjustment would occur in Boise because relative to the size of the local labor force, the flow of migrants would be larger there and smaller in Los Angeles. Such differences are said to be *compensating*—that is, in this hypothetical case, workers in Los Angeles are compensated with higher wages or lower housing costs for living in a city that has, on net, fewer highly valued amenities than disamenities workers want to avoid.

It is an important feature of such compensating income differentials that they do *not* reflect differences in economic well-being. In our example, the higher wages received by workers in Los Angeles compensate them for some combination of the higher cost of living and net disamenities in that city. But we could just as well say that the superior amenity mix in Boise compensates workers there for lower wages. Although their earnings differ, workers in the two cities may be equally well off with the same standard of living, even though the components differ. In Los Angeles, they enjoy more income and fewer net amenities; in Boise, less income but more net amenities. The point is that people move to where the value of the whole package—wages, housing costs, and local amenities—is higher. In locations to which people are moving, the value of the package starts out high but falls; in the places they leave, the value of the package starts out low but rises. Eventually it is a wash, and people stop moving, on net, because they cannot improve their well-being by doing so.[6]

IMPLICATIONS OF GEOGRAPHIC VARIATIONS IN THE QUALITY OF LIFE FOR MEASURING THE STANDARD OF LIVING

The local standard of living is typically measured using the same economic measures used in evaluating the national standard of living: average pay and income, the unemployment rate, and, possibly, the poverty rate. Yet average money income is not an adequate measure of the standard of living because so many nonmarket but valuable aspects of human well-being are not included in that monetary measure (Cobb et al. 1994; Greenwood and Holt, Chapter 1; Power 1994). When it comes to local, state, or regional economies, the problem is even more complex: economic measures such as average pay and income may misrepresent the local standard of living *because* there have been compensating adjustments in pay and cost of living caused by migration of people and economic activity. These differences may be related to climate or other geographic features (proximity to oceans, lakes, or mountains) as well as to the size of an urban area.

But we will stick with our example from the previous section for clarity: smaller cities and less densely settled areas with higher social and natural amenities can be expected to have lower pay levels and therefore lower average income than the national average *because* those areas tend to have a lower cost of living and higher-valued amenities. However, that lower pay and income will not be an accurate measure of economic deprivation suffered by local residents but instead may reflect positive aspects of the local standard of living. As one economist characterized this situation, residents in such an area receive a "second paycheck" in the value of the local amenities and lower cost of living that supplements their monetary paycheck (Whitelaw and Niemi 1989).[7] People making a choice, voting with their feet, to live in such high-amenity, lower-wage areas take this into account in making their decision. Accurate measures of the local standard of living need to also. This is not to suggest that *all* differences in average pay and income among different locales across the nation are compensating differences. But empirical research suggests that these explain much of the difference in pay and income among communities of different size and in different regions of the country.

There *are* substantial differences in average pay and income across the United States. In 2010, per capita income in the highest-ranked state, Connecticut, was about $55,000 while that in the lowest-ranked state, Mississippi, was about $31,000. That is, the "poorest" state had an average income that was only 57 percent of that of the "richest" state. Importantly, eighty-one years earlier, the highest- and lowest-ranked states were the same two states. As Figure 3.1 shows differences in per capita income were quite persistent over most of a century, with per capita income ranking in 1929 explaining 82 percent of 2010 variation. For a fifth of the states, there was no change in ranking; for almost half of the states, the movement was three places or less; and for almost two-thirds of the states, the movement was five places or less.[8]

Figure 3.1 also shows that growth in state real per capita income has largely followed the national average, with some states fluctuating above that national average and some fluctuating below it. Such clustering around the national average is what one would expect in an increasingly integrated national economy. In addition, the percentage differences in state per capita incomes relative to the national average also declined significantly from 1929 to the mid-1970s. Convergence in average incomes would be expected in an integrated economy with relatively free movement of people, businesses, goods, and capital. It is the divergence since the mid-1970s that is *not* what one would expect.

The persistence of large differences in average income over most of a century despite massive movements of population, relocation of industries, and improvements in mobility and information remains somewhat of an economic anomaly. If, in fact, the average standard of living in the state of Connecticut is 71 percent higher than in West Virginia and the economic well-being of a West Virginia resident could be boosted by $23,000 per year or $92,000 for a family of four, one would expect a major migration out of West Virginia into Connecticut. Even more dramatic, if the economic well-being of the average person in Washington, DC, was actually $38,000 per year better than that of the average person living 150 miles away in West Virginia, one would expect to find Washington, DC, filling up with folks from West Virginia. Such migrations from the "poor" states to the "rich" states over a century should have wiped out most of the differences in economic well-being *if* differences in the standard of living of the size indicated by local per capita incomes actually existed.

58

Figure 3.1   Relative Differences in Per Capita Income: Highest and Lowest States

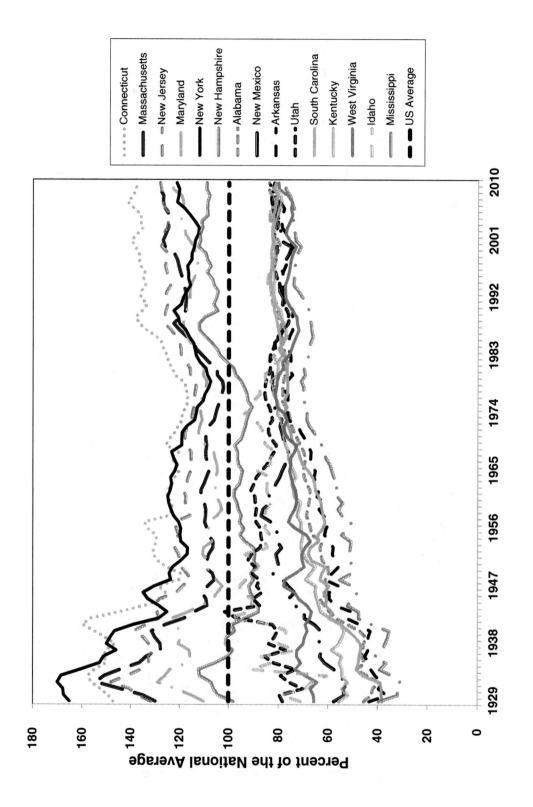

Figure 3.2 State Net Domestic In-Migration Rate, 2000–2009, Versus State Per Capita Income, 2000

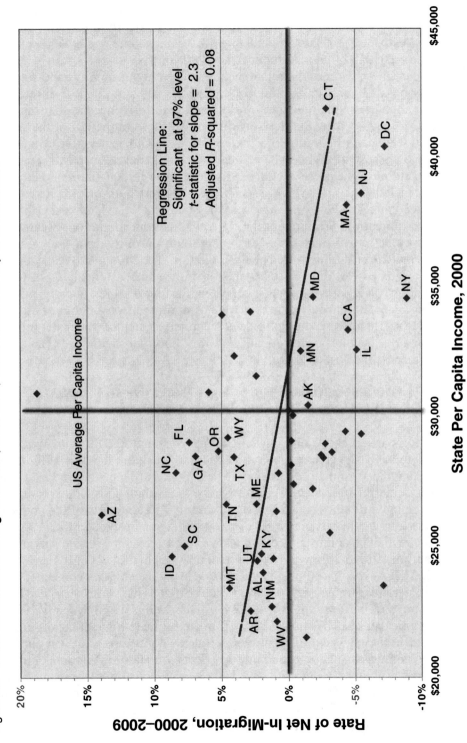

Yet for several decades the direction of migration has been *away* from the "rich" states toward the "poorer" states. What is startling is that the "rich" states have faced net out-migration and the "poorer" states have had net in-migration. That is, people voting with their feet have implied that per capita income was not an accurate indicator of the actual differences in local standards of living.

Figure 3.2 illustrates the relationship between net in-migration to states between 2000 and 2009 and per capita income in those states in 2000. If differences in per capita income among the states represented real differences in the standard of living, one would expect that low-income states (those to the left of the vertical line) would see net out-migration (i.e., net migration would be negative). States with high income (those to the right of the vertical line) would have seen positive net migration. The pattern of data points would be from the lower left quadrant into the upper right quadrant, but that is not what we see. Most of the very high-income states—including Connecticut, New Jersey, New York, Massachusetts, Maryland, and California—had net out-migration. Washington, DC, also had net out-migration. Meanwhile, many low-income states—including North and South Carolina, Tennessee, Florida, Kentucky, and West Virginia—had net in-migration. The Mountain West, which contains many of the lowest-income states outside of the southeastern states, also had net in-migration.[9] This pattern has been persistent for four decades. Clearly, migrants were seeing something about economic well-being in their origin and destination states that per capita income did not reflect accurately. Much of this is the mix of amenities and diasmenities called "quality of life," but a substantial part can also be wide variations in the cost of living.

THE IMPLICATIONS OF GEOGRAPHIC DIFFERENCES IN THE COST OF LIVING FOR MEASURING THE STANDARD OF LIVING

The comparison above of Connecticut and Washington, DC, with West Virginia is likely to have triggered an obvious economic objection: the cost of living is notoriously high in Washington, DC, and in New York's affluent "bedroom," Connecticut. What is missing from the above discussion is something most of us "know": there are geographic differences in the cost of living in different parts of the country as well as between urban and rural areas or between large and small cities.

Some may be confused because, as was made clear above, the per capita income data from 1929 to 2010 were adjusted for changes in the cost of living over that time period. However, that adjustment was made using the *national* consumer price index. The federal government measures how the cost of living varies *over time* but does not measure how the cost of living varies *across locations*. Until the early 1980s, federal economic data agencies made crude efforts to estimate some of the differences in the cost of living between different cities. But for political reasons (in our judgment), a decision was made to abandon those efforts to measure geographic differences in the cost of living.[10] As a result, it is only private consulting companies that seek to gather data from across the nation on a regular basis to measure geographic cost of living differences. Those private data are sold to companies who wish to adjust their employees' pay levels to account for differences in the cost of living or who wish to evaluate potential business costs in particular locations in a way that takes into account the local purchasing power of the dollar (Council for Community and Economic Research, multiple years).

Elsewhere we have used such privately gathered geographic cost of living data, despite their problems and limitations, to determine what part of the differences in regional differences in pay per job could be explained by cost of living differences. Most of the differences in average pay (77 percent in this case) were compensating differences that reflected differences in the local purchasing power of the dollar and not real differences in the standard of living. We found that while pay per job in cities with populations over 2 million was 44 percent higher than in cities with populations less than 500,000, when adjusted for differences in the cost of living, there was only a 10 percent difference in the purchasing power of that pay. This pattern held across the broad range of different-sized metropolitan areas in the United States (Power and Barrett 2001, 112).

Accounting for Differences in the Local Quality of Life[11]

Even after adjusting for cost of living, we did find persistent differences in average pay and income across urban areas in the United States. One other potential explanation for such differences that is also compensating in nature was discussed above: differences in the value of local qualities of life or amenities.

Economists and real estate professionals devoted considerable research effort in the last half of the twentieth century to estimating the value people place on various characteristics of the local residential environment. As real estate agents say, location is everything. Each residential location provides a bundle of different qualities associated with its physical and social environment. Without conducting any formal economic analysis, most people are aware of the fact that property in high-crime, heavily polluted, noisy, congested, or run-down areas commands a lower price or rental value. On the other hand, property that provides access to better schools and parks, that presents lower risks to person and property from crime, or that is located in more aesthetically pleasing neighborhoods commands much higher values.

People who buy homes clearly demonstrate that they are capable of evaluating these qualitative differences and willing to pay tens or hundreds of thousands of dollars in higher housing costs to gain access to more attractive living environments. The aspects of quality of life that come from the local environment are by no means a trivial component of overall well-being. Because people are willing to make major economic sacrifices in pursuit of higher-quality living environments, local environmental quality, both social and physical, is an important consideration in assessing the local standard of living.

By assessing the statistical relationship between the prices paid for homes in different locations and measures of the various environmental features characteristic of those locations, real estate analysts and economists have been able to estimate what people are willing to pay to gain access to particular public amenities or to avoid the particular disadvantages of certain neighborhoods. However, as discussed earlier, paying higher housing prices is just one way in which residents gain access to attractive mixes of public amenities. The other "entry fee" may be acceptance of lower wages and more limited economic opportunities resulting from the excess supply of workers who also want to enjoy those attractive local amenities.

One study used these "hedonic" methods to measure the values Americans placed on sixteen different amenities that varied from one location to another (Blomquist, Berger, and Hoehn 1988). This was done by statistically "observing" what people were willing to pay in higher rents, lower wages, or both in order to have access to those amenities. Those amenities were represented by variables that measured proximity to a coast, crime rate, school quality, and several different dimensions of both climate and environmental quality. These measures of willingness to pay were used to compute a quality of life index; that is, the total value of the package of sixteen amenities that was available in each of 253 metropolitan-area counties across the United States. The authors calculated that an average American family would put a value of almost $8,600 (in 2010 dollars) on the mix of amenities available in the highest-ranked metropolitan county and that in the lowest-ranked county the value of the package was so low that it actually would impose a cost of $4,800 on an average family. As we explained earlier, this means that the average household would be willing to accept up to $8,600 less in pay to receive the net amenities in the first example, but would demand an income at least $4,800 higher than average to live in the lowest-ranked county. The difference between these two was about $13,500 per year in 2010 dollars, or 27 percent of national median household income—not a small economic matter.

When these urban counties' quality of life index is analyzed in terms of the total population of each metropolitan area, as the size of the metropolitan area increased, the average quality of life index fell. In moving from the smallest (less than 250,000) to the largest group of cities (more than 2 million), the value of the package of local amenities fell by almost $1,600. As a measure of relative magnitude, that $1,600 per year represented about 10 percent of the difference in average pay per job between the groups of smaller and larger metropolitan areas.

INTERPRETING REGIONAL DIFFERENCES IN PER CAPITA INCOME AND AVERAGE PAY AS REFLECTING DIFFERENCES IN REGIONAL STANDARDS OF LIVING: A SUMMARY AND SOME CAUTIONS

It appears likely that much of the substantial difference in average pay and income found among various locations within the United States is explained by differences in local cost of living and value of local amenities or qualities of life. In that sense, much of the difference in income does not represent a true difference in the standard of living. The higher pay and income are offset by higher cost of living or lower quality of life. The lower pay and income are offset by lower cost of living and higher quality of life. And these compensating adjustments go beyond income. People who want to live in a particular area because of its local qualities of life, lower cost of living, or any other reason may be willing to accept a more restricted range of employment opportunities, less security in employment, or jobs below what their skill or experience would justify. This is true of many college towns, resort communities, and, as we explain later, areas that exert strong cultural ties, such as Appalachia and reservation lands for Native Americans. For that reason, it is not surprising that these areas have high unemployment rates and high likelihood of underemployment.

None of this should be interpreted to mean that there are not substantial differences in the economic well-being of people. All areas, both high-income and low-income areas, have substantial inequality in income among residents, including a significant portion of the population living in poverty. That is a serious social and economic problem on which public economic policy should appropriately focus. But even in identifying how the intensity of the problem of poverty varies across the nation, income measures are likely to distort our measures of poverty. Ignoring geographic differences in the cost of living and the value of local amenities is likely to understate the problem of poverty in large urban areas and overstate it in smaller cities and rural areas.

It is also possible that there are areas of high and persistent poverty where low-income households are trapped by lack of work-related skills, knowledge of alternatives, personal support systems in other areas, and so on. The federal government has classified parts of Appalachia as suffering from such a syndrome in the past, and the same problem applies to some other rural areas, including Indian reservations with persistent poverty. While poverty and unemployment rates on reservations surely identify real economic deprivation, one has to be careful to look closely at these areas where people have chosen to live because of a commitment to their remnant homeland. The informal economy and indigenous support system should not be ignored or damaged by public economic policies that treat the reservations as simply poverty-stricken areas. Just as an area of natural beauty can be "loved to death" through population growth or industrial-style tourism, an area of cultural significance to its residents can be destroyed by poorly designed economic "improvements."

Our general conclusions should also not be interpreted to mean that *all* geographic differences in average pay and income can be safely ignored. When one finds low-income areas that are also regularly losing population, this combination can certainly be read as a sign of economic distress. Much of the rural Great Plains may currently fall into this category. Other isolated areas far removed from urban trade centers, whether they have spectacular natural amenities or not, may well suffer from a lack of economic opportunity and have a difficult time retaining population or attracting economic activity.

RECOGNIZING LOCAL QUALITIES OF LIFE WHEN CRAFTING LOCAL ECONOMIC POLICY

Recognizing that average pay and income are incomplete and potentially misleading measures of economic well-being and the actual standard of living is a common theme of this book. Because many qualities of life are local in character and vary across the geography of the nation, the use of average pay and income to tell us how well a particular local economy is or is not doing and what policies would improve the standard of living can lead to unique distortions and public economic policy questions. We highlight a few of these below.

SEEING ECONOMIC DEPRIVATION WHERE THERE IS NONE

One of the reasons we emphasize the reality of compensating differences in local pay and income is that local economic development efforts are often driven by a misreading of the relatively low pay and income found in small cities and rural areas. As discussed above, firms in densely settled areas can be expected to pay workers more for both positive and negative reasons. The productivity of many densely settled economic areas will be high because of agglomerative economies, and, as a result, employers will be able to pay workers high wages. However, the demand for centrally located space is likely to drive land and housing costs up and, therefore, the costs of living and doing business. Finally, the cost of the disamenities of very large urban areas may outweigh the value of the urban amenities, at least for a significant part of the population. In order to retain workers in the face of higher cost of living and lower value of amenities, firms will have to raise wages to cover these welfare losses associated with living in these densely settled areas. That will further raise the cost of doing business there. Empirical data confirm these expectations: both worker productivity and wages are higher in densely settled areas (Ciccone and Hall 1996; Power 2001).

If we use metropolitan area population as a proxy for population and economic density, there is a strong correlation between population size and average pay. In general, the smaller the city, the lower the average pay; the larger the city, the higher the pay (see Figure 3.3). The average pay per job in the United States in 2009 of $47,000 per year was significantly above the average pay in most metropolitan areas of the United States and closer to pay for workers living in cities of 2 million or more. Since these cities are larger and have more workers, they dominate the average. As a result, every time pay in a smaller urban or rural area is compared to the national average, it is implicitly being compared to the pay of workers living in a very large city and found wanting.

This economic fact means that across almost the entire geography of the United States, most large cities, small cities, towns, and rural areas have "below average" per capita incomes and average pay, which actually means below the level found in cities of 2 million and more. Since, as we showed above, it is generally necessary to pay more in large cities to compensate for higher housing costs and the disamenities of crowding, using this national average creates the impression that most of the nation has a depressed standard of living. The implication is that many local economies are "failing." As a result, economic development agencies across the nation tend to focus on policies that might raise average pay and income toward the national average. This usually leads to efforts to increase the demand for labor by generating more local jobs, in hopes that that will boost average pay and income.[12]

But if these differences in pay represented real differences in the standard of living in these cities, our smaller cities would have systematically emptied over time and our larger cities would have grown without limit. That is not what has happened. Instead, many of our smaller cities have been gaining population and have become metropolitan areas themselves over time.

If local pay and income are lower because the cost of living is lower and the net value of the area's social and environmental amenities is high, there is nothing eco-

Figure 3.3   Pay per Job in All 366 Metropolitan Areas by Population Size, 2009

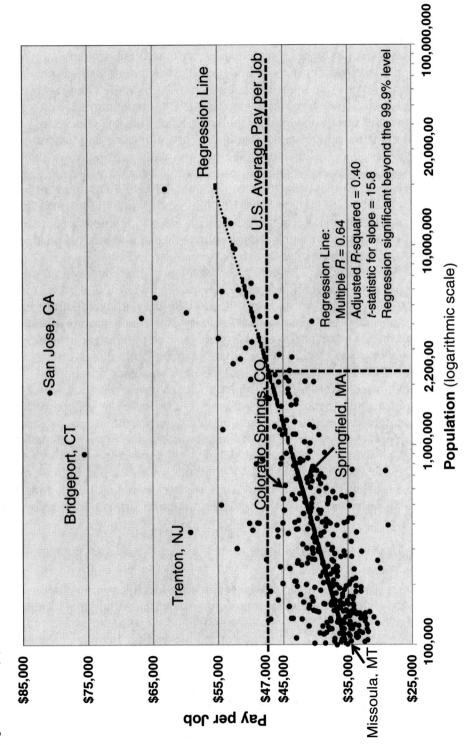

nomically productive that can be done about the "below average" per capita income and pay. However, there are some economically destructive actions that could be taken. Local social and natural amenities could be degraded and the cost of living could be driven up. Policies to do exactly this are often offered in the name of local economic development. Environmentally destructive industries may be subsidized to relocate to the area. Industrial activity may be promoted that creates jobs that are primarily filled by newcomers who migrate into the community rather than by the local unemployed or underpaid population. The result may be the loss of social and environmental amenities and a rise in the cost of housing and the cost of living.

But this reduces the level of well-being for many existing residents who had chosen the area because of its quality of life and lower cost of living. They could lose the very qualities that drew them to the area and held them there, while not getting the benefit of one of the new jobs. In addition, they may find that the higher cost of living reduces the purchasing power of their income. Even if there are compensating changes that finally bring the in-migration to an end, the original residents may have been harmed by the changes.

When evaluating how "poor" or economically disadvantaged an *area* in general is (as opposed to the economic difficulties faced by *particular segments* of an area's population), we have to be careful not to take data on average pay and income as indisputable evidence that the local standard of living is inferior to that of the nation and that, therefore, the local economy, in general, is failing. Such uncritical trust of data on average pay and income can motivate ineffectual or even destructive public economic policies that actually lower the local standard of living.

Rather than join the national competition to entice existing businesses to relocate to or new businesses to locate in a particular area by lowering environmental standards, reducing the business tax base, and putting downward pressure on local wages, the alternative is to play to the strengths an area already has in terms of quality of life and low cost of living. Protecting and enhancing those qualities of life that are directly valuable to existing residents can also be the basis of attracting new residents and businesses. That can be a "cannot lose" strategy as opposed to joining the national race to the bottom of the well in an effort to "bribe" firms to relocate to a particular area.

SUSTAINING AMENITY-SUPPORTED LOCAL ECONOMIC GROWTH

However, even in-migration driven by superior locally specific qualities of life is not necessarily a benefit to the existing local population. Although a local economy that is vital and adaptable enough to offset population loss and business failure is almost always welcomed because it avoids economic decline, there is no general economic principle that says that the more people who live in a particular areas, the higher will be the standard of living. This will only hold in relatively small cities that do not have the critical mass to support the public and private infrastructure and economic opportunities that they would like to have. When that is the case, residents and community leaders may believe that some amount of population growth would be beneficial to the overall community; but most communities do not meet those criteria.

Ongoing amenity-driven in-migration and economic expansion may actually threaten the very social and natural amenities that make the area attractive and boost local economic well-being. Once areas are "discovered" as attractive places to live because the economic opportunity, cost of living, and local amenities make up an attractive economic package, the area can grow rapidly. That growth can continue until those local advantages are effectively destroyed—for example, until congestion and population density, the ongoing turnover in the population and growing number of "strangers," and pressure on public, social, and natural amenities degrades them, and the cost of housing rises, squeezing out previous residents; that is, an area can be "loved to death." The equilibrating economic force is the degradation of the local qualities of life. This is not to say that all areas with attractive mixes of social and natural amenities and more conventional economic attractions, such as low cost of living and ongoing expansion of economic opportunities, are doomed to degradation. Communities that have a clear understanding of what contributes to the local standard of living beyond just "jobs and income" can seek to aggressively and proactively manage that growth. This must be done in a way that minimizes the likelihood that local nonmarket amenities will be degraded or the community overrun and changed in negative ways by visitors or newcomers. That is what the efforts to encourage "smart growth" or "sustainable communities" are all about, although the word "growth" should probably be replaced with a less quantitative concept such as "vitality" or "resilience."

DECREASING THE PRESSURE ON SMALLER COMMUNITIES FROM FAILING LARGER COMMUNITIES

The attractiveness of small cities, suburban areas, and exurban rural locations is only partially tied to the attractiveness of those areas by themselves. Those attractive qualities are the "pull" tending to hold residents there and draw new residents. There is also a set of forces "pushing" residents of other areas toward new residential locations. One important source of these push forces is the degradation of quality of life in some of the more densely settled urban areas. Some of the "resettlement" of the Mountain West by previous residents of California's major cities and the rapid growth of what were once relative small cities in the Mountain West may be an example of this. Growth in New Hampshire, Vermont, and southern Maine driven by in-migrants from the greater Boston area may be another.

Although large urban areas offer a *different* mix of qualities of life, that mix need not, on balance, be an inferior mix to many or most people. Densely settled urban areas do offer social and cultural amenities not found in smaller cities and rural areas. There *are* metropolitan amenities: more diverse populations, cultural amenities in the arts and entertainment, a broader range of educational opportunities, and a broader range of commercial businesses, including restaurants, specialized services, and specialized retail outlets. In addition, of course, metropolitan areas offer economic advantages, which are largely the reasons they have grown so large: a broader range of employment opportunities for specialized and often higher-paid skills, a broader range of economic opportunities in general, the potential for symbiotic development of ideas, skills, and economic opportunities, reduced transportation and communication costs, and so on. In fact, one of the interesting aspects of the vitality of smaller cities and rural areas is that the location of these areas relative to larger metropolitan areas is crucial. Most "amenity migrants" want to "have their cake and eat it too." They want convenient access to large metropolitan areas for the urban amenities they offer as well as the natural and social amenities of smaller cities and rural areas. Large urban areas continue to provide amenities to which a good part of the population wishes to maintain access.

Over time, however, many large urban areas have lost many of the natural and social amenities that are an important part of the quality of life many households seek. Those social amenities include neighborliness, a supportive community, and high-quality public services such as good schools, protection of person and property, clean public areas, and convenient transportation networks. Natural amenities include access to natural areas, the presence of natural vegetation and small wildlife, clean air and water, and open space and open skies. The degradation or absence of these can drive away individuals and families who then pursue them elsewhere.

Residents of large urban areas are well aware of the importance of quality of life in making or maintaining their competitiveness among other big cities. Like their counterparts in smaller cities, city planners in large cities are likely to talk about quality of life as an important economic characteristic of their area. Doing something effective, however, to reduce the congestion, pollution, crime rates, social conflict, general grime, and absence of natural landscapes is much more difficult. Just as in smaller communities, urban leaders are caught between the demands to "create jobs" and the desire to fund public services, plan improvements, and regulate changes to enhance urban quality of life.

It is important for those living in smaller urban areas whose qualities of life are under pressure from amenity-supported residential and business in-migration to understand that improving the quality of life in our largest urban areas is crucial to protecting the quality of life in smaller cities and rural areas. In other words, we are all in this together. Failure of voters in suburban and rural areas, as well as smaller cities, to be willing to support funding to solve urban problems can end up contributing to negative effects in their own nonurban communities.

ENDING (OR MODERATING) THE DANIEL BOONE SYNDROME

European-Americans have been an unusually mobile population. This is not surprising since their ancestors had to take a very long and often dangerous trip simply to reach North America. They then faced what was to become a continental nation with extremely low population density because the indigenous population had been decimated by European diseases and violent conflict with settlers and the army that protected them. European-Americans systematically moved west into what seemed to them almost an "empty" continent, leap-frogging much of the intermountain area as the West Coast was settled and became a significant part of the American economic engine. More recently, since the 1970s, they have turned back to "resettle" the inland West and many other rural areas of the United States.

The Great Recession and the collapse of housing values and markets that began in 2006–2007 slowed that mobility significantly. Economic uncertainty, high unemployment rates across the nation, and the difficulty of selling current homes have led to much more cautious economic behavior, including reduced residential mobility. Given that the growth of the housing market bubble and then its collapse were greatest in some of the areas of the West where amenity-supported economic growth had been strongest, it may be an opportune time to look more closely at the costs of rapid in-migration.

One negative way of characterizing our migratory behavior would be that we, collectively, are constantly moving away from our problems, even the problems that our previous choices and activities have created. Instead of seeking to join together to solve those problems, we individually and collectively walk away from them and seek to start over, often creating a new set of problems at our new location.

The most famous of the early American frontiersmen, Daniel Boone, moved his family from Pennsylvania south along the barrier of the Appalachian Mountains into southwestern Virginia. Ultimately, from there he cut a wilderness road that looped from Virginia into Tennessee and then through the Cumberland Gap into Kentucky, effectively opening up Kentucky to European-American settlement. He later moved on to the new westward access route, the Missouri River in eastern Missouri. From there, he explored deep into what is now considered the American West. Although his move to Missouri was most likely driven by debt and bankruptcy tied to his land speculation in Kentucky, an apocryphal quote has Boone saying that once you can see or hear your neighbors, it is time to move on. Many American families follow, or aspire to follow, the same pattern.

There *is* something quite positive associated with Americans recognizing that noncommercial qualities of life are central to the standard of living they seek and their willingness to sacrifice literally thousands of dollars a year in the pursuit of those noncommercial qualities. This implicit recognition of the value of place and the noncommercial aspects of the standard of living is important to the development of public economic policy. Unfortunately, many Americans who have made considerable economic sacrifices in pursuit of the noncommercial qualities of life they want to be available to their families do not appear to remain self-conscious of how real and important these "qualities of place" are to them. As a result, the social and political pressure needed to protect those qualities is not sustained.

At the same time, moving away from social and environmental problems has had relatively high cost. The shift from our early twentieth-century cities to concentric circles of suburbs is a good example. It led to a hollowing out of the centers of those cities, the isolation of poor minority groups, and a much more fossil-fuel-intensive life-style. As those suburban areas were swallowed up in sprawling megalopolises, many Americans fled to more distant suburbs, smaller cities, and exurban rural areas. This brought an often appreciated economic vitality to many of our smaller cities and rural areas, but also it caused a loss of quality of life for some cities and rural areas.

It is at least worth speculating about what our urban and rural areas would look like if all of the entrepreneurial effort and economic cost that American families devoted to seeking a higher quality of life and, as a result, an enhanced standard of living through individual private actions had been focused on collectively preventing or mitigating the decline in quality of life that ultimately drove them from one location to another to another. Fewer dollars would have gone to the real estate and mortgage industries, and more could have been spent in other areas.

This is not an implicit appeal for strict planning of urban areas or a replacement of entrepreneurial decision making by some sort of urban central planning. As many urban historians and analysts from Jane Jacobs (1961) to Richard Florida (2005) have pointed out, urban areas develop in complex ways as a result of an unpredictable and almost impenetrable tangle of many forces that vary in intensity over time and place. At the same time, we do engage in public economic policy in our urban areas and that has consequences, both good and bad.

Our comments here are more a meditation on the costs and consequences of the individual private pursuit of *existing* public goods, namely the qualities of life found at different locations via migration. Through public policy, communities tend to take action to try to protect their existing positive qualities of life and to create or enhance other qualities. They do this both to benefit their citizens and to be successful in the nationwide competition among communities to attract the "right sort" of new economic activity. This has aspects of a classic open-access public goods problem. That should not be surprising. Urban centers involve people "living on top of one another" and that increases the likelihood of significant external benefits *and* costs associated with their individual behaviors and choices. That complex interaction among residents of densely settled areas is, after all, what makes economic activity in urban areas more productive (agglomeration economies). It is also what generates negative urban results or disamenities, such as higher costs of living, congestion, pollution, and social breakdown.

That is the double challenge we face: working in our existing large urban centers to improve and enhance the qualities of life, both social and natural, so that individuals and families are not driven out to impose burdens on communities that still have an attractive mix of local amenities, and working in the communities receiving the in-migrants to protect the public goods responsible for making them an attractive place to live, work, and raise a family. If either or both types of areas focus only on the "jobs, jobs, jobs" mantra and/or a simplistic "boosting average pay and income" agenda through quantitative growth, there is likely to be a net loss in the local standard of living in both types of areas.[13]

These closing comments are no more than a hope that we will act like the social and political animals that we are and focus more of our energy on trying to improve the places where we live rather than continuing to engage in what is ultimately a "free-rider" strategy of running away from nests we have helped foul in search of someone else's not yet badly fouled nest. That strategy in the end will surely not be sustainable, at least on the aggregate level and across generations.

NOTES

1. Very specific quantities of complex goods and services are produced and sold at very precise and quantitative market prices without great difficulty despite the largely qualitative and subjective character of the decisions that have to be made by all market participants.

2. Worse yet, public economic policy that is only partially informed about the values at stake may actually damage local economic well-being by degrading the local quality of life.

3. This section largely follows part of Chapter 5 in Power and Barrett (2001).

4. Examples of such positive local features include climate, school quality, personal security, cultural and recreational opportunities, and the health of the social and natural environments.

5. This is true, of course, only at the margin for some firms and individuals. Other, inframarginal firms and residents will enjoy net benefits from the location they choose; they will not be on the verge of indifference.

6. Because the adjustment to geographic differences in costs of production and value of amenities takes place through migration of people and economic activity and changes in business costs, land and housing costs, and workers' wages, the overall effects can combine in a way that makes it hard to predict how wages and rents will vary between any two locations. Suppose, for example, that Los Angeles was both a cheap place to do business (thus attracting firms) and an unpleasant place to live (thus repelling workers). Then wages would certainly be higher there, but it would be impossible to predict just how rents might behave. On the other hand, imagine a town with low business costs and outstanding living amenities. Both firms and workers would be attracted to such a place, with an unpredictable effect on wages but an almost certain rise in rents as workers seek housing and firms seek space in which to do business. The important result remains, however, that migration of firms and workers tends to produce a spatial pattern of wages and rents that equalizes both the local standard of living and the cost of doing business between any two localities. Economists have elaborated the theory of local wage and rent differentials in numerous studies. See, for example, Beeson and Eberts (1987); Evans (1990); Harrigan and McGregor (1993); Roback (1982, 1988); and Voith (1991).

7. As our discussion above made clear, the adjustment to local amenities and the cost of doing business are more complex that just an adjustment in residents' "paychecks." Some of the adjustment is in the cost of land and housing and, therefore, in the cost of living.

8. A close look at Figure 3.1 will show that some states did change their relative per capita income position at times. Idaho stands out in that regard, rising from only about 60 percent of the national average to the national average and then falling back to about 80 percent of the national average. Colorado, not shown in Figure 3.1, rose from about twentieth among all the states to the top ten.

9. The Mountain West also had some of the highest-income states: Nevada had the highest per capita income of all the states in 1955 and 1960 and was in the top ten from 1930 to 1980. But the housing bust hit Nevada hard and it fell to thirtieth in 2010. Wyoming was more volatile but stayed in the middle of all the states, around twentieth, until 1995, when it fell to thirtieth, but by 2010 it was seventh. Colorado remained about twentieth from 1930 to 1990, after which it moved into the top ten.

10. There was increased pressure from congressional delegations from large urban areas and urbanized states to index federal payments to states and local governments to the local cost of living so that all areas would get equal purchasing power. Such a change, while equitable, would have had the impact of sending more federal dollars to large urban areas that tend to vote Democratic and fewer dollars to smaller cities and rural areas that tend to vote Republican. The solution to this potentially partisan (but economically rational) outcome was to stop collecting the data that would facilitate any such change in policy. Hence, the gathering of information on geographic differences in the cost of living was halted in the early 1980s and ignorance was chosen over knowledge.

11. This section is an updated version of Power and Barrett (2001, 111–114).

12. Faster growth rates in the local economy, however, do not usually lead to higher levels of per capita income, more rapid increases in per capita income, or lower poverty rates. See Fordor (2012).

13. This is also not a suggestion that we should seek to stop movement among the many different communities that make up a very diverse United States. One emotionally powerful version of that impulse takes the form of an appeal to create more jobs and higher incomes so that our children will not be "forced" to move away from their parents' communities. Although young people and their parents will often give that explanation for their geographic separation, that is often just a more palatable cover from children going through a necessary separation phase from their parents and childhood homes.

Young people exploring the rest of the world and learning to cope on their own with new social and economic settings is an age-old coming-of-age ritual. It is also often followed by a significant return flow of more mature young people as they begin to raise families of their own.

BIBLIOGRAPHY

Beeson, P.E., and R.W. Eberts. 1987. "Identifying Amenity and Productivity Cities Using Wage and Rent Differentials." *Federal Reserve Bank of Cleveland Economic Review* 3: 16–25.

Blomquist, G.C., M.C. Berger, and J.P. Hoehn. 1988. "New Estimates of Quality of Life in Urban Areas." *American Economic Review* 78, no. 1: 89–106.

Borts, G.H., and J.L. Stein. 1964. *Economic Growth in a Free Market*. New York: Columbia University Press.

Ciccone, A., and R.E. Hall. 1996. "Productivity and Density of Economic Activity." *American Economic Review* 86, no. 1: 54–70.

Cobb, C.W., and J.B. Cobb. 1994. *The Green National Product: A Proposed Index of Sustainable Economic Welfare*. Washington, DC: University Press of America.

Council for Community and Economic Research. Multiple years. "Cost of Living Index." Arlington, VA. www.coli.org.

Evans, A.W. 1990. "The Assumption of Equilibrium in the Analysis of Migration and Interregional Differences: A Review of Some Recent Research." *Journal of Regional Science* 30, no. 4: 515–531.

Florida, R. 2005. *Cities and the Creative Class*. New York: Routledge.

Fordor, E. 2012. "Relationship Between Growth and Prosperity in the 100 Largest U.S. Metropolitan Areas." *Economic Development Quarterly* 26, no. 3: 220–230.

Goodstein, E.S. 2011. *Economics and the Environment*. 6th ed. New York: John Wiley.

Harrigan, F.J., and P.G. McGregor. 1993. "Equilibrium and Disequilibrium Perspectives on Regional Labor Migration." *Journal of Regional Science* 33, no. 1: 49–67.

Jacobs, J. 1961. *The Death and Life of Great American Cities*. New York: Random House.

Power, T.M. 1994. "Measuring Local Economic Well-Being: Per Capita Income and Local Economic Health." In *The Green National Product: A Proposed Index of Sustainable Economic Welfare*, C.W. Cobb and J.B. Cobb, 147–167. Washington, DC: University Press of America.

———. 1996a. *Environmental Protection and Economic Well-Being: The Economic Pursuit of Quality*. Armonk, NY: M.E. Sharpe.

———. 1996b. *Lost Landscapes and Failed Economies: The Search for a Value of Place*. Washington, DC: Island Press.

———. 2001. "Economic Structure, Economic Density, and Pay in the Pacific Northwest." Presented at Pacific Northwest Regional Economic Conference, Victoria, British Columbia, May 16–18. www.powereconconsulting.com.

Power, T.M., and R.N. Barrett. 2001. *Post-Cowboy Economics: Pay and Prosperity in the New American West*. Washington, DC: Island Press.

Roback, J. 1982. "Wages, Rents, and the Quality of Life." *Journal of Political Economy* 90, no. 6: 1257–1277.

———. 1988. "Wages, Rents, and Amenities: Differences Among Workers and Regions." *Economic Inquiry* 26, no. 1: 23–41.

Tiebout, C. 1956. "A Pure Theory of Local Expenditures." *Journal of Political Economy* 64, no. 4: 416–424.

Ullman, E. 1955. "Amenities as a Factor in Regional Growth." *Geographical Review* 44, no. 1: 119–132.

Voith, R. 1991. "Capitalization of Local and Regional Attributes into Wages and Rents: Differences Across Residential, Commercial, and Mixed-Use Communities." *Journal of Regional Science* 31, no. 2: 127–145.

Whitelaw, W.E., and E.G. Niemi. 1989. "Money: The Greening of the Economy." *Old Oregon* 68, no. 3: 26–27.

4

Achieving a Brighter Future from the Bottom Up

Activist Laissez-Faire Social Policy

DAVID COLANDER

Most economists use a loose goal of aggregate efficiency as a proxy measure for the policy goal of maximum aggregate output as measured by gross domestic product (GDP). That, in turn, is seen as representing the standard of living portion of welfare that falls under economists' purview. In their introductory chapter to this volume, Holt and Greenwood make it clear that the goal of this book is to question this approach and to explore a broader definition of the standard of living, which includes market, nonmarket, environmental, social, and individual factors that go beyond aggregate or per capita income as the primary indicator of social welfare. While most recent theoretical economic work recognizes that social welfare is determined by a very complicated welfare function, in practice, most economists assume well-being varies directly with material welfare. Holt and Greenwood challenge this view, and I strongly support their challenge. The consideration of the goals of economic policy should be an important part of any discussion of economic policy. If this volume moves the profession in that direction, it will have made an important contribution to the policy debate.

While I agree with the larger issues and goals of the volume, I disagree with the implicit assumption found in some chapters that we can build a meaningful formal measurement of the standard of living. The problem for me is that the GDP measure is so flawed as an adequate measure of the standard of living that to build any other formal measure upon it will not be successful. The quality of life issues embodied in the GDP measure, or any formal measure, are so hopelessly subjective that any measure must be taken with a grain of salt. Therefore, I believe that such measures are an incorrect and inadequate foundation for making policy.

DEALING WITH ENDOGENOUS TASTES

If not GDP, or some other measure, then what measure *does* one use for policy guidance? My answer is that one does not use a formal measure, but rather a variety of informal measures that can be used in a process of reflective judgment. The goal of policy is not to achieve any preset, empirically specified measure but to create a system that encourages people to use their reflective judgment. Thus, I do not see the path to a brighter future lying in a redefinition or modification of the GDP measurement. Instead, I see the path to a brighter future as a change in focus of economic policy analysis from *outcome* to *process*. The goal of economic policy should be a process goal: Get the process right and the outcome of that process will be a better outcome.

The argument to focus on process rather than outcome is based on the observation that tastes are partially endogenous. What people want reflects the institutional structure and culture within which they live. Endogenous tastes and views create a dynamic feedback on any existing specified measure. This feedback so hopelessly distorts it that one cannot use that measure as a value-free normative measure. This means that any measure of welfare based on existing tastes may significantly differ from a measure based on one's reflective, normative values. For example, in our GDP measure, a $300-an-ounce bottle of olive oil gets the same weight as feeding 300 starving infants at a cost of $300. My subjective, normative weights do not give those the same weights. Even though the costs may be the same, the value to society can be quite different. I believe that if people reflected upon it and were given a chance to change the system so that those weights were different, they would also differ in their weighting system. But they are not given that chance. In my view, social policy should be designed to give people a way to let their reflected views determine what constitutes social welfare.

To say that reflective judgment, rather than formal measures, should guide social policy does not mean that informal empirical measures cannot be used as part of reflective judgments. Kept in their place, they can be useful. As I will discuss below, the use of GDP output as a primary measure of social welfare developed when society was poorer and before our society became what J. Kenneth Galbraith in 1958 called an *affluent society*. Galbraith pointed out that in an affluent society the connection between aggregate measures of output and welfare were less direct than in a nonaffluent society; measures of values of output reflected endogenously determined tastes, not uniquely specified biological needs. When the GDP measure was first developed, the problem of endogenous tastes was far less than it is today, but as the economy grew wealthier, the connection between social welfare and GDP became weaker, and we finally found ourselves with an economic infrastructure that was designed to achieve maximum material welfare, not social welfare. As a consequence, when institutions had fulfilled people's obvious material wants, they began influencing people's tastes in order to make people want what businesses were producing. The system then succeeded by fulfilling wants that it created or at least significantly influenced.

The importance of these issues has been noted by economists such as Veblen (1899) and Galbraith (1958), but standard economics has shied away from them with the assumption that tastes are exogenous. The reason economists have avoided endogenous tastes is that they make policy analysis based on any formal measured goal nearly impossible. If tastes are determined by process, it is not only the qualitative aspects of life that are hopelessly subjective and beyond empirical measurement; it is also true of any quantitative measure of GDP. One is left to conduct policy without any formal measure of outcome.

The way one conducts policy without using a formal outcome measure is to focus on process, not outcome. Loose, informal outcome measures are used, but are treated as inputs into a reflective judgment system. My argument is that if we make relatively small changes to our current institutional structure, we can change the process we currently have to one that is more socially desirable. We can thereby significantly change the outcome of our economic system in a direction that most people would agree is more socially desirable, even without specifying just what is a socially desirable outcome.

My focus on process means that this chapter differs substantially from many of the other chapters in the volume. These differences do not mean that I do not share the goals for society that the other contributors have. The goals I see society wanting to achieve are, I suspect, very similar to those of most of the contributors to this volume, as well as the ones I believe most individuals in society want to achieve. We want policy that focuses on more than material welfare; we want policy that will encourage people to develop as complete people and not just one-dimensional materialistic beings; we want a fair system in which all people have as good a chance to succeed as possible. The question is how to get there.

THE CLASSICAL LIBERAL APPROACH AND WHY IT IS STILL RELEVANT TODAY

Most advocates of the goals mentioned above also favor developing measures that better specify those goals, along with developing policies focused on reaching those redefined goals. I do not favor that approach, but instead favor what might be called a classical liberal approach. This is an indirect policy approach in which the policy's goal is to create a set of institutions and cultures, generally classified as an ecostructure, that are conducive to the greatest number of people defining, and achieving, their own brighter future with as little direct government control as possible.

This liberal approach was the essence of classical economics and involved a different way of doing policy analysis than does modern analysis. The classical liberal approach saw policy goals as far too entwined with philosophical issues to be achieved in reference to economic conditions alone. Instead of focusing on measured goals, it focused much more on process, giving individuals as much freedom as possible. This classical liberal policy goal is quite different from the "modern liberal" approach that evolved out of economic thinking captured by Samuelson in his textbook (1976). The "new" modern liberal approach begins by characterizing, defining, and developing a workable measure of broad social goals.[1] Having defined the new proxy, the new modern liberal approach explores how government policies can increase the new proxy measures. These policies include more focus on social and public goods, less on materialistic private goods, and a greater direct role for government in our economy. Given our institutional structure, a greater role for government is the only way we can achieve that alternative focus.

PROBLEMS WITH THE MODERN LIBERAL APPROACH

While I am sympathetic to the need for a greater focus on social goals, I do not see the new modern liberal approach as the appropriate path. My problem is twofold. First, while I agree that we can come to a loosely shared agreement about what is meant by improving the standard of living, I do not believe this standard of living can be formally defined in a useful way for developing public policy. The second problem I have with the new modern liberal approach is that formally defining the standard of living, rather than just accepting that "we will know it when we see it," can contribute to making our future dimmer, not brighter. The reason it can make our future dimmer is that any formalization of the goal implicitly involves making judgments about the policy approach we will use to achieve it—you only need a formalized concept if you are thinking of a control model in which government undertakes policy to directly achieve that goal.

This means that formalizing a social goal implicitly assumes that there will be an increase in government involvement in order to help society to achieve the defined social goal. That goes directly against one of my social goals, which is to leave individuals as free as possible to decide their own future and direction. Achieving that individual freedom goal means reducing the direct role of government in the economy as much as possible. For me, the only way in which society can achieve a higher standard of living is if individuals in society are as free as possible to define and achieve their conception of a better life. This means that, for me, individuals in society must achieve a better life with the minimum of direct direction from government or other agents as possible, because any such direction has the danger of reflecting the other agents', rather than the individuals', conception of a better life.

My focus on individual freedom is a normative goal usually associated with market fundamentalists who argue against government involvement in the economy. But I am no market fundamentalist as that term is usually interpreted. I see myself more in the activist, classical liberal tradition of John Stuart Mill (1848). That tradition involves not only a strong societal commitment to social goals, but also a strong aversion to direct government control. In his writings, Amartya Sen (1999) has carried on with the classical liberal view, arguing that agency and freedom are desirable in their own right, independent of their effect on total output. This approach makes more sense to me.

The question is how to achieve generally shared social goals while using a minimum of direct government involvement. My answer is to see governing as the equivalent of sophisticated parenting or self-control—you give children freedom, but, to the best of your ability, you instill in them a value system that encourages them to use that freedom wisely. That involves creating an infrastructure that supports but does not mandate the actions your reflective self sees as desirable. You rely on the moral sentiments part of Adam Smith's argument (1759), not on the wealth of nations part. You are explicitly trying to influence but leaving the individual free to accept that influence or not.

For Smith, this sense of morality exists in all individuals. He writes, "That we often derive sorrow from the sorrows of others, is a matter of fact too obvious to require any instances to prove it; for this sentiment, like all the other original passions of human nature, is by no means confined to the virtuous or the humane, though they perhaps may feel it with the most exquisite sensibility. The greatest ruffian, the most hardened violator of the laws of society, is not altogether without it" (1759, 1). In the progressive classical liberal approach, the goal of policy was to encourage but not force people to act on these moral sentiments to develop a brighter future.

COMPLEX SYSTEMS AND POLICY

My interest in the classical tradition and in the policies that are associated with it has followed from my work on complex systems and policy (Colander 2011; Colander and Kupers 2014). I have come to believe that having a complexity vision of society provides a different frame for policy—one in which sustainable direct control by government, or by any other agent in the system, is impossible. Because the economy is seen as a continually changing and emerging system, no agent, including government, can control it. In such an evolutionary system, policy is most usefully seen as affecting the evolution of the system, not as controlling the outcomes. Similarly, goals are most usefully seen as emergent and not as a priori. Within a complexity framework, activist government policy involves not direct control of policy, but rather what might be called a natural midwifery policy, designed to assist individuals in creating an ecostructure that fosters the emergence of what individuals collectively see as desirable goals. The social midwifery policy is needed for the same reason that self-control is needed by individuals: we have both immediate desires (we want that chocolate fudge sundae) and long-run desires (we want to remain healthy), and all individuals must blend those desires into actions that they believe are best for themselves. Society must also blend its long-run and immediate desires into social actions. One of the ways society does that is through government.

This is the framework that I believe formed the foundation of classical economic laissez-faire policy. Classical liberal policy was far from a strict market fundamentalist approach. It allowed for an indirect activist role for government and for all individuals in the system to help develop and maintain a framework that allowed all people to achieve a better life as they defined it. Thus, for example, it led to Mill's opposition to slavery and his strong support for women's rights.

Within this complexity framework, government's central policy role is to create an ecostructure that allows individuals to achieve their individual goals as best they can, which means a system in which government has only a small direct role. As I stated at the beginning, the argument in this chapter is that if we make relatively small changes to our current ecostructure, we can significantly change the outcome of our economic system into one that, I believe, most people would agree is more socially desirable, even without specifying what that socially desirable outcome is.

The policy framework here differs from the policy framework that supports a market fundamentalist approach in two ways. First, it sees many different paths that society can follow—there is not a unique equilibrium for the economy or society. Second, it sees the government that has developed as being as natural as the market; the two have coevolved, and thus one cannot talk about the existing market separately from the existing government—both are best seen as part of an organic whole.

GOVERNMENT'S INDIRECT ROLE

Thinking of the economy as a complex system provides a different framework for thinking of government and policy than does thinking of the economy as a system that can be controlled, as is done in the standard policy approach. It creates an indirect role for government that the standard economic policy frame does not capture. That indirect role influences what path society will follow and what kind of institutional framework people will operate in; once on a path, government policy does not control it. Instead, government indirectly nudges people *to reflect upon their choice* and to make sure that they are following what they believe is a preferable path. A central policy goal in the complexity frame is to increase the amount of reflection that individuals give to their choices.

The reasons for these nudges are currently being explored in behavioral economics. As with individual choices, social choices are often guided by short-run impulses, exhibiting hyperbolic discounting, framing effects, and other similar behavioral peculiarities that do not reflect what society would want to do were it governed by long-run considerations. Upon reflection, I suspect most individuals would likely want to guide society's choices. Government's complexity policy role is to provide institutions that encourage that long-run reflection. Policy nudges do not have to be major. Often the actual policy intervention to achieve a major change can be small because complex systems often have sensitive dependence on small variables; a very small nudge at the right time can have an enormous influence on the society's trajectory.

Within a complexity policy frame, government policy involves not only direct government policy, but also an indirect policy designed to influence the future evolution of the ecosystem to foster the type of society one favors. Will society choose materialistic goals, or will it choose more social goals like improving quality of life and sustainability? If one believes that most individuals share similar social goals, but in our current institutional structure are given far too little opportunity to express them within the economic sphere of our lives, then a policy opportunity exists to change the institutional structure to give social goals more focus, thereby nudging individuals to make decisions that put society on a preferable social path. That policy would be designed to change the institutional structure to be more conducive to individuals focusing more on social goals in the economic portion of their lives. If this policy is successful, the direct role for government in achieving social goals can be significantly reduced, even as the society better achieves these goals.

I believe that this was the framework that J.M. Keynes (whom I see as being within the classical liberal tradition) was referring to in his letter (Keynes 1944) to Hayek congratulating him on the *Road to Serfdom* (Hayek 1944). Keynes wrote Hayek that it "was a grand book" and that "morally and philosophically I find myself in agreement with virtually the whole of it: and not only in agreement with it, but in deeply moved agreement." Keynes continued, "What we need therefore, in my opinion, is not a change in our economic programmes, which would only lead in practice to disillusion with the results of your philosophy; but perhaps even the contrary, namely, an enlargement of them. Your greatest danger is the probable practical failure of the application of your philosophy in the United States." He concluded, "I should . . . conclude rather differently. I should not say that what we want is no planning, or even less planning, indeed I should say we almost certainly want more. But the planning should take place in a community in which as many people as possible, both leaders and followers wholly share your own moral position." I interpret this as meaning that Keynes supported planning that would involve designing an ecostructure to minimize government intervention into the market.

HOW ECONOMICS LOST THE CLASSICAL LIBERAL TRADITION

In my view, the direction of policy and policy discussion, which occurred as economics moved from the classical to the neoclassical period, lost sight of that broader, indirect classical policy role of government of guiding society toward what most considered higher goals and leaving individuals free to define those higher goals. Government's indirect guiding role was forgotten, and the policy debate centered on government's direct role. As that happened, society took a path that classical economists had not predicted nor expected, which was a society obsessed with materialistic goals.[2] This presented a dilemma for those who supported social goals, who then turned to direct intervention through government policy to help achieve those social goals. Essentially the government failed in its "guiding" role, and to correct the failure it had to take larger and larger direct control roles in achieving social ends. As that happened, the very definition of liberalism changed. The concept of liberalism, which for classical economists was associated with individual freedom, became associated with expanding direct government intervention to attempt to achieve social goals.

My view of the problem facing society today is quite different from the views held by most modern-day market fundamentalists or most modern-day liberals. Where I disagree with modern liberals is in the idea that social goals can be achieved through direct government action. In my view, government is as inefficient at achieving social goals as it is at achieving material welfare goals. To leave social goals to government in its current form is to undermine any hope of achieving them. Where I disagree with market fundamentalists is on their assumption that achieving individual freedom means that we should leave things just to the market. We are products of our environment, and thus our immediate views reflect that environment. It takes reflection to discover our true views. Individual freedom requires a framework that encourages people to reflect, which our current framework does not. The market only works if the ecostructure underlying the market is the right one, and in my view, our existing underlying ecostructure is not the right one. I believe that most people, if they had the time to reflect, would share that view.

Thus, I see an important policy role for government in creating an ecostructure that encourages reflection, and I believe that the reflected desires of individuals in our society will lead to an ecostructure that encourages much more bottom-up collective action to achieve social goals than currently exists. Governments can aid individuals in achieving that bottom-up collective social action by making it easier for individuals to form these organizations.

My policy goal is for government to concentrate its policy efforts on getting the ecostructure right so that people are encouraged to provide social goods from the bottom up. To the degree that the government is successful in providing an ecostructure that lets individuals carry out their social goals through collective action, government can have a smaller direct role in the social system. If individuals solve problems through bottom-up organizations, they will not need government to attempt to solve the problem with top-down solutions.

EXPANDING THE DOMAIN OF THE MARKET

Achieving the ecostructure I envision is likely to involve some substantial government policy initiatives. But those policy initiatives will not involve more direct government control over individuals or the market. Instead, they will involve an attempt to expand the domain of the market from material goods to social goods in order to turn the power of the market to social rather than just materialistic goals.

My argument is that bottom-up solutions do not have to be restricted to solving problems of a materialistic nature; they can be associated with solving social problems if the ecostructure encourages that. The policy I advocate is what I call a bottom-up policy in which the role of government is to create the infrastructure within which people are encouraged to achieve their desired social ends with extragovernmental organizations that develop from the bottom up and do not involve direct government control. It is a policy not of government control, but rather of government influence and guidance. It is designed to create an ecostructure that encourages individuals to fulfill their social goals as well as their materialistic goals from the bottom up, thereby achieving a brighter future as they see it.

Since almost all of the social problems we face involve public good and externality dimensions, these bottom-up solutions will involve collective action organizations. They will involve a continuous development of social organizations as people work together to solve social problems. This collective effort does not always require government intervention. Elinor Ostrom (2005), a political scientist who developed a "social ecological systems framework" for collective self-governance, gave an outline of how in many situations individuals can develop bottom-up institutions to govern themselves and resolve conflicts.[3] Our complex world requires multifaceted institutions that fit the context of the social system of which they are a part. These institutions compete among each other to solve the social problems as best they can.

I referred earlier to achieving a brighter future as a policy of "as they see it" because what I am advocating does not establish goals as much as process. Instead, it involves aiming at an ecostructure in which individuals decide their future, with what is meant by a better life emerging. The reality that emerges will reflect the brighter future as seen by individuals, not by any one group of individuals such as social science experts. It will emerge without being formally defined.

HOW SOCIETY CAME TO FOCUS ON MATERIALISTIC GOALS

In my view, society is far more materialistic than it desires to be because of a set of decisions made in the evolution of capitalism. Those decisions placed social goals under the purview of government and materialistic goals under the purview of the market. That division led to the creation of an ecostructure that discouraged people's bottom-up social nature and encouraged their material welfare nature. That led to an undesirable "lock-in" on materialistic goals from which society cannot escape without a catalyst. The policies I suggest involve creating catalysts that make it easier for individuals to escape. The bottom-up role of government is to encourage individuals within society to reflect on where we are as a society, and to provide mechanisms to get society out of that lock-in, should we desire to do so. If society does not desire to do so, then the better life that I see is not the better life for society. The collective of individual members of society, as opposed to me, government, or any group of experts, decides on what they want for a better life.

If classical liberal economists such as Sidgwick (1901 [1883]) and Mill (1848) had this broader vision of the goals of economics as part of their analysis, how did economics end up focusing so strongly on material welfare? In my view, it happened through a series of small steps in which the assumptions underlying the classical view were progressively forgotten. Analyzing simultaneously the many goals of the collective will was impossible, so a division of labor in social science was needed. Over time, a subgroup of social scientists, called political economists, working as economic scientists, began to focus on a subset of those goals of a good life—what they called material welfare. Based on their analysis and a wider set of reasoning that included the assumption that achieving material welfare would not negatively impinge on other social goals, they developed a set of policy recommendations for achieving a better materialistic life. The government policy they advocated fostered the creation of an ecostructure that would allow freedom and entrepreneurship to develop. Because their analysis focused on material welfare only, classical economists understood that the results could not be directly transferred to all policy recommendations, since they had assumed away many important issues and only focused on achieving material welfare rather than a broader concept of social welfare.[4] While classical economists emphasized the limitations of this analysis, they also argued that a focus on materialistic goals was acceptable.

Classical economists could justify a focus on material welfare for two reasons. First, the goals of individuals are in many ways lexicographic. If you are starving or freezing in the streets, love, morals, sympathy, and many other goals of a good life lose importance quickly. You do what you can to live and achieve sufficient material welfare goals to survive. Second, for many issues, achieving material welfare goals may not prevent achieving broader social goals also. If there is more to go around, it is probably easier for society to achieve its other social goals than if there is less. But again, although classical economists recognized the limitation of just pursuing material welfare, they never really got around to analyzing how best to achieve social goals or how to develop an ecostructure conducive to individuals achieving those broader social goals.

MATERIALISM AS A TEMPORARY PHASE OF SOCIETIES

A key to understanding classical economists' support of markets, and the materialism associated with them, was that they saw materialism embedded in markets as a temporary phenomenon. They believed that the focus on materialism would fade away as wealth increased and people acquired more materialistic goods than they needed. They did not see the goal of material welfare as sacrosanct, nor did they picture individuals as pursuing only material welfare. Mill, for example, described a stationary state as one in which people had transcended material needs and were concerned with the deeper issues in life such as interrelationships, social justice, and intellectual ideas. Mill pictured a society that was far more concerned with social welfare and far less concerned with material welfare. He saw a society in which "while no one is poor, no one desires to be richer, nor has any reason to fear being thrust back by the efforts of others to push themselves forward" (1848, 369).

Continuing this view, Keynes wrote in "Economic Possibilities of Our Grandchildren" what, in my view, many classical liberals believed:

> When the accumulation of wealth is no longer of high social importance, there will be great changes in the code of morals. We shall be able to rid ourselves of many of the pseudo-moral principles which have hag-ridden us for two hundred years, by which we have exalted some of the most distasteful of human qualities into the position of the highest virtues. We shall be able to afford to dare to assess the money-motive at its true value. The love of money as a possession—as distinguished from the love of money as a means to the enjoyments and realities of life—will be recognized for what it is, a somewhat disgusting morbidity, one of those semi-criminal, semi-pathological propensities which one hands over with a shudder to the specialists in mental disease. All kinds of social customs and economic practices, affecting the distribution of wealth and of economic rewards and penalties, which we now maintain at all costs, however distasteful and unjust they may be in themselves, because they are tremendously useful in promoting the accumulation of capital, we shall then be free, at last, to discard. (1963 [1930], 329)

The view of human nature and of the goals of society embodied in this quotation is far removed from economics as it is practiced and thought about today. But it is a view that is, I believe, shared by many people on both the right and the left. We have materialistic goals and social goals, and we live our lives attempting to achieve balance between both. The balance we achieve is significantly influenced by the ecostructure within which we live. There is a sense that because of the enormous growth our economy has experienced, our current ecostructure puts too great a focus on materialistic goals, a focus individuals find difficult to escape from. In this view of human nature, individuals' division between selfish materialist goals and social goals is not inherent, but reflects the culture within which they develop. I believe individuals would support policies that maintained their freedom to choose but would also lead to an ecostructure that more strongly encouraged achieving social as opposed to materialistic goals than our current ecostructure does.

Thus, Keynes would have been a strong supporter of the premise of this volume—that a renewal of economic growth will not achieve all of society's goals. But I suspect he would not have been a great supporter of the methods being proposed by some here. The problem is that government is not very efficient at achieving social goals, just as it is not very efficient at achieving material welfare goals. To assign government the role of providing social goals is to doom those social goals to failure. The most efficient way to achieve social goals is from the bottom up, letting people's initiative and entrepreneurial spirit be directed toward social as well as materialist goals. Somehow we need to encourage an ecostructure in which incentives drive people's inventiveness toward social rather than just materialistic goals.

WHY MILL'S STATIONARY STATE DID NOT COME ABOUT

To understand how to achieve this, it is useful to consider why Mill's and Keynes's vision did not come about. If anything, we are further away from their vision today than we were 100 years ago, even though our output per capita has increased at a rate they never expected, or even faster. The reason why it did not happen, I suggest, is that in order to take advantage of economies of scale and the market, an institutional structure had to be developed that would allow the market to operate. To take advantage of economies of scale, larger units of production than owner-managed firms were necessary. Government ecostructure policy was designed to develop a legal structure and organizational forms, such as for-profit corporations, that were highly conducive to providing that material welfare.

Within this ecostructure, corporations were state-sanctioned collective action enterprises that allowed expanded, bottom-up collective action to produce material goods; they provided an alternative collective action mechanism to government to undertake certain types of collective action concerned with materialist welfare; they channeled entrepreneurial power and funds into collective organizations that competed among themselves to provide society with increased material welfare.

But these corporations did not develop in a vacuum. For corporations to operate effectively, they needed an institutional and legal framework that allowed them to evolve and develop in order to handle the difficult collective action problems they posed. Over time, that framework developed and the for-profit corporate form became a fixture of Western societies as an alternative source of economic coordination and control within society. They thrived so much that they changed the nature of capitalism from entrepreneurial capitalism to corporate capitalism, as pointed out by Galbraith (1967). In corporate capitalism, government was left in charge of achieving society's social goals, and the corporate-modified private sector was in charge of achieving economic or what economists called material welfare. The corporate structure succeeded admirably, and material living standards increased multifold in Western societies. But as I stated above, early economists, such as John Stuart Mill, had expected that society's focus on material welfare would subside since what they believed was the economic problem had been solved. They envisioned societies switching their focus away from material welfare and toward social welfare, which included material welfare but also included broader concepts of humanistic and nonmaterialistic welfare.

That did not happen. The for-profit corporate form was too strong, and materialistic lock-in set in. Once for-profit organizations had met the immediate material *needs* of society, they learned how to turn material *wants* into material needs that would provide them with additional profit-making opportunities. Whereas material needs are limited, material wants are essentially infinite, so this change gave for-profit corporations an extended, almost unlimited role in an increasingly materialistic society. As that happened, capitalism changed; advertising, marketing, and branding—all mechanisms to keep corporations relevant—became central to capitalist societies, while manufacturing and production became secondary (Galbraith 1958).

There is no doubt that people's measured material welfare has continued to rise in Western market societies, but somehow there is a feeling among many that social welfare has not increased near that amount. In response, people have turned to government to provide that social welfare. Unfortunately, current governmental organizational structures are not set up to efficiently provide that social welfare; while government can often nicely articulate need, it seems unable to contain costs and make the difficult budget decisions that must be made for a sustainable system.

The problem with having the government providing social welfare is the same problem with government providing material welfare. The economy is too complex to deal with in the control framework that social planners implicitly follow. Just as there can be no controller who runs our economic system—the economic system emerges from the infinite number of individual decisions—so too can there be no single controller who runs our social system due to its complexity. Attempts at having government define and achieve social goals, which usually deviate from the aggregated goals of the members of society, are doomed to fail for the same reason that central planning of economies fails.

But that does not mean that government is impotent or unneeded. What government can do is to create a broader ecosystem within which individuals' true preferences—both material preferences and social preferences—can be articulated and acted upon. Classical economists called this policy "laissez-faire," but for them laissez-faire was not a "government should do nothing" policy. Laissez-faire was a policy in which government actively structured the ecosystem in a way that markets could give people the freedom to develop their own conception of the good life, at least to the degree that it did not impinge upon the rights of others. Entrepreneurs operating in a competitive environment by following their own selfish, private material goals would achieve the material goals that society wanted.[5] Classical economists did not explore how social entrepreneurs, operating in a different competitive environment and following their own sense of individual social goals for society, could likewise achieve social goals.

This separation between social goals and material welfare goals is unnatural and highly inefficient. It leads people to compartmentalize their lives, both in their investments and in their employment. Somehow, in their work and investments, people are supposed to be operating in an atmosphere of maximizing profit without concern for broader social goals. Then they put on their social hat, and they turn to what they believe are inefficient governments and inefficient nonprofits to achieve any social goals they have. The result is less success in achieving shared social goals than almost any single member of society wants.

POLICIES TO ESCAPE LOCK-IN

For our society to escape from this materialistic lock-in, we need activist government policy not to directly achieve social goals, but to make it easier for individuals to organize from the bottom up to offset the materialist lock-in that is currently embedded in the corporate structure. This lock-in directs much of our collective social energy toward achieving materialist ends rather than social ends. Essentially, what I am arguing is that individuals' utility function includes both private social goods and private individual goods. Both require collective action to fulfill. Currently, the corporate institutional structure is designed to achieve private individual goods through the market with reasonably efficiency. This means corporate forms focus on achieving profit, rather than on achieving a combination of social and private goals. Thus the entire power of the market is designed to achieve materialistic outcomes— not optimal social outcomes. A different institutional structure would lead to different outcomes.

THE FOR-BENEFIT ENTERPRISE AND SOCIALLY MOTIVATED ENTREPRENEURSHIP

In Colander (2012), I argued that one of the institutional reforms that we need is to make it easier for social entrepreneurs to operate and to develop collective bottom-up organizations to achieve social ends. I argued that the split between social and material welfare concerns is to a large degree a product of the polar way our corporate organizational structure has evolved, allowing for either for-profit or nonprofit organizations and nothing in between. The pure for-profit organizational form is not inherent to the structure of capitalism. Organizational structures do not have to be either for-profit or nonprofit; a more logical structure would include hybrid "for-benefit" organizational structures, which blend the social concerns of a nonprofit with the sustainability concerns (where sustainability means the ability to continue in existence) of a for-profit. Groups such as the Fourth Sector Network have been leading the way in exploring how for-benefit enterprises provide a vehicle for socially motivated entrepreneurs to direct the power of the market to achieving social welfare just as for-profit corporations direct the power of the market to achieving material welfare.[6]

The goal of these for-benefit enterprises is to achieve some combination of profit or sustainability goals and prespecified social goals, where those profit and social goals are spelled out at the formation in the company charter. For example, as I discuss (Colander 2011), one might have a for-benefit school whose goal is to educate students efficiently as measured by a specified metric, while providing a prespecified monetary return, which could be zero or even negative, to investors.[7] Other examples of for-benefit institutions include medical drug companies and media companies.

I see the encouragement of for-benefit institutions as a central way to provide for a brighter future, but not the only way. In Colander and Kupers (2014), I explore other alternatives. The goal of these policies is to create a better future for people without a measure because it will be so much better than the alternative that a formal measure will not be needed. The goal is to create an institutional structure that encourages individuals to work toward achieving what they see as a better future. The aggregate result of those decisions will emerge from the interactions and cannot be specified in advance.

CONCLUSION

Changing the landscape of organizational structures at this fundamental level will not be easy. Changing operating systems is never easy, but the central argument of this paper is that our current operating system is obsolete and has not adjusted for the successes of the system in achieving material welfare. In a complex environment, bottom-up policy that relies on individual initiative works better than direct top-down policy, and changing the environment to encourage bottom-up social policy is our best chance at achieving a better society.

We need to bring to social problems the same incentive dynamic that for-profit corporations and private entrepreneurship brought to the achievement of material welfare. We can do that only by changing the operating system of capitalism to direct social entrepreneurship aimed at solving social problems. Doing so will involve changes in law, accounting procedures, and more generally in our vision of what organizations' goals are. It will not be easy, but it is the direction in which we should be moving.

NOTES

1. I discuss these historical issues in more detail in Colander and Freedman (2011) and Colander and Kupers (2014).

2. As I will discuss below and as I have discussed in Colander (2012), the argument is that for-profit corporations took the easier path to profits, which involved encouraging individuals' materialistic nature through advertising.

3. Ostrom won the Nobel Prize for Economics in 2009. Until her death in 2012, she ran a workshop at Indiana University that studies the problem of common resource management.

4. This approach carried through to Pigou (1920). His *The Economics of Welfare* carefully specified that his focus was only on material welfare and that the analysis was a part of a broader social analysis.

5. As Lionel Robbins (1952, 56) nicely put it, "the invisible hand which guides men to promote ends which were no part of their intentions, is not the hand of some god, or some natural agency independent of human effort; it is the hand of the lawgiver, the hand which withdraws from the sphere of the pursuit of self-interest those possibilities which do not harmonize with the public good."

6. See www.aspeninstitute.org/publications/emerging-fourth-sector-executive-summary for a discussion of the "fourth sector" and its potential importance in the economy. The conception of a for-benefit enterprise that I am presenting here is a broad one—it is an organization that has both social and financial goals that are determined from the bottom up. This means that the actual structure of the for-benefit enterprise will reflect the bargain reached by investors and social entrepreneurs. That bargain might be something quite different from the ideas that I or others currently have. Society's social goals, like its material goals, emerge from the bargaining process and do not exist independently of that process.

7. One can think of a donation as an investment with a 100 percent negative monetary return.

BIBLIOGRAPHY

Colander, D. 2011. "Solving Society's Problems from the Bottom Up: For-Benefit Enterprises." *Challenge* 55, no. 1: 69–85.

———. 2012. The Complexity Policy Narrative and the Future of Capitalism, Keynote Address. "Grand Debate: 21st Century Capitalism." Asian Community Economic Forum, Incheon, Korea, November 7.

Colander, D., and C. Freedman. 2011. "The Chicago Counter-Revolution and the Loss of the Classical Liberal Tradition." Middlebury College Working Paper.

Colander, D., and R. Kupers. 2014. *Complexity and the Art of Social Policy: Solving Society's Problems from the Bottom Up*. Princeton, NJ: Princeton University Press.

Galbraith, J.K. 1958. *The Affluent Society*. Boston: Houghton Mifflin.

————. 1967. *The New Industrial State*. Boston: Houghton Mifflin.

Hayek, F. 1944. *The Road to Serfdom*. Chicago: University of Chicago Press.

Keynes, J.M. 1944. "Letter to Hayek, June 28, 1944." Friedrich Hayek Collection, Hoover Institution, Stanford University.

————. 1963 [1930]. "Economic Possibilities of Our Grandchildren." *Essays in Persuasion*, in *Collected Works*, vol. 9. New York: Norton.

Mill, J.S. 1848. *Principles of Political Economy*. London: Longmans, Green.

Ostrom, E. 2005. *Understanding Institutional Diversity*. Princeton, NJ: Princeton University Press.

Pigou, A.C. 1920. *The Economics of Welfare*. London: Macmillan.

Robbins, Lionel. 1952. *The Theory of Economic Policy in English Political Economy*. London: Macmillan.

Samuelson, P. 1976. *Economics*. 10th ed. New York: McGraw-Hill.

Sen, A. 1999. *Development as Freedom*. New York: Oxford University Press.

Sidgwick, H. 1901 [1883]. *Principles of Political Economy*. 3rd ed. London: Macmillan.

Smith, A. 1759. *Theory of Moral Sentiments*. London: A Miller.

Veblen, T. 1899. *The Theory of the Leisure Class: An Economic Study in the Evolution of Institutions*. New York: Macmillan.

P A R T

II

Lagging Incomes and the Middle-Class Dream

5

The Future of Middle-Class Jobs
Macroeconomic Effects and Shrinking Unions

PAUL J. KOZLOWSKI AND *STEVEN SPIRN*

This chapter deals with the importance of middle-class jobs to the current and future standard of living in the United States. Looking back, these jobs expanded throughout the middle of the twentieth century, greatly widening the middle class. In addition to higher wages, workers also enjoyed better health and pension benefits and improved safety conditions, which all contributed to a better standard of living. This improvement was brought about by the combination of stronger unions and a commitment to macroeconomic stability after the Great Depression. For decades after World War II, large portions of the business community supported improvements in living standards and found ways to be highly profitable while paying workers well and improving working conditions.

However, this support began to weaken in the late 1970s. Private-sector unionism came under fire, full employment fell from being a top macroeconomic priority, and businesses increasingly looked overseas for cheaper labor that would work in less desirable conditions. Moving into the twenty-first century, new models of business profitability arose, along with challenges to public-sector unions and an emphasis on deficit reduction versus employment growth. Each has contributed to lowering the standard of living for large groups of American workers.

We begin the chapter with a brief look at these widespread changes in business behavior, followed by changes in the strength of unions and the widening gap between productivity growth and wage growth. We then consider the impact on jobs and pay as a result of the repeated downswings in the economy that have been followed by historically weak job recoveries. Next, we highlight economic and political responses to the Great Recession of 2007–2009 that occurred in the public sector. These responses weakened the bargaining power of unions representing state and local government workers and had direct impacts on some of the most vulnerable workers. In the last section of the chapter, we identify a range of policies that we argue move in the direction of a brighter future for workers and the middle class. We turn first to the evolving structure of labor markets and business in the "new economy."

CHANGES IN BUSINESS BEHAVIOR AND THE IMPACTS ON WORKERS

Technological change has had both positive and negative effects on the economy. One major effect has been to alter the demand for various types of labor. Some workers have benefited, while others have not. As businesses adjust capital-labor ratios, as the relative demand for various skills changes, and as companies relocate, some workers will experience permanent job losses. If growth of employment requires creation of new positions in different firms and industries, then employers' costs may rise due to the increased time needed to fill positions. Instead of temporary layoffs, more permanent job losses occur in some industries (Groshen and Potter 2003).[1]

Unions actually encouraged temporary layoffs (albeit unintentionally) by supplementing state-provided unemployment insurance with union funds, thus stabilizing income during downturns. While this change added security for workers from the 1950s through the 1980s, it also made it possible for businesses to smooth labor usage over the business cycle by hiring more low-cost temporary workers. Often, growth in temporary and part-time employment reflects labor-inventory adjustments as businesses await reliable signs of increased demand, especially following recessions.

Movements in the rate of outflow (the pace at which workers move from unemployment status) reflect changing business behavior. The rate was at historic lows in the last decade, and workers involuntarily employed in part-time positions hit historic highs (Daly, Hobijn, and Kwok 2009).[2] Slack in the labor market, therefore, was greater in 2009 than in any other year since 1949, a condition we address in more detail when looking at macroeconomic effects later in this chapter.

Businesses are able to pay lower (50–60 percent of full-time) hourly wages to part-time workers, with perhaps no more than one-quarter of such workers receiving health insurance, pensions, or sick leave. Schreft and Singh (2003) estimated that during the 2002 recovery the explicit wage cost of retaining 71,000 workers was about $42 million per week, or only about 4 percent of more than $1 billion paid in overtime. Part-time and temporary positions, along with overtime hours for the regular workforce, also add flexibility and reduce costs for businesses. In the 1980s, the temporary employment services industry was small, filling mostly clerical and temporary vacancies. But by 2000 it accounted for about 2 percent of nonfarm workers, including light industrial, call center, and technical workers. Management and technical consulting jobs also grew (Aaronson, Rissman, and Sullivan 2004). Because unions primarily represent full-time workers, they have had little if any influence on this growing personnel supply services industry.

Employment in temporary services can sometimes be a leading indicator of total employment. This means the economy needs to expand for some time before full-time employment picks up (Segal and Sullivan 1997). While just-in-time labor practices may improve profits, they tend to lower the multifaceted standard of living of wage earners. It is not surprising, therefore, that a high percentage of temporary workers would prefer full-time employment. A key question going forward is this: Are businesses with higher profits actually capable of creating more full-time, well-paying jobs or will we continue to see a divergence between business profitability and the well-being of workers?

THE NEW ECONOMY BUSINESS MODEL VERSUS THE OLD

The old-economy business model (OEBM) generated more stable employment and earnings as workers remained with companies for many years (Lazonick 2009). Unionized workers had protection with collective bargaining agreements, which provided some degree of confidence about job recalls when recessions ended. The 1950 to 1990 period may be regarded historically as an era of relative economic certainty and sustainability of living standards for workers; however, the economic reality for workers has changed.

The new-economy business model (NEBM) outlined by Lazonick reveals a lack of commitment to provide stable employment over long periods in the high-tech industry. The NEBM implies greater *interfirm* than intrafirm mobility for employees, which may work well for workers when demand is rising. Collective bargaining contracts seem to be frowned upon, not only by employers but also by employees, with college-educated technical and administrative professionals preferring not to be represented by unions. Instead, such workers use movement through labor markets rather than union contracts to establish and to maintain individual pay and working conditions. No semiconductor facility in Silicon Valley, for example, was ever unionized.[3] It is not clear whether such behavior would continue if demand drifted downward, as in several recessions followed by slow job recoveries we discuss later in the chapter. We turn next to the role of unions in building a middle class and how that role has changed in recent decades.

UNIONS AND LIVING STANDARDS

From a historical perspective, unions played an important role in moving a significant portion of the US population into the middle class during the twentieth century. A middle-class standard of living includes not just an income range centered on median income, but a safe workplace, the opportunity for advancement, and a degree of economic security.[4] Unions have been important vehicles through which many American families achieved that status.

In the auto industry alone, hundreds of thousands of individuals enjoyed a higher standard of living as a result of negotiated agreements between organized labor and management. Many more experienced improvements in wages, benefits, and working conditions as union effects spilled over to influence conditions in nonunion sectors. Unions are fond of saying that they are "the folks that brought workers the weekend" because collective bargaining formally established forty-hour workweeks on a large scale for many workers, compared to the fifty- and sixty-hour workweeks that had been common before.[5]

Unions have always dealt with the economic insecurity of workers. In 1900, the hourly wage for textile operatives averaged only about one-half that in all manufacturing industries. Low wages combined with unstable employment meant that sometimes the entire family needed to work to achieve a good standard of living. In the textile industry, for example, the male head of the family earned about 54 percent of the family income, children about 29 percent, and the wife 7 percent (Zebroski 1982).

The heterogeneous nature of the workforce sometimes contributed to weak responses by unions. Higher-skilled and better-paid members of craft unions might initiate strikes. Support among newer, less-skilled immigrant workers faded when conditions deteriorated and starvation for families became a real danger. In some cases, management responded by offering training and new positions to unskilled workers as a method of undermining labor solidarity. With no social safety net, some workers eagerly returned, settling for less than they sought initially. At times, poor market conditions led to cuts in full-time work and loss of income as management adjusted by looking for cheaper labor with no unions.[6]

Since a job is a vital source of self-respect and of membership in the community, unions that enhance opportunities also enrich noneconomic quality-of-life aspects for workers. Although varying from contract to contract, union-negotiated provisions have improved job security and alleviated various forms of discrimination by providing members with due-process procedures.

However, history may not indicate how conditions might evolve in the future. Although mass movement of private-sector workers into the middle class occurred during the mid-twentieth century, since the 1980s the middle class has been hollowed out. White-collar and blue-collar middle-skilled jobs disappeared and real wages stagnated or fell (Peck 2011).[7] These changes paralleled the drop in influence of unions. In the private sector, unionization approached 40 percent at one time, but by the beginning of the twenty-first century the share had dropped to about 7 percent. As Figure 5.1 shows, unions held their own primarily in the government sector, with a share of employment over 40 percent in local government and about 30 percent in state government in 2010.

Many factors, including the loss of a strong base in manufacturing, account for the dramatic decline in private-sector unionism. In 1950, for example, about 31 percent of all nonfarm workers were employed in some form of manufacturing; by 2010, that share was only 9 percent. Globalization accounts for some of this decline, but so does movement of work to so-called right-to-work states with statutes that outlaw union shops in which individual workers must join the union after a specified period of time.

"RIGHT-TO-WORK" AND UNION MEMBERSHIP

There is a direct connection between "right-to-work" states and extremely low union membership. Twenty-four states were classified as "right-to-work" states through either the state's constitution or legislative statutes as of 2013. US Department of Commerce (2013) data show that seventeen of those states are in the bottom half of states in terms of per capita personal income. At the bottom is Mississippi, which has "right-to-work" status in its state constitution and only about 3.7 percent of its private-sector workers in unions. "Right-to-work" states weaken unions as an economic force by reducing their ability to bargain with employers, as detailed in AFL-CIO (2014) comments below[8]:

States with "Right to Work" Laws Have Lower Wages and Incomes. In fact, workers in states with these laws earn an average of $5,680 less a year than workers in other states.

Figure 5.1   **Union Membership: Percent of Workers**

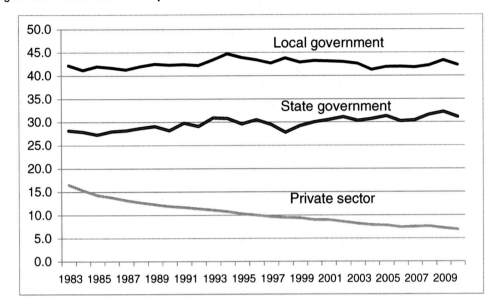

Source: Author generated from data source: Hirsch and Macpherson (2011).

Because of the higher wages, working families in states without these laws also benefit from healthier tax bases that improve their quality of life. Median household income in states with these laws is $6,437 less than in other states ($46,402 vs. $52,839).

Higher Rates of Death on the Job. The rate of workplace deaths is 36 percent higher in states with these laws according to data from the Bureau of Labor Statistics.

Yet by 2012, Michigan and Indiana had joined these poorer states that endorse right-to-work, a demonstration of enormous changes in attitudes about unions. Some of these changes may come from differences in generational attitudes between older workers and the younger entrants into the labor force who are unfamiliar with union history (Fontes and Margolies 2010). Symbolic acts on a grand scale have also influenced attitudes. Presidential action by Ronald Reagan to withhold recognition of the air traffic controllers when they went on strike in 1981 had a chilling effect on unions across the country (Shostak 2009). The message was clear: it is safe to take on the unions. Employers realized they no longer had to settle without a fight.

Management behavior, therefore, shifted fundamentally from defense to offense. The result was a movement of private-sector jobs to "right-to-work" states as well as to other countries, along with the elimination of many jobs through continuous efficiency actions. All of these changes lessened the reliance of business on labor and reduced labor costs. Last but not least, large sums have been donated to state and federal legislators who oppose the laws that have protected the right to unionize for several generations. We turn next to how the rapid decline in union membership and bargaining power has affected opportunities for workers.

MIDDLE-CLASS WOES AND LABOR'S SHARE

The middle-class share of total income slipped from about 53 percent in 1969 to 46 percent in 2009 as union membership fell from 28 percent to about 12 percent (Madland, Walter, and Bunker 2011).[9] While other factors no doubt influenced both, a strong statistical relationship at the state level points to a direct effect on consumer spending and the macroeconomy, as summarized below:

> According to Gallup, from May 2009 to May 2011, daily consumer spending rose 16 percent among Americans earning more than $90,000 a year; among all other Americans, spending was completely flat. The consumer recovery, such as it is, appears to be driven by the affluent, not by the masses. Three years after the crash of 2008, the rich and well educated are putting the recession behind them. The rest of America is stuck in neutral or reverse. (Peck 2011, 62)

Income and wealth have been moving toward the upper end of the income scale, generating a considerable degree of inequality with a high price in both economic performance and social cohesion (Zacharias, Wolff, Masterson, and Eren 2014). Nobel Prize-winning economist Joseph Stiglitz suggests that upper-income groups (the top 1 percent, in particular) have promoted an economic structure that benefits them directly but is neither efficient nor fair for society as a whole (Stiglitz 2012). For example, CEO pay, which was forty-two times that of the average blue-collar worker in 1982, rose to 354 times by 2012, vividly illustrating widening inequality in the United States, which has the widest gap among countries in the Organization for Economic Cooperation and Development (AFL-CIO 2013)[10] One feature of this growing inequality is the effect of education on real wages, as shown in Figure 5.2.

College-educated groups experienced a strong upward trend in real wages, attributable by some to "skill-biased technological change" and globalization (Yellen 2006). Employers and markets rewarded higher skills across professions. A boom in technology raised productivity, but the effects on income were far from equally dispersed across the labor force. Lower-skilled jobs in the private sector have seen real compensation fall. This downtrend in real wages for workers with education below college level is a real issue for both the quality of life in our society and its economic sustainability. However, as we note later in this chapter, even many college-educated workers are now facing declines in job opportunities and in real compensation, particularly if they are employed in state and local governments.

PRODUCTIVITY, EMPLOYMENT, AND WAGE GROWTH

In the late 1970s and the 1980s, sluggish productivity growth was the reason given by many economists for stagnant wages. A resurgence of labor productivity in the late 1990s led to optimism about restoring opportunities and middle-class jobs. Yet the rise in labor productivity failed to stop the upsurge in income inequality. While

Figure 5.2   **Real Hourly Wages by Education, All Genders** (2012 dollars)

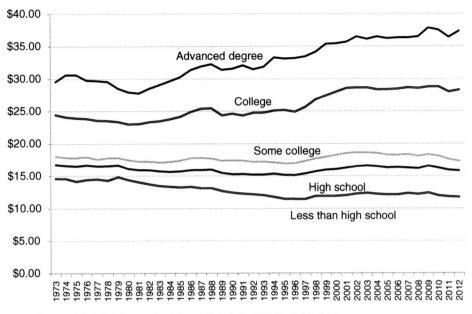

Source: Mishel, Bivens, Gould, and Shierholz (2012), Table 4.14.

nonfarm business-sector productivity advanced about 2.2 percent per year from 1947 to 2010, real hourly compensation rose at only an average 1.7 percent (see Figure 5.3) (Fleck, Glaser, and Sprague 2011). The share of manufacturing output going to labor compensation, about 35 percent in 1987, had dropped to 26 percent by 2010. Over the same period, the share going to capital rose from about 15 percent to nearly 20 percent.[11] We turn next to the relationship between macroeconomic performance and improved worker pay over the last few decades and its effects on mobility and opportunity for membership in the middle class.

RECESSIONS, FINANCIAL CRISES, AND "JOBLESS RECOVERIES"

Emphasis on low inflation and low interest rates, rather than on high aggregate demand, has affected the bargaining power of unions and encouraged the new economy business model discussed earlier. Low interest rates have encouraged purchase of labor-saving equipment over hiring of workers. All of this has significantly affected opportunities and the standard of living for hourly workers.

Along with a widening disconnect between pay and productivity—even when there was strong macroeconomic performance—the United States experienced several recessions. The episode from 2007 to 2009 was the deepest downturn since the Great Depression of the 1930s. There was also a weaker pattern of job growth during recoveries. While there is a long history of financial crises followed by severe economic contractions in the United States (Kindleberger 2000), from 1940 to 2007 recessions were not caused by financial crises and were much shorter and milder than the 1930s Depression.[12]

Figure 5.3 **Productivity and Real Hourly Compensation, Nonfarm Business Sector**

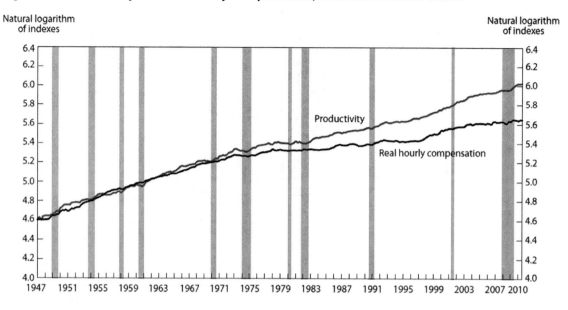

Source: Fleck, Glaser, and Sprague (2011).

In contrast, the Great Recession battered the US economy with sharp declines in jobs, loss of real income, and a fall in the value of real and financial assets. The measures in Table 5.1 show it as the most severe recession since 1950. The output gap, which is the difference between actual real GDP and potential real GDP, was large and reflected an economy operating well below its capacity to produce. Employee compensation also fell more than at any time since the Great Depression of the 1930s.[13]

A weak recovery magnified those downside impacts. As noted in Figure 5.4, weak job recoveries occurred after the recessions of 1990–1991, 2001, and 2007–2009. Twelve months after each recession ended, employment was still below its trough value. A year after the seven earlier recessions, listed in Table 5.1, employment was up about 3 percent.[14]

The lagging pattern of employment marks a significant shift, because in the past, employment typically rose almost simultaneously with output after recessions. In the mild 2001 recession, employment continued down for more than eighteen months after the trough, not rising again until mid-2003. It failed to move above the prerecession peak until early 2005. That is the longest lag on record for employment in the last sixty-five years.

UNRAVELING "JOBLESS RECOVERIES"

The employment pattern after the 1990–1991 and 2001 recessions seemed, at the time, atypical. But the very anemic rebound from the Great Recession deepened concerns

Table 5.1 **Recession Rankings: 1 = Most Severe**

Recession[1,2]	Real GDP	Output gap[3]	National income (deflated)	Corporate profits[4] (deflated)	Employee compensation (deflated)	Nonfarm employment
1953–1954	5	4	3	6	4	9
1957–1958	2	3	2	4	3	5
1960–1961	8	8	7	9	10	6
1969–1970	9	7	9	3	9	8
1973–1975	3	2	5	5	2	7
1980	6	6	10	2	7	3
1981–1982	4	5	4	8	6	2
1990–1991	7	10	8	10	8	4
2001	10	9	6	7	5	10
2007–2009	1	1	1	1	1	1

Sources: US Department of Commerce, Bureau of Economic Analysis (2011); US Department of Labor, Bureau of Labor Statistics (2011).

Notes: 1. Calculations and rankings are by authors.

2. Amplitude computed from peak to trough in specific series. National income, corporate profits, and employee compensation were deflated with the GDP Chain-Type Price Index.

3. Output gap ranking is based on the dollar difference between potential real GDP estimated by the US Congressional Budget Office (2011) and actual real GDP from US Department of Commerce, Bureau of Economic Analysis (2011).

4. Corporate profits with inventory valuation adjustment (IVA) and capital consumption adjustment (CCAdj).

Figure 5.4 **Total Nonfarm Employment Indexes: Trough Value = 1.00**

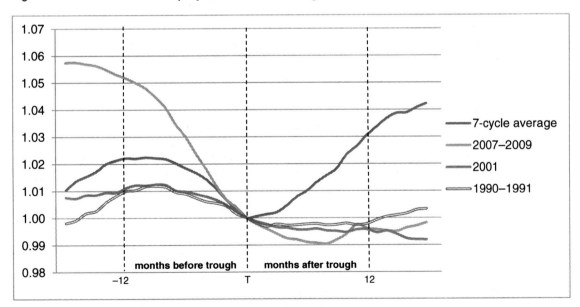

Note: Author generated from data sources. Trough dates (T) specified by the National Bureau of Economic Research (NBER).

that a new pattern was emerging. Comments below from the last three recessions are striking, however, because they underscore a similar pattern:

> By far the most widely noted and puzzling aspect of the current recovery is its failure to create jobs. (Gordon 1993, 271)

> But there remains a dark cloud in this otherwise hopeful picture: the labor market. Employment growth has been unusually weak following the recession, leading some to dub this a "jobless recovery." (Steelman 2004, 10)

> Despite rising real GDP in the third and fourth quarters of 2009, firms continued to shed jobs over the second half of 2009 and the first two months of 2010. (Kliesen 2010, 17)

Table 5.2 lists factors that might explain the observed long lags in job growth. The first, productivity growth, is an economic conundrum. Over long periods of time, productivity-led growth should be good news: efficiency increases, business costs decline, and income rises. Over short periods of time, however, job growth depends on how businesses react. Businesses seemed to underhire for up to two years after the 1990–1991 recession, attempting to correct previous overhiring errors (Gordon 1993). While such behavior was evident in the nonmanufacturing sector, Gordon concluded that the "jobless recovery" in the early 1990s was due primarily to too little stimulus to output: in other words, weak aggregate demand, listed in Table 5.2, rather than a surge in productivity.

Economic performance at the state level supports that conclusion. A majority of states experienced gains in productivity growth from 2001 to 2004, but there was no significant statistical difference in growth rates (Daly and Furlong 2005). States that recovered jobs after the 2001 recession experienced higher growth in output and increased demand for labor. Firms seemed to be making long-lasting improvements in operational efficiencies, including changes in workplace organization. Those with higher labor productivity were able to respond to increased demand for products without adding workers; only those facing even stronger demand added workers.

By 2012, job growth in the private sector was almost offset by declines in public-sector employment. The falloffs in the public sector were driven primarily by cities and states slashing employment to deal with tight revenues and an end to the three-year federal stimulus, which had helped them keep many workers on the payroll. Concern over recession-driven state and local budget deficits led to attention on unionized public employees as a way to control costs (see Table 5.3), including rising debt and unfunded pension liabilities.

THE GREAT RECESSION MEETS PUBLIC-SECTOR UNIONS: 2011–2012

The debate over unions has centered on premises often taken for granted but which we examine carefully here. Unions are assumed to reduce productivity and therefore unnecessarily increase public-sector costs. This assumption has led to a call to privatize some public-sector functions, which we will examine in the final section

Table 5.2 **Explanations for Lagged Timing of Employment in Recoveries**

§ **Growth in labor productivity**
   After a slowdown from 1973 to 1995, productivity growth is relatively high.

§ **Structural adjustments across industries**
   These adjustments are permanent shifts in the distribution of workers throughout the economy with expansions of temporary and part-time workers.

§ **Just-in-time employment practices**
   Increases in temporary and part-time employment add flexibility to business hiring decisions but lower income and benefits for workers.

§ **Old-economy vs. new-economy business practices**
   Intrafirm mobility compared to interfirm mobility exists in some expanding industries, with a lack of commitment to job security.

§ **Inadequate aggregate demand**
   Shocks to the economy from wars, threats of terrorism, and the financial crisis generate caution by businesses and households. Deleveraging constrains private spending as deficits and debt limited government actions at all levels.

of this chapter. But the emphasis in recent years has been on reducing the collective bargaining rights of public-sector workers.

Advocates of restrictions on bargaining for public employees argue that union contracts result in wages, salaries, and benefits that far exceed those received in the private sector. From this perspective, limiting public-sector unions generates positive effects on the bottom line for governmental units, while reducing "excessive" benefits for public employees. But are public employees actually paid better than their private-sector counterparts?

Huffman (2011) cites numerous studies that confirm that public employees are actually paid *less* than their private-sector equivalents. The key to such analyses is an accurate "apples-to-apples" comparison of pay and benefits that accounts for relevant education and experience. Although there is some evidence suggesting that less-educated employees receive better compensation in the public sector, the single largest group of public employees is teachers and administrators. Those positions require, at a minimum, a bachelor's degree, and many require or reward more advanced degrees.

The Employment Policy Research Network (EPRN), composed of academics from more than fifty universities in the fields of labor economics, labor relations, and labor law, produces objective, nonpolitical research on these matters. According to its report:

> Comparisons controlling for education, experience, hours of work, organizational size . . . reveal no significant overpayment but a slight underpayment of public employees when compared to private employee compensation costs on a per hour basis. On average, full time state and local employees are undercompensated by 3.7 percent in comparison to otherwise similar private sector workers. (Keefe 2010)

Thus, the simple solution of removing workers' bargaining rights may be aimed at the wrong problem! Collective bargaining as the direct cause of poor achievement in public education and a run-up in costs, for example, is not well supported by evidence. Unions certainly do provide greater job security by shielding employees from competition in the education market. However, Coulson (2010) observed that salary hikes, wage compression, and dramatic increases in staff-to-student ratios have all occurred in both unionized and nonunionized public school districts.

TURMOIL IN OHIO AND WISCONSIN

Nowhere has the conflict regarding public sector employees been more dramatically played out than in Ohio and Wisconsin with the support of newly elected governors hostile to unions. Both states represent bellwether tales about how public-sector labor issues may proceed and where they may end. After tumultuous and contentious sessions, the legislatures of both states passed bills fundamentally altering the union-management relationship. Strikes were outlawed and arbitration processes in lieu of strikes were eliminated or greatly reduced.

A new Ohio law passed early in 2011 allowed public-sector workers to negotiate wages, but not pensions or health-care benefits. Also, the legislative body that is the highest level of management for the respective entity was given power to decide unilaterally the terms of a future collective bargaining agreement. Collective bargaining in the usual sense was eliminated.

In Wisconsin, where the public-sector unions agreed to accept massive cuts in economic provisions, legislation quickly moved from economic considerations to a power struggle between a chief administrator, the governor, and public unions. Wisconsin Act 10, which became law in 2011, required annual recertification of public-sector unions by absolute-majority voting and banned automatic dues deduction, both of which reduced the political and economic capabilities of unions. The new laws were passed on the belief that government would be more cost-effective with weaker or, potentially, no union representation for state workers. Lost in the battle was a sense of the impact on the standard of living of citizens in the state, especially the most vulnerable.[15]

CHANGING OPPORTUNITIES FOR MINORITY WORKERS

Loss of jobs and restrictions on collective bargaining in the public sector hit minority groups particularly hard. Since the civil rights movement of the 1960s broke many employment barriers, union membership and public employment have both provided important gateways to the middle class for African American and other minority workers. For example, Hispanic men in unions earn wages about 21.9 percent higher than wages earned by nonunion Hispanic men (Yates 2009).

Impacts are even more pronounced for black women. Policy Matters Ohio (2010) found that 19.9 percent of employed black women held jobs in the public sector. Women are more likely to be the sole family breadwinner or to contribute a significant part of total family income in black families. As a result, African Americans have been left much more vulnerable to downside risks in the economy and without the opportunity to rise through the channels that helped earlier disadvantaged groups such as immigrants from southern and eastern Europe during the first half of the twentieth century.[16]

The new laws not only reflected the belief that government would be more cost-effective with little to no union representation for state workers, but also were seen as a way to deal with budget deficits. We now turn to a careful examination of these assumptions.

STATE BUDGET DEFICITS AND PUBLIC-SECTOR UNIONS

Personnel account for the largest share of costs for delivering public services; most estimates put those costs in the range of 60 to 90 percent of total costs. As a result, public officials under pressure to maintain a "no-tax" approach to government finance naturally look to costs of employees for a solution. Table 5.3 shows recent budget deficits and rates of union membership for selected states.

Texas ranked third among all states in budget deficits, but had a low percentage of unionized state workers. Ohio and Wisconsin, two states that passed statutes restricting collective bargaining for state workers, had less than half of the state workforce unionized and ranked in the middle in terms of budget deficits. During the Great Recession, both of those states experienced declines in personal income close to that of Texas and *less* than the drop that occurred in the United States as a whole. The key point is that there are numerous factors beyond collective bargaining that influence state budgets.

There is a high demand in the public sector for the individualized, nonrepetitive tasks performed by teachers, social workers, police, emergency responders, and so on. This contrasts sharply with a factory where mechanized equipment, including robots, can reduce costs on repetitive tasks. Private businesses, especially in goods-producing industries, can invest in new capital equipment and see higher productivity. Comparing these two sectors violates the "apples-to-apples" rule we invoked earlier. In short, there is less opportunity to reduce labor and labor costs in the public sector, and the productivity of workers is much harder to measure than it is in many private-sector jobs.

Another factor to consider when reducing public-sector employment as a solution is the inevitable impacts on local income and spending. Morris (2010) cites estimates that a loss of 100 public-sector jobs will lead to a further loss of thirty private-sector jobs—given the roles of construction, equipment, supplies, and so on—in supporting public-sector functions. While this multiplier effect varies across states, it confirms that the economic impacts of reducing public workers and services go well beyond the public sector.[17]

Efforts to make appropriate long-term adjustments to improve efficiency can get overwhelmed by overly concentrated focus on short-term economic swings, as we have just outlined. We now consider some policy options for a brighter future in the long term as well as for the current standard of living.

POLICY OPTIONS: SHORT-TERM IMPACTS AND LONG-TERM DILEMMAS

No easy fix exists to deal with the many developments cited above that affect the standard of living. Some are related to a weakening labor union movement, some to

Table 5.3 **Budget Gap, Change in Personal Income, and Public-Sector Union Membership for Selected States**

State	Budget gap[1]	Rank 1 = worst	Percent change in personal income (Great Recession)[2]	Union membership (percent)
Nevada	45.2	1	−7.7	39.9
New Jersey	37.4	2	−4.3	59.0
Texas	31.5	3	−2.2	16.9
California	29.3	4	−3.3	56.6
Oregon	25.0	5	−1.8	51.7
Ohio	11.0	25	−2.5	43.1
Wisconsin	12.8	21	−2.5	46.6

Sources: Combs (2011); stateline.org, March 15, 2011; Hirsch and Macpherson (2011); Lenze (2011), Table 1.

Notes: [1]Projected FY 2012 deficit as a percent of 2011 state spending.

[2]Calculations are by authors from specific peak to trough in state current-dollar personal income, 2007–2009.

changes in the business model operating in much of the economy, and some to problems in the macroeconomy. These developments are not separate. Both unions and businesses are influenced by conditions in the overall economy that produce instability, insecurity, inequality, and uncertainty. We start, therefore, with macroeconomic policies that may help to lower the social costs of short-term swings in the economy and then help to improve the long-term prospects for a higher standard of living.

IMPROVING SHORT-TERM MACROECONOMIC PERFORMANCE

Unfortunately, recoveries from severe financial crises take time, longer usually than those following slumps not accompanied by financial distress. In the wake of the Great Recession, the economy was operating more than $800 billion per year below its capacity, and the unemployment rate was high by historical standards. With underutilized resources, businesses were not ready to invest, to produce more, or to hire workers.

Whether organized or not, workers exert little influence over macroeconomic conditions. The burden falls on the Federal Reserve and the federal government to boost aggregate demand, a major factor for lowering cyclical unemployment among workers who lost jobs and are willing to return to work when the economy improves. During the Great Recession and its aftermath, the Federal Reserve and the federal government both focused on minimizing volatility and systemic risk in financial markets rather than restoring employment. The Federal Reserve responded quickly to preserve a financial sector near collapse and then to prevent the entire domestic economy from imploding further. It can be argued that this implosion would have hit workers even harder; thus protecting the financial sector was an important task.

However, by choosing the strategy of monetary easing in the form of quantitative expansions (QE1 and QE2), the Federal Reserve lowered the federal funds rate to nearly zero. While lowering interest rates is traditional monetary stimulus when recessions occur, maintaining lower rates reduces the cost of investing in capital equipment, thereby giving businesses an incentive to substitute equipment for labor. This policy is the opposite of what is needed to encourage businesses to move toward rehiring those who lost jobs or hiring new entrants into the labor force.

Even the incentive of extremely low interest rates was not enough to generate sufficient business investment given the high degree of uncertainty about inadequate aggregate demand.[18] And along with the positive effect of greatly reducing the price of loans, low interest rates had downside effects on the incomes of a growing population of retired individuals, as well as those saving for retirement. In retrospect, considering all these effects, traditional low-interest-rate policy appears considerably less powerful for boosting spending. Given the weak recovery, greater availability of credit at higher risk-adjusted interest rates might be more appropriate.[19]

The Federal Reserve can only ease or tighten credit conditions that influence lending activity, whereas the federal government can boost demand directly through government spending or, to a lesser degree, by cutting taxes. For example, the US Treasury invested a large amount from the Troubled Asset Relief Program (TARP 2008) in financial and nonfinancial corporations, including more than $50 billion to a bankrupt General Motors. Along with loans to Chrysler, that action helped preserve domestic auto production, the supplier network, and union jobs, basically keeping the middle class afloat in Michigan and Ohio during that time.

Government spending for public investment affects the standard of living in two ways: it boosts aggregate demand in the short run and it adds to society's ability to produce in the long run. Expenditures for public infrastructure at all levels (repairing and updating roads, bridges, airports, etc.) provide funds to private businesses that complete construction by hiring union and nonunion workers and boost employment for city, county, and state employees. For policy makers at all levels, these are high-return investments with multiplier effects through communities.

Tax issues are more complicated. Investment tax credits, for example, boost lagging productivity by providing an incentive to imbed advanced technology in newer forms of capital equipment. But a brighter future requires a boost in job opportunities, so employment tax credits would be on target. Implementation through the Work Opportunity Tax Credit Program (WOTC) would reduce costs for businesses hiring workers from specific target groups. Businesses get an incentive to hire in the form of a percentage tax credit for wages; veterans unemployed for six months have a higher wage cap than those unemployed for one month. With employment lagging after the Great Recession, WOTC could be expanded from eight target groups to include former employees, who are excluded under current provisions, but who may have lost a job during the slump and may still be awaiting recall.

At times when the labor market is particularly weak, such tax credits could be extended temporarily for *all* workers. This would expand full-time employment opportunities, with benefits to workers as well as to businesses. To deal with the issue of outsourcing jobs, a result of globalization, an employment tax credit could apply only to businesses that increase employment domestically. Finally, permanent tax cuts for middle-income individuals and households would boost consumer spending by a large segment of the population that is more likely to spend a large portion of its tax cut than are very high-income individuals.

Temporary tax credits can be enacted quickly, but they are much more effective when combined with a boost in aggregate demand. We turn now to why there is resistance to boosting demand through public-sector investments.

PUBLIC INVESTMENTS: SHORT-TERM DEMAND AND LONG-TERM PRODUCTIVITY BENEFITS

Since public investment generates across-the-board economic benefits in both the short and long term, why has it come to be viewed as too "expensive?" After all, physical infrastructure provides the base for development and expansion of private-sector businesses that need to get products to markets. Knowledge-based assets contribute to inventiveness, innovation, and entrepreneurship that are hallmarks of American business. Public investment requires spending from public revenues, however, and the formulation below illustrates the issue in short form for all levels of government.

$$\text{Tax revenue} = (\text{tax rate}) \times (\text{tax base})$$

The tax base at all levels of government was hit hard during the Great Recession: income—down, sales—down, real estate values—down. The reverse occurs during expansions. Tax and/or spending policies that boost aggregate demand lift the base faster, but so does closing tax loopholes. The latter are spread so widely through the tax system that major reforms are necessary. Ignoring issues surrounding the tax base is a prescription for continued weakness in the future because it limits tax revenue that supports economically rational public investments in technology and education. Public policy makers have rejected increases in tax rates for a wide variety of reasons, foremost of which is the historically inaccurate proposition that higher tax rates lead to poorer economic performance.[20] A brighter future for the middle class requires policy makers to find a way out of the financial impasse that restricts the raising of financial resources for important public goods. Improving the tax base is part of this solution. Spending more strategically is another avenue, and privatization of public services has been touted as one way to do that.

FLEXIBILITY IN PUBLIC-SECTOR HIRING: A DOUBLE-EDGED SWORD?

Promoting greater flexibility through competitive markets is an idea for more efficiency that has a long history. While most public-sector jobs cannot be moved to other countries, the "privatizing" of public tasks is advocated by some as an option for lowering labor costs by adding flexibility and increasing efficiency in delivery of public services. The city of Chicago, for example, outsourced many services, including janitorial work and parking. And West Virginia "privatized" its state workers' compensation program. The underlying assumption is that through contracting out (which is usually what "privatization" really means), the quality of public services will remain the same or will improve over time. While it is possible that quality can be maintained or improved, evidence is very mixed on whether the private sector is more cost-effective (Nightingale and Pindus 1997). Public officials need to be aware that performance and effectiveness depend on how private delivery of public services is actually implemented and on whether there is clear accountability. When large corporations seek contracts for public services, the potential advantages of competition may not be sustained for long.

What is clear about privatization is that it reduces employment in the public sector, including many jobs held by union members who oppose privatizing public tasks. Nightingale and Pindus (1997, 1) point out, however, that there is no clear evidence that workers are worse off in terms of employment, wages, or job satisfaction. For policy makers, the main challenge is to ensure effective delivery of public goods and services, which can be done either through the public or private sectors. Unions can address this effectiveness during contract negotiations as long as they maintain the right to represent those who provide public services.

LABOR CONTRACTS AND SPILLOVER EFFECTS

Some policy actions result in changes in institutional arrangements, which are likely to improve the overall standard of living. Long-run impacts on the standard of living of middle-class workers will be positive because domestic auto manufacturers agreed to increase investment in the United States and bring back jobs from other countries. Those contracts will set a standard for future labor agreements and influence conditions for nonunion workers in that industry. This would not have occurred without federal intervention in the auto industry that led to union contracts with profit sharing and signing bonuses instead of traditional annual pay raises for workers. Such adjustments convinced management that costs could be controlled.

However, it is not all about cost control. Failure to share productivity gains with workers adversely restricts consumer spending. A closer link between productivity gains and hourly compensation not only makes workers better off, but also improves the outlook for the whole economy. Spillover effects from the unionized to the nonunionized sector occur, but they are weaker now than when unions represented a larger share of workers. This contributes to longer lags in job recoveries after recessions, a broadly felt cost of "deunionization."

LABOR TRAINING OPPORTUNITIES

Public policies aimed at supporting education also have direct effects on innovation, productivity, and earnings. But not all education occurs in formal institutions such as colleges. Policy makers need to provide support for the kind of business/labor cooperation that provides high-quality vocational training. For example, the Electrical Training Institute (ETI) near Los Angeles is a joint effort of the National Electrical Contractors Association and the International Brotherhood of Electrical Workers. ETI prepares workers for careers in the electrical trades and assures building owners, developers, plant managers, general contractors, architects, and engineers that ETI-trained electricians receive the highest-quality training. Those workers are, therefore, the most efficient at performing a range of basic to highly complex tasks. The ETI also informs electrical workers that continuing education improves quality standards and increases earnings. Institutes like these can contribute to narrowing the gap in earnings by educational level shown in Figure 5.2.

CONCLUDING REMARKS

The fundamental political philosophy of countervailing forces helps to maintain a healthy balance in society. Unions widen the opportunities for a middle-class standard of living by supporting application and enforcement of safe working conditions, improvements in unemployment insurance, trade adjustment assistance, reasonable tax policies, improvements in public infrastructure, and national health insurance. In the words of Madland, Walter, and Bunker:

> Our analysis finds that for every 1 percentage point increase in union membership, the share of aggregate income going to the middle class rises by $153.19 per middle-class household. The upshot: If unionization rates increased by 10 percentage points—about the levels they were in 1980—then every middle-class household's income would be about $1,532 per year higher than it is today, and as a whole, the American middle class would earn $104.43 billion more annually. (2011, 23)

Management may feel empowered to reduce wages and benefits; unions act as a countervailing force against that power. Unions engage with management in collaborative efforts through collective bargaining, a viable option for resolving differences to achieve a broader, common goal. Management and labor can do that in the private sector, and policy makers and public-sector unions should be able to do the same.

For public-sector managers, minimizing costs should not be the sole public policy goal. That will inevitably interfere with improving health, education, open spaces, parks, clean air, and safe neighborhoods—all of which are important and valued aspects of quality of life. As we emphasized above, public-sector workers (teachers, firefighters, and police) contribute to all of those, and unions represent many of them.

We have also emphasized the importance of macroeconomic policies in ensuring a good standard of living, now and in the future. Focusing more on high employment and less on low inflation or low interest rates is important. As noted earlier, low interest rates actually encourage businesses to substitute labor-saving equipment at a time when job creation is what the economy needs. In addition, poor macroeconomic conditions weaken the bargaining power of unions and of workers in general. The failure to sustain pay that reflects productivity gains further weakens the spending power of the middle class and, therefore, the economy.

NOTES

1. Groshen and Potter (2003, 4, 6) showed that in the mid-1970s and early 1980s, cyclical and structural changes accounted for about equal shares of changes in employment. In contrast, they estimated that since 2000 structural changes accounted for 79 percent compared to just 21 percent for cyclical changes. They concluded that permanent job losses eclipsed temporary layoffs and that industries losing jobs during the 2001 recession continued to shrink during the recovery.

2. Daly, Hobijn, and Kwok (2009, 3) stress that labor market data suggested that fewer workers

seemed to be waiting to be called back to jobs. They point to a significant break from past patterns. During the 1981–1982 recession, for example, "the share of unemployed workers on temporary layoffs increased dramatically from 16.1 percent to 20.7 percent. By contrast, between December 2007 and April 2009, the share of unemployed workers on temporary layoffs *fell* from 12.8 percent to 11.9 percent."

3. Under the NEBM, Lazonick (2009, 145) notes that by 2000, "there was a general acceptance among Silicon Valley's high-tech employers that the people, most of them Hispanic immigrants, who cleaned their facilities needed collective bargaining to bolster their meager pay." Union representation did not occur among higher-skilled workers.

4. Middle-class is a concept that often lacks a specific definition. A narrow definition includes the middle quintile (the third of five divisions) for household income—roughly $35,000 to $58,000. A broader definition ranges from the second to fourth quintiles, including many clerical and blue-collar workers as well as highly educated professionals. Surveys from the Pew Research Center (2008) report a current American perception of middle-class status as including 75 to 150 percent of median income. Peck (2011, 65) suggests, on the other hand, that "The true center of American Society has always been its nonprofessionals—high-school graduates who didn't go on to get a bachelor's degree make up 58 percent of the population."

5. The sixty-two-hour workweek at low wages for workers in cotton mills in Lowell, Massachusetts, in 1903 is a good example of hard times in the past (Zebroski 1982, 44).

6. The literature on struggles by unions is extensive. *Surviving Hard Times*, edited by Mary Blewett (1982), includes cases in which cultural phenomena linked to different attitudes by French-Canadian, Greek, Italian, Irish, Polish, and Portuguese immigrants influenced labor organizing, actions, and outcomes during strikes in Massachusetts in 1903, 1912, 1918, and 1933.

7. Peck (2011, 63) notes, for example, "Almost one of every 12 white-collar jobs in sales, administrative support, and non-managerial office work vanished in the first two years of the recession; one of every six blue-collar jobs in production, craft, repair, and machine operation did the same."

8. The AFL-CIO (2014) also points out that "States with 'right to work' laws spend $3,392 less per pupil on elementary and secondary education than other states, and students are less likely to be performing at their appropriate grade level in math and reading." Educational assets are related directly to the overall standard of living.

9. Madland, Walter, and Bunker's (2011, 23) extensive analysis shows that union strength varies greatly among states. In terms of the prosperity of the middle class, they note, "Of the 10 states with the lowest percentage of workers in unions in 2009—North Carolina, Arkansas, South Carolina, Georgia, Virginia, Mississippi, Tennessee, Texas, South Dakota, and Oklahoma—all of them have a relatively weak middle class, with the share of state income going to households in the second, third, and fourth quintiles in these states below the average for all states."

10. The AFL-CIO (2013) points out that wealth distribution is skewed extremely toward the richest 1 percent in the United States, which holds more than one-third of the nation's wealth. Another dramatic example of inequality is the fact that the six heirs of the Wal-Mart empire have wealth of $69.7 billion, which is equivalent to the wealth of the entire bottom 30 percent of US society (Stiglitz 2012, 38). See also Freeman (2007, 50, 86–87) and Peck (2011).

11. The drop in the labor share of manufacturing is attributable to reorganization of production processes that are now more capital-intensive. See Fleck, Glaser, and Sprague (2011, 68–69).

12. A sweeping literature on financial crises exists. Kindleberger (2000) provides a detailed summary with historical and global perspectives. He suggests that a lender of last resort plays a crucial role in mitigating impacts. In his short history of financial events, Galbraith (1993, 19) states, "The world of finance hails the invention of the wheel over and over again, often in a slightly more unstable way."

13. Bruner and Carr (2007) identify seven mutually reinforcing elements that were present 100 years earlier in the Panic of 1907: financial complexity, buoyant growth, inadequate safety buffers, adverse leadership, real economic shock, efficacy of collective action, and undue fear, greed, and other behavior aberrations. The same elements also contributed to the financial crisis that began in 2007.

14. In index form, employment in Figure 5.4 has a value equal to 1.00 at the bottom of recessions

(troughs). A value of 1.03, therefore, represents a 3 percent increase from the recession trough. Values below 1.00 indicate that employment was below the recession low, which can be seen after the 1990–1991, 2001, and 2007–2009 recessions.

15. A larger sense of the common good prevailed as voters in Ohio rejected the new law in November 2011. In Wisconsin, a federal judge ruled that annual recertification of unions and the loss of automatic dues deductions are unconstitutional because they violate the First Amendment rights of affected workers. For more details, see Vielmetti and Marley (2012).

16. In addition to positive impacts on wages for Hispanic and African American workers, Yates (2009, 41) notes "spillover effects" as a strong union presence resulted in higher wages for nonunion workers. Spillover effects have weakened, however, as union density has declined.

17. Morris (2010) cites economic harm linked to cuts in state workers and notes studies at the Economic Policy Institute. For more about public-sector unions, see Orr (2011).

18. John Maynard Keynes pointed out that economic conditions at certain times may not be conducive to releasing "animal spirits" in businesses, so they back off from investing, producing more and hiring workers until conditions improve. Technically, the marginal efficiency of capital is just too low. For a brief summary, see Skidelsky (2010).

19. Changes in federal laws also influence behavior and outcomes in financial markets as institutions adjust accordingly. Outcomes may include unexpected consequences. The Riegle-Neal Interstate Banking and Branching Efficiency Act of 1994, for example, opened the country to rapid development of large interstate banks that dominated the system. A further wave of concentration followed passage of the Gramm-Leach-Bliley Financial Modernization Act of 1999, which effectively repealed the Glass-Steagall Act of 1933 that separated investment banking from retail banking; see Kozlowski (1999, 2006). Financial reform appears unlikely to return to that separation. Instead, the complex Dodd-Frank Wall Street Reform and Consumer Protection Act of 2010 added a network of newer regulations and created the Financial Stability Oversight Council. It also established the Office of Financial Research and the Bureau of Consumer Financial Protection. The policy aim is to protect the public, the middle class included, from unbridled market-driven excesses in financial markets that can generate unacceptable negative externalities. The Consumer Financial Protection Bureau will operate independently of the Federal Reserve and will control financial products and services according to federal law, minimizing adverse effects as financial products evolve.

20. Our discussion of the severity of recessions, illustrated in Table 5.1, and of weak economic performance since 2001 highlights that inaccuracy. So does strong performance during the 1990s. Upper-income groups support that proposition politically so it persists at the cost of greater inequality, as Stiglitz (2012) points out in detail.

BIBLIOGRAPHY

Aaronson, D., E.R. Rissman, and D.G. Sullivan. 2004. "Assessing the Jobless Recovery." *Economic Perspectives*, Federal Reserve Bank of Chicago, 2Q: 2–20.

AFL-CIO. 2013. "Executive Paywatch." www.aflcio.org/Corporate-Watch/CEO-Pay-and-You.

———. 2014. "Right to Work for Less." www.aflcio.org/Legislation-and-Politics/State-Legislative-Battles/Ongoing-State-Legislative-Attacks/Right-to-Work-for-Less.

Blewett, M.H., ed. 1982. *Surviving Hard Times: The Working People of Lowell*. Lowell, MA: Lowell Museum.

Bruner, R.F., and S.D. Carr. 2007. *The Panic of 1907*. Hoboken, NJ: John Wiley.

Combs, D. 2011. "State Budget Gaps: How Does Your State Rank?" The Pew Center on States. March 5. www.stateline.org/live/printable/story?contentId=15158.

Coulson, A.J. 2010. "The Effects of Teachers Unions on American Education." *Cato Journal* 30, no. 1: 155–170.

Daly, M. 2003. "Understanding State Budget Troubles." *FRBSF Economic Letter*, no. 23, August 15: 1–3.

Daly, M., and F. Furlong. 2005. "Gains in U.S. Productivity: Stopgap Measures or Lasting Change?" *FRBSF Economic Letter*, no. 5, March 5: 1–4.

Daly, M., B. Hobijn, and J. Kwok. 2009. "Jobless Recovery Redux?" *FRBSF Economic Letter*, no. 18, June 5: 1–3.

Electrical Training Institute of Southern California. 2013. *Update on State Certification*. www.laett.com.

Fleck, S., J. Glaser, and S. Sprague. 2011. "The Compensation-Productivity Gap: A Visual Essay." *Monthly Labor Review* 134: 57–69. www.bls.gov/opub/mlr/2011/01/art3full.pdf.

Fontes, M., and K. Margolies. 2010. "Youth and Unions." Working Papers, ILR Collection, Cornell University, March 8. http://digitalcommons.ilr.cornell.edu/workingpapers/104.

Freeman, R.B. 2007. *America Works*. New York: Russell Sage.

Galbraith, J.K. 1993. *A Short History of Financial Euphoria*. New York: Viking Penguin.

Gordon, R.J. 1993. "The Jobless Recovery: Does It Signal a New Era of Productivity-Led Growth." *Brookings Papers on Economic Activity* 1: 271–316.

Groshen, E.L., and S. Potter. 2003. "Has Structural Change Contributed to a Jobless Recovery?" *Current Issues in Economics and Finance*, Federal Reserve Bank of New York 9, no. 8 (August): 1–7.

Hakkio, C.S., and W.R. Keeton. 2009. "Financial Stress: What Is It, How Can It Be Measured, and Why Does It Matter?" *Economic Review*, Federal Reserve Bank of Kansas City, 2Q: 5–49.

Hirsch, B.T., and D.A. Macpherson. 2011. "U.S. Historical Tables: Union Membership, Coverage, Density and Employment, 1973-2010." www.unionstats.com.

Huffman, A. 2011. "The Wisconsin Debate: The Basics and Implications of Public Sector Collective Bargaining Legislation." *Georgetown Public Policy Review*. April 11. www.gppreview.org/blog/category/domesticpolicy.

Keefe, J. 2010. "Debunking the Myth of the Overcompensated Public Employee." *E.P.R.N.—EPI Briefing Paper*. September 15: 1.

Kindleberger, C.P. 2000. *Manias, Panics, and Crashes: A History of Financial Crises*. 4th ed. Hoboken, NJ: John Wiley.

Kliesen, K.L. 2010. "National Overview: Signs Point Toward Another Jobless Recovery." *The Regional Economist*, Federal Reserve Bank of St. Louis, April: 17.

Kozlowski, P.J. 1999. "Financial Analysis After the Riegle-Neal Interstate Banking and Branching Efficiency Act." *Journal of Regional Analysis and Policy* 29, no. 1: 74–93.

———. 2006. "Financial Evolution in Core and Peripheral Areas: Tracking Ohio's Metropolitan Experience." *Journal of Regional Analysis and Policy* 36, no. 1: 1–14.

Lazonick, W. 2009. *Sustainable Prosperity in the New Economy*. Kalamazoo, MI: W.E. Upjohn Institute for Employment Research.

Lenze, D.G. 2011. "State and Personal Income and More . . ." *Regional Quarterly Report, Survey of Current Business*, July: 171–190.

Madland, D., K. Walter, and N. Bunker. 2011. *Unions Make the Middle Class*. Center for American Progress Fund, American Worker Project, April. www.americanprogressaction.org/issues/2011/04/pdf/unionsmakethemiddleclass.pdf.

Mishel, L., J. Bivens, E. Gould, H. Shierholz. 2012. *The State of Working America*, 12th Edition. Economic Policy Institute. Ithaca, NY: Cornell University Press. www.stateofworkingamerica.org/subjects/overview/?reader.

Morris, D. 2010. "As Go the Unions So Goes the Nation: End the Assault on Public Sector Salaries and Benefits." *New York Daily News*, September 13. http://articles.nydailynews.com/2010–09–13/news/29441305_1_ public-sector-private-sector-unions.

Mortgage Bankers Association. 2008. "Delinquencies and Foreclosures Increase in Latest MBA National Delinquency Survey." *National Delinquency Survey (NDS)*, March 6, 1–4. www.mbaa.org/NewsandMedia/PressCenter/60619.htm.

National Bureau of Economic Research (NBER). 2012. "U.S. Business Cycle Expansions and Contractions." www.nber.org/cycles.html.

Nightingale, D.S., and N.M. Pindus. 1997. "Privatization of Public Services: A Background Paper." Washington, DC: The Urban Institute. www.urban.org/publications/407023.html.

Orr, A. 2011. "Scapegoating Public Sector Workers." *Economic Policy Institute Commentary*, March 8. www.epi.org/publication/scapegoating_public_sector_workers/.

Peck, D. 2011. "Can the Middle Class Be Saved?" *Atlantic*, September, 60–78.

Pew Research Center. 2008. "Inside the Middle Class: Bad Times Hit the Good Life." A Social and Economic Trends Report, April 9.

Pitts, S. 2011. "Black Workers and the Public Sector." Center for Labor Research and Education, University of California–Berkeley, April 4.

Policy Matters Ohio. 2010. "Public Sector Employs Significant Portion of Ohioans: Women and African Americans More Likely to Be Employed in Public Occupations." *Policy Matters Ohio*, September, 1–2. www.policymattersohio.org/wp-content/uploads/2011/09/SB5_PMO_PressStatement2011.pdf.

Schreft, S.L., and A. Singh. 2003. "A Closer Look at Jobless Recoveries." *Economic Review*, Federal Reserve Bank of Kansas City, 2: 45–73.

Segal, L., and D. Sullivan. 1997. "The Growth of Temporary Services Work." *Journal of Economic Perspectives* 11, no. 2: 117–136.

Shostak, A. 2009. "PATCO's 1981 Strike: Leadership Coordinates—A Unionist's Perspective." *Labor Studies Journal* 34, no. 2: 149–158.

Skidelsky, R. 2010. *Keynes: A Very Short Introduction.* New York: Oxford University Press.

Spence, M. 2011. *The Next Convergence: The Future of Economic Growth in a Multispeed World.* New York: Farrar, Straus and Giroux.

Steelman, A. 2004. "Jobless Recovery." *Region Focus*, Federal Reserve Bank of Richmond, Winter: 10.

Stiglitz, J.E. 2012. *The Price of Inequality.* New York: W.W. Norton.

Troubled Assets Relief Program (TARP). 2008. Division A—Emergency Economic Stabilization Act, Public Law 110-343.

US Department of Commerce, Bureau of Economic Analysis. 2011. GDP, National Income Corporate Profits, Compensation of Employees. http//research.stlouisfed.org/fred2/.

———. 2013. SA1-3 Personal Income Summary, Per Capita Personal Income. www.bea.gov/iTable/iTable.cfm?ReqID=70&step=1#reqid=70&step=1&isuri=1.

US Department of Labor, Bureau of Labor Statistics. 2011. *Wisconsin and Ohio Monthly Labor Force Wage and Salary Estimates.* June 2011.

———. 2011. *Employment Situation.*

———. 2011. *Productivity and Costs.* http://research.stlouisfed.org/fred2/series/PRS85006173. http://research.stlouisfed.org/fred2/series/PAYEMS?rid=50&soid=22.

Vielmetti, B., and P. Marley. 2012. "Federal Court Strikes Down Parts of Union Law." JSOnline, March 30. www.jsonline.com/news/wisconsin/federal-court-strikes-down-parts-of-act-10-4k4qdap-145208985.html.

Yates, M.D. 2009. *Why Unions Matter.* 2nd ed. New York: Monthly Review Press.

Yellen, J.L. 2006. "Economic Inequality in the United States." *President's Speech*, Federal Reserve Bank of San Francisco, November 6, 2006. www.frbsf.org/news/speeches/2006/061106.pdf.

Zacharias, A., E.N. Wolff, T. Masterson, and S. Eren. 2014. "Economic Well-Being in the United States: A Historical and Comparative Perspective." *In A Brighter Future: Improving the Standard of Living Now and for the Next Generation*, ed. R.P.H. Holt, and D.T. Greenwood, 23–50. Armonk, NY: M.E. Sharpe.

Zebroski, S. 1982. "The 1903 Strike in the Lowell Cotton Mills." In *Surviving Hard Times: The Working People of Lowell*, ed. M.H. Blewett, 43–62. Lowell, MA: Lowell Museum.

6 Low-Paid Workers

The Minimum Wage and Employment in the United States and France

David R. Howell, Bert M. Azizoglu, and Anna Okatenko

The rapid growth of good jobs in the United States between the late 1940s and the 1970s produced an extraordinary increase in average incomes. While the middle class experienced an unprecedented expansion, the largest percentage gains actually went to those in the lowest-paid jobs (Goldin and Katz 2008). But this golden age of American capitalism was short-lived: since the late 1970s, the middle class share of total income has declined—a process known as "polarization" (Acemoglu and Autor 2010; Bluestone and Harrison 1990; Howell 2013). After accounting for inflation, both hourly wages and total labor compensation—which includes employment-related benefits—have been essentially flat for the typical (median) worker since the mid-1970s.[1] The performance of the American labor market for hourly wage employees, especially those at the bottom of the wage distribution, also compares poorly with that of many other rich countries, contributing to the failure of low-income families to keep up with their counterparts abroad. For example, between the mid-1980s and the late 2000s, average real (inflation-adjusted) US household incomes at the tenth percentile of the income distribution rose just 0.5 percent per year, less than one-third of France's 1.6 percent rate (OECD 2011c, Table 1).[2]

This poor labor market performance for all but those with top incomes cannot be explained by the failure of the economy to grow. Even after the greatest economic collapse since the Great Depression in 2007–2008, the real value of output per capita in 2010 was 75 percent higher than it was in 1980. As Larry Mishel (2012) of the Economic Policy Institute has shown, there has been a dramatic widening of the gap between American productivity and compensation growth since around 1980. In the words of Joseph Stiglitz (2012, 24) "the American economic engine has given the benefits of that growth to an increasingly small sliver at the top—and even taken away some of what had previously gone to the bottom."

As this chapter will show, the incidence of low pay, defined here as hourly wages less than two-thirds of the median full-time wage, rose particularly sharply for young workers. This should be seen as a serious concern not just for the current well-being of young families, but for future generations as well, mainly because access to good schools almost always depends on a household's ability to pay (mainly via local property taxes). Low wages for young workers today translates into low household incomes, which puts children in these families at a severe educational disadvantage, undermining their ability to compete for the living wage jobs of the future. This close connection between income and educational inequalities helps explain the fact that cross-generational economic mobility in the United States is substantially lower than in most other high-income countries (Krueger 2012).

One obvious policy solution to the problem of low pay for young workers is to redistribute economy-wide productivity gains through the tax and expenditure system—it would be technically easy to level the playing field by redistributing income to the least well-off. This is the idea behind a simple negative income tax, a solution that the libertarian economist Milton Friedman proposed to President Nixon in the early 1970s. Even if this were politically feasible, however, there are strong arguments for relying as much as possible on earnings in the labor market as the way to improve the standard of living of American families. As Robert Solow (2008, 1) has argued, "In a society that values self-reliance, and in which productive work confers identity and self-respect as well as the respect of others, income redistribution unconnected or wrongly connected with work is not the best solution except in special cases. In that kind of society, ours for instance, the persistence of low-wage work is felt as a social problem on its own."

The leading *work-related* tax/transfer policy in the United States that addresses low earnings is the earned income tax credit (EITC)—essentially a wage subsidy from taxpayers to workers with very low earnings. The program, targeted to low-wage workers with children, has been extremely effective for that group, providing a tax credit in 2012 of as much as $5,891 for a married couple earning less than $50,270 with three or more qualifying children. At the other extreme, however, a single worker without qualifying children was eligible for a credit of only $475 and received no benefits once they reached $13,952 in earnings.[3] As a result, while 23 percent of all households with EITC benefits in 2009 had no qualifying children, they received just 2.7 percent of the total amount of credit ($1.6 billion of the total of $59.2 billion).[4]

There are at least three major problems with relying even more heavily on the EITC as a way to improve the take-home pay of low-wage workers. The first is that, as the figures reported in the previous paragraph indicate, the credit offers little to workers without qualifying children. Second, the program is expensive (currently $59 billion), and at least in the near term there is little political support for a substantial expansion of a redistribution program that would add to the federal government's budget deficit and national debt. Third, expansion of the program risks *increasing* the low-wage problem: without a meaningful legal lower boundary on the wage that can be paid, in an economy with a surplus pool of low-skill workers and with collective bargaining unavailable to most workers, increasing the value of the EITC would encourage employers to pay still lower wages (see Wicks-Lim and Pollin 2012). From the employer's perspective, why not just let the taxpayer maintain a socially acceptable wage?

For these reasons, since the Great Depression, a leading policy response to the problem of low pay has been the legal minimum wage. Until recently, the minimum wage was a national one, but with the failure of Congress to legislate increases to keep its real value from falling as consumer prices rise, many states (and other jurisdictions) have imposed legal minimums (Autor, Manning, and Smith 2010). By the early 1990s, nearly all high-income countries had established minimum wages, and a notable exception—the United Kingdom—did so in 1999. Rich countries that have still not established a national minimum wage by law, such as Sweden and Germany, tend to rely heavily on collective bargaining to set wages.

In this chapter, we use the strikingly different minimum wage policies of France and the United States to explore the consequences of alternative institutional and regulatory regimes for the wage and employment outcomes of young, less educated workers—those most vulnerable to low pay and unemployment. With its extremely high and steadily increasing minimum wage, France offers a stark alternative to the American policy of allowing the minimum wage to drop in value to a level that makes it almost irrelevant. After forty years of increases, the French minimum wage reached 60 percent of the median wage in the mid-2000s; after forty years of decline, the US minimum wage fell below 35 percent of the median wage in 2001–2008. In recent years, less than 5 percent of American workers have been paid the national minimum wage, which compares to about 15 percent in France (Gautie 2010; Marx, Marchal, and Nolan 2012).[5]

To offset the effect of these increases in the minimum wage on labor costs, since the mid-1990s France has pursued a policy of scaling back payroll taxes for employers of low-wage workers. This policy helped to significantly reduce labor costs for French workers paid the minimum wage between the early 1980s and the late 1990s (Caroli, Gautie, and Ashkenazy 2008). Still, French labor costs at the minimum wage were far higher than comparable US costs in 2000 in equivalent dollars (about $10.50 compared to about $6.25) and slightly higher as a percent of the labor cost of the average earner (the Kaitz index). In addition, between 2000 and 2005, both labor cost indicators at the minimum wage level (buying power in dollars and the Kaitz index) *rose* for France and *fell* for the United States (Immervoll 2007, Figures 6.2a and 6.2b).

In the conventional account, a minimum wage high enough to make a big difference in the incidence of low wages and in doing so to help maintain high labor costs will cause employers to cut employment, throwing the most vulnerable workers out of the labor market. As the relative levels of the French and US legal minimum wage have sharply diverged and with labor costs for minimum wage workers far higher in France than in the United States, this chapter asks whether aggregate indicators of employment performance show the conventionally predicted US superiority. We point out that there is no ironclad theoretical case for negative (or positive) employment effects of minimum wage hikes. It is well recognized that this is an empirical question, and the literature we summarize makes clear that the evidence is mixed, with much smaller employment effects in the best, most recent published studies. This chapter does not claim that the extraordinary increases in the French minimum wage and the resulting high labor costs have had no employment effects. Rather, it addresses the conventional wisdom that the striking divergence in US and French minimum wage policy since the 1980s is at the root of far superior US employment performance. More specifically, we ask whether the aggregate data support the view that the sharply rising ratio of the French to the US minimum wage, in both absolute terms (buying power) and as measured relative to median pay, explains (the presumed) far worse French unemployment and employment performance for young, less skilled workers.

We present five main findings in this chapter. *First*, we show that the much less regulated US labor market has produced an incidence of low-wage workers about three times larger than France (32 vs. 10 percent), and the gap is even larger for young, less educated workers. The stability of the US low-wage share at around 30 percent over the last three decades has masked enormous increases in low-pay incidence for young workers, especially for young men. *Second*, standard employment indicators of employment performance showed no evidence of worsening as the French minimum wage rose steadily and dramatically between the 1980s and mid-2000s. *Third*, the employment rate of young, less educated men actually rose substantially relative to the rate for similar prime-age men in France between 1994 and 2007, which is inconsistent with the conventional prediction of the effects of large minimum wage hikes. *Fourth*, we find no evidence that French employment performance has worsened relative to the United States; indeed, if there has been a change, it has been in France's favor. *Finally*, we present results for a new indicator of employment performance that accounts for some aspects of job quality as well as the quantity of jobs—the *adequate employment rate*, or AER. This is a more comprehensive indicator of labor market functioning than the unemployment or employment rate, as it measures the share of the labor force employed at wages above the low-pay threshold and not involuntarily part-time. France's performance on the AER has been clearly superior, even for the young, less educated workers most likely to be affected by the high labor costs imposed by the French minimum wage.

We begin with a brief discussion of the incidence of low pay across countries and the importance of labor market institutions in explaining these differences. Section 2 then defines our use of the term *low pay* and outlines the contours of low-paid work in the United States and France. Section 3 describes the evolution of minimum wage policies in the United States and France. Section 4 begins with an overview of what standard theory has to say about predicted employment effects of minimum wage increases and presents a brief summary of the recent evidence. Section 5 compares a variety of aggregate employment indicators for France and the United States. Finally, we present results for an alternative indicator, the adequate employment rate, in Section 6.

Section 7 concludes the discussion. In sum, our results contradict the conventional view that French employment performance for young, less educated workers is poor (relative to the United States) and getting worse. If the French evidence is a useful guideline for US policy—and nearly all commentators believe it is, since we are regularly warned by leading economists and the business press about the dangers of following the French path on minimum wages and job security—our findings suggest that the US minimum wage can be raised substantially to levels that would all but eliminate conventionally defined low pay without observable effects on aggregate employment outcomes for young, less skilled workers. We suggest that this is possible not only by offsetting rising labor costs by lowering payroll charges to employers in low-pay sectors, but because there are many other channels of adjustment available to employers other than slashing employment. We conclude that the minimum wage should play an important role in a "high road" strategy to ensure a living wage for all workers.

LOW PAY AND INSTITUTIONS

We use the Organization for Economic Cooperation and Development's (OECD) definition of *low pay* as an hourly wage below two-thirds of the national median wage for full-time workers (Appelbaum et al. 2010; OECD 2006). Below this level, even full-time work is not viewed as sufficient to provide workers and their families with a socially acceptable level of resources to maintain a standard of living necessary for full participation in their communities. This standard of living from work is increasingly referred to as a "living wage."

There are vast differences among rich nations in the incidence of low wages. Comparing twenty rich countries using a low-wage threshold of two-thirds of the overall median wage for 2009, John Schmitt (2011) reports that the US low-wage share (24.8 percent) was higher than all others except Korea (25.7 percent). While Germany, Canada, and the UK reported rates just over 20 percent, France came in at 11.1 percent, Norway at 8 percent, and Belgium at 4 percent. As reported below, using the OECD's threshold of two-thirds of the *full-time* median wage, we calculate the low-pay incidence in the United States and France in 2009 as 31.3 and 10.1 percent.

The Russell Sage Foundation (RSF) recently completed a six-volume study of low pay in rich countries. Its conclusion was that the incidence of low wages in rich countries is not adequately explained by "economic structural factors," such as changes in production technology, skills, trade, and the offshoring of production. There is, in fact, no relationship between the gross national product and the low-wage share. Rather, the RSF research suggests that the incidence of low pay is determined mainly by "pay setting institutions" like collective bargaining, minimum wage legislation, and labor and product market regulations. The key to reducing the low-wage share of work is the effective presence of "inclusive systems" that "extend outcomes of bargaining by employees with strong bargaining power to those with weaker power" (Bosch, Mayhew, and Gautie 2010; Schmitt 2011).

LOW PAY IN THE UNITED STATES AND FRANCE

We begin with a breakdown of low-paid US workers by demographic group and then turn to a comparison with France. Figure 6.1 shows the low-wage share of employment from 1979 to 2010 by age group. For the entire workforce, age 16 to 64, the incidence of low pay fluctuated around 30 percent from 1979 to 2007. This stability also characterized the low-pay rates for teens (age 16 to 19, not shown) and workers 35 to 54 years old. But substantial long-run increases can be seen for young workers: those 20 to 24 (from 41 to 60 percent in 2007) and 25 to 34 (from 20 to 32 percent). At the same time, the incidence of low pay decreased modestly for those 55 to 64 between the late 1990s and 2007.

The explanation for the stability in the overall low-wage share at a time of large increases for young workers (20 to 34 years old) is mainly demographic: while there has been a sharply rising incidence of low wages among younger workers, their share of total employment has been falling: from 16 to 10 percent of total employment for 20- to 24-year-olds and from 28 to 23 percent for 25- to 34-year-olds. The increasing size of the 55- to 64-year-old group, which has experienced a declining low-wage

Figure 6.1 **The Low-Wage Share of US Employment by Age Group, 1979–2010**

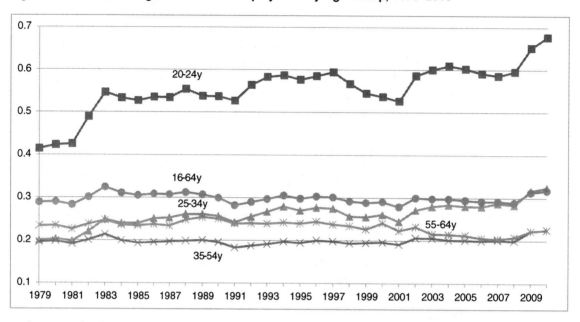

Source: Authors' calculations of CPS Outgoing Rotation Group Uniform Extracts, downloaded from the Center for Economic and Policy Research (CEPR) website, http://ceprdata.org.

employment share, has helped to offset the rising incidence for much younger workers. These offsetting demographic trends have produced a relatively stable overall low-wage share since the late 1970s.

Table 6.1 reports the incidence of low-wage workers by age, gender, and educational attainment for five dates between 1979 and 2010. These include four business cycle peaks (1979, 1989, 1999, and 2007) and 2010, the most recent year for which the data were available.[6]

The first column repeats the low-wage share for the entire 16 to 64 age group that appears in Figure 6.1 and highlights the effects of the recent economic crisis: the low-pay rate increased from 29 to 32 percent between 2007 and 2010. Column 2 shows that the incidence of low pay for young workers rose fairly steadily from 28 percent in 1979 to 43 percent in 2010. Even more striking has been the increase of 22 percentage points for young male workers (from 18 percent in 1979 to 34 percent in 2007 and 40 percent in 2010) shown in column 3. These increases nearly closed the gap with young female workers (column 4), whose low-pay rate increased modestly and only since 2000.

Like the results for young workers, columns 6 to 8 show that the rise in the incidence of low pay among prime-age workers was driven by the increases for men in the 1980s (from 9 to 15 percent) and since 2000 (from 15 to 21 percent). The incidence of low pay among female prime-age workers was lower in 2010 than 1979 (from 34 to 31 percent). It is also notable that there has been a fairly steady rise in the low-wage share of workers with more than a high school degree (columns 5 and 9). For these better-educated young workers, the low-pay incidence rose from 22 to 34 percent

Table 6.1   **Incidence of Low Wages by Age, Sex, and Education Group in the United States, 1979–2010***
(in percent)

| | 16–64 | 20–34 | | | | 25–54 | | | |
	1. Total	2. Total	3. Male	4. Female	5. Above HS	6. Total	7. Male	8. Female	9. Above HS
1979	29	28	18	41	22	20	9	34	11
1989	31	34	28	41	26	23	15	32	13
1999	29	34	29	40	26	21	15	29	13
2007	29	38	34	43	29	23	18	29	14
2010	32	43	40	47	34	26	21	31	17

Source: Authors' calculations using CPS Outgoing Rotation Group Uniform Extracts prepared by CEPR.
*For example, the 18 percent figure in column 3 for 1979 would be read: "18 percent of all young male workers were paid low wages in 1979."

Table 6.2   **Distribution of Low-Wage Workers by Age, Sex, and Education Group in the United States, 1979–2010*** (in percent)

| | Ages 20–34 | | | | Ages 25–54 | | | |
	1. Total	2. Male	3. Female	4. Above HS	5. Total	6. Male	7. Female	8. Above HS
1979	42	15	27	17	43	11	32	11
1989	47	21	26	19	53	19	34	16
1999	41	18	23	18	55	20	35	20
2007	44	21	23	21	56	23	33	22
2010	45	22	23	23	58	25	33	24

Source: Authors' calculations using CPS Outgoing Rotation Group Uniform Extracts prepared by CEPR.
*For example, 27 percent in column 3 for 1979 would be read: "27 percent of all low-wage workers (ages 16 to 64) were young females in 1979."

(column 5); for prime-age workers, the incidence of low pay for those with more than a high school degree rose from 11 to 17 percent (column 9).

Whereas Table 6.1 shows the low-wage share of workers for each demographic group, Table 6.2 shows the *distribution* of low-wage workers among these groups. The low wage workforce became increasingly male over this period: young men (20 to 34) increased from 15 to 22 percent of all low wage workers (column 2); prime-age men (25 to 54) accounted for 11 percent of low-paid workers in 1979, rising to 25 percent in 2010 (column 6). And there has been a substantial increase in the share of low paid workers who have more than a high school degree. By 2010, almost one-quarter (24 percent) of low-wage workers (ages 16 to 64) were prime-age with more than a high school degree, an increase from just 11 percent in 1979 (column 8).

Our comparison of the low-wage share of employment in France and the United States makes use of comparable data (the main household survey in each country), a threshold that follows the Organization for Economic Co-operation and Development's (OECD) definition and similar populations (wage and salary employment).[7] Figure 6.2 reports the annual low-wage share time series for workers for the United States (1979–2010) and France (1993–2010). The US trend is the same as appeared in Figure 6.1: a fairly stable level of about 30 percent. In contrast, the French low-wage

Figure 6.2   **Incidence of Low Wages for US (1979–2010) and French (1993–2010) Workers**

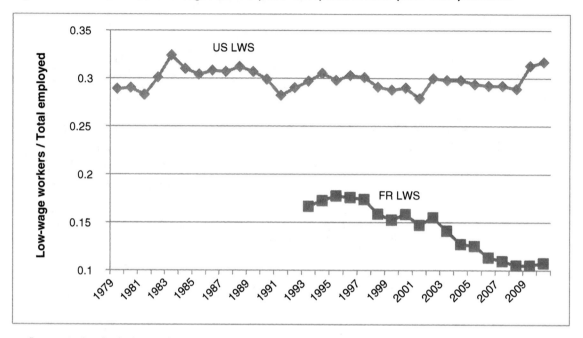

Source: Authors' calculations for United States based on CPS Outgoing Rotation Group Uniform Extracts prepared by CEPR and for France based on French Labour Force Survey [Emploi (en continu) version FPR (1990–2002, 2003–2009, and 2010), produced by INSEE, distributed by Centre Maurice Halbwachs].

Note: French LFS underwent a major redesign in 2003 when the annual survey usually conducted in March was replaced with a continuous one providing quarterly results. Caution is required when comparing trends before and after 2003.

share has clearly fallen since 1997, and quite dramatically between 2002 and 2007. Notably, the increases since the 2007 crash have been large for the United States and barely visible for France.

Figure 6.3 shows that behind the aggregate stability in the United States low-pay share there has been a huge, long-run increase in the share of young, less educated workers (age 20 to 34, high school degree only) paid low wages between 1979 and 2010. The increase in low-pay incidence in the United States has been much larger for these young men (about 32 percentage points, from 17 to 49 percent) and women (about 20 points, from 46 to 66 percent). The entire increase between 1979 and 2010 for both men and women took place during and shortly after each economic downturn: 1981–1983, 1992–1994, 2001–2003, and 2009–2010. In contrast, the performance of the French labor market for young, less educated workers could not have been more different: steady *declines* in the share paid low wages between 1997 and 2007 (from 25 to 18 percent for women and from 20 to 11 percent for men).

Figure 6.4 reports huge differences between French and US low-pay rates for young workers by gender and educational attainment for 2010, the most recent year for which we had data. For example, 86 percent of US female workers with less than a high school degree were paid low wages against just 24 percent for similar French workers; for female high school graduates, the US-French low-pay gap was 47 per-

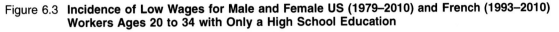

Figure 6.3 **Incidence of Low Wages for Male and Female US (1979–2010) and French (1993–2010) Workers Ages 20 to 34 with Only a High School Education**

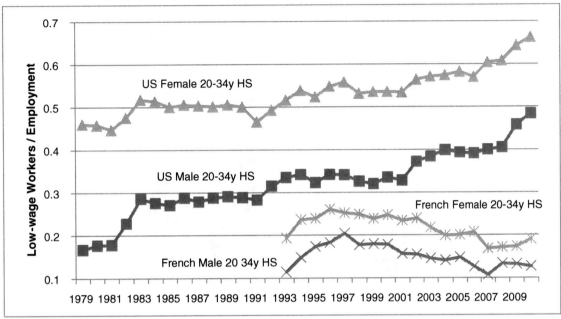

Source: Authors' calculations for the United States based on CPS Outgoing Rotation Group Uniform Extracts prepared by CEPR and for France based on French Labour Force Survey [Emploi (en continu) version FPR (1990–2002, 2003–2009, and 2010), produced by INSEE, distributed by Centre Maurice Halbwachs].

Note: French LFS underwent a major redesign in 2003 when the annual survey usually conducted in March was replaced with a continuous one providing quarterly results. Caution is required when comparing trends before and after 2003.

centage points (66 percent vs. 19 percent); for female workers with some college, 57 percent were paid low wages in the United States compared to only 7 percent in France. The gaps are only slightly smaller for male workers.

Differences Between the US and French Minimum Wage

In the 1960s, as the French collective bargaining system was increasingly recognized as incapable of protecting workers from unacceptably low wages, political support grew for strengthening the minimum wage law, which was first established in 1950. The 1970 revision, the *saliare minimum interprofessionel de croissance* (SMIC) relied on three mechanisms: (1) automatic adjustments for changes in the cost of living; (2) automatic increases reflecting a portion of the inflation-adjusted increase in average blue-collar pay; and (3) the "coup de pouce"—which refers to the discretionary power by the government to set the SMIC at higher levels (Gautie 2010).[8]

The United States, in sharp contrast, has no automatic mechanisms designed to maintain, much less to increase, the real value of the minimum wage. Changes in the federal minimum wage take place only by congressional vote and are not automatically tied to inflation or to economy-wide productivity gains. The consequences of these different approaches to setting minimum wage levels are reported in Figures 6.5a and 6.5b.

Figure 6.4 **Low-Wage Shares for Educational Groups of Ages 20 to 34 for the United States and France, 2010**

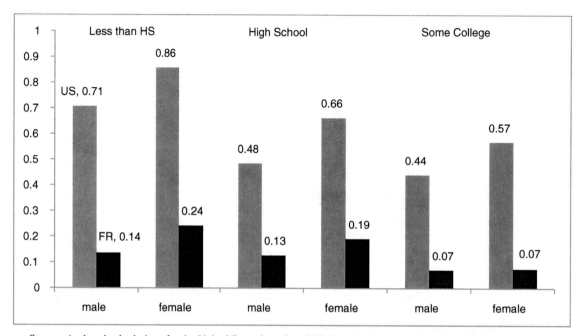

Source: Authors' calculations for the United States based on CPS Outgoing Rotation Group Uniform Extracts prepared by CEPR and for France based on French Labour Force Survey [Emploi (en continu) version FPR (1990–2002, 2003–2009, and 2010), produced by INSEE, distributed by Centre Maurice Halbwachs].

In 2010, the French SMIC was more than 40 percent higher than the US federal minimum wage—a gap of about $3. As Figure 6.5a shows, adjusting the federal minimum for the higher minimum wages legislated by some individual states makes little difference for the overall trend and gap with France; the main effect of accounting for state minimum wages was to reduce the decline in the value of the federal minimum between 1999 and 2008. But it should be underscored that this adjusted minimum wage is an average: the federal minimum continued to govern in most states.

Figure 6.5b shows the minimum wage relative to the median wage in each country (known as the "Kaitz index"). While the US Kaitz index fell from 50 to 55 percent in the 1960s to below 35 percent between 2000 and 2008, the French index shows a strong and steady increase, from about 34 percent in the mid-1960s to about 60 percent in the late 2000s.

This long commitment by France to an increasing absolute and relative value of the minimum wage has sharply reduced the incidence of low pay. Figure 6.6 plots the value of the SMIC and the French low-wage threshold (two-thirds of the median full-time wage) in inflation-adjusted euros. The SMIC shows a substantial and fairly steady increase, from 5.4 euros in 1993 to just under 7 euros in 2010, whereas the low-wage threshold remained between 6.5 and 6.75 in the 2000s. Remarkably, this figure shows that since 2005 the SMIC would—if universally applied and enforced— effectively outlaw the payment of low wages. The third trend line shown in Figure 6.6

Figure 6.5a   **Purchasing Power of the US and French Minimum Wage, 1960–2010**

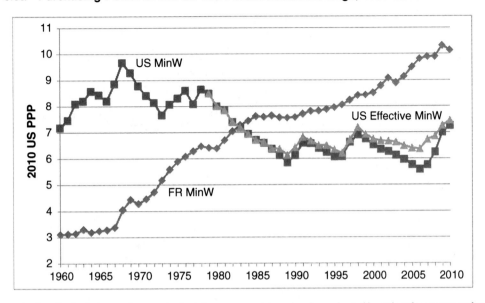

Source: Authors' calculations using nominal minimum wage data series denominated in national currency and purchasing power parity series from OECD.Stat; values are deflated using the CPI-W from the BLS. State minimum wages are taken from Autor, Manning, and Smith (2010); the Current Employment Statistics Survey is the source for state employment levels. The effective minimum wage is calculated using state-specific employment as weights.

Figure 6.5b   **Relative Values of the Minimum Wage (the Kaitz Index) for France and the United States, 1960–2009**

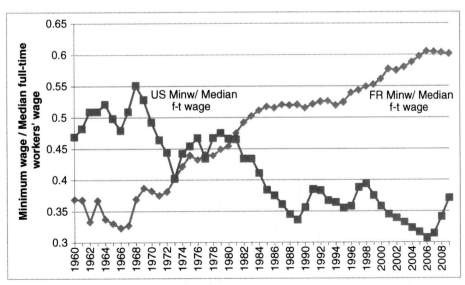

Source: Authors' calculations based on data from OECD.Stat.

Figure 6.6 **The French Low-Wage Threshold, Low-Wage Mean, and the Minimum Wage (SMIC), 1993–2010**

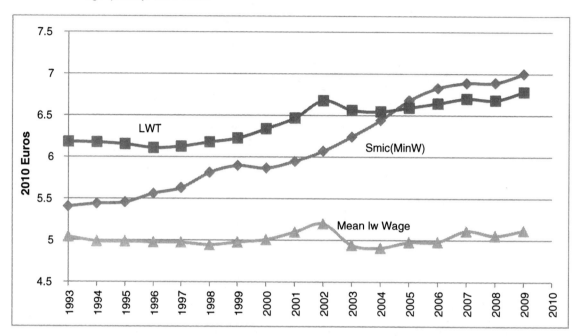

Source: Authors' calculations using French Labor Force Survey (Enquête Emploi) [Emploi (en continu) version FPR (1990–2002, 2003–2009, and 2010), produced by INSEE, distributed by Centre Maurice Halbwachs].

Note: French LFS underwent a major redesign in 2003 when the annual survey usually conducted in March was replaced with a continuous one providing quarterly results. Caution is required when comparing trends before and after 2003.

The minimum wage is provided by the National Institute of Statistics and Economic Studies (INSEE) and is deflated with the consumer price index from the International Monetary Fund (World Economic Outlook Database, September 2011).

presents our calculation of the average wage for those earning below the low-wage threshold.[9]

The relationship between the low-wage threshold and the minimum wage in the United States has been entirely different. As shown in Figure 6.7, the low-pay threshold fluctuated around $11 (2010 dollars) between 1979 and 1997, rose to $12 in 2002, and stayed at that level until the onset of the economic crisis in 2007 (the subsequent increase probably reflects disproportionate job loss in the bottom half of the distribution). This figure shows that the federal minimum wage has been set at a much lower level than the low-pay threshold—even after the higher minimum wages in some states have been accounted for (the "effective minimum wage"). In addition, this gap has steadily widened over the last three decades: the federal minimum wage was 77 percent of the low-wage threshold in 1979 and just 50 percent in 2007. As a result, large numbers of low-wage workers in the United States have remained far below the low-pay threshold. Figure 6.7 shows that the average wage paid to low-wage workers has ranged between $8 and just over $9 since 1979.

Because the SMIC is set so high relative to the median wage (Figure 6.5b), it directly affects pay setting for a relatively large share of the French workforce. French

Figure 6.7 **The US Low-Wage Threshold, Low-Wage Mean, and Federal Minimum Wage, 1979–2010**

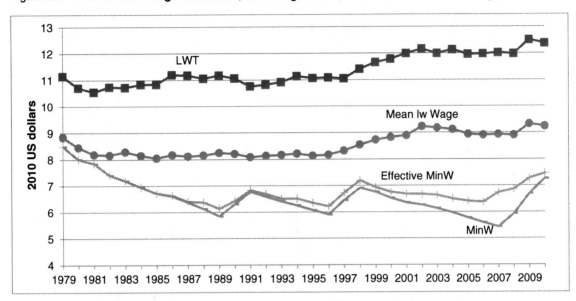

Source: Authors' calculations using CPS Outgoing Rotation Group Uniform Extracts prepared by CEPR. The federal minimum wage is taken from the Department of Labor (www.dol.gov/whd/minwage/chart.htm). State minimum wages are from Autor, Manning, and Smith (2010). Minimum wages are deflated with the CPI-W from the BLS. The Current Employment Statistics Survey is the source for state employment levels. The effective minimum wage is calculated using state-specific employment as weights.

workers with a base hourly wage set by the SMIC accounted for 13 to 16 percent of total employment in 2004–2006, about three times the 4 to 5 percent share of workers paid the minimum wage in the United States (Gautie 2010; Marx, Marchal, and Nolan 2012). It should also be noted that not only has this base SMIC risen far above the US minimum wage, but many SMIC base wage workers actually have much higher earnings due to a variety of premiums and bonuses. As Gautie (2010, 152) states "For instance, in 2002 the hourly earnings of 26 percent of minimum wage earners were at least 30 percent above the hourly minimum wage."

The Rising SMIC and French Employment Outcomes

The French minimum wage has compressed the bottom of the wage distribution and substantially raised the hourly pay of minimum wage workers. If these minimum wage increases also raise labor costs per hour and employers operate in highly competitive product markets and there are no alternative channels of adjustment (but see Hirsch, Kaufman, and Zelenska 2011; Schmitt 2013), the conventional textbook model would predict corresponding declines in employers' demand for labor. Under these circumstances, the consequences should be declining employment, rising unemployment, and perhaps rising nonemployment as well (as discouraged workers drop out of the labor force). These negative effects are expected to disproportionately affect young workers entering the labor market or having little seniority. As exemplified by the following passage, this has long been the conventional wisdom, especially in the business press. "The French, it seems, would rather live with nearly 25 percent youth unemployment than see the minimum wage or rigid job protection for incumbent workers eroded. And many are unwilling to see any connection between the two" (Taylor 2012).

However, as Hirsch, Kaufman, and Zelenska (2011, 1) point out, alternative predictions follow from other labor market models (monopsony and institutional/behavioral); channels of adjustment other than through employment levels include "hours, prices, profits, training, work effort, human resource practices, operational efficiencies, and internal wage structure." As the OECD (1998) has emphasized, these theoretical considerations have several implications for the empirical study of the employment effects of minimum wages. First, it is important to allow for the possibility of both positive and negative employment responses. Second, there may be a certain degree of nonlinearity in employment responses, with positive effects occurring for minimum wages below a certain level, but job losses occurring thereafter. Third, employment effects may vary according to a worker's age, skills, industry, and region of employment. In particular, the possibilities of substitution between workers of different skill levels imply that aggregate job losses may be more muted than for specific groups of workers. Finally, it is important to distinguish between short-run and long-run employment effects (OECD 1998, 44). In sum, as an important study by Dolado et al. (1996, 330) concluded, "The key point is that economic *theory* has no unambiguous prediction about the employment effects of minimum wages. Empirical research is required."

Yet, remarkably, it is common to find assertions about the negative employment effects of minimum wages—especially regarding the French SMIC—*without* so much as mention of empirical evidence. Surprisingly, given the OECD's position just summarized, a good example of the role of such theoretical blinders can be found in the OECD's biannual Country Survey reports for France. The 2005 report (OECD 2005, 34) asserts that it "is clear that the SMIC is high relative to the potential productivity of a significant part of the workforce." The implication is that unemployment rates for young workers can be reduced *only* by reducing labor costs via lowering the SMIC. Indeed, this claim is made explicit in the next issue of the *Survey of France* (OECD 2007, 117): "given the limited fiscal room for maneuver, the only way to further lower low-skilled unemployment is likely to be to reduce the SMIC relative to the average wage, e.g., by blocking any real increase in the SMIC in the coming years." Similar assertions can be found in more recent *Surveys* (OECD 2009; OECD 2011b) and in the OECD's annual *Going for Growth* volumes. For example, without a single reference to evidence, France is grouped with Greece, Indonesia, Slovenia, and Turkey as countries that "should limit the increase in their minimum wages" to increase "the jobs available for young workers and the low-skilled" (OECD 2011a, 37).

What does the empirical evidence actually show? The strongest results in favor of the conventional prediction can be found in early studies that showed modest negative effects for less skilled teenagers (OECD 1998, 47–48). As the OECD noted in its 2006 *Employment Outlook* assessment (86), "pinning down the size of employment losses that result from minimum wages has proven to be difficult and there is considerable uncertainty concerning how many jobs might be lost due to minimum wages set at the levels actually observed in different countries." A recent, highly influential cross-country study by the OECD failed to find any impact of minimum wages on unemployment rates (Bassanini and Duval 2006). In a survey of the evidence for Europe, the International Labour Organization (ILO) concluded, "While the minimum wage—under the condition that it is adjusted in a progressive and regular manner— has not been found to adversely affect employment," it has unquestionably reduced the incidence of low-pay and wage inequality (Vaughan-Whitehead 2010). Leading studies on the United States and United Kingdom have come to similar conclusions.[10] Indeed, the results of a recent study of the UK minimum wage found little or no effect on employment but large effects on the inequality in the bottom half of the wage distribution[11]—consistent with our interpretation of the results we present below for the effects of the French SMIC.

If there are negative minimum wage employment effects, they should be readily apparent in post-1970 France, where minimum wage increases have been extreme by international standards. But the published evidence for France is not very compelling. In the major study of the pre-1990 period, Dolado et al. (1996, 343) conclude that "low-wage regions did relatively well in the period 1967–1985, a period when minimum wages were raised very dramatically. . . . In conclusion, French evidence suggests that the substantial rise in the SMIC to the mid-1980s had no adverse effect on employment." But another study (Abowd, Kramarz, and Margolis 1999) that was also focused on the 1980s found that both US and French workers who were paid exactly at the minimum wage were significantly impacted by changes in the minimum wage (more employment for US workers after a real minimum wage decline; less employment for French workers after a minimum wage increase).[12] The authors conclude that their findings "contrast sharply" with the highly influential studies of Card and Krueger (1994, 1995) for US workers. But in a subsequent unpublished "extensive extension" of this work, Abowd et al. (2005) find no minimum wage effects for the United States, so these new results, according to the authors, are now "compatible with the results of Card and Krueger." In this revised version, the results for France remain strongly negative, but no effort is made in the text to reconcile these findings with the Dolado et al. (1996) conclusion of no employment effects.

In sum, unlike the literature on minimum wage effects in the United States, there are few published studies for France, especially using data from the 1990s and after, and the evidence is mixed.[13] Nevertheless, from the popular press to the OECD (see above) and leading economics textbooks, high French youth unemployment rates are simply assumed to reflect the effects of the very high SMIC on employment opportunities. If this is right, we might be expected to see the evidence in the aggregate data. The next section asks whether trends in French employment and unemployment rates suggest worsening labor market outcomes for less skilled French workers and whether there is any evidence of a widening gap between French and US employment performance.

FRENCH AND UNITED STATES EMPLOYMENT PERFORMANCE

The French government has been concerned with the possible employment impacts of rising labor costs caused by increases in the SMIC. As a result, mandated employer contributions similar to the US Social Security tax have been reduced since the mid-1990s for *all* low-wage workers with wages up to 1.3 times the SMIC (Caroli, Gautie, and Ashkenazy 2008; Gautie 2010). Still, according to the OECD, in 2005 the minimum labor cost to employers (wages, benefits, and taxes) for full-time minimum wage workers in France was the third-highest among twenty-one OECD countries, at about $11.40 (in 2005 US dollars at market exchange rates), up from about $10.60 in 2000; the comparable figure for the United States in 2005 was about $5.60, down from about $6.25 in 2000 (Immervoll 2007). How has this higher labor cost affected the employment of low-wage workers in France? We turn next to a variety of aggregate employment performance indicators for France.

Figures 6.8 and 6.9 plot the standard unemployment rates for 15- to 19-year olds and 20- to 24-year-olds, separately for males and females, from 1990 to 2010. As these figures indicate, over this period the ratio of the SMIC to the median full-time wage rose from 51 percent to 60 percent, the highest among OECD countries. At the same time, real labor cost, in both absolute terms (US dollars) and relative to the average earner, increased between 2000 and 2005, even though France was already among the highest in the OECD on both indicators (Immervoll 2007). Despite these high and rising labor costs, Figures 6.8 and 6.9 show that the male and female unemployment rates for these two age groups (15 to 19 and 20 to 24) were *lower* in 2008 (before the current global crisis hit France) than in 2000 and about the same (for males) or lower (for females) than in the early 1990s.

It is true that by the conventional measure of unemployment—the unemployed share of the labor force—youth unemployment remains very high by international standards. But Figures 6.10 and 6.11 show that another unemployment indicator, the unemployment-to-population rate (UPOP), tells a very different story. Figure 6.10 reports that the French UPOP for teens has remained quite stable since 1989, fluctuating between 3 and 5 percent and well *below* the US rate. Similarly, Figure 6.11 reports that the UPOP rate for French 15- to 24-year-olds has ranged between 4 and 10 percent since the late 1980s, closely tracking the US rate (except in the mid-1990s). In sum, the unemployed share of the young French population shows long-term stability at levels much below the United States for teens and at about the same levels as the United States for the larger 15 to 24 age group.

Why is the UPOP rate an appropriate measure of youth unemployment? The answer is that employment rates for young people enrolled in school will depend not just on job opportunities, but also on school hours and social norms regarding working while in school. To illustrate, assume two otherwise identical locations, A (e.g., Paris) and B (e.g., New York City). If location A strongly discourages employment of young people while they are enrolled in school (via school hours, homework time, jobs designed for part-time unskilled workers) while location B encourages and facilitates student employment, the denominator of the standard unemployment indicator (the labor force, equal to the employed plus those not working but actively seeking employment) will be smaller in location A. This will automatically raise its unemployment rate compared to location B, even though the number of unemployed and number of those in the working-age population are the same.

In the numerical example below, we compare these two hypothetical regions, calling one New York City (US) and one Paris (France), assuming that each has the

Figure 6.8 **The French Minimum Wage (Kaitz Index) and Unemployment Rates for Male and Female French Workers Ages 15 to 19, 1990–2010**

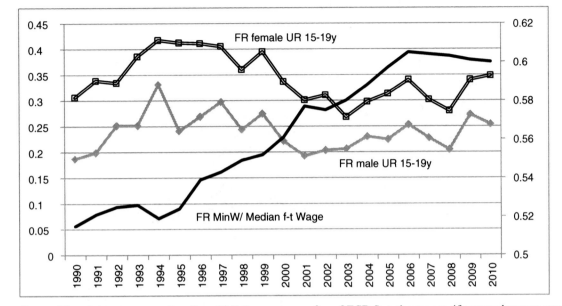

Source: The minimum wage and median of full-time wages are from OECD.Stat; the age-specific unemployment rates are the authors' calculations based on data from OECD.Stat.

Figure 6.9 **The French Minimum Wage (Kaitz Index) and Unemployment Rates for Male and Female French Workers Ages 20 to 24, 1990–2010**

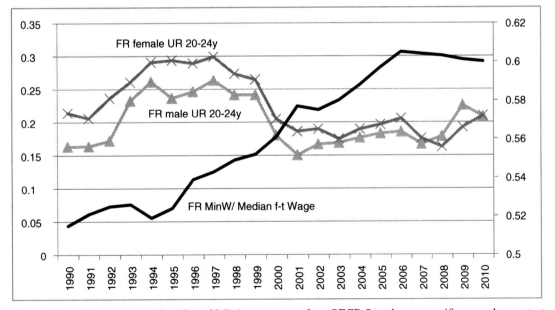

Source: The minimum wage and median of full-time wages are from OECD.Stat; the age-specific unemployment rates are authors' calculations based on data from OECD.Stat.

Figure 6.10 **Unemployment-to-Population Ratios for Male and Female Workers Ages 15 to 19, France and the United States, 1983–2010**

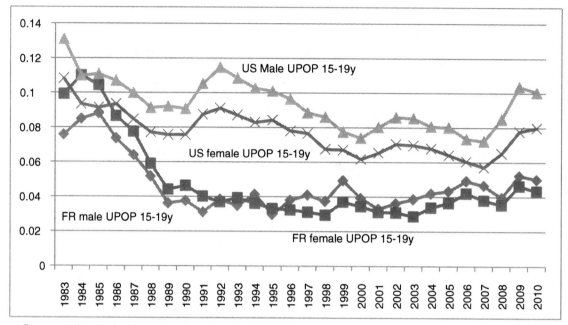

Source: Authors' calculations based on data from OECD.Stat.

Figure 6.11 **Unemployment-to-Labor-Force and Unemployment-to-Population Indicators for France and the United States, Ages 15 to 24, 1983–2010**

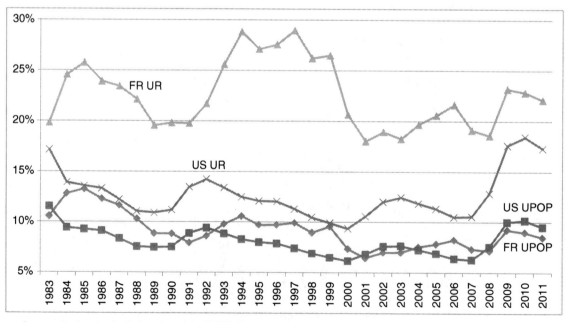

Source: Authors' calculations based on OECD.Stat.

Table 6.3 **Calculating the Unemployment Rate: A Measure of the Labor Force or the Population?** (an illustration that assumes identical numbers of individuals in the working age population and the same number of unemployed workers)

	United States	France
Population (POP)	100	100
Labor force (LF)	60	40
Employed	50	30
Unemployed (U)	10	10
Not in the labor force	40	60
U/LF	16.7%	25%
U/POP	10%	10%

same number of 15- to 24-year-olds and the same number of unemployed workers in this age group. However, an important difference exists in the social institutions and customs of the two countries that explains a large part of the difference in labor market outcomes. In New York City, student employment is socially acceptable and facilitated by the school schedule, while in Paris it is not. Table 6.3 shows how this scenario will produce a much higher conventional unemployment rate in France (25 percent compared to 16.7 percent), but an identical unemployment-to-population rate (10 percent).

As it turns out, French teens almost never work while enrolled in high school and rarely even when enrolled in college. While similar shares of 15- to 19-year-olds in France and the United States were enrolled in school in 2003 (83.8 and 82.9 percent), the employment rates of enrolled teens were strikingly different. In the United States, 23.1 percent of enrolled teens held jobs compared to only 1.8 percent of French teens (Howell and Okatenko 2010). It is notable that the employed share of enrolled students in France has been remarkably stable over the last four decades, spanning periods of very low and high overall unemployment, which suggests that these low employment rates for enrolled students are not just a reflection of the lack of job opportunities.[14] So while the blame for relatively low employment rates of enrolled teens in France is often blamed on an inadequate number of jobs, it is in fact much more a reflection of the length of the school day and social mores about being employed while enrolled in high school. Cross-country comparisons of youth unemployment should either use the unemployment-to-population rate or exclude students from the sample.

Turning to employment rates, this conventional indicator of employment performance also offers no support for the orthodox prediction that a high and rapidly rising SMIC has priced young, less educated workers out of the labor market. As shown in Figure 6.12, the employment-to-population (EPOP) rate for young (20- to 34-year-old) male workers with just a high school degree rose fairly steadily from about 55 percent in the mid-1990s to more than 68 percent just before the 2008 global crisis. Young, less educated female workers also showed a substantial increase in employment, from about 51 percent to 56 to 58 percent over this period.

Finally, if the rising value and cost of the SMIC were pricing young, less educated workers out of the labor force, their employment rate would be falling relative to the employment rates of prime-age workers. But here too there is no

Figure 6.12   **The French Minimum Wage (Kaitz Index) and the Employment-to-Population Ratio for Male and Female French Workers with Only a High School Education, Ages 20 to 34, 1993–2010**

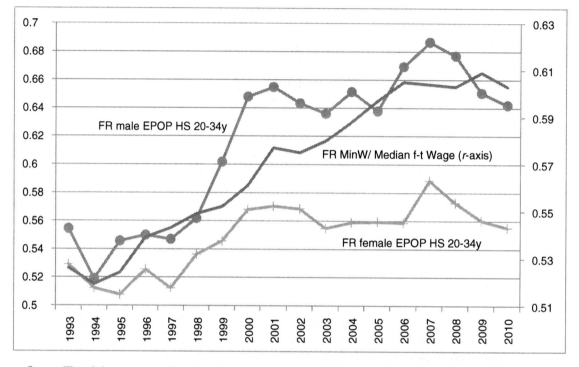

Source: The minimum wage and median of full-time wages are from OECD.Stat; the age, gender, and education-specific employment-to-population ratios are authors' calculations based on French Labour Force Survey [Emploi (en continu) version FPR (1990–2002, 2003–2009, and 2010), produced by INSEE, distributed by Centre Maurice Halbwachs].

Note: French LFS underwent a major redesign in 2003 when the annual survey usually conducted in March was replaced with a continuous one providing quarterly results. Caution is required when comparing trends before and after 2003.

supportive evidence for the conventional wisdom. For French males, the ratio of the EPOP for young, less educated workers to all prime-age workers *increased* from 60.3 percent in 1994 to 78.1 percent in 2007. For French women, this ratio fell slightly (from 76.6 to 75 percent). This was *not* due to a decline in the EPOP for young, less educated female workers (which increased from 51 to 57 percent), but rather reflected the large increase in employment for prime-age females (from 66.6 to 76 percent).

In sum, we find no evidence in the aggregate data that the rising value of the SMIC has reduced either absolute or relative employment performance of young, less educated workers compared to the US. The conventional indicators shown in Figures 6.8 to 6.12 fail to show the predicted employment effects since the mid-1990s on four counts. First, standard unemployment rates have fallen; second, employment rates have risen; third, the ratio of employment rates of young, less educated workers to prime-age workers has increased substantially for male workers (and fallen only slightly for female workers because of a huge increase in prime-age female employment rates);

and fourth, not only have UPOPs been stable at very low levels, they are far *lower* for French teens than those in the United States and have closely tracked the US rates for 15- to 24-year-olds. Of course, it is possible that these indicators of employment performance could have been more impressive without the large increases in the SMIC. But at a minimum, this evidence shows that the French effectively eliminated low-wage work while maintaining or improving aggregate employment performance for their most vulnerable workers.

THE ADEQUATE EMPLOYMENT RATE: AN INDICATOR FOR QUALITY OF EMPLOYMENT

We now turn to a look at a more comprehensive indicator of employment performance, one designed to take some account of the *quality* of employment, measured in terms of adequacy of pay and hours of work (Howell and Okatenko 2010). The AER measures the share of the working-age population employed at jobs that pay more than the low-wage threshold with inadequate hours of work (working involuntarily part-time due to a lack of full-time job opportunities). Figure 6.13 shows the AER for 20- to 34-year-old French and US workers (males and females) with only a high school degree. By this measure, the French labor market has outperformed the United States for both groups.

The AER for young US men with just a high school degree fell drastically between 1979 and 2007, from 74 percent to just 48 percent. It has since fallen further, to 34 percent in 2010. In contrast, the comparable French male AER rose from 43 percent (1994–1997) to 60 percent in 2007, before falling during the Great Recession to 55 percent. At the 2007 peak, the French labor market outperformed the US market for young, less educated men by 12 percentage points (60 vs. 48 percent); two years later, this gap had increased to 19 percentage points (55 vs. 36 percent).

Figure 6.13 also shows that the AER for young high-school-educated US women remained nearly unchanged between 1979 and 2001 at around 30 percent but has declined steadily since to 24 percent in 2007 and 18 percent in 2010. The French female AER, on the other hand, *increased* from 36 percent in 1995–1996 to 44 percent in 2007 before falling slightly in the recession to 41 percent. For young women, the labor market performance gap in France's favor rose from 6 percentage points in the mid-1990s to 20 points in 2007.

CONCLUSIONS

France and the United States have taken diametrically opposed approaches to minimum wage policy. In the 1960s, the French legal minimum was set at 30 to 35 percent of the median wage, well below the United States's 50 percent; by the 2007, just prior to the global financial crisis, the French minimum had reached 60 percent while the US rate was just 35 percent of the median (Figure 6.5a). In terms of buying power, minimum wage workers in France now earn 40 percent more than their counterparts in the United States. Whereas the US minimum has been roughly stable at just around 60 percent of the of the low-wage threshold since the 1970s, around 2005 since 2005,

Figure 6.13 **Adequate Employment Rates* for Male and Female, French and US Workers with Only a High School Education, Ages 20 to 34, 1979–2010 (United States) and 1993–2010 (France)**

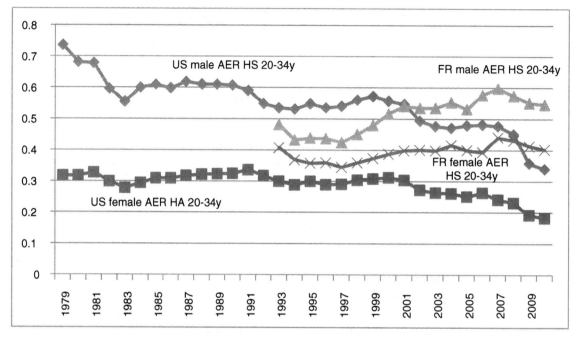

Source: Authors' calculations for United States based on CPS Outgoing Rotation Group Uniform Extracts prepared by CEPR and for France based on French Labour Force Survey [Emploi (en continu) version FPR (1990–2002, 2003–2009, and 2010), produced by INSEE, distributed by Centre Maurice Halbwachs].

*Employed but not earning low wages (< 2/3 of the full-time median) and not working involuntarily part-time as a share of the civilian population (ages 20 to 34).

Note: French LFS underwent a major redesign in 2003 when the annual survey usually conducted in March was replaced with a continuous one providing quarterly results. Caution is required when comparing trends before and after 2003.

the legal minimum in France steadily converged to the low-wage threshold and since 2005 has surpassed it, effectively outlawing the payment of low wages, by the official definition of two-thirds of the median wage (Figures 6.6 and 6.7). This striking difference in the trajectories of the French and US minimum wage systems has played an important role in the sharp divergence between them in the share of workers paid low wages. While low wages have been effectively eliminated in France, close to one-third of all US workers are paid low wages, the highest proportion in the rich world (Figure 6.2).

For the standard of living of future generations, the most significant dimension of the US low-wage problem is the extraordinarily high—and rising—low-wage share for *young* workers. This chapter showed that there is a large and still expanding gap between French and US low-pay incidence for young workers with only a high school degree. In the decade 1997 to 2007, the low-pay share for young (20- to 34-year-old) less educated US men more than tripled from 17 to 49 percent, but for comparable French men this share fell to almost half its 1997 value, from 20 to 11 percent. For young women without a high school degree, the US low-pay rate rose by 20 points, from 46 to 66 percent; in France, it fell by one-third, from 25 to 18 percent (see Figure 6.3).

In conventional accounts, a high minimum wage that helps keep labor costs high is disastrous for employment performance, whether measured by unemployment or employment rates. Despite the French government's efforts to reduce labor costs for employers of low-wage workers by reducing payroll taxes, French labor costs for minimum wage workers have remained extremely high even by European standards and the gap with US labor costs has steadily widened. Yet our results show no support for the orthodox prediction that French labor market performance has been wrecked by minimum wage hikes: standard aggregate employment indicators for young, less educated workers have been stable or have improved between the mid-1990s and 2010; the pay gap between young, less educated male workers and all prime-age workers in France has fallen, not risen as would have been expected; and French employment and unemployment rates for young, less educated workers show no long-run worsening relative to the United States.

At the same time, there can be little doubt that the rising value of the SMIC has increased the *quality* of French employment for the most vulnerable workers. The adequate employment rate measures the share of the workforce paid adequate wages and not working involuntarily part-time (see Howell and Okatenko 2010). By this measure, French labor market performance has been unequivocally superior to that of the United States, and its superiority has been growing over time. For example, the AER for young US men with just a high school degree fell from 74 percent in 1979 to just 48 percent in 2007, while the young French male AER rose from 43 percent (1994–1997) to 60 percent in 2007 (Figure 6.13).

Economists and policy makers have long preferred supply-side solutions to the low-pay problem, believing that it is possible to educate and train our way out of bad jobs. But the last five decades of experience show little support for this path: the incidence of low pay for young workers in the United States has steadily increased despite rising educational attainment, and this trend is expected to continue. According to the US Bureau of Labor Statistics, most employment growth over the coming decade will be in very low-skill and poorly paid jobs. Four of the top six jobs with the largest projected growth between 2010 and 2020 paid a median annual wage of under $21,000 in 2010 (US Department of Labor 2012). This preponderance of low-wage rather than "middle-class" jobs in occupational employment projections suggests that the United States is on a path that will make it an even more extreme outlier among rich nations in the near future. The consequences of a growing incidence of low pay and an increasing gap between these workers and those with top incomes can be expected to have strongly negative effects on the quality of American life through its effects on families, children, and upward mobility in the United States.

Based on our analysis of the data available from the French minimum wage experiment, a far more promising path is to directly increase the quality of jobs in the bottom half of the wage distribution. This cannot realistically be achieved within the next decade without a large increase in the federal minimum wage, preferably in conjunction with a more generous EITC (Wicks-Lim and Pollin 2012). According to the Economic Policy Institute, raising the federal minimum wage to $9.80 (which would still be far below the low-wage threshold of the French minimum wage) would affect roughly 28 million workers and increase aggregate wage incomes by $40 billion (Hall and Cooper 2012).

Following France's example of mandating a "living wage" would help ensure that American workers now struggling with low pay could not only afford the material necessities of life but also enjoy the self-respect and social standing that come with a middle-class standard of living generated by productive work. These improvements have important consequences for the well-being of the next generation, since higher incomes, self-respect, and social standing of current workers will help their children prepare for a life of decent jobs and improve their prospects of participating in the American dream.

NOTES

1. The average hourly wage for production and nonsupervisory workers peaked at $17.88 in 1972, fell steadily to just $16.13 in 1992, and did not return to its 1972 level until 2006, when it reached $17.83 (in 2009 dollars) (Economic Policy Institute 2009). Compensation growth, which includes employer health spending, rose just 10.7 percent for the median production and nonsupervisory worker between 1973 and 2011. "Excluding 1995–2000, median hourly compensation grew just 4.9 percent between 1973 and 2011" (Mishel 2012).

2. For example, between 1980 and 2009, median production worker compensation in manufacturing increased by just 4 percent in the United States, compared to 42 percent in Germany, 43 percent in France, and 56 percent in Sweden (see Howell 2013, Figure 16). Measured by the 90/10 ratio, the OECD (2011c, Figure 1.2) reports that for twenty-three countries, with the exception of Poland and Hungary, US wage inequality increased the fastest from 1979 to 2007. Apart from Spain, only France showed a decline. The difference between the United States and France was equally large for household income inequality. Whether measured by cash disposable income or as "extended income" (disposable income adjusted by the money value of services in education, health care, social housing, and the care of children and the elderly), household income inequality was far higher for the United States than France: of the twenty-seven countries examined, only Mexico's was higher than the United States, while France was nearly as low as Norway and Denmark and only modestly above the lowest, Sweden (OECD 2011c, 39, Figure 11).

3. The figures are taken from Internal Revenue Service (2012).

4. When a household owes less in income tax than the value of the credit, it receives the difference in the form of a cash transfer. For the year 2009, "of the $51 billion in EITC credits, the federal government sent more than $44 billion to families in the form of EITC refund checks. The average EITC check sent to households was therefore $2,308 in 2009" (Wicks-Lim and Thompson 2010).

5. More specifically, according to the study by Autor, Manning, and Smith (2010), taking into account the twenty-seven states with a higher state than federal minimum wage, the share of hours worked at or below the minimum wage was 5 percent (Table 1b); for females and males it was 6 percent and 4 percent, respectively (Table 1a).

6. We use ages 25 to 54 because it is the convention for "prime-age" workers. With limited space in this chapter, we chose to focus on adult workers most likely to be heads of households and not marginally attached to the labor force, so we excluded both teens (16 to 19) and older workers (over 65). This also facilitates comparisons with France, whose institutions (schools, retirement policies) are designed to strongly discourage employment for workers in either of these age groups. Since the conventionally measured prime-age group does not include 20- to 24-year-olds and because 25- to 34-year-olds can reasonably be considered "young" workers, we created another category for those 20 to 34 (and thus overlapping with the conventional 25 to 54 category).

7. It should be noted that the French wage figures must be calculated by dividing reported monthly earnings by estimated hours of work, while the US Current Population Survey asks respondents directly for their hourly wage (in the "outgoing rotation group" surveys).

8. Part of the explanation for the rapid rise in the SMIC between 1997 and 2005 reflects the commitment by the government to keep the weekly earnings of minimum-wage workers from falling (via the "coup de pouce" mechanism) with the reduction in work hours from thirty-nine to thirty-five hours per week mandated by the Aubry laws I and II (Caroli and Gautie 2008, 53).

9. That there remain workers tabulated as paid low wages (see Figure 6.2) is explained in part by exemptions for teens (a lower minimum applies to 16- to 17-year-olds) and apprentices, as well as measurement error (inaccurately reported hours and wages by survey respondents) and systematic violations of the law by employers who do not pay for overtime, a problem that appears most commonly for immigrant workers in small hotels and retail stores. "These de facto violations of minimum wage regulations are facilitated by the low number of labour inspectors in charge of monitoring compliance, and the weakness—and often absence—of trade unions in small and medium-sized firms, and therefore the absence of a countervailing power to ensure that the regulations are respected" (Gautie 2010, 151).

10. Examining effects using differences across US state borders, Dube, Lester, and Reich (2010, 962) conclude, "These estimates suggest no detectable employment losses from the kind of minimum wage increases we have seen in the United States." Further analysis fails to find effects even for teens: "In this paper we show that the absence of a disemployment effect generalizes beyond the restaurant sector, and holds also for teenage workers" (Dube, Lester, and Reich 2011, 25). Similarly, the UK's Low Pay Commission also found no significant negative effect of the minimum wage, which was introduced in 1999, on employment (Vaughan-Whitehead 2010, 26).

11. "Research suggests that, at the levels set in countries such as the US and the UK, minimum wages have no detectable impact on employment but they do seem to have sizeable impacts on wage inequality that stretch beyond those workers directly affected, i.e., there are spillover effects. . . . Our estimates suggest that for young workers something over half of the change in the log 50/5 from the period 1998–2010 can be ascribed to the NMW (National Minimum Wage) and 40 percent of the change in the log 50/10. . . . We also presented evidence that the impact of the NMW reaches up to 40 percent above the NMW in 2010 which corresponds to the 25th percentile" (Butcher, Dickens, and Manning 2012, 21).

12. As the authors put it, "In France, as the real SMIC increased over the period from 1981 to 1989, a certain share of young French workers had real wages that fell between the increasing consecutive real minimum wages. For workers in this situation, subsequent employment probabilities fell significantly" (Abowd, Kramarz, and Margolis 1999, 23).

13. It is perhaps revealing that in their study of low wages in France, Caroli and Gautie (2008) do not attempt to estimate minimum wage effects and do not cite recent studies that suggest robust negative impacts on employment, and Gautie (2010) references only the Abowd, Kramarz, and Margolis study (1999).

14. "It might be argued that the extremely low employment rates (and high conventionally defined unemployment rates) for French teenagers were due to the lack of job opportunities, but the data suggest otherwise. In the early 1970s, when the French male youth unemployment rate was just 3 to 4 percent, about the same share of 16 to 19 year old students held jobs as in 2000–2002 (less than 1 percent), when the standard unemployment rate hovered around 22 to 23 percent" (Howell and Okatenko 2010, 340).

BIBLIOGRAPHY

Abowd, J.M., F. Kramarz, and D.N. Margolis. 1999. "Minimum Wages and Employment in France and the United States." NBER Working Paper #6996 (March).

Abowd, J.M., F. Kramarz, D.N. Margolis, and T. Philippon. 2005. "Minimum Wages and Employment in France and the United States." (unpublished manuscript).

Acemoglu, D., and D. Autor. 2012 "What Does Human Capital Do? A Review of Goldin and Katz's 'The Race Between Education and Technology.'" *Journal of Economic Literature* 50, no. 2: 426–463.

Appelbaum, E., G. Bosch, J. Gautie, G. Mason, K. Mayhew, W. Salverda, J. Schmitt, and N. Westergaard-Nielsen. 2010. "Introduction and Overview." In *Low-Wage Work in the Wealthy World*, ed. J. Gautie and J. Schmitt. New York: Russell Sage.

Autor, D., A. Manning, and C.L. Smith. 2010. "The Contribution of the Minimum Wage to U.S. Wage Inequality over Three Decades: A Reassessment." FEDS Working Paper #2010–60, Federal Reserve Board.

Bassanini, A., and R. Duval. 2006. "Employment Patterns in OECD Countries: Reassessing the Role of Policies and Institutions." *OECD Economic Studies* 42, no. 1: 7.

Bluestone, B., and B. Harrison. 1990. *The Great U-Turn: Corporate Restructuring and the Polarizing of America*. New York: Basic Books.

Bosch, G., K. Mayhew, and J. Gautie. 2010. "Industrial Relations, Legal Regulations, and Wage Setting." In *Low-Wage Work in the Wealthy World*, ed. J. Gautie and J. Schmitt, 91–146. New York: Russell Sage.

Brookings Tax Policy Center. 2009. Table, "Distribution of Earned Income Tax Credit by Size of Adjusted Gross Income and Number of Qualifying Children, 2009." http://taxpolicycenter.org/taxfacts/displayafact.cfm?Docid=559.

Butcher, T., R. Dickens, and A. Manning. 2012. "Minimum Wages and Wage Inequality: Some Theory and an Application to the UK." CEP Discussion Paper No. 1177 (November).

Card, D., and Krueger, A.B. 1994. Minimum Wages and Employment: A Case Study of the Fast-food Industry in New Jersey and Pennsylvania." *American Economic Review*, September, 772–793.

———. 1995. *Myth and Measurement: The New Economics of the Minimum Wage*. Princeton: Princeton University Press.

Caroli, E., and J. Gautie. 2008. "Low-Wage Work: The Political Debate and Research Agenda in France." In *Low-Wage Work in France*, ed. E. Caroli and J. Gautie, 16–27. New York: Russell Sage.

Caroli, E., J. Gautie, and P. Ashkenazy. 2008. "Low-Wage Work and Labor Market Institutions in France." In *Low-Wage Work in France*, ed. E. Caroli and J. Gautie, 28–87. New York: Russell Sage.

Dolado, J., F. Kramarz, S. Machin, A. Manning, D. Margolis, and C. Teulings. 1996. "Minimum Wages: The European Experience." *Economic Policy,* October, 319–372.

Dube, A., T.W. Lester, and M. Reich. 2010. "Minimum Wage Effects Across State Borders: Estimates Using Contiguous Counties." *Review of Economics and Statistics* 92, no. 4: 945–964.

———. Reich. 2011. "Do Frictions Matter in the Labor Market? Accessions, Separations, and Minimum Wage Effects." IZA DP No. 5811, June.

Economic Policy Institute, State of Working America. 2009. http://stateofworkingamerica.org/charts/hourly-wage-and-compensation-growth-for-production-non-supervisory-workers-1959–2009/.

Gautie, J. 2010. "France: Towards the End of an Active Minimum Wage Policy?" In *Minimum Wage Revival in the Enlarged EU*, ed. Daniel Vaughan-Whitehead, 149–178. Geneva: International Labour Organization.

Goldin, C., and L.F. Katz. 2008. *The Race Between Education and Technology*. Cambridge, MA: Harvard University Press.

Hall, D., and D. Cooper. 2012. "How Raising the Federal Minimum Wage Would Help Working Families and Give the Economy a Boost." *Economic Policy Institute Issue Brief #341*, August 14.

Hirsch, B.T., B.E. Kaufman, and T. Zelenska. 2011. "Minimum Wage Channels of Adjustment." Andrew Young School of Policy Studies, Working Paper 11–34 (November).

Howell, D.R. 2013. "The Great Laissez-Faire Experiment: American Inequality and Growth from an International Perspective. Center for American Progress, December.

Howell, D.R., D. Baker, A. Glyn, and J. Schmitt. 2007. "Are Protective Labor Market Institutions at the Root of Unemployment? A Critical Review of the Evidence." *Capitalism and Society* 2, no. 1: 1–71.

Howell, D.R., and A. Okatenko. 2010. "By What Measure? A Comparison of French and US Labor Market Performance with New Indicators of Employment Adequacy." *International Review of Applied Economics* 24, no. 3: 333–358.

Immervoll, H. 2007. "Minimum Wages, Minimum Labor Costs, and the Tax Treatment of Low-Wage Employment." *Social Employment and Migration Working Papers* 46. Paris: OECD.

Internal Revenue Service. 2012. "EITC Income Limits, Maximum Credit Amounts and Tax Law Updates." www.irs.gov/Individuals/EITC-Income-Limits,-Maximum-Credit-Amounts-and-Tax-Law-Updates.

Krueger, A.B. 2012. "The Rise and Consequences of Inequality." Congressional Testimony (January 12, 2012). www.whitehouse.gov/sites/default/files/krueger_cap_speech_final_remarks.pdf.

Marx, I., S. Marchal, and B. Nolan. 2012. "Mind the Gap: Net Incomes of Minimum Wage Workers in the EU and the US." GINI Discussion Paper 56 (July).

Mishel, L. 2012. "The Wedges Between Productivity and Median Compensation Growth." Economic Policy Institute, *Issue Brief #330* (April 26).

OECD. 1998. *Employment Outlook*. Chapter 2: "Making the Most of the Minimum: Statutory Minimum Wages, Employment and Poverty." Paris: OECD.

———. 2005. *OECD Economic Surveys: France*. Chapter 1: "Key Challenges Facing France." Chapter 3: "Improving Labour Market Performance." Paris: OECD.

———. 2006. *Employment Outlook*. Chapter 3: "General Policies to Improve Employment Opportunities for All." Paris: OECD.

———. 2007. *OECD Economic Surveys: France*. Chapter 2: "Combating Poverty and Social Exclusion." Paris: OECD.

———. 2009. *OECD Economic Surveys: France*. Chapter 2: "Progress in Labour Market and Other Reforms." Paris: OECD.

———. 2011a. *Economic Policy Reforms: Going for Growth*. Chapter 1: "An Overview of Going for Growth Priorities in 2011." Paris: OECD.

———. 2011b. *OECD Economic Surveys: France*. Chapter 1: "Securing a Lasting Recovery." Paris: OECD.

———. 2011c. *Divided We Stand: Why Inequality Keeps Rising*. Chapter 1: "An Overview of Growing Income Inequalities in OECD Countries: Main Findings." Paris: OECD.

Schmitt, J. 2011. "Low-Wage Lessons from the Wealthy World." Conference Draft, Korea Labor Institute Seminar (November 16, 2011).

———. 2013. "Why Does the Minimum Wage Have No Discernible Effect on Employment?" Center for Economic and Policy Research (February).

Solow, R. 2008. "The French Story." In *Low-Wage Work in France*, ed. E. Caroli and J. Gautie, 1–15. New York: Russell Sage.

Stiglitz, J.E. 2012. *The Price of Inequality*. New York: W.W. Norton.

Taylor, P. 2012. "French Are Too Comfortable to Consider Reform." *New York Times*, May 1.

US Department of Labor, Bureau of Labor Statistics. 2012. "Fastest Growing Occupations." *Monthly Labor Review*, January. www.bls.gov/emp/ep_table_103.htm.

Vaughan-Whitehead, D. 2010. "Minimum Wage Revival in the Enlarged EU: Explanatory Factors and Developments." In *Minimum Wage Revival in the Enlarged EU*, ed. Daniel Vaughan-Whitehead, 1–53. Geneva: International Labour Organization.

Wicks-Lim, J., and R. Pollin. 2012. "Making Work Pay: Combining the Benefits of the EITC and Minimum Wage." Political Economy Research Institute, University of Massachusetts-Amherst (April).

Wicks-Lim, J., and J. Thompson. 2010. "Combining Minimum Wage and Earned Income Tax Credit Policies to Guarantee a Decent Living Standard to All US Workers." Political Economy Research Institute, University of Massachusetts-Amherst (October).

7

Opportunity and Mobility
The American Dream and the Standard of Living

Daphne T. Greenwood and *Richard P.F. Holt*

Belief in opportunities to "pull oneself up by the bootstraps" is an important part of what Americans expect of their standard of living, according to a Pew Research Center poll. It showed 31 percent of Americans believing they have already achieved the American dream and another 37 percent expecting to during their lifetime. Yet it also shows declining confidence among parents that their children will move up the economic ladder, along with strong support for more governmental action to ensure future opportunities.[1]

Although opportunity cannot be easily measured, one of its results—mobility—can be. Several recent studies have shown less mobility in the United States than in many other countries, although belief in mobility is much stronger in the United States than elsewhere.[2] Whether mobility is less now than it was in the past remains a point of contention among researchers, and is addressed later in this chapter.[3]

We begin with a discussion of why opportunity and mobility are important to the standard of living. Next, we summarize the research findings on mobility in the United States and in other affluent countries. Third, we take a close look at several barriers to opportunity and mobility in the United States. These include changes in the economic and social landscape, the effects of geographic and economic segregation, and the uniquely different history of African Americans. Finally, we look at new policies to increase opportunity and mobility.

Several themes are emphasized: the effects of both economic growth and economic inequality, investments in various kinds of capital, the importance of specific institutions and the role of path dependence. All are important for understanding the possibilities for achieving the American dream. We turn first to how opportunity and mobility are integral parts of a good standard of living.

WHAT GOES AROUND COMES AROUND: THE IMPORTANCE OF OPPORTUNITY

Our broader definition of the standard of living (see Chapter 1 in this volume) emphasizes the roles of quality of life and sustainability along with income. Each underlies one of three quite different reasons that opportunity is important. First, standard economics emphasizes that opportunity leads to more efficiency and productivity, since a meritocracy supports income growth. Without equality of opportunity our economy will not be as productive as others that draw on the full pool of talent. (Another way to broaden the pool is to import skilled workers, but that does not address the quality of life of those left behind economically).

Second, opportunity to develop innate capacities affects individual quality of life. Income transfers and other assistance can raise the level of household consumption but are not a substitute for the ability to develop full human potential at work and in society. This matters because the way income is earned is part of quality of life according to philosopher Martha Nussbaum (2011) and economist Amartya Sen (1999).

Third, political and social stability are at risk without opportunities that live up to "belief in America's essential fairness" (Stiglitz 2012, 17). Mobility functions as a safety valve that allows people to reconcile meritocracy and inequality with other standards of fairness because it implies the existence of relatively equal opportunity. Less intergenerational mobility in the United States may lead to declines in the faith Americans have in their public and private institutions. That could lower motivations to invest in human and social capital and diminish creativity and vitality. We turn now to the empirical evidence about mobility.

MOBILITY AND PERSISTENCE: THE EVIDENCE

While opportunity cannot be easily quantified, mobility can be measured quite precisely. But it is important to keep in mind that there are three different kinds of economic mobility.[4] First, each individual's experience typically includes movement up the rungs of the income and wealth ladders in what could be called *life-cycle* mobility. Second, when economy-wide productivity gains are broadly shared, most people experience *absolute* mobility: that is, having a higher real income at a particular age than their parents had. The third, *relative*, or intergenerational, mobility means movement up and down the rungs of the income or wealth ladder.[5] It is the primary focus of this chapter, since it most affected by the extent of opportunity in a society. Staying at the same rung on the ladder across the generations—persistence—is the opposite of mobility and implies less access.

Individual effort and family circumstances greatly affect the life cycle, absolute, and relative mobility of any particular individual. But these interact in any society with the *external structure* of opportunity, as illustrated in Figure 1.1 of Chapter 1. This includes possibilities for education, for employment, and for accumulating assets (such as housing equity) along with the overall economic situation that individuals confront. Public investments in capital stocks, such as transportation infrastructure to reduce geographic isolation, are an example of an external factor. So are social safety nets such as unemployment insurance, which helps to prevent the downward mobility that may follow from job loss.

Constant movement up and down the income distribution, sometimes called "churning," is often mistaken for mobility. For example, 60 percent of families with heads of household 25 to 44 years of age move from one income quintile to another in a typical decade (Haskins and Sawhill 2009, 69). But since most people earn considerably less when they are young than in midlife, this could show nothing but life cycle mobility. If there is economic growth and the distribution of income is relatively stable, widespread *absolute* mobility also raises income. Movement from one level to another may or may not reflect intergenerational mobility.

From the 1940s through the mid-1970s, absolute mobility was quite common. A median-income family in 1970 brought in 63 percent more income (even after adjusting for inflation) than the median income their parents might have had some twenty years earlier.[6] By 1970, 40 percent of adults had income within 75 percent to 150 percent of the median—a common criteria for being "middle-class." Today, 53 percent of families *define* themselves as middle-class, but only 35 percent actually fall in the middle (Pew Charitable Trusts 2008). Absolute mobility is lower, and many studies find there is also less movement to different rungs on the income ladder than in the decades after World War II.[7]

MORE STICKINESS AT BOTH ENDS OF THE LADDER

Children's success as adults has always been affected by their parents' income, wealth, and education, but the effects are far stronger today than in the 1970s. Measures of persistence (the opposite of mobility) have risen by close to 50 percent over just a few generations.[8] Children born near the top of the income and wealth ladders, as well as children born at the bottom, are much more likely to remain there than in the past.[9]

What explanations are there for this change? After World War I, expanded access to public education made years of school completed less dependent on parents' economic rank (Hauser and Featherman 1976) and led to more mobility. But since 1975 additional years of school have been more highly rewarded (Katz and Murphy 1992) and this has widened income inequality. However, not only do the highly educated receive a greater income premium than in the past, they also are much more likely to marry other high earners (Harding et al. 2005, 108–109). Together these contribute to parental education having an even greater effect on children's mobility than it did in earlier generations.

The widening gap between the highly educated and the less educated is often presented as the inevitable result of market forces. But all around the world labor markets have been affected by changes in technology and greater rewards for more education. While this has led to rising inequality in most countries, the change has been less than in the United States and the effects on mobility have been less. For example, the transmission of economic position from parent to child is much lower in many Western European nations than it is in the United States.[10]

Figure 7.1 reproduces the "Great Gatsby curve" first mentioned by economist Alan Krueger (2012). It shows measures of persistence between the generations plotted against measures of income concentration (Gini coefficients). A strong positive relationship between inequality and persistence of economic position from its parents to children is clear in Figure 7.1. Most of continental Europe—along with Australia, New Zealand, and Japan—has both less inequality and more mobility than the United States.

Figure 7.1 **The Great Gatsby Curve**

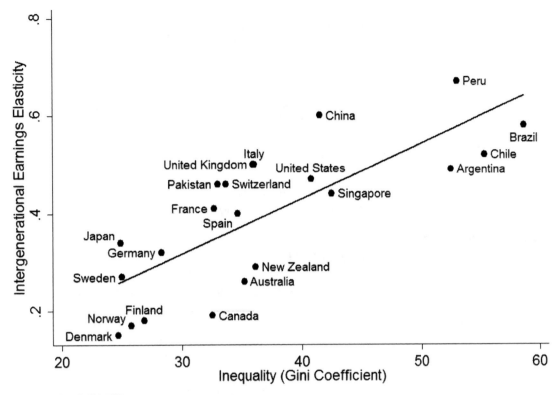

Source: Corak (2013b).

Cultural values are often cited as a reason why inequality and mobility differ between countries. But recent surveys show quite a bit of similarity between the United States and Canada about what constitutes "the good life" and the importance of individual efforts to success. Canadians, as well as Americans, place much more importance on equality of opportunity than equality of outcome (Corak 2010). In both countries, people show less concern about passing on advantages at the top than about whether the children of the poor are doomed to stay in their parent's situation.

Yet intergenerational mobility is quite different. As shown in Table 7.1a, 26 percent of American sons born to fathers in the top tenth of earnings stay there as adults, while in Canada only 18 percent remain. In the United States, 22 percent of sons born to low-earning fathers are low earners as adults, while in Canada the rate of persistence is only 16 percent. In both cases, "stickiness" is almost 50 percent higher in the United States than in Canada. Moving a little farther up to include the bottom third of the population in Table 7.1b, 38 percent of Canadian sons born there move to more than median income as adults, while only 30 percent in the United States make it into the top half.

Why would there be more persistence in economic position across the generations in the United States—long described as the "land of opportunity"—than in Canada or

Table 7.1   **Mobility of Sons in the United States and Canada**

a. Rates of persistence in earnings of fathers and sons

	United States	Canada
Top tenth	26	18
Bottom tenth	22	16

b. Born into bottom third but earning above median income

United States	Canada
30	38

Source: Corak (2010).

many parts of Western Europe? We turn now to examining various kinds of barriers that differ across countries to see if they provide an explanation.

BARRIERS TO OPPORTUNITY: ECONOMIC, SOCIAL, RACIAL, AND GEOGRAPHICAL

Some barriers in the United States are historic. Racial discrimination and geographic isolation are centuries old, but their effects still linger. In contrast, other barriers stem from more recent changes in social behavior and in the economy. The interaction of all these barriers impacts the availability of opportunities. We begin with the economic.

THE EFFECTS OF GROWTH AND INEQUALITY ON OPPORTUNITY AND MOBILITY

Rising returns to human capital and the "winner-take-all" aspects of global markets have increased the spread between high-skilled and less-skilled jobs, contributing to less upward mobility and increasing the likelihood of downward mobility in the United States. But slower rates of gross domestic product (GDP) growth and rising inequality have also affected opportunity.

Absolute mobility in the post–World War II decades was the product of relatively high rates of GDP growth combined with a stable distribution of income. Since then, not only has the growth of GDP slowed, but the fruits of that growth have been concentrated in an increasingly small group, as Chapter 1 outlined. Both slower economic growth and an increasingly concentrated income distribution (where productivity gains flow primarily to the top) explain less absolute mobility. As Richard Freeman observed, if the United States had kept the income distribution of the early Reagan era, "the average American family would have over $4,000 more income each year than it does now" (2007, 42).[11] The majority of families have seen increases in real income since 1980, but they have been smaller increases than in the past and usually depend on a second or third wage earner (Pew 2012, 12).

Theoretically, inequality and mobility do not have to move together. Two different societies, one with much more inequality in income than the other, could have the same degree of mobility—if people moved up and down the ladder in each but the share of income held by each decile (or the top 1 percent) remained the same. But in fact, more inequality does appear to result in lower intergenerational mobility (Corak 2013a; DiPrete and Ehrich 2006; Solon 2004). The following paragraphs explain the process through which this happens.

First, the more concentrated family resources are, the more concentrated parental investments in children are likely to be. Second, greater inequality among families leads to more economic segregation by neighborhood and political jurisdiction and therefore to differences in access to important local public goods and job opportunities. Third, rising inequality seems to result in less public support for programs that help low-income children and families, including policies targeted to low-wage workers. We turn first to differences in parental investments.

High-income families now spend seven times more a year on average than low-income families to develop their children's learning skills (Greenstone et al. 2013).[12] Without some balancing from additional public resources, the gap between rich and poor students will widen. Housing patterns, along with the way schools and other local public goods are financed in the United States often magnify differences in parental investments rather than leveling them out (Woolhouse 2013).

The top 10 percent and bottom 10 percent of families are much more geographically isolated from middle-class families than in earlier decades (Massey and Fischer 2003) and this has caused "economic segregation." Poor people used to live in greater proximity to rich people in order to get to the jobs that involved serving them. But the automobile has permitted people to live far apart, often in different towns and suburbs within a metropolitan area, with consequences for the distribution of opportunity.

It is not only geographic separation that matters; so does living in different political jurisdictions. Many metropolitan areas encompass several counties and a host of different cities, towns, and school districts, each with its own tax base and level of spending on schools, transportation infrastructure, and neighborhood (Glaeser, Scheinkman, and Shleifer 2003; Leonhardt 2013; Reardon and Bischoff 2011; Swanstrom et al. 2006). "Fiscal zoning" is technically illegal, but many communities use lot size and regulatory barriers to keep out multifamily housing or affordable housing and preserve high levels of service (or low tax rates) for the better-off while excluding residents who would use lots of schooling or other public services (Greenwood and Holt 2010).

Households have also become more segregated (even within race and income groups) into neighborhoods of owners and neighborhoods of renters. This has a profound influence on the civic quality of the community (Hoff and Sen 2005). Zoning and regulatory differences lead to variations in environmental quality, which affect children's development (Currie 2011). This contrasts with the post–World War II United States where the "rising tide" of absolute income gains led to *more* equal access to local public goods such as libraries, parks and recreation centers, public schools, and community events.

Third—and perhaps related to economic segregation—is the weakening of social capital and support for public programs, especially those targeted to low-income children. Politicians increasingly find it pays to support "middle-class programs" whose benefits go primarily to families in the top deciles of the distribution.[13] In many other affluent countries where inequality is less there is more help both for children (Mayer and Lopoo 2008) and for low wage workers. With fewer universal programs in the United States and less support for targeted programs, rising income inequality has had more effect on opportunities and mobility than it has in many other countries. But changes in family structure and behavior are also frequently cited as reasons why poverty is intergenerational. Let us look next at the evidence.

CHANGING SOCIAL BEHAVIORS: FAMILIES AND WORK

One important change in family behavior over the last three decades has been greater labor force participation by mothers of young children. It is not surprising that higher wages for college graduates kept many married women with degrees in the labor force after they had children. But married women with less education, low wages, and children at home also began to stay in the labor force in much greater numbers. Many of them worked in order to maintain household income, since wages for men with less education were falling.

In addition, fewer women were getting married or staying married, a trend most visible at low incomes. By 2004, 36 percent of all births were to single women, compared to 5 percent in 1960 (Cancian and Reed 2009). Divorce, single parenthood, and out-of-wedlock births are often attributed to the influence of mass media and pop culture on moral standards. But economic status, including long spells of unemployment, may be more important (Edin and Reed 2005; Kearney and Levine 2009, 2012).

For example, although teen births have fallen considerably in the United States since the 1950s, they continue to be high in certain regions. There is a clear "teen birth belt" from New Mexico to Mississippi, with two and half times as many births per teenage woman as there are in the Northeast (Florida and Johnson 2013). Since rates are also relatively low in the Northwest and the upper Great Plains, one could be forgiven for asking if it is something about the weather! But economic circumstances provide a better explanation: across the United States, the teen birth rate is negatively correlated with income (−.53) and wages (−.35) and is much higher in states with greater poverty.[14]

In the United States today, women whose first birth occurs as a teen are more likely to give birth outside of marriage, less likely to finish high school or attend college, and more vulnerable to downward mobility. Higher rates of divorce also leave many mothers and children with low income, although the economic effects are muted when mothers remarry (Morrison and Ritualo 2013, 560). But single parents—whether divorced or never wed—are disproportionately poor and downwardly mobile if the mother is a low earner and there is little child support. Fewer job opportunities for men without college degrees has led to lower rates of marriage and higher rates of divorce. The result is that more children are in female headed households, often with low incomes.

While major social changes in family structure have affected opportunity, we turn next to an area where change has been slower in coming. Although some barriers for historically disadvantaged groups, such as African Americans, Native Americans,

Mexican Americans in the Southwest, and whites in Appalachia, have been greatly reduced, their effects linger on. Other historic barriers are still alive.

GEOGRAPHY, RACE, AND HISTORY: THE PATH DEPENDENCE OF MOBILITY

Poverty, like teen births, is often attributed to family and culture. But children often face the same economic, political, and social barriers (or advantages) that their parents faced. That can explain much about intergenerational poverty. Many Americans believe we are in a post-racial society where discrimination is a thing of the past. Political commentator and comedian Stephen Colbert likes to say to his African American guests, "I don't see race." And recognizing economic barriers is almost as taboo as recognizing race. Mentioning either can elicit a cry of "playing the race card" or "class warfare." In this section we explore the long-term effects of denying civil rights as well as full educational and economic opportunities to African Americans. We look at the similar effects of growing up poor and white in geographically isolated regions of Appalachia. Some of these effects are also present for other minority groups in America.

After coming to the United States in what resembled an American nightmare more than an American dream, Africans became slaves rather than paid workers. Most were forbidden to read or write and could not save money or buy property. The promise of forty acres and a mule to accompany their freedom quickly evaporated after the Civil War. Many turned to sharecropping on their old plantations and living at subsistence level.[15] At the same time, during the late nineteenth and early twentieth century, many European immigrants used job ladders not available to African Americans to climb from poverty to the middle class.

The civil rights legislation of the 1960s and 1970s opened up many of those ladders, rapidly increasing opportunities for the "talented tenth"[16] of African Americans and gradually bringing others into the middle class. However, for African Americans without much formal education, a chance at the American dream required more than getting rid of restrictions on education, employment, and housing choices. Behind President Lyndon Johnson's "War on Poverty" was the realization that intergenerational patterns would be quite slow to change without widespread use of programs like Head Start.

However, the timing of other economic forces—rapidly changing technology, more demand for highly educated workers, factory jobs moving overseas, and competition from new immigrants—made it difficult for those at the bottom to take the old routes to mobility. On the heels of the civil rights laws, a major change in immigration policy in 1965 opened the door to more low-skilled immigrants from low-wage countries. This widened the earnings gap between workers who were college educated and those who were not. Real wages and benefits fell for many African American workers along with opportunities for moving up the job ladder from lower-skilled positions (Borjas, Grogger, and Hanson 2010, 256). In the 1980s, many of the factory jobs blacks held moved abroad.

It is not surprising that two-thirds of African Americans are still raised at the bottom of the income ladder given lackluster efforts to broaden opportunity after the end of the Jim Crow laws. It took decades to get school funding within the states equalized, and it still varies widely between the states. Combined with changes in the economy that sent more manufacturing jobs overseas and with policies that encouraged the immigration of low-skilled workers, the situation worked against mobility for anyone at the bottom, and there were additional historical barriers for African Americans.

More than half of blacks raised at the bottom remain there as adults, while only one-third of whites are.[17] Blacks are also much more likely to be downwardly mobile from the middle (56 percent) than are whites (32 percent), according to Pew (2012).[18] Race is the differentiating characteristic researchers have chosen to measure here—and depending on one's point of view, the wide differences in outcomes can be interpreted as evidence of racial discrimination or of behavioral differences connected to race and upbringing. But it is easy for advocates of either position to oversimplify their analysis based on the characteristic of race and forget the historical reasons why race is often associated with other disadvantages.

As we have emphasized throughout this chapter, parents' education and income influence children's opportunities and achievement. But even after controlling for both, Thomas Hertz (2005) found a 25 to 30 percent gap in income achievement for black children relative to white. Is this evidence of continuing racial discrimination? It might be. But modern-day disadvantage may be as much about "white privilege" as about overt discrimination. Recent research shows the importance of social and economic networks, to which blacks and whites have very different access (DiTomaso 2013).

To use race as the primary way to categorize disadvantage is also misleading. The education and economic resources of parents, extended families, neighbors, and communities affect the development of human and social capital. That in turn affects mobility (Greenstone et al. 2013). There is a component of "economic privilege" and even "regional privilege" that also affects access to networks and opportunity. For the first time in American history, all nine Supreme Court justices come from Ivy League schools and many of them grew up around New York City. That is just one high-profile example of the complexity of privilege in the United States today.

The explanation for why African Americans—at every income level—have greater likelihood of downward mobility than whites in the United States today probably lies in a combination of racial, geographic, institutional, and historical factors.[19] However, other racial and ethnic minorities—as well as increasing segments of white America—are experiencing many of the same problems. But comparable historical data on other minorities, such as Latinos or Native Americans, is not available for similar analysis.[20]

White Americans with a long legacy of poverty are simply averaged with all whites because they lack a noneconomic characteristic on which they can be separated. But being white does not make their experience and opportunities the same as the majority of white Americans. The geographic and cultural isolation of Appalachian whites provides a case study of path dependence that does not depend on racial or ethnic exclusion, but illustrates why opportunity and mobility are less likely for some Americans than others. Some lessons learned by observing the effects of historic poverty and immobility in Appalachia can be applied to whites across the United States who live in towns or neighborhoods that are increasingly economically segregated.

In central Appalachia, where geographic and cultural isolation have persisted longest, post–World War II economic growth did little to reduce poverty and deprivation. Since Appalachia is almost exclusively Anglo-Saxon white, the explanations could not lie in racial factors or discrimination. But inadequate diet and health care, geographic isolation from better jobs, and lower educational levels converged in a "poverty trap," just as they have for a large share of the African American population. The roots of the war on poverty lay in recognizing the need for positive outreach to all people—including children—with a long legacy of poverty. Head Start and the food stamp program were first introduced into poor counties in central and northern Appalachia (Ziliak 2012, 27) before being extended into the rest of America.

Since then, changing family structures have made the incidence of poverty in Appalachia worse than it would have been otherwise.[21] The same can be said for intergenerational poverty outside Appalachia. Economic opportunity affects family structure in all parts of the country and for whites and nonwhites. But family structures have been affected by a continued lack of economic opportunity. It is important to address geographic and economic, as well as racial, disparities.

Poverty rates have remained stubborn at best since the 1980s, and children are the most likely age group to be in poverty. Changes in childbearing and labor force participation among women have been heavily influenced by rising inequality and have further contributed to more inequality and less mobility. Increased inequality has raised barriers to opportunity and mobility for millions of Americans who already suffered from geographic isolation or racial-ethnic discrimination.

We turn next to opportunity-oriented policies that have the potential to moderate the effects of low parental income, locational and racial disparities, and even individual choices. Some of these have changed substantially over the last half-century, and many are quite different from the policies in other affluent countries. Perhaps that explains why mobility is lower in the United States than in many other countries, and than it was here in the past.

PATHWAYS OUT OF POVERTY AND UP FROM THE MIDDLE CLASS: THAT WAS THEN, THIS IS NOW

In the last section, we compared the pathways available to youth after they leave high school with those from an earlier time. These have changed substantially, along with changes in the structure of the US economy and labor markets. Unions represent a far smaller share of workers. Many jobs that paid well but required little education have moved overseas. More jobs require a college degree, and almost all require high school graduation. At the same time, budget pressures on states have caused college to be less affordable. But mobility requires additional ports of entry into the middle class besides college. We begin with the military.

THE MILITARY AS GATEWAY TO ADULT EMPLOYMENT

For most of American history, less than 1 percent of adult males served in the military during peacetime (Segal and Segal 2004, 4–5). Teenage males joined the military in large numbers from 1951 into the 1970s (Sider and Cole 1984, 11). Many got a new start after dropping out of high school or having a minor brush with the law, and then returned to civilian life after their service with better job and life skills. Most of them were white. Figure 7.2 shows how enlistment rates have changed over the last several decades, at the same time that the racial composition of youth was changing.

Figure 7.2 **Percentage of Young Men in US Military**

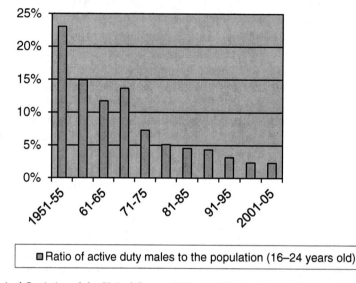

□ Ratio of active duty males to the population (16–24 years old)

Sources: Historical Statistics of the United States: Millenial Edition Vol. 1. Ed. Susan B. Carter et al.; US Census Bureau, Population Division; US Census Bureau, *Statistical Abstract of the United States;* Washington Headquarters Services (DoD) Directorate for Information Operations and Reports. *Selected Manpower Statistics.*

The proportion of young men in the armed forces dropped from 23 percent in the early 1950s to less than 5 percent in 1980 and roughly half that by 2005 (even with active wars in Iraq and Afghanistan). By the 1980s, a new emphasis on completing high school raised the average age of new enlistees. At roughly the same time, the racial composition of the military also changed significantly. While nonwhites were underrepresented as late as 1970 (Sider and Cole 1984, 11), their representation among active duty military personnel rose above their share of population to 23 percent in 1984 and 29 percent in 2011.[22]

African Americans and Hispanics who had a high school education and no criminal record began to have greater opportunities in the military than they had earlier. But these opportunities no longer extended to more disadvantaged individuals of *any* race. In earlier times, along with providing national defense, the army effectively functioned as an educational and social program that gave a second chance to many of its members. As force size shrank and standards for acceptance rose, that path was less available to those at the bottom. These were now disproportionately minority youth.

For youth who were accepted into the military, educational programs had evolved to better target the disadvantaged. But monthly allowances had far less purchasing power than was given to veterans of World War II.[23] Only since 2002 has the real value of these programs come close to Vietnam-era values, and it is still a fraction of what it was in the 1950s (Bowman 1973, 786–790). But the value of veterans' educational benefits depends not only on the dollar value but also on charges for tuition, fees, and books. These have increased in both public and private institutions. Let us turn next to how shifting more costs onto students has affected opportunity and mobility.

THE LINKS BETWEEN EDUCATION, TRAINING, AND OPPORTUNITY

In this section we compare the investments in lifelong education being made in the United States today with those in other countries and with the past. After briefly discussing the critical roles of early childhood education and K–12, we will focus on access to post-secondary education.

Of course, in an earlier era it was not necessary to graduate from high school to stay out of poverty (or even to get some "middle-class" jobs), and preschool education was virtually unknown. But as the world economy and labor markets changed with new technologies and globalization, the public education system in the US lagged behind many other countries in adapting to those changes.

One of the best ways to increase opportunity is through high-quality preschool programs for low-income children, which increases success rates in the K–12 system (Tomer 2014). A lack of these programs in the United States compared to widespread adoption in Western Europe may help explain why almost one-fourth of US students fail to graduate from high school, compared to 15 percent in the European Union (OECD 2011, 54). Even the United Kingdom, which has income inequality almost as high as ours, has much more upward mobility for children in poverty: 70 percent to our 58 percent.[24] This has been attributed to progress in early childhood education in the UK (Waldfogel and Washbrook 2011).

But it is not just a matter of instilling good attitudes and a foundation for school in early childhood. The K–12 system in the United States does have more resources per pupil than in the past, and it also directs a greater share of them to low-income children. However, other affluent countries have done much more (Mayer and Lopoo 2004). In the United States, even poor children with good academic performance are less likely to graduate from high school than richer children with weaker performance (Stiglitz 2012, 19). Something is going on in their lives and their schools that reflects poorly on opportunity in the United States today. Unless we target more public investments in health, safety, and early education to low-income children, attempts to reform K–12 education will do little to increase upward mobility.

Yet the political system has been slow to respond to two decades of evidence on the high rate of return to early childhood education or K–12 investments for low-income children. This failure to act may be due to declining social capital and less willingness to invest in "other people's children." It could also be a function of a highly fragmented system of school districts and school funding in the United States relative to other countries. While the US Supreme Court has decided that states must provide relatively equal education to all their students, that equality stops at the state border. Some states are poorer than others, and education funding is not equalized in the way that funding is for Medicare, Social Security, or food stamps. States that spend more on K–12 have both higher graduation rates and more mobility from the bottom up (Mayer and Lopoo 2005). Since these positive effects are intergenerational, impacting the health and education of the next generation of children (Greenwood 1997), this is an issue of long-term sustainability.

Once students graduate from high school, an increasingly important step is attending college. According to the Pew mobility project, a four-year college degree was *most* important to upward mobility for children raised in households with low incomes (the bottom 40 percent). Having a college degree tripled their chances of rising from the bottom of the income ladder to the top. But a college education is also important for lowering the odds of *downward* mobility, even for those higher up the income ladder; 51 percent who had a college degree stayed at least where they were on the income ladder, while only 25 percent without a college degree did (Pew 2011b, 23–25).

POSTSECONDARY EDUCATION: WHO PAYS?

Although more students want to attend college, state funding for higher education has not kept pace. As a result, an increasing share of costs has been shifted to students.[25] Tuition costs have gone up, on average, even faster than health-care costs (Stiglitz 2013). In 1971, the average family spent 12 percent of income for tuition at a four-year public school, but that more than tripled to 40 percent by 2008 (Heller 2011, 22). And for several decades, need-based federal programs have not kept up with rising costs.[26]

For example, the maximum Pell grant covered tuition and fees at the average public four-year college in 1992, but less than two-thirds of the bill in 2012 (Baum, Ma, and Payea 2012, Figure 14). Plus, completing college successfully requires more than paying tuition. Textbooks and supplies must be purchased, along with room and board for students who are not able to live at home. As a result, students are working more hours while in college *and* taking on more debt.

Borrowing increased by 55 percent in real terms between 2001 and 2011 (Baum, Ma, and Payea 2012), with student loan debt the only form of debt increasing since the financial crisis (Federal Reserve Bank of New York 2013). Students held $1 trillion in education-related debt by 2012—more than all credit card debt in the US economy—according to the Consumer Financial Protection Bureau, which made several special reports to Congress (2012a, 2012b). Just as mobility differs across income and wealth groups, patterns of debt and ability to repay also differ—calling into question the equality of access in the United States today.

Family income has a larger effect on attending a four-year college than performance on standardized entrance exams. Fewer low-income high school seniors with high scores ever enroll than high-income seniors with only average test scores (Stiglitz 2012, 19). Family income also affects the likelihood that students who attend college will graduate (Haveman and Smeeding 2006) and the likelihood of carrying student loans. One-third of all students graduating with a bachelor's degree do so without student loans, but almost 13 percent of student borrowers owe more than $50,000. These are not all medical or law students—almost one-fifth of the students who had borrowed $75,000 or more were at for-profit vocational schools (Baum, Ma, and Payea 2012).

Many of the students with high student loans are first-generation college students who come from low-income or minority families, and only 15 percent of them complete a four-year degree within six years (Johnson, Van Osten, and White 2012, 14). Along with concerns over student indebtedness, it is important to revisit the educational options students have today. Restoring opportunities to move up to the middle class—and stay there—requires high-quality and affordable vocational training as well as access to traditional colleges and universities.

VOCATIONAL TRAINING: MORE COSTS AND LESS VALUE

There is still strong demand for workers with specialized vocational skills, demonstrated by the fact that one-fifth of all noncollege graduates earn more than the average college graduate (Mariani 1999). But as traditional channels of vocational training in high school, the military, and union apprenticeships have narrowed, their replacements have fallen short on both quality and affordability. Public community colleges are less expensive than four-year colleges but have also raised tuitions as state support faltered. Many for-profit technical schools have low completion rates, with their students more likely to default on loans. Often, the training they give does not help students get a good job (U.S. Senate, Committee on Health, Education, Labor and Pensions 2012).

Tuition at for-profits is far higher than at community colleges, but enrollments at these schools have tripled between 2000 and 2009. Aggressive recruitment programs targeted students eligible for federal loans and grants, who make up 86 percent of the student body at for-profits. They lack counseling on how their debt compares to earnings potential. Students at for-profits also sign up for direct private loans at twice the rate of all other students, often unaware of lower-cost loan options. These loans have been packaged into asset-backed securities by some of the largest financial institutions in the United States, many familiar names from the mortgage securities crisis. They are part of a system that Stiglitz (2013) has called "a leech on the poor," because banks and investors profit, while many students are left with crippling debt.[27]

Opportunity and mobility require that students get the skills they need without debts that cannot be paid from future earnings. But even when students are able to get a good education, there is substantial evidence that it is not enough to close the inequality gap (Wolff 2006) or to achieve mobility. The *high-achieving* children of the poor are still worse off, on average, than the *low-achieving* children of the rich. Fewer children born into the lowest fifth who graduate from college (19 percent) make it to the top fifth of the income ladder than children from the highest income group (23 percent), who stay at the top despite never even graduating from high school (Stiglitz 2012, 19). Stickiness at the top and bottom is not simply a matter of education and hard work. We turn now to policies that can reinvigorate opportunity throughout American society.

INCREASING OPPORTUNITIES FOR MOBILITY: A BROAD POLICY OUTLINE

Economic growth is often expected to "trickle down" to Americans in all social and economic strata. But with less trickle than there was in the decades after World War II, growth in GDP is not an adequate strategy for increasing mobility. A "percolate up" approach requires focusing on people and how their marriages, births, education, and work affect their economic outcomes. Let us look first at decisions about family.

PERCOLATING UP TO AFFECT FAMILY DECISIONS

It is conventional wisdom that "babies have babies" because their mothers did. In fact, opportunities for education or employment are far more important indicators of early pregnancy. Living in a community with large gaps between the poor and middle class raises teen pregnancy rates substantially (Kearney and Levine 2009). Out of wedlock births at all ages are greatly influenced by economic circumstances.[28] Focusing on birth control methods and access will "only make dents around the edges of the problem without addressing the root cause" (Kearney and Levine 2012). Increasing economic opportunity for young women and young men has the potential to significantly reduce teen pregnancy and out-of-wedlock births.

Since other "noneconomic" decisions like marriage and divorce also have deep roots in the economic environment, policies to improve the economic situation of struggling families help the standard of living in three ways. First, they raise parental income, which contributes to a better standard of living for the entire family. Second, there is evidence that a better economic situation improves family stability. And third, they improve quality of life by increasing the opportunities of parents and children to fully develop their innate capabilities and participate in the American dream. Let us look at some specific policies that might improve the economic opportunities of children and young adults, turning first to education.

PERCOLATING UP TO MAKE EDUCATION MORE AFFORDABLE

It is not just a matter of how much is spent on education; the way it is spent is also important. Below, we look at (1) inadequate focus on vocational training in high schools, (2) an inefficient system of for-profit technical schools, (3) a poorly designed student loan program, and (4) decreased funding for higher education in most states.

First, too much emphasis on "college prep" in today's high schools ignores both the wide distribution of students' ability levels and interests and where the jobs are. Although only half of US students graduating from high school enter college, vocational courses receive less attention in high school than they did a generation or two ago. In contrast, Germany's high-quality vocational programs teach reading and writing skills closely related to the training and their students graduate with *better* mathematical, statistical, and computing skills, on average, than many students in the United States (Lerman 2008). The skills these students acquire during training are highly transferable across different occupations (Fedorets and Spitz-Oener 2011). Pairing privately paid apprenticeships (such as unions used to provide) with high school based vocational preparation would give students more options.

Second, grants and loans to students need to be more efficiently targeted and administered. While federal grant aid to postsecondary students more than *tripled* in constant dollars between 2001 and 2011 (Baum, Ma, and Payea 2012), it went disproportionately to private technical schools. Although only 10 to 12 percent of students are enrolled at for-profits, they receive 25 percent of the funds. They are also responsible for 47 percent of student debt defaults. Sixty-three percent of students who enroll in a two-year program leave without a degree and even many with degrees cannot find employment in the field for which they trained (U.S. Senate, Committee on Health, Education, Labor and Pensions 2012, 1–2). After pursuing education they believed would advance their job opportunities, they instead have two strikes against them. The first is a debt that cannot be discharged even in bankruptcy; the second, little to no improvement in their career potential.

For-profit institutions have been allowed to establish their own accrediting agencies and criteria for accreditation with little state oversight. They can then charge high tuition that is paid through Pell grants and federal student loan programs. The schools make high profits but students often do not get the training that would help them in the job market. This seems to be a recurring problem, as many of the same things happened in the 1980s and early 1990s. That led to Congressional reforms that were largely undone after 2001. But it was not only for-profits that were unleashed.

After 2001, the student loan program became a way for banks to profit at the expense of students. Reforms have been proposed that make it harder for schools and lenders to market deceptively to students. The challenge is whether the Obama administration reforms will be undone, this time by a court ruling.[29] But even more changes are needed. For example, an income-contingent repayment program like Australia's, administered through the federal income tax system, would be fairer to students while lowering the costs of monitoring and collection, writes Joseph Stiglitz (2013). Another important reform, proposed during the Clinton presidency, would set national standards and oversight for the accrediting agencies so that schools with really poor performance either cannot operate or are not eligible for federal student aid.

However, along with better vocational education and improved targeting of loans and grants, affordability of higher education is an issue. The much publicized increases in tuition have been greatest at exclusive private universities. That makes it all the more important that good students from low and middle income families have an alternative in high quality public universities and colleges. States could support access and affordability in three ways. The first is to restore state support to higher education to the levels that helped previous generations attend college. The second is to change the mix of state scholarships to target more low-income students. The third is to enforce standards and accountability at for-profit technical schools—both to help their students and to prevent the waste of public funds that could be better spent elsewhere.

However, in a rapidly changing global economy, the task is not over once college or vocational training is completed. Worker-oriented programs are also important. Below we give examples of how to provide more opportunity for workers in general and address specific barriers and challenges.

PERCOLATING UP THROUGH WORKER-ORIENTED PROGRAMS

Many worker-oriented programs used to be provided through unions. As well as providing training, unions helped ensure enforcement of health and safety laws. While they are still important institutions in most affluent countries, unions have seen a real decline in power and representation in the United States. Whether unions help to create stronger state economies or whether people in high-income states feel able to afford the protections they give to workers, unions are clearly compatible with a vibrant economy

(Florida 2011). Across the United States, higher average state income is correlated with more support for collective bargaining (Pantuosco, Parker, and Stone 2001).

Surveys show that most workers want *more* representation than they have today, not less. Thirty-two percent of workers without a formal union want one and another 46 percent would like an organization that helps resolve workplace issues outside of collective bargaining (Freeman 2007, 83). Yet federal and state laws today are less friendly to worker organization than they were in the time of more upward mobility.

With fewer workers protected by union contracts, a larger share of the labor force depends on the laws and programs that apply to all of us. Some are general, while others are targeted to specific employment barriers. For example there are many "family-friendly" employment policies that can increase the likelihood workers with young children will remain at their jobs and move up to better paying positions. Flexible use of sick days, release time for school conferences, and on-site child care are examples (Waldfogel 2007). Along with parental leave (Pressman and Scott 2014) these not only help today's working families, they provide a better foundation for the next generation.

There are other specific barriers to opportunity such as physical disabilities, drug and alcohol addiction, mental health problems, and past criminal records. The share of Americans with disabilities is growing, but their employment rate is no higher than when the Americans with Disabilities Act passed in 1990 (Khadaroo 2007). Some countries require businesses above a certain size to hire a specified percentage of their workforce from the disabled population. That is a different way of spreading costs across society. It has the additional benefit of increasing quality of life for the moderately disabled through access to productive work.

Drug and alcohol abuse are also major barriers to success on the job. Offenders generally must pay for rehabilitation, which means judges can only require very low-cost programs that often have poor track records. The right treatment and monitoring of drug and alcohol dependency could bring important increases in labor force productivity and lower dependency rates. Much the same holds for people with mental illness—treatment and monitoring could result in more opportunities for themselves and their children.

Criminal records are another hurdle. With more nonviolent crimes classified as felonies, a criminal record is now a barrier for more who seek work (Raphael 2008). The difficulties faced by workers with a criminal record, who are often ineligible for security clearances or occupational and business licenses also affect their families. All of these examples underline the fact that different programs and policies are needed to address different barriers.

Opportunity requires more than increasing graduation rates in high school or college.[30] To begin with, there will always be a large share of the labor force that does not attend college. But alternatives like the military or union apprenticeships are less available to them than in the past. Without these, other pathways are needed to fill the vacuum. Americorps (national service) is quite small but could be expanded. The highly successful Civilian Conservation Corps of the 1930s could also provide a model for a program. Since many youth who attend college also have a rockier transition to a career than in the past, more programs are needed to help them. In addition, since workers at all educational levels can have disability, mental illness, substance abuse, or a criminal record, programs to address these should be expanded.

CONCLUDING REMARKS

Throughout this chapter we emphasized the path dependence of opportunity as well as the importance of formal and informal institutions in altering the structure in which people make decisions. Social and economic sustainability depend on reviving the promise of the American dream: the opportunity to improve one's circumstances regardless of race, place of residence, or family of origin. Generations of immigrants came to the United States in pursuit of opportunity. Abundant land, labor shortages, and relatively open social and political institutions attracted them.

A different institution—slavery—caused a very different start for African Americans. Slavery ended, but for 100 years discriminatory laws and practices created a radically different opportunity structure for blacks than for white immigrants. In the last few decades, opportunity for all low- and middle-income Americans has weakened. Some of this decline is a result of global economic changes largely beyond the control of any one country.

While the same economic forces have been present around the world, many other affluent nations have instituted very different policies, thus improving opportunity and mobility (Sawhill and Morton 2007). By instituting high-quality preschool, vocational training in high school, a more equal education in K–12, and affordable higher education, they provide examples of how to start youth on an opportunity path. And by guaranteeing universal health coverage, family leave, and basic rights for workers, they have helped mobility from the bottom up.

Fifty years ago, Michael Harrington's *The Other America* and John Kenneth Galbraith's *The Affluent Society* led to support for President Lyndon Johnson's "War on Poverty." Not long after, court cases required greater equality in K–12 funding and Pell grants helped broaden access to higher education. Many people were helped by these and other programs. But by the 1980s, the poverty rate ceased falling—even in good times—and mobility lagged behind Canada and much of Western Europe. In *Creating an Opportunity Society* (2009), Ron Haskins and Isabel Sawhill analyze the successes and failures of anti-poverty programs. They conclude that some very good programs with high success rates were underfunded and did not reach enough people. But other programs were poorly targeted and failed to reach the people who most needed them. Still others were not well designed, in light of current knowledge about how people really behave. Haskins and Sawhill suggest building on past successes by expanding some programs, but also modifying programs as new information about their effectiveness becomes available.

Unfortunately, rather than taking a pragmatic and evidence-based approach to restoring opportunity, many people link the American dream with stock market performance or the lifestyles of the rich and famous. But the success seen in those realms has not trickled down to the average American. Not only has more inequality directly affected people's pocketbooks, it has also had indirect effects, some of which we outlined in Chapter 1 in this volume. When gaps between the top and bottom are smaller, there seems to be more support for opportunity policies that help people further down the income ladder.

The GI bill and other programs that helped build a large middle class were enacted after World War II at a time of "shared purpose" in America. In contrast, many dollars earmarked for opportunity in recent decades have been quickly diverted to the already well off. A dramatic example can be found in the re-direction of spending marked to help students attend college. Much of it went to large investors and banks through a newly designed student loan program. A large share also went to for-profit technical schools.

Productivity growth provides another example of redirection. In the decades after World War II (when mobility was high and inequality much lower) growth in productivity supported wage increases for the average American worker as well as those at the top. Over the last few decades, income gains from higher productivity have gone mostly to the top. Few workers have had increases much above inflation, and many have fallen behind. As a result, even when more family members worked, median household income rose slowly, if at all.

A third example of redirection was the evolution of easy credit as a substitute for low income growth. What was pitched as making housing affordable and creating jobs in construction and real estate was actually a giant transfer of wealth to banks and investors. It did nothing for the long-term economic mobility of most American households.

At the same time, greater economic segregation is creating new social and geographic barriers for many people across the country. Areas that have historically suffered from these barriers, such as Appalachia or inner-city ghettoes, continue to provide inhospitable environments for mobility. But economic segregation is increasing in the suburbs and in almost every metropolitan area as well (Swanstrom et al. 2006).

The chances of being upwardly mobile are far less for children who are poor than for the better off, even if they get an education. A high school degree (or even a college education) is not the guarantee of a good job that it was in the past. Postsecondary education often carries much more debt. And African American children are several times more likely to persist in poverty than white children who are born there. A better standard of living depends on broadly based opportunity that makes mobility possible for all race and income groups in all parts of the United States.

Yet there is at least one bright spot in the future of American mobility. Belief in the American dream continues even today, probably because cultural fluidity is higher than in many older, more established countries. Better public policy can build on the openness of American society and continue to provide increased opportunity and mobility.

NOTES

1. Results of the 2011 mobility poll show the number of parents who expect their children to do better falling sharply from 62 percent in 2009 to 47 percent in 2011 and 83 percent saying government needs to do more to promote opportunity (Pew 2011a).

2. Haskins and Sawhill (2009, 64) compare polling results from twenty-seven countries.

3. The Pew Charitable Trust is a nonprofit organization that sponsors regular polling and reports on social and economic issues. More information about the mobility project can be found on its website.

4. Longitudinal data, such as the Panel Study of Income Dynamics, has linked the economic circumstances of parents to their adult children since the 1960s. Cross-country comparisons rely on similar longitudinal data. While differences in data and time periods make exact comparisons difficult, the consistent pattern that emerges has been deemed sufficient to draw conclusions (Mazumder 2005, 80).

5. This contrasts with static measures of inequality at any one point in time. Opportunity and mobility are dynamic processes.

6. This example is taken from Greenwood and Holt (2010).

7. Some studies find a decline in intergenerational mobility (Ferrie 2005; Levine and Mazumder 2007), while others see no change since the 1970s (Chetty et al. 2014; Lee and Solon 2009). The answer depends in part on whether intergenerational mobility in the past was actually as high as was commonly believed. See Smeeding, Erickson, and Jantti (2011) for a review of the research.

8. In a pure opportunity society, intergenerational elasticities between parents and children's economic outcomes would be zero, while an estimate of 1 shows complete persistence across generations. Using several longitudinal data sets, the elasticities for succeeding cohorts of adult sons in the United States (relative to their fathers at the same age) have risen quite substantially from .4 for earlier cohorts (Solon 1992) to .6 for more recent ones (Chau 2011). This means that 60 percent (rather than 40 percent) of the earnings gap now remains after each generation and that parental background will affect earnings for the next four generations, rather than for two (Mazumder 2005, 80–82).

9. In low-income families, almost half of children remain at the bottom as adults. In the top deciles of income and wealth, 40 percent raised there remain as adults, with only 8 percent falling to the bottom according to Acs (2011, 13–15) analysis of the Pew mobility project. It was based on the Panel Study of Income Dynamics (PSID), which begins with adults in the 1960s. The somewhat different conclusions of Chetty, et al. (2014) are based on data starting with children born in 1971. The youngest would have been teenagers in the 1980s and adults in the 1990s, a very different period than experienced by children born in the 1940s–1960s.

10. Intergenerational elasticities in Germany are two-thirds as strong as in the United States (Chau 2011), and mobility is much higher for children at the bottom in Sweden, Denmark, Finland, Norway, and the United Kingdom (Duncan 2011; Haskins and Sawhill 2009, 66).

11. For those concerned that more equality would mean a more slowly rising GDP and therefore less total income to be divided, see Chapter 1 of this volume for a review of the evidence.

12. Parental wealth is actually more important than parental income in relative mobility (Smeeding, Erikson, and Jantti 2011), but most research on mobility deals with the effects of income. This is probably due to greater availability of data on income than on wealth.

13. An example is allowing taxpayers to deduct tuition as a strategy to make college affordable; 60 percent of the tax savings went to households with incomes between $100,000 and $160,000. The benefits of many other "middle-class programs," like deductibility of medical expenses and mortgage interest, are even more concentrated at the top. This reflects higher voter turnout and issue awareness at the top of the distribution, as well as increased dependence on campaign contributions (Hacker and Pierson 2010, 150–151).

14. There is a correlation of .72 between teen birth and the state poverty rate, and rates are actually far *higher* in more conservative states, with a correlation of .65 to the share of state residents who say they are "very religious," further calling into question the role of declining moral values. Reduced access to birth control and stronger pro-life values in highly religious states may explain this, according to Charlotte Melander of the Martin Prosperity Institute (Florida and Johnson 2013).

15. While their earnings were often still near subsistence, African Americans who had formerly been slaves now legally "owned" themselves and their children—a major step forward. In the late 1800s and early twentieth century, some blacks were able to save and buy property, but that property was frequently seized on weak pretenses by more powerful whites who coveted it. Others moved

gradually to higher-paying jobs outside the South where discrimination exerted less power over their economic circumstances.

16. DuBois (1903) used this phrase to refer to exceptional black Americans already capable of leadership despite restricted access to schooling and other benefits of middle-class life at the time.

17. Black children born into poverty between 1949 and 1972 were two and a half times more likely to remain poor as adults than white children born in poverty at the same time (Hertz 2005, 165); also Pew (2012, 18–20).

18. "The percentage of black families at the top two rungs of the family income and wealth ladders is so small that median and absolute mobility estimates cannot be calculated with statistical certainty. As a result the absolute mobility and median wealth figures report mobility estimates for blacks only on the bottom three rungs of the ladder" (Pew 2012, 18–20).

19. In contrast, for family wealth, "more than two-thirds (68 percent) of blacks raised in the middle fall to the bottom or second rung as adults, compared with just under a third (30 percent) of whites" (Pew 2012, 18–20).

20. Even if this were possible, the results would not be "apples to apples." Census data differentiates by race or Spanish surname, but it does not allow a separate look at children whose families have long historical roots in the United States relative to those of recent immigrants. Similarly, the native American category may include many individuals who are only one-eighth native American (the legal minimum by Federal standards) and have had little to no contact with reservations or predominantly native American communities. Despite sharing a Census category, their experiences are likely very different.

21. For example, poverty rates in Appalachia would have been 15 to 20 percent in 2009 if family structures had stayed the same over the previous two decades, according to estimates by Ziliak (2012, 10).

22. The percentage was as high as 34 percent in 2000 (Lutz 2008, 177).

23. "At the time, the subsidy for tuition and books was sufficient to cover the charges of traditionally expensive schools like Harvard University or Williams College. Moreover, the monthly stipends were about half the opportunity cost of not working for a single veteran and about 70 percent of the opportunity cost for a married veteran, based on the monthly median income for the population in 1947" (Bound and Turner 2002, 790).

24. When children born in the Unites States move out of poverty, it is typically in smaller steps than progress for children in the United Kingdom (Stiglitz 2012, 19).

25. While tuition charges vary considerably from state to state, over the past twenty years all states have shifted more costs into tuition and provided less from the state budgets (Davis 2000, cited in St. John 2003, 182–183). Taxpayer revolts limited tax increases and the existing budgets shifted more dollars to Medicaid. Between 1989 and 2009, the average state budget almost doubled the share allocated to Medicaid, from 11.5 percent to 20.7 percent (Mumper and Freeman 2011, 47).

26. Only since 2008 have the real values of individual grants equaled what they were in 1976 (Baum, Ma, and Payea 2012, Figure 13a).

27. More information on private direct loans to students is available in the Consumer Financial Protection Bureau reports, listed in the bibliography.

28. Marriage does not necessarily mean stability. Americans marry at higher rates than Swedes, but they also change partners more often. Twelve percent of American children have lived in three or more parental partnerships by age fifteen, compared to 3 percent of Swedish children. Other western European countries have much lower rates of partner changes (Cherlin 2005, 45). Whether inside or outside of formal marriage, more frequent changes of partners lead to more emotional and locational disruption for American children than in many other countries.

29. "Under the new rules, schools had to meet one of three tests, or lose their eligibility for federal student aid: at least 35 percent of graduates had to be repaying their loans; the typical graduate's estimated annual loan payments could not exceed 12 percent of earnings; or the payments could not exceed 30 percent of discretionary income. But in 2012, a federal judge struck down the rules as arbitrary; the rules remain in legal limbo" (Stiglitz 2013).

30. Portions of this section are taken from Greenwood and Holt (2010, Chapter 5).

BIBLIOGRAPHY

Acs, G. 2011. *Downward Mobility from the Middle Class: Waking Up from the American Dream.* Pew Charitable Trusts. www.pewtrusts.org/uploadedFiles/wwwpewtrustsorg/Reports/Economic_Mobility/ Pew_PollProject_Final_SP.pdf.

Baum, S., J. Ma, and K. Payea. 2012. "Trends in Public Higher Education: Enrollment, Prices, Student Aid, Revenues, and Expenditures." *Trends in Higher Education Series*, College Board, May.

Borjas, G.J., J. Grogger, and G.H. Hanson. 2010. "Immigration and the Economic Status of African American Men." *Economica* 77, no. 306: 255–282.

Bound, J., and S. Turner. 2002. "Going to War and Going to College: Did World War II and the G.I. Bill Increase Educational Attainment for Returning Veterans?" *Journal of Labor Economics* 20, no. 4: 784–815.

Bowman, J.L. 1973. *Educational Assistance to Veterans: A Comparative Study of Three G.I. Bills. Final Report.* Princeton, NJ: Educational Testing Service.

Cancian, M., and D. Reed. 2009. "Family Structure, Childbearing, and Parental Employment: Implications for the Level and Trend in Poverty." *Focus* 26, no. 2: 21–26.

Chau, T.W. 2012. "Intergenerational Income Mobility Revisited: Estimation with an Income Dynamic Model with Heterogeneous Age Profile." *Economics Letters* 117, no. 3: 770–773.

Cherlin, A.J. 2005. "American Marriage in the Early Twenty-First Century." *Future of Children* 15, no. 2: 33–55.

Chetty, R., N. Hendren, P. Kline, E. Saez, and N. Turner. 2014. "Is the United States Still a Land of Opportunity? Recent Trends in Intergenerational Mobility." *NBER Working Paper* 19844.

Consumer Financial Protection Bureau. 2012a. Private Student Loans. August 12. http://files.consumerfinance.gov/f/201207_cfpb_Reports_Private-Student-Loans.pdf.

———. 2012b. The Next Front? Student Loan Servicing and the Cost to Our Men and Women in Uniform. October 18. www.consumerfinance.gov/reports/the-next-front-student-loan-servicing-and-the-cost-to-our-men-and-women-in-uniform/.

Corak, M. 2009. *Chasing the Same Dream, Climbing Different Ladders: Economic Mobility in the United States and Canada.* Economic Mobility Project, Pew Charitable Trusts.

———. 2013a. "Income Inequality, Equality of Opportunity, and Intergenerational Mobility." *Journal of Economic Perspectives* 27, no. 3: 79–102.

———. 2013b. "Inequality from Generation to Generation: The United States in Comparison." In *The Economics of Inequality, Poverty, and Discrimination in the 21st Century*, ed. Robert Rycroft. Santa Barbara, CA: ABC-CLIO, LLC.

Currie, J. 2011. "Inequality at Birth: Some Causes and Consequences." *American Economic Review* 101, no. 3: 1–22.

DiPrete, T.A., and G.M. Ehrich. 2006. "Cumulative Advantage as a Mechanism for Inequality: A Review of Theoretical and Empirical Developments." *Annual Review of Sociology* 32: 271–297.

DiTomaso, Nancy. 2013. "How Social Networks Drive Black Unemployment." *New York Times* May 5. http://opinionator.blogs.nytimes.com/2013/05/05/how-social-networks-drive-black-unemployment/?php=true&_type=blogs&_r=0.

DuBois, W.E.B. 1903. "The Talented Tenth." From *The Negro Problem: A Series of Articles by Representative Negroes of To-day.* New York. www.yale.edu/glc/archive/1148.htm.

Duncan, G., and R. Murnane. 2011. "The American Dream, Then and Now." In *Whither Opportunity? Rising Inequality, Schools, and Children's Life Chances*, eds. Greg J. Duncan and Richard J. Murnane. New York: Russell Sage.

Edin, K., and J.M. Reed. 2005. "Why Don't They Just Get Married? Barriers to Marriage Among the Disadvantaged." *Future of Children* 15, no. 2: 117–137.

Federal Reserve Bank. 2013. "Student Loan Debt by Age Group: Data as of Fourth Quarter 2012." March 29. www.newyorkfed.org/studentloandebt/.

Fedorets, A., and A. Spitz-Oener. 2011. "Flexibility and Adaptability of the Employees with a Dual Vocational Training Degree." *Journal for Labour Market Research* 44, nos. 1–2: 127–134.

Ferrie, J.P. 2005. *The End of American Exceptionalism? Mobility in the US Since 1850.* No. w11324. National Bureau of Economic Research.

Florida, R. 2011. "Unions and State Economies: Don't Believe the Hype." *The Atlantic*, March 10. www.theatlantic.com.

Florida, R., and S. Johnson. 2013. "The New Geography of Teen Mothers." *The Atlantic Cities*. May 22. www.theatlantic.com.

Freeman, R. 2007. *America Works: The Exceptional Labor Market.* New York: Russell Sage.

Galbraith, J.K. 1969. *The Affluent Society.* 2nd ed. Boston: Houghton Mifflin.

———. 1997. *The Good Society: The Humane Agenda.* Boston: Houghton Mifflin.

Glaeser, E., J. Scheinkman, and A. Shleifer. 2003. "The Injustice of Inequality." *Journal of Monetary Economics* 50, no. 1: 199–222.

Greenstone, M., A. Looney, J. Patashnik, and M. Yu. 2013. "Thirteen Economic Facts About Social Mobility and the Role of Education." Policy Memo. The Hamilton Project. www.hamiltonproject.org/files/downloads_and_links/THP_13EconFacts_FINAL.pdf.

Greenwood, D.T. 1997. "New Developments in the Intergenerational Impact of Education." *International Journal of Educational Research* 27, no. 6: 503–511.

Greenwood, D.T., and R.P.F. Holt. 2010. *Local Economic Development in the 21st Century: Quality of Life and Sustainability.* Armonk, NY: M.E. Sharpe.

Hacker, J.S., and P. Pierson. 2010. *Winner-Take-All Politics: How Washington Made the Rich Richer and Turned Its Back on the Middle Class.* New York: Simon & Schuster.

Harding, D., C. Jencks, L. Lopoo, and S. Mayer. 2005. "The Changing Effect of Family Background on the Incomes of American Adults." In *Unequal Chances: Family Background and Economic Success*, ed. S. Bowles, H. Gintis, and M. Groves, 100–144. Princeton, NJ: Princeton University Press.

Harrington, M. 1997 [1967]. *The Other America.* New York: Scribner.

Haskins, R., and I. Sawhill. 2009. *Creating an Opportunity Society.* Washington, DC: Brookings Institution Press.

Hauser, Robert, and David Featherman. 1976. "Equality of Schooling: Trends and Prospects." *Sociology of Education* 49: 99–120.

Haveman, R.H., and T.M. Smeeding. 2006. "The Role of Higher Education in Social Mobility." *Future of Children* 16, no. 2: 125–150.

Heller, D.E. 2011. "Trends in the Affordability of Public Colleges and Universities." In *The States and Public Higher Education Policy: Affordability, Access, and Accountability*, 2nd ed., ed. D.E. Heller, 11–38. Baltimore: Johns Hopkins University Press.

Hertz, T. 2005. "Rags, Riches and Race: The Intergenerational Mobility of Black and White Families in the United States." In *Unequal Chances: Family Background and Success*, ed. S. Bowles, H. Gintis, and M. Groves, 165–191. Princeton, NJ: Princeton University Press.

Hoff, K., and A. Sen. 2005. "Homeownership, Community Interactions, and Segregation." *American Economic Review* 95, no. 4: 1167–1189.

Johnson, A., T. Van Osten, and A. White. 2012. "The Student Debt Crisis." Center for American Progress, available at www.americanprogress.org.

Katz, L.F., and K.M. Murphy. 1992. "Changes in Relative Wages, 1963–87: Supply and Demand Factors." *Quarterly Journal of Economics* 107, no. 1: 35–78.

Kearney, M.S., and P.B. Levine. 2009. "Subsidized Contraception, Fertility, and Sexual Behavior." *The Review of Economics and Statistics* 91, no. 1: 137–151.

———. 2012. "Why Are Teen Birth Rates So High in the U.S. and Why Does It Matter?" *Journal of Economic Perspectives* 26, no. 2: 141–163.

Khadaroo, S.T. "Disabled Americans: Jobless Rate Still High 22 Years After Landmark Law." *Christian Science Monitor*, June 17, 2013. www.csmonitor.com/USA/2012/0726/Disabled-Americans-Jobless-rate-still-high-22-years-after-landmark-law.

Krueger, A.B. 2012. *The Rise and Consequences of Inequality in the United States.* Report to Council of Economic Advisers, January 12. www.whitehouse.gov/sites/default/files/krueger_cap_speech_final_remarks.pdf.

Lee, C.I., and G. Solon. 2009. "Trends in Intergenerational Income Mobility." *Review of Economics and Statistics* 91, no. 4: 766–772.

Leonhardt, D. 2013. "In Climbing Income Ladder, Location Matters." *New York Times*, July 22. www.nytimes.com/2013/07/22/business/in-climbing-income-ladder-location-matters.html?hp&_r=0.

Lerman, R.I. 2008. "Are Skills the Problem? Reforming the Education and Training Systems in the United States." In *A Future of Good Jobs? America's Challenge in the Global Economy*, ed. T. Bartik and S.N. Houseman, 17–80. Kalamazoo, MI: Upjohn Institute for Employment Research.

Levine, Phillip, and Melissa Kearney. 2013. "Forget Plan B: To Fight Teen Pregnancy, Focus on Economic Opportunity." www.theatlantic.com.

Levine, D., and B. Mazumder 2007. "The Growing Importance of Family: Evidence from Brothers' Earnings." Industrial Relations 46, 1: 7–21.

Lutz, A. 2008. "Who Joins the Military? A Look at Race, Class, and Immigration Status." *Journal of Political and Military Sociology* 36, no. 2: 167–188.

Mariani, M. 1999. "High-Earning Workers Who Don't Have a Bachelor's Degree." *Occupational Outlook Quarterly* 43, no. 3: 9–15.

Massey, D.S., and M.J. Fischer. 2003. "The Geography of Inequality in the United States, 1950–2000." *Brooking-Wharton Papers on Urban Affairs*, 1–40.

Mayer, S.E., and L.M. Lopoo. 2004. "The Effect of Maternal Employment on Teenage Childbearing." *Journal of Population Economics* 17, no. 4: 681–702.

———. 2005. "Has the Intergenerational Transmission of Economic Status Changed?" *Journal of Human Resources* 40, no. 1: 169–185.

———. 2008. "Government Spending and Intergenerational Mobility." *Journal of Public Economics* 92, nos. 1–2: 139–158.

Mazumder, B. 2005. "The Apple Falls Even Closer Than We Thought: New and Revised Estimates of the Intergenerational Inheritance of Earnings." In *Unequal Chances: Family Background and Economic Success*, ed. S. Bowles, H. Gintis, and M. Groves, 80–99. New York: Russell Sage.

Morrison, D.R., and A. Ritualo. 2013. "Routes to Children's Economic Recovery After Divorce: Are Cohabitation and Remarriage Equivalent?" *American Sociological Review* 65, no. 4: 560–580.

Mumper, M., and M.L. Freeman. 2005. "The Causes and Consequences of Public College Tuition Inflation." In *Higher Education: Handbook of Theory and Research*, 307–361. Netherlands: Springer.

Nussbaum, M.C. 2011. *Creating Capabilities: The Human Development Approach.* Cambridge, MA: Harvard University.

OECD. 2011. Education at a Glance: OECD Indicators. www.oecd.org/dataoecd/61/2/48631582.pdf.

Pantuosco, L., D. Parker, and G. Stone. 2001. "The Effect of Unions on Labor Markets and Economic Growth: An Analysis of State Data." *Journal of Labor Research* 22, no. 1: 195–205.

Pew Charitable Trust. State and Consumer Initiatives, Economic Mobility Project. Overview. www.pewstates.org/projects/economic-mobility-project-328061.

Pew Charitable Trust. 2008. *Inside the Middle Class: Bad Times Hit the Good Life.* www.pewsocialtrends.org/2008/04/09/inside-the-middle-class-bad-times-hit-the-good-life. April.

———. 2011a. *Economic Mobility and the American Dream: Where Do We Stand in the Wake of the Great Recession?* July.

———. 2011b. *Does American Promote Ability as Well as Other Nations?* November.

———. 2012. *Pursuing the American Dream: Economic Mobility Across Generations.* July.

Pressman, S., and R. Scott. 2014. "Reducing Child Poverty in America: The Effects of a Paid Parental Leave Policy." In *A Brighter Future: Improving the Standard of Living Now and for the Next Generation*, ed. R.P.F. Holt and D.T. Greenwood, 165–186. Armonk, NY: M.E. Sharpe.

Raphael, S. 2008. "Boosting the Earnings and Employment of Low-Skilled Workers in the United States: Making Work Pay and Removing Barriers to Employment and Social Mobility." In *A Future of Good Jobs? America's Challenge in the Global Economy*, ed. T. Bartik and S.N. Houseman, 245–304. Kalamazoo, MI: Upjohn Institute for Employment Research.

Reardon, S.F., and K. Bischoff. 2011. "Income Inequality and Income Segregation." *American Journal of Sociology* 116, no. 4: 1092–1153.

Sawhill, I., and J.E. Morton. 2007. "Economic Mobility: Is the American Dream Alive and Well?" Washington, DC: Pew Charitable Trusts, Economic Mobility Project. www.brookings.edu/views/papers/sawhill/200705.pdf.

Segal, D.R., and M.W. Segal. 2004. *America's Military Population* 59, no. 4. Washington, DC: Population Reference Bureau.

Sen, A. 1999. *Development as Freedom*. New York: Alfred A. Knopf.

Sider, H., and C. Cole. 1984. "Changing Composition of the Military and the Effect on Labor Force Data." *Monthly Labor Review* 107: 10.

Smeeding, T.M., R. Erikson, and M. Jantii, eds. 2011. *Persistence, Privilege, and Parenting: The Comparative Study of Intergenerational Mobility*. New York: Russell Sage.

Solon, G.R. 1992. "Intergenerational Income Mobility in the United States." *American Economic Review* 82, no. 3 (June): 398–408.

———. 2004. "A Model of Intergenerational Mobility Variation over Time and Place." In *Generational Income Mobility in North America and Europe*, ed. M. Corak, 38–47. Cambridge, UK: Cambridge University Press.

St. John. E. P. 2003. *Refinancing the College Dream: Access, Equal Opportunity, and Justice for Tax Payers*. Baltimore: Johns Hopkins University Press.

Stiglitz, J.E. 2000. "Reflections on Mobility and Social Justice, Economic Efficiency, and Individual Responsibility." In *New Markets, New Opportunities*, ed. N. Birdsall and C. Graham, 36–65. Washington, DC: Brookings Institution Press.

———. 2012. *The Price of Inequality*. New York: W.W. Norton.

———. 2013. "Student Debt and the Crushing of the American Dream." *New York Times*, May 12. http://opinionator.blogs.nytimes.com/2013/05/12/student-debt-and-the-crushing-of-the-american-dream/?ref=josephestiglitz.

Swanstrom, T., P. Dreier, C. Casey, and R. Flack. 2006. "Pulling Apart: Economic Segregation in Suburbs and Central Cities in Major Metropolitan Areas, 1980–2000." In *Redefining Urban and Suburban America: Evidence from Census 2000*, vol. 2, ed. A. Berube, B. Katz, and R. Lang, 143–166. Washington, DC: Brookings Institution Press.

Tomer, J. 2014. "Improving the Standard of Living Through Investments in Intangible Capital." In *A Brighter Future: Improving the Standard of Living Now and for the Next Generation*, ed. R.P.F. Holt and D.T. Greenwood, 229–247. Armonk, NY: M.E. Sharpe.

United States Senate, Committee on Health, Education, Labor and Pensions. 2012. *For Profit Education: The Failure to Safeguard the Federal Investment and Ensure Student Success*.

Waldfogel, J. 2007. "Work-Family Policies." In *Reshaping the American Workforce in a Changing Economy*, ed. H.J. Holzer and D.S. Nightingale, 273–292. Washington, DC: Urban Institute Press.

Waldfogel, J., and E. Washbrook. 2011. "Income-Related Gaps in School Readiness in the United States and the United Kingdom." In *Persistence, Privilege, and Parenting: The Comparative Study of Intergenerational Mobility*, ed. T. Smeeding, R. Erikson, and M. Jantti, 175–207. New York: Russell Sage.

Wolff, E.N. 2006. *Does Education Really Help? Skill, Work and Inequality*. Oxford: Oxford University Press.

———. 2013. "The Asset Price Meltdown, Rising Leverage, and the Wealth of the Middle Class." *Journal of Economic Issues* 2: 333–342.

Woolhouse, M. 2013. "Wealth Gap Limits Equality of Education." *Boston Globe*, July 5. www.bostonglobe.com/business/2013/07/04/inequality-among-students-rises/AuUbN6qkLDb684uiUysqFP/story.html.

Ziliak, J. 2012. *Appalachian Legacy: Economic Opportunity After the War on Poverty*. Washington, DC: Brookings Institution Press.

8

Reducing Child Poverty in America

The Effects of a Paid Parental Leave Policy

STEVEN PRESSMAN AND *ROBERT H. SCOTT III*

Over several decades, substantial economic growth has failed to improve the standard of living for those near the bottom of the income distribution. In addition, economic growth has failed to generate policies that provide aid to families with children. Since the 1970s, child poverty rates in the United States have consistently been much higher than the poverty rates for other age groups. Child poverty in the United States has also been much higher than child poverty in other developed countries. In this regard, the United States remains far behind the rest of the world. Our focus here will be on one policy that can do much to help such families and especially their children—paid parental leave.

Paid parental leave has two important consequences that lead to improved living standards. First, it supplements the income of families who have reduced earnings capacity due to the birth of a child. Second, it enables parents to spend more time with their very young children, improving both parental well-being and the quality of life of their children. These benefits have further consequences for national living standards through reduced crime, less violence, and greater social mobility (see Duncan and Magnuson 2013; Heckman 2011).

This chapter begins with a review of the long-term consequences of child poverty for workforce development, public health, social equity and stability, and other socioeconomic factors. It next demonstrates that official US poverty measures underestimate the problem by ignoring how many children are in families that are "debt-poor." We then discuss paid parental leave programs and their many benefits. Finally, we address the costs of adopting a paid parental leave policy in the United States and conclude that it can be both affordable and effective in reducing poverty rates among very young children.

THE CONSEQUENCES OF CHILD POVERTY: TODAY AND IN THE FUTURE

Child poverty has many negative consequences. Many of these are both large and long-term, affecting future sustainability of the standard of living in addition to reducing it today. These costs have been documented extensively over the past twenty years. In the early 1990s, economist Robert Solow calculated the many economic losses associated with child poverty and estimated the total cost at 3 percent of gross domestic product (GDP) (CDF 1994, xix). Even without including future costs of greater unemployment and health problems, Solow found the annual current cost of child poverty to be about 1.5 percent of GDP. Two decades later, both child poverty and health-care costs have risen. The Center for American Progress, a Washington, DC, think tank, estimated costs of child poverty at $500 billion per year, or nearly 4 percent of GDP (Holzer et al. 2007). This includes the effects of lower productivity (and hence income), as well as higher crime rates and health expenditures. Each of these factors contributed about one-third to the overall cost.

The negative income tax experiments provide another way to estimate the overall cost of child poverty (see Munnell 1986; O'Connor 2001). These were a set of controlled experiments conducted during the 1970s. Households were randomly divided into two matched groups. One received a guaranteed minimum income; the other did not. This study then measured the effects of providing an income floor. Besides looking at the immediate effects on work, marriage, and other social factors in a household, the study also looked at long-run consequences such as the income levels of children as adults. On average, each year spent in poverty as a child reduced expected lifetime earnings by nearly $6,800 in the 1970s. In today's dollars (2013), the loss comes to $33,000. With 15 million poor children in the United States, one year of child poverty costs $400 billion, or nearly 3 percent of current GDP. This estimate includes the costs of future unemployment (which is reflected in the earnings figures), but not the additional health-care costs due to child poverty. Using the Center for American Progress figure on additional health expenditures, child poverty cost a little more than 4 percent of GDP in the United States (Holzer et al. 2007). When you add in the increased costs of higher crime rates as a result of poverty, the total cost exceeds 5 percent of GDP.

There are also important costs of child poverty that go beyond lost GDP or lost income. These involve the impact of poverty on child development and its relationship to long-term social and economic sustainability. The first attempt to measure these consequences of growing up in poverty was undertaken by John Spargo (1907) in the early twentieth century. Much subsequent work has been done using better data and controlling for the many intervening factors that affect the consequences of growing up poor. This work falls into an examination of three somewhat overlapping categories: (1) the educational and intellectual development of the child; (2) current and future health problems of the child; and (3) the social and psychological development of the child.

EDUCATION AND INTELLECTUAL DEVELOPMENT

Educational attainment is important not only because of its relationship to a child's future earnings but because of its impact on civic participation, health status, participation in criminal activity, and other elements of what Greenwood and Holt (see Chapter 1 in this volume) have described as nonmarket aspects of the standard of living. Income rises sharply with years of schooling, and intellectual development impacts future earnings. If growing up poor keeps children from completing school and/or impairs their cognitive ability or mental functioning, it will have long-run negative consequences. Several researchers (see Duncan and Magnuson 2013; Heckman 2011) have sought to estimate the magnitude of these effects. For example, children in low-income households are less likely to attend school, do less well in school, and are less likely to continue their education than nonpoor children (Birch and Gusson 1970; Heckman 2006).

Studies using data from the negative income tax experiments have concluded that school attendance was higher for children from low-income households that received guaranteed incomes (Manheim and Minchilla 1978; McDonald and Stephenson 1979). Since school attendance is correlated with success in school, it is reasonable to infer that school performance also improves with higher income. This conclusion is supported by other studies (see Duncan and Magnuson 2013; Heckman 2006). Poor children are twice as likely as nonpoor children to repeat a grade (29 percent vs. 14 percent), twice as likely to be suspended or expelled from school (12 percent vs. 6 percent), and twice as likely to be high school dropouts (21 percent vs. 10 percent) (CDF 1994).

Using longitudinal data and controlling for variables such as parental education and neighborhood characteristics, several studies have found that growing up in poverty has a small, yet statistically significant effect on high school graduation rates and the years of schooling completed (Haveman and Wolfe 1994, 1995; Teachman et al. 1997). A US Department of Education study found that each year spent in poverty increases by 2 percent the likelihood that a child will not progress in school (Haveman et al. 1991).

One important conclusion from this work is that the time spent in poverty matters, as does the age of the child. Children who are poor for several years do much worse than the transient poor in terms of years of schooling completed and high school graduation rates. Deeper poverty and longer bouts of poverty are also more harmful to the development of cognitive abilities. Smith, Brooks-Gunn, and Klebanov (1997) found that children in families whose incomes were less than half the poverty line scored six to thirteen points less on standardized tests than children in families with incomes between one and a half to two times the poverty line. Children in families with incomes falling between half the poverty line and the poverty line also did worse than these nonpoor children in families with incomes up to twice the poverty line. In addition, Smith, Brooks-Gunn, and Klebanov (1997) found that children in persistently poor families (experiencing four to five years of poverty) scored nine points lower on standardized tests than children who never experienced poverty; transient poor children scored four points lower than never-poor children.

Duncan et al. (1998) found that the age of the child was important in determining the effect of poverty on educational achievement. Childhood poverty is more important than adolescent poverty, and early childhood poverty appears more important than later childhood poverty (see also Baydar, Brooks-Gunn, and Furstenberg 1993). This is why we focus on poverty for very young children and paid parental leave, a policy that mainly benefits families with very young children.

CURRENT AND FUTURE HEALTH PROBLEMS

Health is one of the most important determinants of one's standard of living. Health problems can begin even before birth, due to inadequate prenatal care or the lack of adequate nutrition in poor mothers. Problems continue after birth due to poor nutrition, lack of a decent living environment, and lack of immunizations and proper infant care (Monheit and Cunningham 1992). As found in studies on the impact of growing up poor on education, persistent poverty seems to lead to greater health problems, as does poverty for very young children (Korenman and Miller 1997). Poor children experience more asthma, more anemia, more ear infections, and more hearing loss (Klerman 1991b, 3). These conditions are known to lead to lower IQ scores and to generate greater learning disabilities (Goldstein 1990).

It is well established that poor women are more likely to give birth to premature babies, to babies with low birth weight, and to babies who die in the first year of life (Klerman 1991a). Taking just one example, Binsacca et al. (1987) found that California women experiencing financial problems during pregnancy were nearly six times more likely to have a low-birth-weight child than other women, even after controlling for other variables. Low birth weight has many negative consequences that extend far into the future, including a greater probability of grade failure, lower achievement in school, and more behavior problems (Klebanov, Brooks-Gunn, and Duncan 1994).

The Children's Defense Fund (1994, 14f.) reports that poor children ages one to five were less likely to receive the recommended daily dietary allowance of twelve nutrients. Particularly important, they were more than three times more likely than their nonpoor counterparts to have low levels of iron. Low iron levels have been shown to reduce the ability of children to concentrate and to solve problems and are associated with a long-term reduction in IQ scores.

Poor children are also likely to show up at school hungry, which will adversely affect learning. These children do worse in school because they are less able to concentrate (Birch and Gusson 1970). Malnutrition has been shown to lead to lower brain size (given body weight) among children (Frost and Payne 1970) and may be why poor children stand a greater chance of becoming mentally retarded than children who do not grow up poor (Hurley 1969). Inadequate food intake causes the body to conserve energy. First, cognitive and social activities get limited—children do not play or learn. Then, the body limits the energy needed for growth. Stunted growth (falling below the fifth percentile of height for age) occurs in poor children at twice the rate as nonpoor children (Lewit and Kerrebrock 1997).

The US food stamp program (recently renamed SNAP), which began in 1961, attempts to deal with this problem. By most estimates, SNAP has reduced food insecurity for families (Bhattacharya, Currie, and Haider 2002). However, it has not eliminated the problem because the benefits are small compared to household needs: only 69 percent of eligible recipients enroll in the program. One reason is the cost of enrolling and reenrolling in the program. Another reason is that many people are not aware that they are eligible for the program and so do not apply (Currie 2003).

Growing up poor also means greater exposure to environmental hazards, a nonmarket quality-of-life factor that has negative impacts beyond those of low income.

Exposure to lead during pregnancy or in early years of life has a strong impact on children, leading to a greater probability of neurological problems and a lower IQ. Lead can enter the bloodstream in many ways—through the air, water pipes, exhaust fumes, toys, jewelry, or lead dust from the workplace brought into the home via clothing. Poor children are much more likely to be exposed to lead. For children aged six months through five years, lead concentration in the bloodstream was negatively and strongly associated with family income (Mahaffey et al. 1982; Niles and Peck 2008).

All these problems are exacerbated by the inadequate health care received by the poor. Some of this is due to the lack of services available to low-income households. Medicaid, which was enacted in 1964 to provide medical care for the poor, does not cover dental care, glasses, or hearing aids. Poor children are less likely to receive such needed services than nonpoor children. Another problem is that, as with food stamps, not all eligible families avail themselves of Medicaid benefits. Selden, Banthin, and Cohen (1998) estimate that 5 million children, nearly half of those without health care benefits, are eligible for Medicaid but have not been signed up by their parents.

SOCIAL AND PSYCHOLOGICAL DEVELOPMENT

An extensive literature has also documented the negative effects of poverty on mental health (Dougherty et al. 1987; Gould, Wunsch-Hitzig, and Duhrenwend 1981), especially if the poverty is persistent (Makosky 1982). Child poverty contributes to low self-esteem and a greater incidence of depression (Bolder et al. 1995; McLeod and Shanahan 1993). Some of this stems directly from growing up poor, some is the result of hunger and malnutrition (Weinreb et al. 2002), and some comes from the stress that poverty puts on parents and how this affects their relationship with their children (Hanson, McClanahan, and Thomson 1997; McLoyd and Wilson 1991).

Mothers in poor households report that their children have more behavioral problems than mothers from nonpoor households. These problems include greater moodiness, more tantrums, greater anxiety, and increased aggression (Smith, Brooks-Gunn, and Klebanov 1997). Examining an experimental welfare program in Minnesota, Morris and Gennetian (2004) found that increased income improves the engagement of children in school as well as their behavior.

Child poverty also leads to increased rates of juvenile delinquency (Berrueta-Clement et al. 1984) and to greater chances that an individual will engage in criminal activity (Holzer et al. 2007). This may be related to several studies that show a link between child poverty and a greater likelihood of risky behavior such as early sexual activity (Afxentiou and Hawley 1997) and a greater probability of teenage out-of-wedlock births (Hogan and Kitagawa 1985; Klerman 1991a).

UNDERMEASUREMENT OF CHILD POVERTY: INCLUDING DEBT-POOR FAMILIES

As mentioned earlier, child poverty has been a serious problem in the United States for many decades, averaging about 20 percent since the late 1970s. Unfortunately, traditional measures of child poverty fail to address two significant issues. First, the official US government child poverty estimates are not broken down by age. Yet a substantial literature makes it clear that very young children (from birth to two years old) have a greater incidence of poverty than older children. Second, because families with very young children are more likely to earn low wages, have less stable employment, and experience household start-up costs such as the first purchase of durable goods, they are also more likely to accumulate revolving consumer debt. Many child-rearing costs are new to families with young children: day care, high medical expenses, and greater housing costs for a larger family. Many growing families need two earners to meet their financial expenses, and that means day-care costs. If a family with a new baby instead sacrifices one paying job (sometimes for many months or years) to have and care for a child, that also reduces income. Either way, these families often deal with the financial stresses by accumulating debt.

High consumer debt has a long-run negative financial impact on families and makes them more vulnerable to other income shocks (job loss, illness, and unexpected costs) as well as to family breakup (Kelso 1994). Also, financial problems are an impetus for many divorces, and divorce is one reason that many children grow up in poor families since poverty rates are much higher for female-headed, single-parent families (Amato 2000).

Our focus here, however, is on income. Consumer debt means accumulating interest burdens—potentially affecting a family's balance sheet for many years. As a result, many families have incomes above their respective poverty thresholds, but because of interest payments on their consumer debt (payments that do not pay off the principal), their available incomes should classify them as poor. Our earlier work (Pressman and Scott 2009a, 2009b) defines people in this situation as "debt-poor."

When calculating whether someone is debt-poor, we only count consumer debt. This includes mostly credit cards, installment loans, motor vehicle loans, medical debt, and student loans. Because a home is in part an investment, loans associated with housing are not factored into our estimates (unless rent is put on a credit card and does not get repaid immediately). We sum each person's consumer debt and then find the interest rates on that debt in order to compute how much the person is paying in interest. Then we factor out any portion of each interest payment that goes toward repaying principal since we are only interested in the amount of money people pay to maintain their debt. Finally, we subtract interest payments on past consumer debt from their income and compare this modified income to their respective poverty threshold to see if they are now poor.

POOR AND DEBT-POOR CHILDREN

The following estimates rely on the Federal Reserve Board's (2009) "Survey of Consumer Finances" datasets. These data include detailed financial information on roughly 4,500 randomly selected American household units. The information is collected triennially. To measure the number of debt-poor children from birth to two years old, we use two methods. The first follows the official US government calculations developed by Mollie Orshansky in the 1960s. This approach uses family size to determine poverty thresholds. Our estimates include (1) one head of household with one child, two children, three children, four children; and (2) two heads of household with one, two, three, four, and five children. This approach covers more than 95 percent of all families with children two years old and younger in each sample. We use the Orshansky poverty thresholds for each family type to find the number of poor young children. The percentage of poor young children is shown in the second data column of Table 8.1. Then we subtracted interest payments on consumer debt from annual household income. If this number falls below the household poverty threshold, the household and its young children are counted as debt-poor. Column 3 of Table 8.1 shows the percentage of debt-poor young children.

The second method we use to calculate the poverty rate of young children relies on a relative measure of poverty. In this case, incomes are adjusted for household size to take account of the fact that two people can live more cheaply than one, three can live more cheaply than two, and so on. So, as with the Orshansky definition, families of different sizes have different income needs and different poverty lines. We adjust for family size using the original Organisation for Economic Co-operation and Development (OECD) recommendations for adjusting income by household size because they best track the Orshansky poverty lines used in the official US government definition of poverty.[1] Once we identify poor households, it is a simple matter to calculate the number of poor children and the percentage of children that are poor. Column 4 presents the poverty rate for young children using the relative income method, and column 5 is the poverty rate of young children plus those young children who are debt-poor.

According to our estimates, interest on consumer debt added 1.5 percentage points to the government's official poverty metric in 2007 for children two years old and younger. Expressed another way, more than 100,000 young children that year were debt-poor—that is, not counted as poor, but because of interest payments on consumer debt, their incomes fell below their respective poverty thresholds. Using the relative method, in 2007 we estimate that 7.6 percent of young children were debt-poor, which equals more than 500,000 young children in the United States. Using either the Orshansky method or the relative income method underestimates young children in poverty. The problem is the interest that households pay on past consumer debt. This reduces the income available to support living standards in the current year. It should be clear from Table 8.1 that over time families with young children have increasingly relied on consumer debt in order to maintain their living standards. Many more young children are becoming debt-poor; their standard of living has declined even though their measured income level may have increased.

Child poverty rates are high in the United States because poverty rates among young families are high, particularly for single heads of household. Not all parents are working, even under Temporary Assistance for Needy Families (TANF), and some work part-time or part-year. Our focus in this chapter is on just one of many reasons for high child poverty rates in the United States—the lack of paid parental leave for parents who *are* working. This policy would be a long-term investment in children that would help to improve and sustain the standard of living now and in the future. It allows parents to spend more time with their children and promotes the parental bonding that enables their children to become better functioning adults as well as

Table 8.1 **Poverty Rates for Young Children** (0–2 years old; in percent)

SCF surveys	Child poverty rate	Poverty rate for young children	Poverty rate for young children including debt-poor	Relative method poverty rate for young children	Relative method poverty rate for young children including debt-poor
1989	19.6	20.0	20.6	26.1	27.0
1992	22.3	21.5	22.2	29.8	31.7
1995	20.8	18.8	19.3	30.7	33.2
1998	18.9	20.1	20.5	24.0	29.2
2001	16.3	17.5	18.8	26.3	29.8
2004	17.8	18.6	20.0	27.5	37.5
2007	18.0	18.4	19.9	30.2	37.8

Sources: Federal Reserve Board of Governors (2009), "Survey of Consumer Finances," weighted data.
Note: Households' incomes in the "Survey of Consumer Finances" are based on the year prior to when the data were collected.

relieving financial pressures on young parents. Parental attention in the early years of life is essentially an investment in human capital that leads to greater well-being in the future as well as greater income (Heckman 2000). Following a discussion of the policy, we present several options for fully funding this program.

HELP FOR THE WORKING POOR AND THEIR INFANTS: PAID PARENTAL LEAVE

The following question originally appeared in the *Wall Street Journal* on June 23, 2010: "What do the countries of Lesotho, Papua New Guinea, Swaziland, and the United States have in common?" The answer is that these are the only countries in the world with no policy of paid parental leave.[2]

Giving birth involves significant costs. There are the obvious medical expenses, such as seeing a doctor during pregnancy and going to a hospital to give birth. Some, but not all, of these expenses may be covered by insurance. There is another person (or more than one) to feed, clothe, shelter, and educate. Given a fixed income, this increase in family size reduces the standard of living of the family and increases the probability that the family will be poor.

There are also large opportunity costs. Working women stand to lose many weeks of work and a good deal of income if they take off from work because of pregnancy, birth (or adoption), and caring for newborns and very young children. Plus, they risk losing their job, as well as possibilities for promotion and higher pay. If they do return to work after giving birth, child-care arrangements must be made. To compensate families for the costs of raising the next generation of citizens, most developed countries have put into place two policies—birth grants and paid parental leave.

Birth grants (or baby bonuses) are fixed payments made to families when a child is born or adopted. Most countries provide these grants as cash payments; however, some nations provide an in-kind benefit package that includes such things as diapers, lotions, and pacifiers. Today, about half of the OECD nations provide birth grants to new parents. Generally, birth grants do not involve a great deal of money. Finland provides €140 ($200) per child or a slightly more generous package of goods. However, in some nations the payments are more substantial. Italy pays new parents €1,357.80 ($1,947) spread over a period of five months. For the median Italian household with children, birth bonuses provide more than 5 percent of their annual disposable income.[3]

Paid parental leave is the more important policy that aids families with newborn children. This policy developed as a means to replace lost wages around the time of birth or adoption. The money received from paid leave makes it easier for mothers *and fathers* to take time off from paid employment in order to care for a new child with less income loss. It also helps new parents seeking to balance the demands of work and the demands of being a new parent. Not until the latter part of the twentieth century did middle-class female labor force participation become the norm rather than the exception. Some reasons for this are economic in nature—the extra income helped families survive and maintain their usual standard of living. In the United States, the percentage of mothers with children working in the paid labor force increased sharply from 17 percent in 1948 to 40 percent in the early 1970s and then to 70 percent in the 1990s. Even many women with infants are working. At the start of the twenty-first century, the labor force participation rate for married women with infants whose husbands' earnings are in the middle three income quintiles was 64 percent (Cohany and Suk 2007). For 2004, using the Luxembourg Income Study (LIS) database and adjusted household incomes, we computed similar figures for the middle income quintiles. But for the lowest quintile, only 40.7 percent of married women with young children were in the labor force (either working or looking for employment). While the LIS data showed female labor force participation increasing for the middle income quintiles over time, for the bottom quintile female labor force participation has remained at about 40 percent since the late 1970s.

Female labor force participation is complicated by the birth of a child. For health reasons, many women need to take some time off from work before they give birth. Studies have consistently shown that when women return to work shortly after giving birth, their health is adversely affected; they suffer from increased fatigue, depression, and anxiety (Hock and DeMeis 1990; Hyde et al. 1995). While paid leave was originally thought of as a way to aid mothers who might damage their health by working immediately before and after giving birth, concern has shifted from the mother's health to the well-being of the child.

A rather large scholarly literature has demonstrated that maternal employment in the first year following birth has at least four negative consequences for a newborn child.

First, maternal employment can cause increased stress to the child, and high stress levels in children have been linked to slower learning, reduced attention, and worse motor skills (Boyce 1985). Second, maternal employment has been linked to behavior problems in children at age four and to lower scores on language and cognitive skills tests, possibly because it harms the social bonding or attachments between mother and child (Belsky and Eggebeen 1991). Third, working parents are unable to provide their very young children with the amount of nurturing, oversight, and bonding that their children need (Brooks-Gunn, Hun, and Waldfogel 2002; Waldfogel, Han, and

Brooks-Gunn 2002). Finally, health-care providers strongly recommend that infants be breast-fed because of the health benefits to children, but working mothers are much less likely to breast-feed their children if they start working soon after giving birth—mostly because few companies allow time and space for mothers to breast-feed (Blau, Guilkey, and Popkin 1996; Roe et al. 1999; Ryan and Martinez 1989).

Historically, Germany was at the forefront of the movement for paid parental leave. It began a policy of three weeks *un*paid leave after the birth of a child in 1878 in order to protect the mother and the child (Erler 2009, 121). The German Imperial Industrial Code of 1891 set maximum work hours for new mothers and prohibited the employment of women within four weeks of childbirth. Amendments in 1903 and 1911 increased the leave period to six weeks and also required *paid* time off two weeks before expected delivery (Frank and Lipner 1988). France soon followed the lead of Germany. In 1913 it gave low-income mothers a benefit of four weeks prior to and four weeks after giving birth on the condition that the child be breast-fed (Fagnani and Math 2009).

Parental leave programs in Western Europe started expanding in the 1970s, although (beginning in the mid-1990s) the trend is one of large increases in the Nordic countries, Belgium, and Germany and small declines in the Netherlands and Italy (Ruhm 1998). In June 2000, the International Labour Organisation recommended that companies offer paid maternity leave of fourteen weeks, including six weeks after the birth of a child, and that the replacement rate be at least two-thirds of previous earnings plus health benefits.

Most developed nations have followed these recommendations. However, provisions vary from nation to nation in terms of the amount of paid leave and the extent to which the payments replace lost wages. In more than half of the OECD nations, the benefit replaces between 70 and 100 percent of the prior wage, up to some maximum (Kamerman 2000). The United Kingdom provides six weeks of benefits at 90 percent of previous wages and another twelve weeks of parental leave at a low flat rate. Canada provides new parents twenty-five weeks of paid leave, at about 55 percent of previous wages up to a maximum possible payment. Slightly more generous is Denmark, which provides twenty-eight weeks of paid leave at 60 percent of previous wages, and Finland, which provides forty-four weeks of leave at about 70 percent of previous wages. Even more generous are Norway and Sweden, which provide an entire year of leave at 80 percent of previous wages (Kamerman 2000).

For workers to qualify for paid parental leave, most countries require some prior work history and make benefits contingent on the length of time employed. The money to pay for these benefits usually comes from both the government and the employer, although several countries also require workers to make contributions.

THE COSTS OF EXISTING PARENTAL LEAVE PROGRAMS

Of course, the cost of any paid parental leave program depends on the generosity of the benefits provided—the fraction of previous wages that get replaced, the maximum possible benefit, and the length of time during which people are eligible for benefits. In most developed nations, the cost of parental leave programs is relatively small, less than 1 percent of GDP. The main exception is Sweden, where paid parental leave approaches 2 percent of GDP (Coré and Koutsogeorgopoulou 1995)—mainly due to the long time period (one year) that young parents are eligible for paid leave.

Part of the reason this program costs so little is that only women with very young children are eligible for these benefits. A second reason is that not all women with very young children are eligible for paid leave. Women without recent employment histories and women earning high salaries are generally not entitled to paid leave. Furthermore, it is easier for women in high-paying jobs to afford child care, so they are more likely to return to work as soon as possible. Besides the income loss (even with child-care expenses), many women believe that taking time off will hurt their careers and future incomes.

Despite the relatively small overall cost, the benefits of paid parental leave are rather extensive, as we detail below. This is why virtually every country in the world has adopted a policy of paid parental leave. Australia only recently joined the club. Following more than eleven years of rule by the conservative Liberal and National Parties, the Australian Labour Party returned to power in 2007. Its electoral success stemmed in large part from emphasizing the needs of working families as well as the importance of early childhood education and child-care services. Labour Party candidates campaigned on a promise to make paid leave available to all mothers, without imposing costs on businesses. After assuming office, the new Labour government asked the national Productivity Commission[4] to examine several possible programs and identify their costs and benefits. The commission recommended eighteen weeks of paid leave at the Australian minimum wage to be funded by general government revenues; alternatively, parents could receive the existing $5,000 birth bonus. On Mother's Day (May 11) in 2009, Australia announced a policy of paid maternity leave, to begin January 1, 2011. Primary caregivers are eligible for eighteen weeks of benefits if they worked at least ten of the previous thirteen months and had an annual income below $150,000 (AU).[5] The new Australian program left the United States as the only developed nation without paid family leave—leading the *Wall Street Journal* to pose the question that began this section.

PARENTAL LEAVE IN THE UNITED STATES

The United States does have a family leave policy, but it is not funded. Congress began debating legislation to give women time off from work (without pay) around the birth of a child during the 1970s. However, no laws made it through Congress until the 1990s. In 1990 and again in 1991, Congress passed a parental leave bill but lacked the votes to override vetoes by President Bush. In February 1993, just one month into his presidency, President Clinton signed the Family and Medical Leave Act (FMLA). It ensures that women who take time off to give birth have some job protection. It requires employers to provide workers with twelve weeks of unpaid, job-protected leave to deal with the birth of a child, adoption, or a serious health problem faced by a close relative.

However, FMLA has many exceptions for employers. It excludes all part-time workers, workers who have not been with their present company for at least a year (a typical situation for young workers), and anyone working for firms employing less than fifty workers. Key workers, generally the highest-paid 10 percent of employees, can also be denied this benefit if their employer claims it would create "substantial and grievous injury" to the firm. Most important, although parents are entitled to the leave, the leave is not paid. To take leave means doing without regular income for an extended period of time.

A paid leave program took effect in California beginning in July 2004, with new parents eligible for six weeks of benefits (at a maximum of $987 per week) by 2011. New Jersey followed the lead of California by establishing a paid leave program providing two-thirds of weekly pay up to a maximum of $561 beginning in 2010. Such programs are the exception rather than the rule in the United States. The lack of a national paid parental leave program in the United States has serious negative consequences in terms of children and poverty.

CHILD POVERTY AND THE IMPACT OF PAID PARENTAL LEAVE

Table 8.2 computes child poverty rates for several countries using Wave 6 of the Luxembourg Income Study.[6] Households are regarded as poor if they have adjusted income that is under 50 percent of adjusted median household income. For international comparisons, a relative definition of poverty is more appropriate than the absolute Orshansky measure because of the difficulties in comparing living standards when two different currencies are involved. We adjust incomes for family size the same way as in Table 8.1. Table 8.2 shows that the United States has by far the highest child poverty rates among the countries listed. In fact, except for the UK, the US rate is more than double the rate of these other countries.

One reason the United States does so badly is clear in column 2—the income from paid parental leave and baby bonus payments makes a big difference for families with children. Unfortunately, for many countries, baby bonuses and paid parental leave are lumped together. Since baby bonuses are just a small part of the total in most cases, we have used the combined payments in our empirical work. This column recalculates child poverty rates after leave and bonus payments to young parents get subtracted from household income. On average, excluding the United States, child poverty was reduced by more than 3 percentage points. In several countries, the decline exceeded 4 percentage points.

The numbers are even more striking for households with very young children, or those with children below the age of two. This is the main target group of paid parental leave programs, since leave is available in most countries for six months to a year or so, but it can be spread out over a longer period of time if parents are willing to accept less government aid for leave. For this age group, the child poverty rate in the United States is nearly triple that of other developed countries. However, when we subtract paid leave and baby bonus income out of household income, much of the difference disappears.

One conclusion to draw from Table 8.2 is that large differences in child poverty for very young children in the United States and in other developed countries result from the income available through public support to young parents. Moreover, as discussed above, this gap has consequences for families and for children that extend

Table 8.2 **Child Poverty Across Countries** (in percent)

Country and year	Poverty rate of children	Less parental leave (and baby bonuses)	Poverty rate of young children	Less parental leave (and baby bonuses)
Australia (2003)	14.7	21.3	16.7	23.7
Denmark (2004)	5.1	6.6	8.9	14.2
Finland (2004)	5.5	10.4	10.4	26.5
Germany (2004)	12.9	13.9	19.0	23.4
Norway (2004)	6.3	10.7	10.1	22.9
Sweden (2005)	6.7	11.2	9.2	25.9
UK (2004)	16.9	16.9	22.4	22.6
US (2004)	26.2	26.2	34.6	34.6
Averages (unweighted)	11.8	14.7	16.4	24.2
Averages (without US)	9.7	13.0	13.8	22.7

for many years. The accumulated debt could effectively put families into poverty for many years, even though the government does not count them as poor. For many reasons, their children have worse lives as a result of growing up in poverty.

THE BENEFITS OF PAID PARENTAL LEAVE

There are many long-run benefits for children from paid leave (Brooks-Gunn, Han, and Waldfogel 2002; Waldfogel, Han, and Brooks-Gunn 2002). Christopher Ruhm of the University of North Carolina at Greensboro found that parental leave positively impacts pediatric health and appears to reduce infant and child mortality; these results alone could make the program cost-effective (Ruhm 2000). Probably these effects arise because it is easier for parents on paid leave to ensure that their children see doctors and get immunized and because of a greater probability of breast-feeding (Berger, Hill, and Waldfogel 2005; Blau, Guilkey, and Popkin 1996; Roe et al. 1999; Ryan and Martinez 1989). But there is more. By improving the health of children, parental leave improves their earnings when they become adults (Ruhm 1998).

The long-term costs of child poverty are 4 to 5 percent of US GDP, as noted earlier in this chapter. Cutting child poverty rates by 25 percent (the average decline in Table 8.2, without the United States) should result in savings of between 1 and 1.25 percent of US GDP annually. If we did this with paid leave (and small baby bonuses) that roughly followed the average plan of the European countries listed in Table 8.2 (which runs from three months in Germany to one year in Denmark and Sweden) in terms of structure and cost, this would cost less than 1 percent of US GDP (probably much less, since the United States has higher per capita income levels and would need a smaller percentage of that income to fund programs similar to those in Europe). Financially the United States would come out slightly ahead, but still remain behind other developed countries in terms of child poverty. A more generous paid leave program, akin to that of Sweden (which, as noted earlier, provides about a year of leave at 80 percent of previous wages) would cost close to 2 percent of US GDP and reduce child poverty by 40 percent (bringing us close to the average of the developed world). This should also save close to 2 percent of US GDP.

PAYING FOR PAID PARENTAL LEAVE

Still, paid parental leave has up-front costs, so even with the overwhelming evidence that it would provide a positive return over a generation, funding such a program would be controversial. This is especially true at present, when politicians are unwilling to undertake programs that add to the federal deficit. There are three simple ways to incorporate paid parental leave into the US Social Security system, financing the program with payroll taxes. The suggestions and estimates below are for a rather stingy program compared to the rest of the world, providing benefits for much less time than the paid parental leave programs in the developed world and below the recommendations of the International Labour Organisation. Nonetheless, they provide a good benchmark for estimating the costs of something more similar to European systems (which provide on average about twice as much parental leave).

First, Randy Albelda and Alan Clayton-Matthews (2006) estimate that we could fund paid parental leave, covering 100 percent of earnings over twelve weeks for new mothers, with just a 0.3 percentage point increase in the Social Security payroll tax for both employer and employee. Paying 75 to 80 percent of previous earnings seems a reasonable alternative given work-related costs (commuting, food eaten at work, and work clothes), child-care expenses, and higher marginal tax rates for couples with a second income. This would put the program more in line with the replacement rates for Western European programs. It would also lower the needed tax increase proportionately, or it would allow for a proportionately longer period of leave at a similar cost.

Second, instead of increasing Social Security tax rates, we could fund twelve weeks of paid leave at 100 percent of earnings by increasing the wage level to which Social Security taxes apply. Raising the Social Security wage base by about 10 percent (to $120,000 from the 2011 limit of $108,600) would also accomplish this, according to the estimates of Heather Boushey (2009). Again, replacing only 75 to 80 percent of previous earnings would reduce the needed base increase or allow for longer periods of paid leave.

Third, delaying the date at which people can collect full Social Security benefits if they take paid parental leave would also provide the needed funds. Twelve weeks of paid leave for any one parent could result in both parents working an extra six weeks later in life in order to collect their full Social Security benefit upon retirement. For a family with two children, each parent would need to work an extra twelve weeks or three months to collect full benefits. Parents could also have the option of retiring at normal retirement age and collecting lower monthly payments from Social Security after they retire. By either delaying retirement or accepting slightly smaller benefits at retirement, they could effectively shift the time they pay for parental leave in order to have valuable time at home with a very young child.

These suggestions are all inexpensive. The first two would cost only 0.6 percent of the Social Security wage base and an even smaller percentage of US GDP. The last would cost nothing except a slightly longer work life for the parents. Each option would finance a program with many short-run benefits for families and young children as well as long-term gains that, alone, would pay for the entire program.

By reducing US child poverty to near Western European levels, paid parental leave would become an important investment in the future.

SUMMARY AND CONCLUSIONS

Child poverty in the United States far exceeds child poverty in all other developed countries, whether or not we include the debt-poor. The statistics are especially disconcerting when we consider children two years of age or less. These children are the most vulnerable to poverty and suffer most from its effects, according to research we presented above. The long-run impact of even a short bout of poverty can damage children's physical, psychological, and intellectual development and negatively affect both economic and social sustainability. Many young children are in poverty because their parents are not financially stable and may lack the foresight or ability to plan for all the expenses a new baby brings.

When most married women with young children worked in the home rather than the paid labor market, a family could use that division of labor to meet their financial needs—the husband could work longer hours or take a second job while the wife took care of the children. Today, with falling real wages for the majority of Americans, it often takes two income earners to maintain the same family income level of thirty years ago. Families with young children are, therefore, income constrained more than ever before because of child-care costs, rising medical expenses, and higher real estate costs. These expenses lead them to accrue revolving consumer debt. We showed above that when interest payments to maintain consumer debt are subtracted from household income, the number of young poor children increases significantly.

The United States remains far behind the rest of the world in keeping young children out of poverty. As we outlined above, parental leave costs much less than prolonged poverty among the youngest Americans because of its impact on the future standard of living of all our citizens. Other developed countries have much lower child poverty rates—especially among young children. One policy that these other countries have in common is paid parental leave, a policy that accommodates the changing economy in which many married women are working and in which many more mothers are single. The terms and generosity of leave vary widely among countries, but in all of them the parents of young children are more able to take time away from work because a fraction of their prior wages is replaced. As we have shown, paid parental leave policies (even the less generous ones) are largely responsible for the much lower child poverty rates in other developed countries. These lower rates of poverty for young children translate into many long-term benefits for themselves and for society.

NOTES

1. According to the OECD recommendations, the income needs of additional adults are 70 percent of the needs of the main adult and the income needs of children are 50 percent of the income needs of the main adult in the household.

2. Some states and companies in the United States do have a form of paid parental leave. California was the first state to pass paid parental leave in 2002. Washington and New Jersey also have policies. State paid leave operates through state unemployment insurance programs. According to Appelbaum

and Milkman (2011), most employers said the law had no effect or a positive effect on their business and their employees. Nearly 10 percent of the businesses surveyed thought that the law led to cost savings by reducing labor turnover and/or benefit costs. Consistent with studies from other nations, paid parental leave increased the mean duration of breast-feeding and had a positive effect on the ability of new parents to care for their children and make child-care arrangements.

3. Authors' calculations from the Luxembourg Income Study (LIS) database. Unfortunately, it is not possible to divide out these two programs using the LIS. Since baby bonuses are eligible only at the birth of a child, while paid parental leave continues for several years, and since baby bonuses tend to be very small (see the figures for Finland and Italy above) relative to paid parental leave, almost all of the decline in poverty in Table 8.2 stems from paid parental leave.

4. This is a nonpartisan research and advisory board in Australia similar to the US Congressional Budget Office.

5. Productivity Commission (2008). At current exchange rates, this is about $159,396 (US).

6. Our figures come from the Luxembourg Income Study (LIS), an international micro database containing income and sociodemographic information for several dozen countries over the past thirty years. Data are centered about particular years, called waves. Each wave is around five years apart, with Wave #1 beginning in the early 1980s. Wave #6 covers around the year 2004. LIS data for each country at each point in time contain extensive detail regarding income sources as well as a wealth of sociodemographic information. Data come from national surveys of a random sample of households and then get processed to ensure that the economic and sociodemographic variables are as comparable as possible from one country to the next. Those interested in more information about the LIS can consult a number of excellent summaries (Smeeding, Schmaus, and Allegra 1985; Smeeding et al. 1988) or the LIS homepage at www.lisdatacenter.org.

BIBLIOGRAPHY

Afxentiou, D., and C.B. Hawley. 1997. "Explaining Female Teenagers' Sexual Behavior and Outcomes: A Bivariate Probit Analysis with Selectivity Correction." *Journal of Family and Economic Issues* 18, no. 1: 91–106.

Albelda, R., and A. Clayton-Matthews. 2006. *Sharing the Costs, Replacing the Benefits: Paid Family and Medical Leave in Massachusetts.* Boston: University of Massachusetts at Boston, Labor Resources Center.

Amato, P. 2000. "The Consequences of Divorce for Adults and Children." *Journal of Marriage and the Family* 62, no. 4: 1269–1287.

Appelbaum, E., and R. Milkman. 2011. *Leaves That Pay: Employer and Worker Experiences with Paid Family Leave in California.* Washington, DC: Center for Economic and Policy Research.

Baydar, N., J. Brooks-Gunn, and F. Furstenberg. 1993. "Early Warning Signs of Functional Illiteracy: Predictors in Childhood and Adolescence." *Child Development* 64, no. 3: 815–829.

Belsky, J., and D. Eggebeen. 1991. "Early and Extensive Maternal Employment and Young Children's Socioemotional Development: Children of the National Longitudinal Survey of Youth." *Journal of Marriage and the Family* 53: 1083–1098.

Berger, L., J. Hill, and J. Waldfogel. 2005. "Maternity Leave, Early Maternal Employment and Child Health and Development in the US." *Economic Journal* 115, no. 501: F29–F47.

Berrueta-Clement, J., L. Schweinhart, W. Barnett, A. Epstein, and D. Weikart. 1984. *Changed Lives: The Effects of the Perry Preschool Program on Youths Through Age 19.* Ypsilanti, MI: High/Scope Press.

Bhattacharya, J., J. Currie, and S. Haider. 2002. "Food Insecurity or Poverty? Measuring Need-Related Dietary Adequacy." Institute for Research on Poverty Discussion Paper #1252-02.

Binsacca, D., J. Ellis., D. Martin, and D. Petitti. 1987. "Factors Associated with Low Birthweight in an Inner-City Population: The Role of Financial Problems." *American Journal of Public Health* 77, no. 4: 505–506.

Birch, H., and J. Gusson. 1970. *Disadvantaged Children: Health, Nutrition, and School Failure*. New York: Harcourt, Brace and World.

Blau, D., D. Guilkey, and B. Popkin. 1996. "Infant Health and the Labor Supply of Mothers." *Journal of Human Resources* 31: 90–139.

Bolder, K., C. Patterson, W. Thompson, and J. Kupersmidt. 1995. "Psychosocial Adjustment Among Children Experiencing Persistent and Intermittent Family Economic Hardship." *Child Development* 66, no. 4: 1107–1129.

Boushey, H. 2009. *Helping Breadwinners When It Can't Wait: A Progressive Program for Family Leave Insurance*. Washington, DC: Center for American Progress.

Boyce, T. 1985. "Stress and Child Health: An Overview." *Pediatric Annals* 14, no. 8: 539–542.

Brooks-Gunn, J., W. Han, and J. Waldfogel. 2002. "Maternal Employment and Child Cognitive Outcomes in the First Three Years of Life: The NICHD Study of Early Child Care." *Child Development* 73, no. 4: 1052–1072.

Children's Defense Fund (CDF). 1994. *Wasting America's Future*. Boston: Beacon Press.

Cohany, S., and E. Suk. 2007. "Trends in Labor Force Participation of Married Mothers of Infants." *Monthly Labor Review* 130: 9–16.

Coré, F., and V. Koutsogeorgopoulou. 1995. "Parental Leave: What and Where?" *The OECD Observer* 195: 15–21.

Currie, J. 2003. "US Food and Nutrition Programs." In *Means Tested Transfer Programs in the United States*, ed. R. Moffitt, 199–290. Chicago: University of Chicago Press.

Dougherty, D., L. Saxe, T. Cross, and N. Silverman. 1987. *Children's Mental Health*. Durham, NC: Duke University Press.

Duncan, G., and K. Magnuson. 2013. "Investing in Preschool Programs." *Journal of Economic Perspectives* 27, no. 2: 109–132.

Duncan, G., W. Yeung, J. Brooks-Gunn, and J.R. Smith. 1998. "How Much Does Childhood Poverty Affect the Life Chances of Children?" *American Sociological Review* 63: 406–423.

Erler, D. 2009. "Germany: Taking a Nordic Turn?" In *The Politics of Parental Leave Policies: Children, Parenting, Gender and the Labour Market*, ed. S. Kamerman and P. Moss, 119–134. Bristol, UK: Policy Press.

Fagnani, J., and A. Math. 2009. "France: Gender Equality a Pipe Dream?" In *The Politics of Parental Leave Policies: Children, Parenting, Gender and the Labour Market*, ed. S. Kamerman and P. Moss, 102–116. Bristol, UK: Policy Press.

Federal Reserve Board of Governors. 2009. "Survey of Consumer Finances." www.federalreserve.gov/PUBS/oss/oss2/scfindex.html.

Frank, M., and R. Lipner. 1988. "History of Maternity Leave in Europe and the United States." In *The Parental Leave Crisis*, ed. E. Zigler and M. Frank, 3–22. New Haven, CT: Yale University Press.

Frost, J., and B. Payne. 1970. "Hunger in America: Scope and Consequences." In *The Disadvantaged Child: Issues and Innovations*, 2nd ed., ed. J. Frost and G. Hawkes, 70–83. Boston: Houghton Mifflin.

Goldstein, N. 1990. *Explaining Socioeconomic Differences in Children's Cognitive Test Scores*. Cambridge, MA: Kennedy School of Government, Harvard University.

Gould, M., R. Wunsch-Hitzig, and B. Duhrenwend. 1981. "Estimating the Prevalence of Childhood Psychotherapy: A Critical Review." *Journal of the American Academy of Child Psychiatry* 20: 462–476.

Hanson, T., S. McClanahan, and E. Thomson. 1997. "Economic Resources, Parental Practices and Children's Well-Being." In *Consequences of Growing up Poor*, ed. G. Duncan and J. Brooks-Gunn, 190–238. New York: Russell Sage.

Haveman, R., et al. 1991. "Childhood Events and Circumstances Influencing High School Completion." *Demography* 28, no. 1: 133–157.

Haveman, R., and B. Wolfe. 1994. *Succeeding Generations: On the Effects of Investments in Children*. New York: Russell Sage.

———. 1995. "The Determinants of Childhood's Attainments: A Review of Methods and Findings." *Journal of Economic Literature* 33, no. 4: 1829–1878.

Heckman, J. 2000. "Policies to Foster Human Capital." *Research in Economics* 54, no. 1: 3–56.

———. 2006. "Skill Formation and the Economics of Investing in Disadvantaged Children." *Science* 312, no. 5782: 1900–1902.

———. 2011. "The Economics of Inequality: The Value of Early Childhood Education." *American Educator* 35: 31–47.

Hock, E., and D. DeMeis. 1990. "Depression in Mothers of Infants: The Role of Maternal Employment." *Developmental Psychology* 26, no. 2: 285–291.

Hogan, D.P., and E.M. Kitagawa. 1985. "The Impact of Social Status, Family Structure and Neighborhood on the Fertility of Black Adolescents." *American Journal of Sociology* 90: 825–855.

Holzer, H., D. Schanzenbach, G. Duncan, and J. Ludwig. 2007. *The Economic Costs of Poverty in the United States: Subsequent Effects of Children Growing Up in Poverty.* Washington, DC: Center for American Progress.

Hurley, R. 1969. *Poverty and Mental Retardation: A Causal Relationship.* New York: Random House.

Hyde, J., M. Klein, M. Essex, and R. Clark. 1995. "Maternity Leave and Women's Mental Health." *Psychology of Women Quarterly* 19, no. 2: 257–285.

Kamerman, S. 2000. "Parental Leave Policies: An Essential Ingredient in Early Childhood Education and Care Policies." *Social Policy Report* 14, #2.

Kelso, W. 1994. *Poverty and the Underclass: Changing Perceptions of the Poor in America.* New York: New York University Press.

Klebanov, P., J. Brooks-Gunn, and G. Duncan. 1994. "Does Neighborhood and Family Affect Mothers' Parenting, Mental Health and Social Support?" *Journal of Marriage and the Family* 56: 441–455.

Klerman, L. 1991a. *Alive and Well?* New York: National Center for Children in Poverty.

———. 1991b. "The Association Between Adolescent Parenting and Childhood Poverty." In *Children in Poverty*, ed. A. Huston, 79–104. Cambridge, UK: Cambridge University Press.

Korenman, S., and J. Miller. 1997. "Effects of Long-Term Poverty on Physical Health of Children in the National Longitudinal Survey." In *Consequences of Growing Up Poor*, ed. G. Duncan and J. Brooks-Gunn, 70–99. New York: Russell Sage.

Lewit, E., and N. Kerrebrock. 1997. "Population-Based Growth Stunting." *Children and Poverty* 7: 149–156.

Mahaffey, K., J. Annest, J. Roberts, and R. Murphy. 1982. "National Estimates of Blood Levels: United States, 1976–1980." *New England Journal of Medicine* 307, no. 10: 573–579.

Makosky, V.P. 1982. "Sources of Stress: Events or Conditions?" In *Lives in Stress: Women and Depression*, ed. D. Belle, 35–52. Beverly Hills, CA: Sage.

Manheim, L., and M. Minchilla. 1978. *The Effects of Income Maintenance on the School Performance of Children: Results from the Seattle and Denver Experiments.* Princeton, NJ: Mathematica Policy Research.

McDonald, J., and S. Stephenson. 1979. "The Effect of Income Maintenance on the School Enrollment and Labor Supply Decisions of Teenagers." *Journal of Human Resources* 14, no. 4: 488–495.

McLeod, J.D., and M.J. Shanahan. 1993. "Poverty, Parenting, and Children's Mental Health." *American Sociological Review* 58: 351–366.

McLoyd, V., and L. Wilson. 1991. "The Strain of Living Poor." In *Children in Poverty*, ed. A. Huston, 105–135. Cambridge, UK: Cambridge University Press.

Monheit, A., and C. Cunningham. 1992. "Children Without Health Insurance." *The Future of Children* 2: 154–170.

Morris, P., and L. Gennetian. 2004. "Identifying the Effects of Income on Children's Development Using Experimental Data." *Journal of Marriage and the Family* 65, no. 3: 716–729.

Munnell, A., ed. 1986. *Lessons From the Income Maintenance Experiments.* Boston: Federal Reserve Bank of Boston.

Niles, M., and L. Peck. 2008. "How Poverty and Segregation Impact Child Development: Evidence from the Chicago Longitudinal Study." *Journal of Poverty* 12, no. 3: 306–332.

O'Connor, A. 2001. *Poverty Knowledge*. Princeton, NJ: Princeton University Press.

Pressman, S., and R. Scott. 2009a. "Consumer Debt and the Measurement of Poverty and Inequality in the US." *Review of Social Economy* 67, no. 2: 127–146.

———. 2009b. "Who Are the Debt Poor?" *Journal of Economic Issues* 43, no. 2: 423–432.

Productivity Commission. 2008. Paid Parental Leave: Support for Parents with Newborn Children. Canberra, Australia: Productivity Commission.

Roe, B., L. Whittington, S. Fein, and M. Teisl. 1999. "Is There Competition Between Breast-Feeding and Maternal Employment?" *Demography* 36, no. 2: 157–171.

Ruhm, C. 1998. "The Economic Consequences of Parental Leave Mandates: Lessons from Europe." *Quarterly Journal of Economics* 15, no. 1: 285–317.

———. 2000. "Parental Leave and Child Health." *Journal of Health Economics* 19, no. 6: 931–960.

Ryan, A., and G. Martinez. 1989. "Breast-Feeding and the Working Mother: A Profile." *Pediatrics* 83, no. 4: 524–531.

Selden, T., J. Banthin, and J. Cohen. 1998. "Medicaid's Problem Children: Eligible but Not Enrolled." *Health Affairs* 17, no. 3: 192–200.

Smeeding, T., L. Rainwater, B. Buhmann, and G. Schmaus. 1988. "Luxembourg Income Study (LIS) Information Guide." LIS-CEPS Working Paper #8.

Smeeding, T., G. Schmaus, and S. Allegra. 1985. "An Introduction to LIS." LIS-CEPS Working Paper #1.

Smith, J.R., J. Brooks-Gunn, and P. Klebanov. 1997. "The Consequences of Living in Poverty for Young Children's Cognitive and Verbal Ability and Early School Achievement." In *Consequences of Growing Up Poor*, ed. G. Duncan and J. Brooks-Gunn, 132–189. New York: Russell Sage.

Spargo, J. 1907. *The Bitter Cry of Children*. New York: Macmillan.

Teachman, J., K. Paasch, R. Day, and K. Carver. 1997. "Poverty During Adolescence and Subsequent Economic Attainment." In *Consequences of Growing Up Poor*, ed. G. Duncan and J. Brooks-Gunn, 382–418. New York: Russell Sage.

Waldfogel, J., W. Han, and J. Brooks-Gunn. 2002. "The Effects of Early Maternal Employment on Child Cognitive Development." *Demography* 39, no. 2: 369–392.

Weinreb, L., C. Wehler, J. Perloff, R. Scott, D. Hosmer, L. Sagor, and C. Gundersen. 2002. "Hunger: Its Impact on Children's Health and Mental Health." *Pediatrics* 110, no. 4: 1–9.

PART

III

Policies to Improve Quality of Life and Sustainability

9 | Raising US Living Standards by Controlling Climate Change

Robert Pollin

To maximize opportunities for all people to enjoy a decent living standard, now and into the future, requires an agenda for environmental protection that is fully integrated with an economy's overall trajectory around jobs and economic growth. There are many crucial issues on the environmental agenda relating to air and water pollution, the maintenance of viable habitats for plant and animal species, and the fair distribution of both environmental benefits and costs tied to economic growth. But the most fundamental environmental issue now facing humanity, in the United States and globally, is climate change. At present, an overwhelming majority of climate scientists contend that our environment faces a severe—and perhaps even existential—threat if we do not control the changing climatic conditions that result from the emissions of greenhouse gases (Emanuel 2012). It is hard to conceive of what might constitute a decent living standard into the future if we do not take control over this major threat to the future of humanity.

It is possible, of course, that the research done by this majority of climate scientists is wrong. After all, scientific matters are never settled on the basis of majority rule. However, their warnings are both credible and serious enough that it makes sense to take concerted action to control greenhouse gas emissions, as opposed to continuing to play a game of Russian roulette with the future of our planet. This means that we need to mobilize both public and private investments to dramatically restructure the energy infrastructure in the United States and throughout the world.

We can think of these investments as constituting an environmental insurance policy. Though we cannot know for certain just how serious is the threat to our future living standards, we do know enough to understand that the statistical probability that we are advancing toward an environmental disaster is not trivial. We purchase insurance to protect ourselves in the event of automobile accidents and house fires. The need for climate insurance is also compelling. The only real question is how much we should be willing to pay for this insurance. The main aim of this paper is to examine the costs for the United States to purchase "climate change insurance" by investing in energy efficiency and renewable energy, in particular.

Since 2009, the Obama administration has maintained as an intermediate goal that the US economy should emit no more than about 4,200 million metric tons (mmt) of greenhouse gas emissions by 2030 as part of our "insurance policy." This is an extremely ambitious goal given that, in 2010, the US economy emitted about 6,800 mmt of greenhouse gases into the atmosphere, with 5,600 mmt—that is, about 80 percent—coming from burning fossil fuels to produce energy. The other 1,200—20 percent—came from nonenergy sources, including methane, nitrous oxide, and other less significant sources of greenhouse gases. The focus of this chapter is on the 80 percent of emissions generated by consuming fossil-fuel energy.

The Obama administration's goal entails cutting emissions by nearly 40 percent in 2030 relative to 2010 and achieving this without imposing unsustainable costs on incomes, job opportunities, and other basic aspects of economic well-being. Focusing on the 80 percent of emissions coming from energy sources, action must be taken on two fronts to have a serious chance of reaching the 2030 target. First and most important are investments to dramatically improve the efficiency with which energy is consumed in the US economy. It will not be possible to achieve major cuts in emissions without these investments. Second, the United States must undertake a major expansion in its use of renewable sources of energy that do not generate greenhouse emissions. Without major advances in the two critical areas of efficiency and renewables, the only other plausible path to significantly reducing greenhouse gas emissions would be to increase dependence on nuclear power. But the meltdown of the Fukushima nuclear power plant in Japan in 2011 as a result of the massive 7.0 Richter scale earthquake provided a dramatic and tragic reminder of the severe public safety risks associated with nuclear power (Schreurs and Yoshida 2013).

This chapter describes an economically realistic agenda for reaching the goal of a 40 percent reduction in US emissions by 2030. First, I examine the investments needed to improve energy efficiency. Second, I look at what is needed to increase the production of clean renewable energy based on what future requirements in the United States are likely to be. Third, I explore the effects of both of these on employment opportunities at all levels of the US economy. Investing in a green US economy raises both the labor intensity and domestic content of energy production and consumption relative to a fossil-fuel–based economy. Finally, I review the evidence on how cap-and-trade measures to reduce carbon emissions are likely to affect long-term gross domestic product (GDP) growth.

Based on this analysis, I conclude that something akin to the "green energy" agenda outlined here can serve as a major foundation for achieving significant improvements in living standards in the United States over the next generation. Rather than considering specific policy proposals in detail, I present here a broad, macro framework for hitting the emissions targets and then describe the impacts on jobs and incomes of pursuing those targets.

INVESTMENTS FOR ENERGY EFFICIENCY

The United States has made significant advances over the past forty years in raising energy efficiency standards. The average per capita consumption of energy was 308 million BTUs

(British thermal unit) per year in 2009, 7 percent *lower* than in 1970.[1] Such long-term improvements in energy efficiency are impressive. However, in considering environmental impacts, we need to focus on the absolute level of greenhouse gas emissions, not simply improvements in efficiency. Any gains in efficiency can be offset by an expanding level of economic output as well as population growth. Thus, the absolute level of energy consumption in 2009 of 95 quadrillion BTUs (hereafter Q-BTUs) was 36.5 percent higher than 1970. This increase in total energy consumption translates into more greenhouse gas emissions. Greenhouse gas emissions were about 7 percent *higher* in 2009 relative to 1970, a response to a doubling of real per capita GDP during this period.

Despite improvements, the level of energy consumption and greenhouse gas emissions from energy is substantially higher in the United States than in almost all other advanced economies. Per capita, the United States consumes roughly twice as much energy as France, Germany, Japan, and the United Kingdom. In terms of greenhouse gas emissions, France, Germany, Japan, and the UK are all between 48 and 64 percent lower than the United States in carbon emissions per capita.

The long-term trend in the United States toward rising efficiency levels, along with the fact that most other advanced economies already operate at roughly double the efficiency level of the United States, make clear the feasibility of major gains in efficiency over the next twenty years. Indeed, this conclusion is built into the reference case model for US energy consumption produced by the US Energy Information Administration (EIA), an agency of the Department of Energy (EIA 2011, 2012). Thus, the EIA's reference case projecting that US energy consumption will be 111.2 Q-BTUs (an increase of 16.2 Q-BTUs relative to the 2009 level of 95 Q-BTUs) as of 2030 amounts to an average annual increase of 0.7 percent—that is, an improvement from the 0.9 percent rate of increase in energy use between 1970 and 2009.[2]

However, even with this slow rate of increase in energy consumption, the US economy will still be emitting about 6,200 mmt of CO_2 into the atmosphere through energy-based sources and a total of 7,700 mmt as of 2030 (EIA 2011, 2012). This figure is 83 percent above the 4,200 mmt target for 2030. The National Academy of Sciences (NAS 2010), along with other research groups, has developed scenarios for energy efficiency investments that can deliver gains beyond the EIA reference case for 2030. These measures span all areas of energy consumption—in buildings, industry, and transportation.

In buildings, the key efficiency investments highlighted by the NAS study are improvements in insulation systems, in cooling and heating systems, and in lighting systems by switching to either compact fluorescent (CFL) or light-emitting diode (LED) systems. In industry, the NAS study cites combined heat and power (CHP) systems as the single biggest opportunity for efficiency gains. CHP systems are units that transform a fuel into electricity and then use the hot waste gas steam for processes such as space and hot-water heating or industrial and commercial processes. There is also a range of industry-specific measures available to substantially improve efficiency in high energy-intensive sectors, including chemicals, refining, paper, and steel. In transportation, the single most important area for making large efficiency gains is by raising the fuel efficiency standard for automobiles and light trucks.

The NAS study does not fully quantify the impact on emissions of all the measures it describes. However, it does present an overview of the potential impacts of the full range of energy efficiency investments that it proposes. Through this combination of proposed investments, the NAS concludes that, as of 2030, the United States could operate at a level of energy consumption about 30 percent below the EIA reference case of 111 Q-BTUs. This would represent a dramatic improvement in energy efficiency in the US economy—indeed, an absolute decline in the level of energy consumption of 11 percent relative to the actual 2009 level of 95 Q-BTUs.

However, even with this ambitious agenda to improve energy efficiency by about 25 percent relative to the EIA reference case, it still follows that the US economy would be generating about 4,900 mmt of CO_2 through consuming energy, and a total of 6,500 mmt, including nonenergy sources, as well. This is based on operating at an 85 Q-BTU level of consumption and with roughly the same mix of energy sources as at present. The result? The level of CO_2 emissions would still be fully 55 percent above the 2030 target of 4,200 mmt.

My analysis does not assume any technological breakthroughs in carbon capture and sequestration (CCS) technology for fossil fuels. The idea behind CCS is that it will allow for the indefinite heavy reliance on fossil fuels as energy sources, since the CCS technology will lead to a dramatic reduction in greenhouse gas emissions from burning fossil fuels. However, to date, there is no evidence that CCS technologies are capable of operating at competitive costs on a large scale. To bring these technologies to the point where they are cost-competitive would entail capital expenditures at least at the level we discuss for efficiency and renewables, and with far less certainty as to the returns on these investments. In addition, assuming the CCS technology could be made cost-competitive, it would then still require that the carbon captured at the point where coal, petroleum, and natural gas are being burned be transported and stored *permanently* under Earth's surface. Given these issues, I assume that investments in research and development of clean energy over the next generation would be much more effectively allocated by concentrating on efficiency and renewable energy.[3]

Therefore, the most basic question we need to address is how to make still further improvements in energy efficiency in the United States, beyond the types of improvements projected in the NAS study. Indeed, for the United States to succeed in reaching the goal of 4,200 mmt of greenhouse gas emissions by 2030, it is almost certainly the case that the overall level of energy consumption in the US economy will need to be pushed down to about 65 to 70 Q-BTUs—that is, to a level that is roughly one-third below the actual level for 2009 and 40 percent below the EIA's reference case for 2030.

TOTAL ENERGY EFFICIENCY INVESTMENT NEEDS

Table 9.1 details the data on the levels of investment spending needed to achieve a 65 Q-BTU level of overall energy consumption in the United States by 2030, considering separately the building, industry, and transportation sectors.

Buildings

To bring the building sector down to a level of about 32 Q-BTUs of energy consumption by 2030, NAS estimated that investment of about $440 billion over

Table 9.1　**Summary Estimates for Creating a High-Efficiency Economy by 2030**

	EIA reference case consumption level for 2030 (Q-BTUs)	Consumption levels for high-efficiency economy (Q-BTUs)	Reduction in consumption in high-efficiency case (percent)	Investment costs through 2030 for high-efficiency economy ($billion)	Average investment costs per year for 20 years ($billion)
Buildings	47	25	−46.8	650	32.5
Industry	33	20	−39.4	370	18.5
Transportation	31	17	−45.2	785	39.2
Total	111	62	−44.1	1.8 trillion	90

Sources: US Energy Information Administration (2011); discussion in text.

twenty years is needed. This would reduce energy consumption in buildings about 25 to 30 percent below what the Energy Information Administration's calls its "reference case" (i.e., its most likely scenario, based on current information) of 45 Q-BTUs.

I then assume that the costs of lowering energy consumption in buildings further, to about 25 Q-BTUs, would be proportional to the costs of achieving a 32 Q-BTU level of consumption. There is strong evidence that there could be increasing returns to these efficiency investments in buildings, in part because the returns on investment in building efficiency are high. To date, the growth in building efficiency investments has been held up because the financial and market infrastructure remains undeveloped. The system of financing and risk-sharing that enables businesses and homeowners to capture the benefits of the high returns without having to carry the full burden of initial financial risk remains immature. Developments in these areas should come rapidly once the initial set of business and financial innovations takes hold. To operate on the basis of a linear cost function for investments in building efficiency is therefore a conservative working assumption. It follows that the total costs of reaching a 25-Q-BTU level of consumption in the building sector would be $650 billion in investments, or $32.5 billion per year.

Industry

Based on the Energy Information Administration's econometric forecasting model, my colleagues and I (Pollin, Garrett-Peltier, Heintz, and Hendricks 2014) have estimated total new investments in CHP systems at $123 billion to reduce energy consumption by 2.3 Q-BTUs over twenty years. In addition, another $85 billion will be necessary to achieve 5.5 more Q-BTUs in efficiency improvements in all non-CHP areas within industry, including increasing the efficiency of operations in chemical, paper, and steel production, as well as oil refining. This averages to a cost of about $30 billion per Q-BTU of energy savings in industry, including both CHP and investments and those in chemicals, paper, steel, and oil refining. Thus, to bring total industry energy consumption from the EIA's reference case of 33 Q-BTUs to 20 Q-BTUs by 2030 will require $370 billion in investments, or $18.5 billion per year.

Transportation

In Pollin, Garrett-Peltier, Heintz, and Hendricks (2014), we focused our estimate on the agreement achieved between the Obama administration and US automakers to achieve an average fuel efficiency standard for automobiles and light trucks of 54.5 miles per gallon (mpg) as of 2025. As of 2010, the average fuel efficiency level for the US auto fleet was 29.2 mpg. Working from NAS estimates of the incremental retail cost of purchasing a high-efficiency vehicle relative to a standard gasoline car in 2035, we estimated that the total cost of replacing the US auto fleet with high-efficiency cars in twenty years would be $740 billion. We also allow for other modes of transportation—including especially freight trucks and airplanes—to increase efficiency by 5 to 10 percent relative to the Energy Information Administration's reference case for 2030. In total, these investments would bring the transportation sector to an energy consumption level of 17 Q-BTUs by 2030. The total cost would be $785 billion, or $39 billion per year for twenty years.

In addition to the opportunities for improving transportation efficiencies through automobiles and light trucks, it is also crucial to give careful attention to the prospects for dramatically expanding public transportation offerings throughout the United States. Over time, a shift to more public transportation options would provide a wide range of social as well as environmental benefits to increase US living standards. These include reduced costs for transportation, lowered congestion and pollution, and less suburban sprawl. However, public transportation is so small a fraction in overall energy consumption figures for the transportation sector that in the short term we cannot rely on it as a significant factor in lowering greenhouse gas emissions.

TOTAL EFFICIENCY INVESTMENT REQUIREMENTS

Our total spending figure—including all areas of energy efficiency investments in buildings, industry, and transportation—requires up to $1.8 trillion in order to achieve energy consumption efficiencies at about 44 percent below the EIA reference case of 111 Q-BTUs in 2030. This $1.8 trillion in new investments would span out over twenty years. This amounts to a rate of roughly $90 billion per year for the full twenty years. The average cost of saving relative to the EIA's reference case would be about $37 billion per Q-BTU of energy saved. The net result would be to push the level of energy consumption in the United States to about 62 Q-BTUs.[4]

FINANCING THE ENERGY EFFICIENCY TRANSFORMATION

A key driver in this analysis of energy efficiency is that these investments will be generating substantial savings over time. NAS estimates the payback period for energy efficiency investments in buildings at less than three years. We have estimated that the savings on fuel costs for operating an energy-efficient auto rather than a conventional gasoline-powered car should be about 35 percent per year. This means a payback period of less than three years to purchase a more fuel-efficient car. Estimates on payback periods for investments in CHP systems and other types of industrial efficiency measures are within this same range (Pollin, Garrett-Peltier, Heintz, and Hendricks 2014).

Given such major opportunities for cost savings, there need to be innovative financing packages to provide savings to investors at the time they make their investment purchases. For example, a viable strategy for minimizing the impact of the higher initial purchase price of fuel-efficient automobiles would be for policy makers to establish lower financing costs for consumers who purchase cars that are above a given efficiency threshold. The idea behind such arrangements would be to enable consumers to capture some of the long-term savings through the terms of their auto financing loans.

Since efficiency investments generate high rates of return at low risk, the main requirement for public policy is to foster the development of effective financing opportunities that allow up-front costs to be spread over time. Beyond this, the need for direct public subsidies should be modest.

EXPANDING THE PRODUCTION OF CLEAN RENEWABLE ENERGY

Renewable energy sources—including biofuels and biomass, along with hydro, wind, geothermal, and solar power—vary widely in their basic feedstock (the means by which they generate energy) and their environmental impacts. Hydro, wind, solar, and geothermal power produce no greenhouse gas emissions. Of these, only hydro is currently producing energy on a significant scale. However, it is neither likely nor desirable that large-scale hydropower will expand significantly beyond its current capacity level. One limiting factor is that the most favorable sites in the United States for constructing large-scale dams are already built out and operating at capacity. Additional dam construction would also be likely to cause serious disruption in existing communities and ecosystems. However, small-scale hydro projects do offer significant promise. These are projects built into rivers or strong-running streams. They generate energy through the force of the current running through a turbine located on the side of a river or stream.

The most heavily consumed biofuel at present is corn ethanol, but producing corn ethanol means using a food crop to produce energy. This drives up global food prices, which is clearly undesirable, especially for poor countries. In addition, when fossil-fuel energy is used to refine the corn into ethanol, the resulting level of greenhouse gas emissions becomes comparable to those from burning oil to power automobiles.

By contrast, biofuels can be a carbon-neutral source of energy if the raw materials are wastes and nonfood crops and if these raw materials are refined by the use of renewable sources, such as wind- or solar-power-generated heating. The challenge for expanding renewable energy becomes clearer in the context of specific conditions in this sector at present. As of 2009, all renewable energy sources generated about 7.5 Q-BTUs of energy in the United States—about 7.9 percent of the total energy supply that year. As noted in Table 9.2, the biggest source of renewable energy is biomass and biofuels, with corn ethanol being the most important component here. In combination, biomass and biofuel sources provided 3.9 Q-BTUs in 2009, 52 percent of the total renewable energy supplied. Hydroelectricity produced an additional 2.7 Q-BTUs in 2009, which amounted to 36 percent of all renewable energy that year.

In combination, as presented in Table 9.2, biofuels, biomass, and hydroelectricity accounted for 88 percent of all renewable energy in 2009—52 percent for biofuels and biomass and 36 percent for hydro. Wind, geothermal, and solar power in total

Table 9.2 **US Renewable Energy Consumption in 2009**

	Total Q-BTUs	Percent of total
Renewable energy—all sources	7.5	100.0
Biomass and biofuels—all sources	3.9	52.0
Hydroelectric—all sources	2.7	36.0
Wind	0.7	9.3
Geothermal	0.3	4.3
Solar—all sources	0.04	0.5

Source: US Energy Information Administration (2011).

accounted for only 12 percent of total renewable energy and less than 1 percent of all US energy supply in 2009, with wind the largest contributor. The contribution of solar power in 2009 was negligible. From all solar sources, including both thermal and photovoltaic power generation, the total supply was 0.04 Q-BTUs.

In its reference case, the Energy Information Administration estimated that production of renewable energy will expand substantially over the next twenty to twenty-five years, roughly doubling its supply of energy to 15 Q-BTUs by 2030. The EIA also developed a "low-cost technology case" for renewables, as of 2035. In this case, the EIA (2011, 2012) projected renewable supply to reach about 20 Q-BTUs total, an increase of over 150 percent relative to the actual 2009 production level.

Working within the framework of a 65-quad level of total energy consumption for the United States by 2030, if all renewable sources are able to reach 20 Q-BTUs of supply by 2030, it will be possible for the United States to achieve the 4,200 emissions target for that year. It would also be possible to hit this target if renewables grew to only 15 Q-BTUs total by 2030, depending on two other factors. The first is the specific mix of renewable energy sources, given that some forms of biofuels and biomass produce only modest gains in terms of lowering emission levels; the second is the extent to which the United States relies on nuclear power as a backup energy source (as opposed to coal, oil, or natural gas). Among the nonrenewable sources, nuclear power is the only one that does not generate greenhouse gas emissions in generating energy, even while it presents its own set of severe problems, especially as regards public safety.

As a way to underline the overall needs for renewable energy over the next twenty years, let us work with the simplifying assumption that the United States is able to produce 15 Q-BTUs of renewable energy from emissions-free renewable sources. Among these, we also assume energy from hydropower will remain fixed at its current level of about 3 Q-BTUs. This would mean 12 Q-BTUs total from wind, solar, geothermal, and clean biofuels. I turn now to what this means in terms of capital investments and overall costs.

ESTIMATING CAPITAL INVESTMENTS AND OPERATING COSTS OF RENEWABLES

The EIA provides estimates of what it terms the "levelized costs of new generation resources." This is a summary measure that represents the present value of the total cost of building and operating an electricity generating plant over an assumed financial life and duty cycle.[5] Table 9.3 shows the EIA estimates for total levelized costs for

Table 9.3 Estimated Levelized Costs of Renewable Energy Electricity Generation for Plants Entering Service in 2016
(in billions of 2009 dollars per Q-BTU of electricity)

	Levelized capital costs	Fixed operations and maintenance	Variable operations and maintenance, including fuel	Transmission investment	Capacity factor, in percent	Total system levelized costs
Hydro	25.0	1.3	2.0	0.6	53	28.8
Wind onshore	26.5	3.0	0	1.1	34	30.6
Geothermal	24.6	3.8	3.0	0.3	91	31.8
Biomass	17.6	4.4	13.5	0.4	83	35.9
Solar PV	62.1	3.8	0	1.3	25	67.2
Wind offshore	66.8	9.0	0	1.9	34	77.6
Solar thermal	82.7	14.8	0	1.8	18	99.4

Source: US Energy Information Administration, Supplement to *Annual Energy Outlook*, http://205.254.135.24/oiaf/aeo/electricity_generation.html.

renewable sources of electricity, expressed in terms of billions of dollars to produce one Q-BTU of delivered electricity.

We focus on Table 9.3 and the first column of figures, which shows capital costs. The EIA estimates annual capital expenditures at $25 billion to produce one extra Q-BTU of hydropower capacity and $26.5 billion for a Q-BTU of onshore wind power (EIA 2010). By contrast, solar photovoltaic power requires $62.1 billion in capital expenditures to generate one Q-BTU of delivered electricity and solar thermal power requires nearly $83 billion to generate a Q-BTU of delivered electricity.[6] Both require much more capital investment per unit of electricity than hydro.

To roughly estimate the capital costs of expanding clean renewable sources, I make the following two assumptions:

1. Beginning from the base of the existing capital stock, the level of new investment in renewable energy capital equipment will be about 10 Q-BTUs total. This includes 7.5 Q-BTUs to reach the target of 15 Q-BTUs in total, relative to the current level of 7.5 Q-BTUs of renewable energy. It also includes 2.5 Q-BTUs that would provide clean renewable capacity to substitute for burning corn ethanol and other less environmentally benign renewable sources.
2. The expansion of the clean renewable sources will be 4 Q-BTUs of wind power and 2 Q-BTUs each of clean biofuels, solar power, and geothermal. I also assume that the expansion of wind and solar capacity is concentrated on the less expensive technologies, onshore wind and photovoltaic solar, as opposed to offshore wind and thermal solar.

Based on these two assumptions, the overall capital costs of expanding the capacity of clean renewables by 10 Q-BTUs will be about $400 billion. Over a twenty-year period, this would amount to an average of $20 billion per year.

COMPARING OPERATING COSTS FOR RENEWABLE AND NONRENEWABLE ELECTRICITY

It is illuminating to compare overall levelized costs, as well as capital costs, for renewable sources relative to nonrenewables. I present this comparison in Table 9.4, showing costs of generating electricity with coal, natural gas, and nuclear power relative to hydro, wind, and geothermal power. Hydro, wind, and geothermal are all cost-competitive at present with coal and are significantly less costly than nuclear power. The renewable sources are about 30 percent more expensive than natural gas. However, expanding the natural gas supply also faces serious constraints. These include both high costs and environmental impacts of expanding the extraction and transportation infrastructure, including the costs and impacts of the use of hydraulic fracking technology.[7]

This indicates that hydro, wind, some biofuels, and geothermal are *already* cost-competitive with nonrenewable sources apart from any additional public subsidies to them or any policies to raise the costs of fossil fuels to reflect their environmental impact. The capital markets should therefore soon be poised to begin financial expan-

Table 9.4   **Levelized Costs of Hydro, Wind, and Geothermal vs. Fossil Fuels and Nuclear**

	Total system levelized costs (billions of dollars per Q-BTU of electricity)	Total costs relative to hydro (in percent)	Total costs relative to onshore wind (in percent)	Total costs relative to geothermal
Conventional coal	30.3	+5.2	−1.0	−4.7%
Natural gas— conventional combined cycle	20.7	−28.1	−32.3	−53.6
Advanced nuclear	36.3	+26.0	+18.6	+14.2

Source: US Energy Information Administration, Supplement to *Annual Energy Outlook*, http://205.254.135.24/oiaf/aeo/electricity_generation.html.

sion on a large scale. The primary role of public policy in these areas should be to help organize investment activity into these new areas and to promote the expansion of the market, just as we found earlier with efficiency investments.

More active industrial policies will still be needed, most especially with respect to solar power, which at present is not yet cost-competitive with nonrenewable sources. The focus here should be on research and development to nurture both small- and large-scale solar technologies to the point where they are cost-competitive. In addition, the electrical grid system needs to be upgraded so that it can transmit energy from wind and solar power much more efficiently than is attainable at present.

FUTURE REQUIREMENTS FOR NONRENEWABLE ENERGY

Following the previous discussion on energy efficiency and clean renewables, it is reasonable to assume that by 2030 the United States will need to supply approximately 50 Q-BTUs of energy through nonrenewable sources or relatively dirty renewable sources such as corn ethanol. Our focus here is on how to meet this demand and still maintain overall emissions levels at about 3,200 mmt from all energy-based sources and 4,200 mmt in total from all sources.

The first issue in proceeding with this goal is to establish the demand for liquid fuels to meet transportation needs, based on the federal government's auto efficiency standard for new cars and light trucks of 54.5 mpg by 2025. Assuming that electric cars, biofuel-powered cars, and public transportation will continue to make relatively modest contributions to overall US transportation needs during the next twenty years, this means a relatively inflexible demand for petroleum for transportation of about 20 Q-BTUs even with a doubling in the efficiency standards.[8]

Working with the constraint of a 20 Q-BTU demand for petroleum to power automobiles in 2030, we can then proceed with estimating emission levels by meeting the remaining 30 Q-BTUs of overall energy demand through various combinations of nonrenewable sources. To proceed with such calculations, we need to work with the levels of greenhouse gas emissions that result from the alternative nonrenewable energy sources. These figures are shown in Table 9.5: coal generates the heaviest emissions at

Table 9.5   **Average Greenhouse Gas Emissions by Fuel Source**

Fuel source	Greenhouse gas emissions per quad of energy
Coal	95
Petroleum	63
Natural gas	52
Nuclear power	0

Source: US Energy Information Administration, "Greenhouse Gas Emissions," www.epa.gov/climatechange/emissions/index.html#ggo.

95 mmt of carbon per Q-BTU of energy. Petroleum is next at 63 mmt, and natural gas is relatively clean at 52 mmt. Nuclear power produces no greenhouse gas emissions.

THE EFFECTS OF ALTERNATIVE COMBINATIONS OF NONRENEWABLES

In Table 9.6, we consider four alternative scenarios for delivering 50 Q-BTUs of energy from nonrenewable sources and calculate the overall emissions levels generated by each scenario. In the four scenarios, we first vary the level of the nuclear energy supply—using 5 Q-BTUs, 10 Q-BTUs, and two scenarios with no nuclear power. In the two cases that assume no nuclear power, we then cover the loss of nuclear power by increasing either the coal or the natural gas supply.

As we see in the final row of these tables, if we allow for nuclear power to provide between 5 and 10 Q-BTUs of the overall US energy supply, the United States can achieve a level of greenhouse gas emissions from energy sources below 3,000 mmt. This would enable the country to achieve the overall 2030 emissions target of 4,200 mmt.

However, if we allow for no nuclear energy, it becomes much more difficult to keep overall emissions from energy sources below 3,200 mmt. Since natural gas is the cleanest-burning among fossil fuel energy sources, it becomes possible to stay close to or perhaps even below a 3,200 mmt threshold only if the use of natural gas is maximized. However, we have already alluded to significant obstacles to increased reliance on natural gas.

The first set of concerns is about supply constraints and infrastructure demands. These issues were summarized in a study by the US Government Accountability Office (2008, 5 and passim), which concluded that "fuel switching to natural gas . . . poses challenges related to existing infrastructure, including limited pipeline and storage capacity and technical and regulatory barriers to the conversion of existing coal plants. Large-scale fuel switching would require substantial investments in pipeline and storage capacity and new terminals to process imported natural gas—all of which would require regulatory approval." In addition, there is serious debate about the effects of extracting natural gas supply through hydraulic fracking technology.[9] These concerns are not likely to be resolved in the near future. This means that expanding the natural gas supply will present environmental problems of its own as well as more conventional sorts of supply constraints.

Table 9.6 **Emissions Levels from Alternative Combinations of Energy Consumption Exclusive of Transportation Sector Consumption** (figures are total Q-BTUs of energy per year)

Scenarios 1 and 2: Mid-range and maximum nuclear power

	5-Q-BTUs nuclear		10-Q-BTUs nuclear	
	Nonrenewable energy supply (Q-BTUs)	Emissions levels (mmt)	Nonrenewable energy supply (Q-BTUs)	Emissions levels (mmt)
Petroleum	20	1,260	20	1,260
Coal	10	950	10	950
Natural gas	15	780	10	520
Nuclear	5	0	10	0
Totals	50 Q-BTUs	2,990	50 Q-BTUs	2,730

Scenarios 3 and 4: No nuclear power with coal or natural gas substitution

	No nuclear with coal substitution		No nuclear with natural gas substitution	
	Nonrenewable energy supply (Q-BTUs)	Emissions levels (mmt)	Nonrenewable energy supply (Q-BTUs)	Emissions levels (mmt)
Petroleum	20	1,260	20	1,260
Coal	15	1,425	10	950
Natural gas	15	780	20	1,040
Nuclear	0	0	0	0
Totals	50 Q-BTUs	3,465	50 Q-BTUs	3,250

MANAGING EXCESS CAPACITY IN NONRENEWABLES

Assuming we are able to achieve an overall level of energy consumption by 2030 of about 65 Q-BTUs, and that 15 of those Q-BTUs will be provided by clean renewable energy sources, the unavoidable conclusion is that the US economy will have *excess* capacity in coal, natural gas, and nuclear power. With petroleum, the solution will be to simply cut back on the roughly 20 Q-BTUs of imported supply that is projected for 2030 in the EIA reference case. As a baseline for establishing the degree of excess capacity of coal, natural gas, and nuclear power, the 2009 production levels were as follows: natural gas, 23 Q-BTUs; coal, 20 Q-BTUs; and nuclear, 8.4 Q-BTUs. The EIA reference case figures for 2035 are roughly the same amounts as 2030.

Determining the most appropriate mix of nonrenewable sources for 2030 depends on how one assesses a combination of environmental, public safety, economic, and social priorities, since all of these contribute to the standard of living.

Oil Imports

The good news is that minimizing petroleum consumption beyond the roughly 20 Q-BTUs necessary for the transportation sector can reduce dependency on oil imports significantly. The EIA's reference case for oil imports in 2030 is 18.3 Q-BTUs, with another 5.3 Q-BTUs in imports for liquid fuels and other petroleum products. This is in addition to 12.5 Q-BTUs of domestic production in 2030 under the reference scenario, which is the same level as the actual production level of 2009. If domestic oil production is at 12.5 Q-BTUs in 2030, then this could mean that oil imports could fall to 7.5 Q-BTUs—a reduction of between 60 and 70 percent, depending on what we count in the oil import mix. There should be positive spillover effects on the economy and foreign policy from less dependence, including, of course, less reliance on the unstable Middle East for supplying oil to the United States.

Environment

There is a variety of environmental concerns to be addressed in comparing different nonrenewable sources of energy. Even "clean coal" is not all that clean. Natural gas contributes less to greenhouse gas emissions than coal or oil, but the use of hydraulic fracking technology for expanding natural gas production has been demonstrated to contaminate drinking water with methane gas in aquifers overlying the Marcellus and Utica shale formations of northeastern Pennsylvania and upstate New York (see Osborne et al. 2011). Is the overriding priority the minimization of greenhouse gas emissions? If so, a scenario that maintains nuclear power at a high level (perhaps as much as 10 Q-BTUs of energy by 2030) will be the appropriate choice.

Public Safety

However, nuclear power brings a unique set of concerns about public safety. Once we get to a 65-quad level of energy efficiency, the US economy can operate without any nuclear power supply, if this is the priority. To do so, while still remaining comfortably within the overall emission standards, will entail maintaining a high level of natural gas consumption. This then brings us back to the problem of the expanding use of hydraulic fracking technology for extracting natural gas from shale rock deposits.

Jobs

Since none of the scenarios requires significant expansion in nonrenewable fuel sources, it follows that there will not be any new sources of job creation in that sector. Instead, there are likely to be job losses in these industries.

Regional Impacts

Reducing production of nonrenewables will have differential impacts on different regions and communities throughout the country. For example, Appalachia will obviously be harmed most seriously by a reduction in coal production, although many western states also produce coal. Texas, Louisiana, Oklahoma, and the Rocky Mountain region will be affected by cutbacks in domestic petroleum or natural gas production. The boom in North Dakota has been based on the spread of fracking technology to extract natural gas. Differential impacts on regions and communities need to be weighed when considering the alternative scenarios. Some areas can more easily transition to an emphasis on wind, solar, or geothermal than others.

In order to align policies needed to limit climate change with broadly based increases in the standard of living, environmental, public safety, economic, social, and regional impacts should all be considered when determining how to set priorities in the extent to which we rely on alternative conventional energy sources. It is important to focus on how clean energy will create jobs as well as where it eliminates them and to balance the regional impacts as much as possible.

HOW THE CLEAN ENERGY AGENDA CREATES JOBS

Spending money in any area of the US economy will always create jobs, since people are needed to produce any good or service that the economy supplies. This is true regardless of whether the spending is done by private businesses, households, or a government entity. However, spending directed toward a clean energy investment program will have a much larger positive impact on jobs than spending in other areas, including, for example, within the oil industry—including all phases of oil production, refining, transportation, and marketing—or the coal industry. This is true regardless of whether the spending—on clean energy or fossil fuel energy—is done by households, private businesses, or the government. As such, a clean energy investment program will be a net source of job creation in the United States relative to spending the same amount of money on fossil fuels. We can anticipate that there will be a significant net increase in jobs coming from clean energy investments as long as the project of constructing this new energy infrastructure continues. This is likely to be a roughly twenty-year project. If it takes longer, we will clearly not be able to meet the greenhouse gas emission reduction targets by 2030 or thereabouts.

There are three sources of job creation associated with any expansion of spending—direct, indirect, and induced effects. For purposes of illustration, consider these examples of investments in energy-efficient building retrofits or constructing wind turbines:

1. **Direct effects**—the jobs created by retrofitting homes to make them more energy-efficient or by building wind turbines
2. **Indirect effects**—the jobs associated with industries that supply intermediate goods for the building retrofits or wind turbines, such as lumber, steel, and transportation
3. **Induced effects**—the expansion of employment that results when people who are paid in the construction or steel industries spend the money they have earned on other products in the economy

Figure 9.1 shows the total number of jobs—direct, indirect, and induced—that we estimate would be created from spending $1 million in a combination of six clean energy investment areas. Three of these are energy efficiency investment areas: building retrofits, transportation, and upgrades of the electrical grid. The other three are renewable energy areas: solar power, wind power, and biomass fuels.[10] As shown

Figure 9.1   **Job Creation Through $1 Million in Spending: Clean Energy Investments vs. Fossil Fuels**

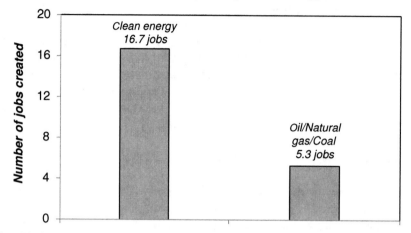

Source: Pollin, Heintz, and Garrett-Peltier (2009).

here, this combination of clean energy investments in efficiency and renewables will generate about 16.7 jobs per every million dollars of spending.

By contrast, we can use our same estimating model to generate figures for the total job creation from spending $1 million within the fossil fuel industries (i.e., oil, natural gas, and coal). As Figure 9.1 also shows, the total job creation in this case is 5.3 jobs per $1 million in spending on fossil fuels. In short, spending a given amount of money on a clean energy investment agenda generates more than three times the number of jobs within the United States as does spending the same amount of money within the fossil fuel sectors.

Why does the clean energy investment program create more jobs than spending within the fossil fuels industry? Three factors are at work:

1. **Relative labor intensity.** Relative to spending within the fossil fuel industries, the clean energy program utilizes far more of its overall investment budget on hiring people and relatively less on acquiring machines, supplies, land (either on- or offshore), and energy itself.
2. **Domestic content.** The clean energy investment program relies much more on products made within the US economy and less on imports than spending within the fossil fuel sectors. Thus, about 97 percent of total spending on public transportation will remain within the US economy, while, for the oil industry, about 83 percent of spending is domestic and 17 percent purchases imports.
3. **Pay levels.** Clean energy investments produce far more jobs at all pay levels—high-paying as well as low-paying jobs—than the fossil fuel industry. Clean energy investments also produce more jobs per dollar of expenditure, since the average pay for these jobs is less than the average for fossil fuel industry jobs. This is actually a positive for today's US economy, in which unemployment rates and income growth for middle- and lower-paying jobs have been worse than for higher-paying positions.

NET JOB GAINS THROUGH A CLEAN ENERGY INVESTMENT AGENDA

To illustrate the potential for clean energy investments as a net source of job creation, let us assume that the total amount of clean energy investments is about $110 billion per year—that is, $90 billion for efficiency and $20 billion for renewables. These are the spending levels for efficiency and renewables derived in the previous two sections to achieve both an overall level of energy consumption at 65 Q-BTUs and a level of 15 Q-BTUs supplied by clean renewable sources. This clean energy investment agenda will generate about 1.8 million jobs.

Now let us also make a simple assumption that spending within the fossil fuel sector of the US economy is reduced by the same $110 billion annually—that the increase in clean energy investments is exactly matched by a reduction in spending on fossil fuels. The decline in employment in the fossil fuel sector would then be about 600,000 jobs. However, as shown in Table 9.7, the net effect of this transfer of resources from fossil fuels to clean energy would result in a net gain in overall employment of 1.2 million jobs.

This is a healthy net increase in job creation, but it is small in relationship to the overall US labor market of about 150 million people. Nevertheless, creating this net increase in labor intensity within the US economy, on its own, could reduce structural unemployment in the United States (i.e., unemployment that is not due to the ups and downs of the business cycle) by nearly 1 percent, from, say 7 to 6 percent. Achieving this could also enable macro policies supporting a full-employment economy to be implemented more easily than would be the case with the more capital-intensive, fossil-fuel-dominant energy sector (see Pollin 2012 for further discussion), where there would be fewer jobs generated in the production of energy.

CARBON TAXES AND CARBON CAPS: ENVIRONMENTAL POLICY AND GDP GROWTH

Environmental regulations aimed at directly reducing fossil fuel consumption operate by both raising fossil fuel prices and limiting supply. One approach is a carbon tax, which directly raises the price so as to indirectly limit supply. The other approach is a carbon cap, which mandates reductions in fossil fuel production by specified amounts. The explicit limit on supply would then also be expected to raise prices. Cap-and-trade legislation is one variant of a carbon cap; but the "trade" feature of such a measure—that is, the capacity to buy or sell rights to produce the limited amount of overall fossil fuel supply—is a secondary effect which, at least in principle, will not alter the impact of the cap itself.

What is likely to be the impact of any such measures on economic activity in general? While forecasts are notoriously unreliable, especially over an extended period of time, it is useful to study the forecasting that has been done to obtain a sense of the range of effects that researchers anticipate.

With this limited ambition in mind—as opposed to presuming one can accurately forecast the future growth rate of the economy over the next generation—let us consider now several forecasts generated to estimate the effects on long-term GDP

Table 9.7   **Net Employment Effect of a $110 Billion Shift from Fossil Fuels to Clean Energy Investments**

1. Job creation through $110 billion spending on clean energy	1.8 million jobs
2. Job losses through $110 billion reduction in spending in fossil fuel sector	600,000 jobs
3. Net job creation through shift to clean energy (row 1 − row 2)	1.2 million jobs

Source: US Bureau of Labor Statistics and IMPLAN.

growth of the most recent piece of cap-and-trade legislation that was considered in Congress. The American Clean Energy and Security Act, or Waxman-Markey bill (named for its two sponsors in the House of Representatives), passed the House of Representatives in May 2009, but failed to pass in the Senate.

Table 9.8 shows the results of alternative forecasts of the impact of the Waxman-Markey bill that were generated by the Energy Information Administration, the Environmental Protection Agency, and the American Council on Capital Formation/National Association of Manufacturers (ACCF/NAM). The latter is a business lobbying group that was strongly opposed to Waxman-Markey. I present in Table 9.8 only the worst-case scenario generated by the ACCF/NAM model, its "high-cost case."

The results of these modeling exercises can be summarized quickly. In the models produced by the EIA and EPA, the effects of Waxman-Markey on GDP growth would be virtually indiscernible statistically. That is, the difference between their baseline GDP forecast and that in which cap-and-trade legislation was in effect is in the range of 1/20th of 1 percentage point of GDP growth. For example, in the first case shown in Table 9.8 (the EIA reference case) the difference is between a 2.71 and a 2.67 average annual growth rate between 2010 and 2030.

What is remarkable is that the worst-case scenario from ACCF/NAM, those strong opponents of cap-and-trade legislation, is not far from the same conclusion as the EIA and EPA models. Under their worst-case scenario, cap-and-trade legislation would reduce average GDP growth by only one-tenth of a percentage point (2.21 vs. 2.31 average annual growth).

This basic finding is even more notable considering that all these models omit significant factors that tend to encourage long-term growth. The positive effects of higher employment, the benefits of a higher level of domestic production and thus a reduced trade deficit from oil imports, the possibilities for major technological breakthroughs in areas such as solar power, and lower risks for natural disasters as greenhouse gas emissions are reduced would each be expected to raise the expected rate of economic growth.[11]

Moreover, as other chapters in this volume outline, faster GDP growth is not an adequate proxy for higher living standards without taking other factors into account. But creating more decent job opportunities and a dramatic reduction in carbon emis-

Table 9.8   **Comparison of Alternative US GDP Growth Forecasts Under Baseline and with Cap-and-Trade Legislation**

Average annual growth rate forecasts for specified time periods

	1. Baseline GDP forecast	2. GDP forecast under Waxman-Markey cap-and-trade bill	3. Difference between baseline and cap-and-trade growth forecasts (column 1 – column 2)
Energy Information Administration (basic scenario, 2010–2030)	2.71	2.67	0.04
Energy Information Administration (high-cost scenario, 2010–2030)	2.71	2.66	0.05
Environmental Protection Agency-1 (ADAGE model, 2015–2050)	2.41	2.36	0.05
Environmental Protection Agency-2 (IGEM model, 2015–2050)	2.38	2.32	0.06
ACCF/NAM (high-cost case, 2007–2030)	2.31	2.21	0.10

Sources: US Energy Information Administration (2009b); Environmental Protection Agency (2009); American Council on Capital Formation/National Association of Manufacturers (2009).

sions relative to current levels is surely part of improving living standards. What these GDP forecasting exercises suggest is that two cornerstones of a brighter future—good jobs and a sustainable environment—are achievable without having to assume that even conventionally measured GDP needs to be reduced as a result.

CONCLUDING REMARKS

The US economy will need to undertake a major transition of its entire energy infrastructure in order to both raise and sustain the living standard of US residents over the next generation. That energy transformation will entail three major projects:

1. *Investments to raise energy efficiency in buildings, industry, and transportation.* Reducing overall energy consumption in the United States by about 30 percent, from its current level of about 95 Q-BTUs to about 65 Q-BTUs, can be handled in part by improved efficiency standards. These will also provide for the expansion of good job opportunities and rising average incomes.

2. *Investments in clean renewable energy sources.* Clean renewable sources—including wind, solar, geothermal, and clean biofuels—will need to supply about 15 Q-BTUs of the total 65 Q-BTUs needed to power the United States economy in order to reach

the reduced emissions target. The proposal described here achieves the necessary shift while also expanding job opportunities.

3. *Delivering about 50 Q-BTUs of total energy through traditional sources.* The primary challenge will be to manage the excess capacity with nonrenewable energy sources (oil, coal, natural gas, and nuclear power) that will result from reduced energy use and more supply from clean renewables. Crucial considerations here include emission levels, other environmental impacts, job creation, public safety, minimizing oil imports, and the economic and social impacts on communities dependent on traditional energy as its use declines.

The transition to a clean energy economy will be greatly bolstered by two basic findings presented in the last two sections of this chapter. First, the transition to a clean energy economy will be a major new engine of job creation. Investments in clean energy generate about three times more jobs than similar spending within the fossil fuel sector. If the United States spends about $110 billion a year on investments in efficiency and expanding capacity of clean renewables and if that level of investment is exactly matched by declines in fossil fuel spending, the net effect will be to increase overall US employment by 1.2 million jobs. Second, even the estimates of those opposed to carbon limits show very little negative effect on GDP growth of policies limiting the supply of fossil fuels.

Overall, then, what emerges through our examination of these questions about undertaking major public and private investments in clean energy (i.e., energy efficiency and clean renewables) in the US economy is that it will produce major gains for the living standards of people in the United States. US residents will be able to live in a cleaner and safer environment, and the process of improving our environment will also bring an expansion of job opportunities and rising average incomes.

APPENDIX 9.1: DEMAND FOR PETROLEUM IN THE TRANSPORTATION SECTOR

I reach the conclusion that the US transportation sector will require about 20 Q-BTUs of petroleum in 2030, assuming a fuel efficiency standard of 54.5 mpg for new cars and trucks as of 2025. This is based on the following considerations:

1. **Reference case energy demand for cars and light trucks.** For its 2030 reference case, the EIA assumes that cars and light trucks will consume 17.6 Q-BTUs of energy; that is, about 60 percent of the total for the transportation sector.
2. **Cars and light trucks energy demand with higher fuel efficiency standards.** The Obama fuel efficiency standard for 2025 represents a 50 percent improvement over the 36.2 mpg standard assumed by the EIA for 2030. The average age for cars is now about ten years, a peak figure over the past fifteen years. The figure is likely to be lower as the economy moves out of the recession. In any case, the average mileage for the mix of new and used cars by 2030 will be around 50 mpg. However, it is also the case that even with the lower 36.2 mpg standard for 2030, the average age of cars would have

remained about the same as with the higher standards. In short, it is reasonable to assume that the level of fuel consumption for cars and trucks by 2030 will be 50 percent lower than under the EIA reference case. This means energy consumption for cars and light trucks of 8.8 Q-BTUs as of 2030.

3. **Demand from other transportation modes.** If, conservatively, we assume no efficiency improvements in other areas of transportation, the most important of which are freight trucks (6.0 Q-BTUs) and air travel (3.0 Q-BTUs), then total energy consumption as of 2030 in transportation will be 21.7 Q-BTUs. We round up to 22 Q-BTUs.

4. **Prospects for electric vehicles.** In the EIA reference case, about 97 percent of all energy in transportation is supplied by petroleum products of various sorts. It is possible that some share of this energy could be replaced by the use of electric vehicles. However, even in this case, electric cars could be powered by coal, nuclear power, or natural gas, in which case the overall environmental benefits would be few, if any.

5. **Prospects for biofuels.** Biofuels are the only other feasible alternative to petroleum for providing a large supply of affordable liquid fuels. However, as noted in the main text, there are also significant environmental problems associated with corn ethanol, which is at present the largest source of biofuels.

APPENDIX 9.2: GLOSSARY OF ACRONYMS AND TECHNICAL TERMS

BTUs/Q-BTUs (British thermal units)—A BTU is a standard unit of energy in a wide range of applications. It refers to the amount of energy needed to heat one pound of water by one degree Fahrenheit. Q-BTUs refers to one quadrillion BTUs.

CCS (carbon capture and sequestration)—The purpose of this technology is to capture waste carbon dioxide (CO_2) from large point sources, such as fossil fuel power plants, and transport the CO_2 to a storage site, which is normally an underground geological formation. This way the CO_2 emissions will not enter the atmosphere. As discussed in the main text, CCS technology remains, to date, unproven on a commercial scale.

CHP (combined heat and power)—As discussed in the main text, CHP systems are units that transform a fuel into electricity and then use the hot waste gas steam for processes such as space and hot-water heating or industrial and commercial processes. CHP systems are in widespread commercial use at present. But these systems could be used to a much greater extent in a range of industrial settings.

Geothermal energy—Geothermal energy is stored under Earth's surface in the form of heat. The most common current way of capturing the energy from geothermal sources is to tap into naturally occurring hydrothermal convection systems where cooler water seeps into Earth's crust, is heated up, and then rises to the surface. When heated water is forced to the surface, it is then captured as steam and can drive an electric generator.

Small-scale hydropower energy—Small-scale hydropower projects operate without requiring the construction of a dam or reservoir. They operate by the insertion of a water wheel or turbine into a stream or river. This produces a powerhouse whose tailwater returns the working flow back into the stream or river. Small-scale hydro projects have a generating capacity of thirty megawatts or less per site.

Solar photovoltaics (PV) technology—Solar PV technology generates electrical power by solar radiation converting into electricity using semiconductors. PV technology employs solar panels composed of a number of solar cells containing photovoltaic material—that is, material that generates an electric current upon exposure to sunlight.

Solar thermal technology—Solar thermal technology uses solar radiation primarily for directly generating heat through panels that collect the heat from radiation. Solar thermal panels are classified as low-, medium-, or high-temperature collectors. High-temperature collectors can also be used for electric power production, though this technology is not at present in widespread commercial use.

NOTES

1. Appendix 9.2 provides a glossary of technical terms used in this paper, including BTUs (British thermal units).

2. The 111.2 Q-BTU figure for total US energy consumption is the EIA's reference case forecast taken from the 2011 edition of the EIA's *Annual Energy Outlook*. In the 2012 edition of *Annual Energy Outlook*, the EIA's reference case forecast for total US energy consumption was adjusted downward to 104.3 Q-BTUs. Unless explicitly noted otherwise, throughout this paper, when referring to the "EIA reference case" figures, I will be citing the 2011 reference case estimates, including the 2011 estimate that total US energy consumption will be 111.2 Q-BTUs in 2030.

3. These points are developed in more depth in Pollin, Garrett-Peltier, Heintz, and Hendricks (2014).

4. It is notable that the $37 billion figure we have generated for total costs per quad of energy saved in the United States is very close to the $38 billion per year estimated by a 2009 study by the McKinsey management consulting and research firm (Granade et al. 2009), even though our figure and the McKinsey figure were generated independently of each other and based on different methodologies.

5. The figures are converted to equal annual payments and expressed in real annual dollar terms.

6. With solar photovoltaic technology, the energy from solar radiation is converted into electricity. Solar thermal technology uses solar radiation primarily to directly heat water. Both solar photovoltaic and solar thermal technologies can be and are used both for small-scale projects, such as generating electricity and hot water for private homes, and for large-scale projects, such as producing electricity that can be distributed over the power grid.

7. The most careful study on the negative environmental effects of hydraulic fracturing, including drinking water contamination, is Osborne et al. (2011).

8. I explain how I reach this figure in Appendix 9.1.

9. The debate is described, for example, in a *New York Times* article by Mike Soraghan (2011). See Osborne et al. (2011) for an in-depth analysis of the environmental effects of fracking.

10. The allocation of total investment funds that we are working with is 40 percent retrofits; 20 percent transportation; and 10 percent each for grid, wind power, solar power, and biomass fuels. Adjusting the budgetary allocations would affect the job total estimates, but not by a dramatic extent. The details for deriving these job figures are presented in Pollin, Heintz, and Garrett-Peltier (2009).

11. Pollin, Garrett-Peltier, Heintz, and Hendricks (2014) discuss these considerations at length.

BIBLIOGRAPHY

American Council for Capital Formation/National Association of Manufacturers. 2009. *Analysis of the Waxman-Markey Bill "The American Clean Energy and Security Act of 2009" (H.R. 2454) Using the National Energy Modeling System.* Washington, DC. http://accf.org/wp-content/uploads/2009/10/accf-nam_study.pdf.

Emanuel, K. 2012. *What We Know About Climate Change.* Cambridge, MA: MIT Press.

Granade, H.C., J. Creyts, A. Derkach, P. Farese, S. Nyquist, and K. Ostrowski. 2009. Unlocking Energy Efficiency in the US Economy. www.mckinsey.com/Client_Service/Electric_Power_and_Natural_Gas/Latest_thinking/Unlocking_energy_efficiency_in_the_US_economy.

National Academy of Sciences (NAS). 2010. *Real Prospects for Energy Efficiency in the United States.* Washington, DC: National Academies Press.

Osborne, S.G., A. Vengosh, N.R. Warner, and R.B. Jackson. 2011. "Methane Contamination of Drinking Water Accompanying Gas-Well Drilling and Hydraulic Fracturing." *Proceedings of the National Academy of Sciences Early Edition.* www.pnas.org/content/early/2011/05/02/1100682108.abstract.

Pollin, R. 2012. *Back to Full Employment.* Cambridge, MA: MIT Press.

Pollin, R., J. Heintz, and H. Garrett-Peltier. 2009. *The Economic Benefits of Investing in Clean Energy.* Washington, DC: Center for American Progress and Political Economy Research Institute. www.peri.umass.edu/fileadmin/pdf/other_publication_types/green_economics/economic_benefits/economic_benefits.PDF.

Pollin, R., H. Garrett-Peltier, J. Heintz, and B Hendricks 2014. *Green Growth: A Program for Controlling Climate Change and Expanding U.S. Job Opportunities.* Washington, DC: Center for American Progress.

Schreurs, M.A., and F. Yoshida, eds. 2013. *Fukushima: A Political Economic Analysis of a Nuclear Disaster.* Sapporo, Japan: Hokkaido University Press.

Soraghan, Mike. 2011. "Baffled About Fracking? You're Not Alone." *New York Times.* www.nytimes.com/gwire/2011/05/13/13greenwire-baffled-about-fracking-youre-not-alone-44383.html?pagewanted=all.

US Energy Information Administration (EIA). 2009a. *Energy Market and Economic Impacts of H.R. 2452, the American Clean Energy and Security Act of 2009.* August. Washington, DC: US Department of Energy. www.eia.gov/oiaf/servicerpt/hr2454/pdf/sroiaf(2009)05.pdf.

———. 2009b. *EPA Preliminary Analysis of the Waxman-Markey Discussion Draft.* April 20. www.epa.gov/climatechange/economics/pdfs/WM-Analysis.pdf.

———.2010. "Levelized Cost of New Generation Resources in the Annual Energy Outlook 2011." Washington, DC: US Department of Energy. http://205.254.135.24/oiaf/aeo/electricity_generation.html.

———. 2011. *Annual Energy Outlook 2011, with Projections to 2035.* Washington, DC: US Department of Energy. www.eia.gov/oiaf/aeo/demand.html.

———. 2012. *Annual Energy Outlook 2012, with Projections to 2035.* Washington, DC: US Department of Energy. www.eia.gov/forecasts/aeo/pdf/0383(2012).pdf.

US Environmental Protection Agency (EPA). 2009. "EPA Analysis of the American Clean Energy and Security Act of 2009. H.R. 2454 in the 111th Congress, Appendix. 6/23/09: Washington, DC: US Environmental Protection Agency, www.epa.gov/climatechange/Downloads/EPAactivities/HR2454_Analysis_Appendix.pdf.

US Government Accountability Office (GAO). 2008. "Economic and Other Implications of Switching from Coal to Natural Gas at the Capitol Power Plant and at Electricity-Generating Units Nationwide." May. www.gao.gov/products/GAO-08-601R.

Food, the Environment, and a Good Standard of Living

EMILY NORTHROP

Throughout this volume it is argued that a meaningful definition of the "standard of living" extends beyond market income and production to include quality of life and sustainability. This chapter follows that theme by highlighting modern industrial-style practices in the production, distribution, and consumption of food that are not environmentally or economically sustainable and that have diminished the quality of diets. Failures in the modern food system underscore limitations in using the market valuations of output as the only indicator of well-being, because they ignore the externalities and public goods that will be outlined later in this chapter. Fortunately, numerous proven avenues for improvement exist. This chapter makes a wide range of policy recommendations, each of which is built upon a successful precedent.

I begin with a review of agricultural practices that have become conventional over the last century. These practices harm the environment and contribute to the depletion of irreplaceable natural resources by eroding the potential for growing food in the future. The chapter then shifts to other connections between food and quality of life, including limited access to full-service supermarkets, the aesthetics of fast-food dining, and the increased occurrence of obesity. These rising obesity rates have raised the specter of a shortened American life expectancy, an outcome that makes for a dramatic reduction in the nation's living standard. I also address the concern of achieving global food security in light of projections that the world population will grow to 9 billion people by midcentury. The final sections provide an economic analysis of the issues raised in this chapter and recommend several policies that have already been demonstrated to be effective.

INDUSTRIAL AGRICULTURE, ENVIRONMENTAL DEGRADATION, AND RESOURCE EXHAUSTION

To achieve improvements in sustainable farming, we need to look back at the historical development of industrial agriculture in the United States. The first push toward modern methods of industrial agriculture came in response to the farm crisis of the 1920s and was further reinforced by the post–World War II Green Revolution. This major transformation of farming did not begin from the bottom up, but by a combination of effective product promotion by chemical and biotech firms, increased concentration of farm input suppliers, and various government policies that promoted larger-scale operations. Thus, conventional modern farming came to rely on heavy mechanization, crop hybrids, monocultures, and intensive use of fertilizers, pesticides, and water. Although this approach has yielded agricultural production sufficient to meet the caloric needs of the current global population of 7 billion, failures in economic, political, and social systems of distribution have left 925 million people undernourished (FAO 2010) and approximately 49 million Americans who are "food insecure" (USDA Economic Research Service 2011). As the world population and global demand for food continue to grow, it is easy to look for a continuation of industrial farming to provide the necessary future increases in food output. Unfortunately, this method of agriculture, which is the dominant method in the United States, causes tremendous environmental degradation and is unsustainable (Gliessman and Rosemeyer 2010).

At a basic level, industrial agriculture techniques erode precious topsoil. Even after significant improvement in the 1980s and 1990s, as of 2007, the United States was still losing 1.7 billion tons per year (USDA Natural Resources Conservation Service 2010), a rate far beyond nature's ability to replace it (Pimentel and Kounang 1998). Since 1950, erosion problems have prompted the abandonment of about one-third of the nation's cropped land (Warshall 2002). In the cornbelt, vast monocultures are a culprit, and the problem has been aggravated by the intensification of storms. It is widely observed that this loss of topsoil is reducing the nation's capacity to grow food in the future. In addition, many of the remaining soils have been degraded by the applications of nitrogen and phosphorus (Jackson 2010).

The extensive use of water is another unsustainable element of industrial farming. Roughly 20 percent of the irrigated area of the United States is supplied by groundwater pumped at a faster rate that it is replenished by nature (Tilman et al. 2002). Farming is also a major polluter of both ground and surface water. One of the most obvious and egregious results is the annual "dead zone" in the Gulf of Mexico caused by fertilizer runoff from across the Midwest. The nutrients in the runoff feed the Gulf algae, which in turn "bloom" and rob the rest of the sea life of oxygen, including seafood for humans. In 2011, the zone was nearly 6,800 square miles (17,600 square kilometers), roughly the size of New Jersey (NOAA 2011).

This chemical-laden runoff contributes significantly to the loss of biodiverse aquatic systems and threatens the survival of a variety of species. Heavy sediment from this runoff compounds the problem. Biodiversity is further weakened by the extensive monocultures that disrupt and reduce the number of insect species. To the extent that agriculture has claimed or fragmented habitat, it has scattered, divided, and reduced populations of species and made them more vulnerable to extinction (Badgley 2002). A different sort of threat to biodiversity comes from government support for livestock producers, which has resulted in the near extermination of the wolf population. Livestock production also causes significant ecological damage—

because as animals graze they often cause destruction to native vegetation, wildlife habitats, soils, stream banks, and aquatic habitats, all of which takes a significant toll on various species (Center for Biological Diversity 2012).

Another key resource constraint confronted by industrial agriculture is its heavy reliance on fossil fuels. The principle uses include the production of chemical inputs, especially fertilizers that rely on natural gas, the production and use of heavy capital equipment, and the transportation of inputs and products. It is often noted that between seven and ten calories of fossil fuel input are required to provide an average calorie of food (Bomford 2010). Since fossil fuels are nonrenewable resources, by definition the current system of industrial agriculture cannot be sustained indefinitely using these types of fuels. The heavy use of fossil fuels also works against sustainability efforts on another front, namely the attempts to maintain the global climate. The significant level of greenhouse gas emissions from agriculture is fully commensurate with the significant expenditures of these fuels. According to one estimate, the amount of CO_2 emitted by obtaining the average American diet is roughly comparable to that associated with the average person's transportation needs (Eshel and Martin 2006).

Because Americans on average eat a hefty 270 pounds (125 kilograms) of meat each year (FAO 2009), it is essential to recognize that the environmental repercussions of industrial agriculture are compounded by this dietary preference. The fundamental issue is that grains are an input into industrially produced animal products. A pound of grain is a pound of human food if it is directly eaten. Alternatively, it can be fed to livestock, but food potential is lost in the conversion to meat. For example, after a cow arrives in a feedlot, it takes 7 pounds (3 kilograms) of corn to generate one additional pound of body weight, not all of which is edible (Jacobson et al. 2006). This means more farmland, soil, chemicals, fuel, and water are needed to produce meat relative to what is needed for grains.

Contributing to the water intensity of meat production is the water needed for direct animal consumption. As a result, the total water requirement for a pound (.45 kilograms) of industrially farmed broiler chicken is 415 gallons (1,575 liters), while for beef it is 5,000 gallons (19,300 liters). In comparison, 240 gallons (900 liters) is needed for a pound of soybeans and 75 gallons for a kilogram of corn (Pimentel et al. 2004). Water pollution from "concentrated animal feeding operations" (CAFOs) is another serious problem. The concentration of animals makes for a concentration of animal wastes, and the common practices of waste management make for water resources polluted with pathogens, excessive nutrients, pharmaceuticals, and heavy metals that exist in the excreta. Manure "lagoons" are intended to contain the contaminants, but these holding areas leak, seep, and overflow, affecting both surface and ground waters (Burkholder et al. 2007).

The energy input differential between meat and plant food is also significant. For example, a calorie of chicken requires about 5.5 calories of fossil fuel input and a calorie of grain-fed beef takes about 15.6 calories, while for corn and apple, the fossil fuel caloric requirements are 0.4 and 0.9, respectively (Eshel and Martin 2006). In contrast, a vegetarian diet requires about one-third less fossil energy than the typical American diet (Pimentel and Pimentel 2008). Accompanying the higher use of fossil fuel is the increased generation of CO_2. In addition, meat production emits significant quantities of other much more powerful greenhouse gases, including methane, a product of animals' digestive processes, and nitrous oxide, which is emitted when bacteria digest livestock waste. It is common for the impact of these additional emissions to be expressed in "CO_2 equivalents" (CO_2e), which provide a single indicator for emissions of various potencies. Employing this measure, the impact of eating a diet heavy in red meat rather than a plant-based diet of equal calories is comparable to the typical American driver choosing an SUV over a Toyota Prius (Eshel and Martin 2006).

The practices of conventional agriculture described here were promoted by a spectrum of government policies. Agricultural subsidies encouraged the industrial production methods that rely heavily on off-farm inputs of capital, pesticides, and fertilizers, which have allowed US farmers to sell their output at artificially low prices. Publicly funded research and development has focused narrowly on promoting the industrial model for higher yields per acre (Reganold et al. 2011). Agricultural exemptions from the environmental regulation of water and long-standing government tax incentives to promote the use of fossil fuels have also been foundational to industrial agriculture (US Senate 2012). To make the agricultural system sustainable will require changes in all of these policies. There is a lot of evidence that these changes will improve rather than reduce the quality of life, certainly over time.

HEALTHY COMMUNITIES, HEALTHY CONSUMERS

Food affects the quality of our lives, and hence our standard of living, in innumerable complex and interconnected ways. For example, consider that the grueling, low-paid efforts of migrant farmworkers not only affect their own well-being and that of their employers and all who enjoy affordable fruits and vegetables, but also morph into this nation's divisive debate around immigration. This section elaborates on the ways that modern production, marketing, and consumption of food have harmed communities and individual consumers. It begins with the reduced vitality of rural communities, including the surprising lack of access to healthy food. Focus then shifts to some of the aesthetics of fast foods, the obesity epidemic, and the sophisticated methods of engineering food.

HEALTHY COMMUNITIES

Quality of life is certainly affected by the vitality of communities, and many connections to food can be readily made. The preeminent example in the era of capital-intensive agriculture is the cost incurred by rural communities that have experienced a decline in the number of farmers. Resultant erosions of economic and community vitality have reduced rural opportunities for future generations.

Another connection between community vitality and food is the availability and affordability of groceries, and it is noteworthy that many households in rural areas have "restricted food access" as defined by the US Department of Agriculture (USDA); that is, 1.1 million rural households live more than a mile (1.5 kilometer) from a supermarket and have no access to a vehicle. Restricted options to shop for food are commonly associated with the "food deserts" of urban communities, and there are indeed 1.3 million households in nonrural areas with this limited access to food (USDA Economic Research Service 2011). Given the US systems of food production and distribution, quality of life is clearly diminished when a community lacks a super-market or families have difficulty getting to one. Paradoxically, if these households had access to a nearby supermarket, the effect could be to decrease gross domestic product (GDP). That is, by relying less on fast-food restaurants and convenience store groceries, consumers might well spend fewer dollars on food, thereby reducing the dollar value of purchases that comprise GDP. The importance of food to quality of life and the examples above provide stark illustrations of how market production, prices, and income are incomplete indicators of a society's living standard.

AESTHETICS OF FOOD

A different case for broadening our concept of well-being beyond the GDP measure can be developed from some of the diverse aesthetics associated with food. To begin, many of the important aesthetics created by the production and consumption of food are not captured by a market exchange. For example, concentrated animal feeding operations literally reek, thereby imposing a huge aesthetic burden on their neighbors, a burden for which the neighbors are uncompensated. The aesthetic cost (i.e., the loss of clean air) is not reflected in the market price of the meat, a pricing issue I discuss more completely later in the chapter.

Fast-food restaurants provide convenience and low prices that often overwhelm other factors that make fast-food dining less aesthetically pleasing, such as eating from paper and Styrofoam containers. Experiments by behavioral economists have demonstrated that unadorned food presentations such as these actually diminish the ratings that diners give to how food tastes (Ariely 2008). Some argue that this is a trade-off customers knowingly make and that the low price accurately reflects how little the product is valued. But this presumption ignores the power of marketing to encourage humans to make irrational decisions, as discussed later in this section.

Eating meals in a vehicle rather than around a family dining table can not only diminish the dining aesthetic, but also affects family relationships. Regular family meals at home have been shown to result in lower incidences of child and teenage smoking, drinking, drug usage, depression, and eating disorders, as well as better school performance and delayed sexual activities (National Center on Addiction 2011). It is a stretch to assume that all parents recognize that they are making this trade-off when they allow their teenagers to pick up a fast-food dinner on the way home from an afternoon school event. When these detriments to children are accounted for, the low market price of the fast-food meal exaggerates the benefits to society's well-being.

In addition, fast-foods meals are less healthful, due in part to being typically laden with excess calories (Todd, Mancino, and Lin 2010). But on a per calorie basis, calorie-dense foods like those served in fast-food restaurants have a lower market price than healthier alternatives such as lean meats and fresh vegetables (Drewnowski 2004). However, to the extent that the low price and convenience of these foods promote unhealthy and even gluttonous consumption, there is a decided loss to the beauty as-sociated with the eating experience. This loss may well be omitted from a consumer's calculations when choosing the meal, a possibility underscored when recognizing that the Food and Drug Administration (FDA) nutrition labeling requirements are only now being extended to fast-food offerings (US FDA 2012). So, to the extent that people are unaware of, but care about, any negative nutritional consequences of their food purchases, the market price again overstates the benefits of its consumption. Since obesity is a food-related problem with colossal implications, including for quality of life, I will elaborate on this health concern.

OBESITY AND THE AMERICAN DIET

Obesity was publicly declared to be an epidemic in the United States in the late 1990s (Mokdad et al. 1999), but sounding the alarm did not protect the nation. Due largely to the methods of industrial agriculture, food has become more plentiful—a daily increase in the marketplace of 600 calories per person since 1970—and the evidence is clear that Americans are eating more. Between the early 1970s and 2008, obesity among children two to five years old doubled to 10 percent, for children between six and eleven years old it increased fivefold to 20 percent, and for adolescents of twelve to nineteen years old it tripled to 18 percent (USDA and USDHHS 2010). Over those years, adult obesity more than doubled to reach 34 percent. The combined percentages of overweight and obesity have reached 64 percent for women and 72 percent for men (Flegal et al. 2010).

This epidemic affects not only those directly afflicted, but also others who are forced to shoulder the financial burden. Excessive body weight has many costly adverse health effects, including coronary heart diseases, type 2 diabetes, various cancers, hypertension, stroke, and sleep apnea. For adults under sixty-five, medical expenditures are 36 percent higher for obese individuals than for those who are of normal weight (Sturm 2002). Between 1999 and 2005, childhood hospitalizations attributed to a diagnosis of obesity nearly doubled, with a roughly commensurate increase in costs; in 2005, the bill was $237.6 million (Trasande et al. 2009). A recent estimate of the medical cost associated with obesity approached $147 billion for 2008 (Finkelstein et al. 2009). It is important to point out that half of the cost of obesity was paid by taxpayers through the Medicaid and Medicare programs (Centers for Disease Control 2004), and much of the rest was shared through higher private insurance premiums.

These medical expenses do not include the indirect costs of lost market production and premature deaths, so again losses are not borne solely by the individual, but extend to society at large as well as to family and loved ones. One study found that among obese 40-year old nonsmokers, women lost 7.1 years of life and men lost 5.8 years (Peeters et al. 2003). Because of the combination of an increase in the incidence of obesity at all ages and the health-related concerns brought on by obesity, one group of researchers asserts that we are on track for the American life span to be shortened by up to five years over the coming decades. They conclude that "the steady rise in life expectancy during the past two centuries may soon come to an end" (Olshansky et al. 2005). This prospect is the most dramatic indication of how our modern food system is reducing the national standard of living.

Behind this obesity epidemic are the concerted efforts by food manufacturers to advertise their brands to promote the consumption of their products. But the lengths to which food processors go extend well beyond these (more or less) transparent efforts. They include the activities of a small group of food scientists whose work is to engineer foods that are "palpable," by which the scientists mean foods that exaggerate the sensory pleasures of eating. Furthermore, these foods actually stimulate the appetite, rather than satisfy it, thereby triggering additional eating. David Kessler, former head of the FDA, reports the brain research showing that eating hyperpalatable foods can maintain dopamine levels (as does cocaine use), thereby changing the operation of neural circuits to amplify the reward provided by the food. There is substantial scientific evidence that the manufactured hyperpalatability of food is conditioning Americans, and increasingly others around the globe, to overeat (Kessler 2009).

This successful engineering of foods that stimulate appetite can also be understood as the successful engineering of a new consumer demand for these foods. To view the manufacturers' activities in this way is to invite a recurrent question of economic philosophy concerning whom the market system ultimately serves. In this context, the focus is whether the market directs producers to *meet* the needs of consumers or whether to some extent firms *create* consumer needs in order to meet their own goals. It is an assumption of mainstream economics, summarized as "consumer sovereignty," that consumer demand originates with consumers and that firms work to serve that demand. A critique of that assumption, referred to as "producer sovereignty" (Galbraith 1971), is a policy-relevant contrast that I will return to below.

It is important to recognize that all of the threats to quality of life raised in this section have evolved in the presence, or absence, of potent government policies. Obesity has been abetted by the presence of tax deductions for the marketing of sugary sodas and the promotion of USDA dietary guidelines that have obfuscated critical elements of a healthy diet (Nestle 2002). Nutrition education requirements and healthful and attractive lunch options in public schools have been noticeable in their absence, although this is beginning to change. There are many policies to promote improvement, even in the very personal choices about what people eat.

SUSTAINABILITY, DIET, AND GLOBAL FOOD SECURITY

The two broad issues of sustainability and dietary preferences are critical to the prospects for achieving food security for the 9 billion global inhabitants expected by midcentury. Given the unknowns that lie ahead, there is no consensus that the goal will be reached. Among the uncertainties are the rate and extent to which the climate will change and the concomitant impacts on yields, the rate and extent to which natural resources are degraded and exhausted, the amount that is invested in developing alternative sustainable farming methods, the rate of dissemination of these methods, and their potential yields. Also relevant are the degrees of continued urbanization and a veritable host of institutional parameters including international trade rules, credit availability for small growers, and the expansion of opportunities for women peasant farmers (Evans 2009; Worldwatch Institute 2011).

As people around the globe achieve middle-class status, their diets tend to mimic that of Americans, with lots of fat, sugar, and processed carbohydrates. As of 2000, there were already as many overnourished people on the planet as undernourished people (Gardner and Halweil 2000). "Globesity" has entered the lexicon in response to a global epidemic of obesity that extends to individuals in moderate- and low-income nations. Predictably, the so-called Western diseases such as diabetes and heart disease associated with that diet are following the obesity trend. Another central component of the diet is meat, and as outlined earlier in this chapter, the production of meat amplifies the detrimental environmental effects of food production. In addition, in an era of increasing food scarcity, the use of grain as animal feed will be increasingly consequential. Thus the extent to which people adopt American-like diets is another factor central to the potential achievement of global food security in the coming decades.

Given the uncharted complexities of achieving this food security, no reliable prediction can be made concerning the cost of achieving it. In the same vein, the benefits of obtaining global food security are also impossible to quantify. Chief among those benefits are the countless human lives that will be spared undernourishment and starvation. And in the decades ahead, even if the national riches of the United States are used to protect its citizens from experiencing emaciated bodies, the nation will nevertheless be affected. In fact, global food security issues have already affected the United States.

The availability and price of food have geopolitical ramifications that impact US national interests. The Arab Spring uprisings of 2011 are a ready illustration. As measured by the Food and Agricultural Organization (FAO) Food Price Index, in February 2011, global food prices were at a historic high, double the level of prices in 2005 (FAO 2014). While the unrest had deep and perennial causes, including inadequate political freedom and economic opportunity, researchers have connected the timing of the street protests to this historic spike in food prices (Breisinger et al. 2012). Clearly the uprisings demanded the attention of Washington, even including direct military involvement in Libyan battles.

An earlier preview of the geopolitical possibilities comes from 2008. Global food prices had risen by nearly 60 percent in two years, reaching a then unprecedented level. Hunger spread among the poor, especially in the global south, and the gains of the global middle-class were eroded. A wave of protests, which occurred in at least thirty nations, was explicitly motivated by these high food prices. Scores of people died in riots, and governments, both weak and strong, were under intense pressure; in Haiti, the government was brought down (Lacey 2008).

It is apparent that the inability of a government to ensure a food supply for its citizens is a lightning rod for social unrest. Since the United States is a global actor in the economic, military, and humanitarian spheres, insufficient global food security will impinge on US interests and well-being in multiple areas. Once again the traditional definition of standard of living, one that ignores the social and environmental sustainability of production, is far too narrow.

HOW "CHEAP" FOOD IS A BAD DEAL

Applying the standard economic concepts of "externalities" and "public goods" to the issues raised in this chapter provides some interesting insights into what is thought of as a personal activity (eating). First, though industrially produced food is lower priced, when all environmental and health costs are accounted for, it is no bargain. Second, public policies are needed to improve the environment, as well as to improve personal diets. These lessons from the application of mainstream economics will then be underscored by some unorthodox but warranted modifications of mainstream theory. Namely, four key assumptions of conventional economics will be relaxed. These assumptions are that suitable substitutes can be developed to supply the services provided by natural resources, that people can be counted on to behave rationally, that consumers are "sovereign," and that consumer preferences are stable.

The concept of externalities is central to basic economic theory. Applying it to industrial agriculture brings into focus the fact that significant costs associated with the negative environmental effects described above are not paid by the direct producers and consumers of the food, but rather are externalized, or passed along, to third parties. For example, neighbors and people downstream from farms often must deal with polluted groundwater and waterways. Since these environmental costs are not reflected in the market price of food, current food prices understate its true cost of production. Methods that mitigate the environmental harm of modern food production are typically costly to farmers. To the extent that they are adopted, these methods would lead to higher food prices as some of those extra production costs would be passed along to direct consumers.

This is a critical insight. Organic foods are more "expensive" because more of the production costs are internalized by the growers, rather than spilling onto third parties. When costs are internalized, there is less incentive to use environmentally destructive growing methods, and equity is enhanced as costs are shifted away from third parties. From this standpoint, having consumers pay for the full cost of their meals is socially desirable. An essential exception is for those with incomes insufficient to pay the higher prices, but in these cases the subsidy should not come from externalizing environmental costs. The need to be able to afford the real cost of healthful food provides another argument for increasing the pay of low-wage workers, as outlined by David Howell and others in this volume. Short of this, means-tested public support may be needed along with larger allocations for those who receive food stamps.

That said, it is entirely possible that in the future, the market price of sustainably produced foods could fall *relative to* the price of conventional foods. This prospect looms particularly feasible when considering the unsustainable reliance on oil of conventional farming methods. Today's cost advantage in favor of conventional agriculture is based on today's oil prices and the externalization of the environmental cost associated with its use. But oil prices will surely rise in the future, and presumably at some point governments will more forcefully address climate change and shift the cost of CO_2 emissions toward the direct emitters; both developments will shift the cost advantage away from conventional agriculture. This follows because the oil-based production methods will incur increasing production costs, while food grown with more sustainable methods that use less oil will have relatively less upward pressure on costs of production. This narrowing of production costs makes for a narrowing of the price differential between the products. Furthermore, we can expect that at some high threshold price for oil, the cost advantage of conventional methods will disappear altogether, thus bringing the transition to sustainable agricultural methods.

The problem of rising "globesity" also suggests that many foods are underpriced, because their full costs are not internalized to either consumers or producers. That is, those who are most responsible for the obesity-related medical bills are the companies who effectively promote consumption of unhealthful and addictive food products, as well as the consumers who overeat. But who pays the medical bills? They are primarily shifted to healthier individuals in private insurance pools or to taxpayers when government programs pay the bills.

Finally, it is important to understand that today's low food prices are actually being subsidized by future generations. To be specific, environmentally degrading agricultural methods that keep present-day prices low shift some of the costs to future generations. To achieve "a brighter future," the vision of this volume, requires moving away from feeding people today using methods that harm the prospects of future generations. Instead, production methods that maintain the natural capital required for people in the future to feed themselves should be used even if they are more expensive in the short run. Intergenerational equity dictates that today's consumers pay the full cost of their meals.

The industrial food system is often heralded for providing Americans with cheap food. The concept of externalities sheds a new light on the claim that the food is "cheap." When negative environmental and health impacts are accounted for, it is apparent that the food is appreciably less affordable than the price tag indicates. Government policy is required to force the internalization of the costs of producing and consuming food.

Applying the economic concept of "public goods" reinforces the market failures present in today's outcomes and the need for improvement. A stable climate and healthy biodiversity are two principal public goods related to agriculture. These are public goods in that one individual's consumption of the good does not reduce the amount available for others, and no one can be excluded from consuming the good. Because of this nonexclusivity, private sector firms find it unprofitable to provide public goods. The market also invites free-rider behavior, leaving to others the burdens of protecting biodiversity and minimizing climate change even though the free riders will themselves benefit from these provisions. It is not surprising that a stable climate and rich biodiversity are being underprovided by pure market forces and that collective action through public bodies is needed to provide these public goods.

The presence of both public goods and externalities means that government policies are needed to improve on market outcomes. This conclusion is further reinforced when some key conventional economic assumptions are relaxed. Standard economics tends to deemphasize, or even implicitly take for granted, natural resources. For example, microeconomic production models commonly highlight just the two inputs of labor and capital, with an emphasis on their substitutability and with no finite limits applicable to either. Applying this production theory to farming obfuscates the unique contributions of topsoil and water, as well as the finite limit of fossil fuels. It leads to the careless expectation that industrial agriculture can be maintained by developing substitutes for these natural resources and that no public policies are needed to ensure their stewardship. To the extent that these resources cannot be replaced, government action is needed to discipline their private exploitation.

Another fundamental assumption of microeconomic theory is that individuals will act in their own best interests to maximize their personal satisfaction. This implies that even unhealthful levels of food intake maximize the "utility" of the consumers, because if their choices failed to enhance their well-being, they would simply choose otherwise. This formulation for decision making is a direct contradiction of the fact that many people have eaten their way into the decidedly unhappy state of being overweight or obese, and it is a policy-relevant falsehood. That is, if individuals are "rational" and reliably act in their own self-interest, public health initiatives to tackle obesity are (beyond efforts to internalize externalities) unwarranted. It is more accurate and constructive to see some dietary choices as lacking rationality and to explore how policy can act to improve individuals' consumption choices.

The assumption of rational behavior is related to the presumption of "consumer sovereignty," introduced above, and the orthodox approval that markets receive when they are portrayed as mechanisms that motivate firms to satisfy, rather than to create, consumer needs and desires. If, in contrast, firms in the food industry are able to employ the rigorous methods of psychology and chemistry to manipulate consumer decisions, then a market emerges in which buyers are to some extent bending to the "sovereignty" of the producers (Galbraith 1971). An outcome consistent with this type of producer influence would be for consumers to irrationally eat themselves into poor health and premature death, just as is apparent in the United States today. This is not a well-behaved market, and it is ripe for government mediation.

Apart from any decisive influence of firms on consumer demand, the mere understanding that consumer preferences *can change* is itself the relaxation of another assumption of standard economics that considers people's preferences to be "relatively unchanging" or "stable." In her book *Plenitude*, Juliet Schor (2010) draws on "behavioral economics, cultural evolution, and social networking . . . [and] interdisciplinary work in psychology, biology, and sociology," all of which point to "a view of humans as far more malleable." She continues, "As we transform our lifestyles, we transform ourselves. Patterns of consuming . . . that may seem unrealistic or even negative before starting . . . become feasible and appealing." It is both hopeful and realistic to include diet among the types of consumption for which tastes and preferences can change, and this perspective adds legitimacy to government efforts to assist consumers in improving their diets.

There are significant food-related impediments to sustainability and quality of life that are multifaceted and disparate, thus requiring responses on multiple levels. Fortunately, in many of the policy-relevant matters central to agricultural methods and public health, constructive responses already exist as precedents upon which society can build. So the obstacles are less about designing government policies than about summoning the wisdom and will to undertake them. I now turn to specific policy options.

THE MULTIFACETED FARM BILL

An obvious and arguably necessary place to begin a policy discussion is with the farm bill, the national omnibus legislation that is renegotiated about every five years.

An examination of the legislation reveals that government support largely fails to promote, and often deters from, a healthy environment, healthy communities, and healthy bodies. But much more hopefully, it also reveals positive directions for the development of policies.

The farm bill is the legislation that fashions agricultural subsidies. The structure of these subsidies is commonly criticized, very often because the distribution of payments is not consistent with the aspiration of supporting the small family farms that are vital to rural communities. The Environmental Working Group has scrutinized the massive USDA records of subsidy payments and confirms that the payments are concentrated among recipients, with the richest 10 percent of the beneficiaries obtaining 74 percent of the funds. This group averaged subsidies of $447,873 over the sixteen-year period of 1995 through 2010. The total payment to those in the bottom 80 percent averaged $8,682. The contrast is even sharper between the $2,069,453 received just in 2009 by the single business entity of SJR Farms and the 62 percent of all farmers who received no subsidies at all. As these figures suggest, the distribution has promoted increased concentration in farming, and in turn, the loss of farms has contributed to economic and social declines in rural America.

The public is paying large subsidies to obtain undesirable effects. Commodity subsidies amounted to $167.3 billion from 1995 through 2010, with another $39.2 billion providing subsidies for crop insurance. In recent years, about 70 percent of the subsidies have gone to support only five crops: corn, wheat, cotton, rice, and soybeans, with corn receiving more assistance than the sum of any two of the other principal crops (Environmental Working Group 2011). About 80 percent of all US-grown corn (and another 30 million tons of soybeans) is fed to animals (Environmental Protection Agency 2009), turning the crop subsidy program also into a meat subsidy program. Notably missing from the list of major subsidized crops are fruits and vegetables. Thus there are many sound bases for rethinking crop subsidies.

The farm bill could also be redirected to give incentives to improve the environment rather than to despoil it. While there is current federal support for conservation through a variety of programs, these budgets are in the millions, rather than billions, of dollars. Current conservation initiatives were designed to maintain farm and ranch land in their agricultural uses (rather than sacrificed to development), conserve natural resources on working farms and ranches, promote environmental innovations, facilitate cooperation of farmers and community groups in addressing concerns about natural resources, and preserve wetlands. The Environmental Quality Incentives Program (EQIP) is the USDA's primary conservation program. It provides farmers with the educational, technical, and financial assistance needed to develop and implement conservation plans for their working lands (Environmental Working Group 2011). This is an example of the type of program that should be maintained and generously expanded.

Another existing effort is the National Institute for Food and Agriculture (NIFA), which has the "unique mission to advance knowledge for agriculture, the environment, human health and well-being, and communities by supporting research, education, and extension programs in the Land-Grant University System and other partner organizations" (NIFA 2011). Experts writing in *Science* argue for a redirection of NIFA and other public dollars from researching incremental changes in farming practices to investigations that will "transform" agriculture. They advocate that funding support transdisciplinary approaches to advance sustainability, broadly defined to include the well-being of farmers, agricultural workers, and rural communities in addition to the environment. These scientists observe that current developments toward transformative agricultural practices are coming mainly from the fields of farmers and nonprofit organizations, not from conventional research institutions. They recommend that the government provide instrumental support to these efforts, for instance, by gathering and facilitating the exchange of information among these small independent innovators. The scientists also recommend publicly funded pilot projects to develop and advance sustainable options (Reganold et al. 2011). All of these recommendations have implications for the research and extension programs of agricultural schools. Given the acute and impending challenge of feeding a more crowded planet, a strong commitment needs to be made to publicly finance research and development in order to achieve sustainable production.

Outside the farm bill, but central to a healthy environment, is the national Clean Water Act (CWA). This legislation is unfortunately on the sideline for critical farming issues since agricultural storm and irrigation runoff, the largest source of water pollution in the United States, is exempt from the CWA. The regulation of runoff has been left to the states, and collectively they have fallen well short of adequate protection. However, a recent analysis of various existing state programs discerned "five individual agricultural management practices, each of which is commonsense, widely applicable, and readily required by state regulation." The five regulations are requiring vegetative buffers along all surface water, restrictions on which substances can be applied to land within 100 feet (30 meters) of surface water, restrictions on applying manure in winter, prohibitions on applying some commercial fertilizers during the fall, and prohibiting livestock access to surface water (Dexter and Ettinger 2010). So long as the CWA maintains its agricultural exemption, states need to impose these proven measures.

POLICIES TO PROMOTE HEALTHY EATING

Turning to public efforts that promote healthier diets is to return the discussion to the crop subsidies, and most obvious is that these dollars could be redirected to support the production of fruits and vegetables. Again we have a model upon which to build. The USDA Specialty Crops Block Grant program initiated in 2004 awards monies to states to encourage the production of vegetables, fresh and dried fruits, and nuts. Among the efforts supported have been "buy local" campaigns that promote the sale of produce to local consumers, including schools, people with low incomes, and underserved communities, with farmers' markets being one type of venue. The annual monetary commitment of this program has never reached even $100 million, a small fraction of the support for the major crop recipients (Congressional Budget Office 2012). Greater support for specialty crops would encourage healthier eating and an improved quality of life.

The farm bill also includes the Supplemental Nutrition Assistance Program (SNAP, previously known nationally as the food stamp program), and under its auspices in 2010 nearly $65 billion went to aid more than 40 million people (USDA Food and Nutrition Service 2011a). This program is key to the collective efforts that address the issue of domestic food security, but beyond that, its repeated stated intention is to help households "purchase *healthier* foods" (USDA Food and Nutrition Service 2010; italics added). From the standpoint of public health, it is unfortunate that the program also pays for *less* healthy foods, including sugary sodas, cookies, candies, and chips. The program need not do so.

SNAP would be vastly improved if it followed the precedent of the USDA's Women, Infants, and Children program (WIC), which distinguishes between foods that are clearly healthy and those that do not warrant public support; for example, only breads that contain at least 51 percent whole wheat or whole grain are WIC approved (USDA Food and Nutrition Service 2011b). The WIC experience demonstrates that the contentious decisions concerning which foods to subsidize and which to leave unsubsidized can be made in ways that promote better health. Since the means-tested allotments are calculated to only supplement spending on food, households may continue to buy cookies and soda, but simply not with the government subsidy intended to support the consumption of "healthier foods."

Because healthful foods are often more expensive than an unhealthy alternative, a move to restrict SNAP payments to these foods would need to include an increased level of benefits. To the extent that diet-related illnesses were reduced, there would be some offsetting declines in government spending on medical assistance. An alternative suggestion is to encourage SNAP recipients to spend more on fruits and vegetables by allowing the dollar value of the assistance to be doubled when spent on those foods (Nestle 2010). While this would be an improvement over the current system, it would presumably be less effective than restricting eligible foods to healthful options. However, this type of reform would directly acknowledge and address the reality that healthier foods often cost more.

A third monetary incentive to encourage healthy eating has become recurrent in public debate since it made a high-profile appearance in the *American Journal of Public Health* in 2000. The proposal by Michael Jacobson and Kelly Brownell was to tax "foods of low nutritional value." In making their case, they reported that eighteen states and the city of Chicago already taxed soft drinks, snack foods, chewing gum, and/or candy. With tax rates ranging up to 7.5 percent on colas in California, the levies generated more than $200 million annually in revenues in each of the big states of California, Texas, and New York, and nationally they added about $1 billion to government coffers. Typically, the funds were added to the governments' general revenue pools. Jacobson and Brownell urged state and local governments to levy more taxes on these foods and devote all proceeds to programs that promote public health. They pointed out that at the time of their writing the National Cancer Institute spent about $1 million annually on the "5-A-Day" campaign urging people to eat five servings of fruits and vegetables each day, while 600 times that amount was spent on cola advertising each year (Jacobson and Brownell 2000).

A more specific version of this tax plan has been recently proposed by the Urban Institute which recommended a tax of 10 percent on "fattening food of little nutritional value" that could be expected to raise $500 billion over a decade (Engelhard, Garson, and Dorn 2009). However, the effects of this policy on obesity are not assured. Studies that have estimated the impact of food prices on consumers' body weight have found the expected negative relationship, but over the short term it is estimated to be very slight (Chou et al. 2004). There is, however, some evidence that the effect is more significant over the course of several years (Goldman, Lakdawalla, and Zheng 2009). Yet even if a sizable tax, broadly applied, ended up being only a small deterrent to eating "fattening food," it might nevertheless prove beneficial in combating obesity if the revenues were used to support a variety of anti-obesity campaigns. Since this tax would be regressive, it would be important to ensure that its revenues benefit people in low-income areas. These benefits could range from providing needed transportation to residents of the nation's food deserts to expanding nutrition education in schools and creating parks and walkable spaces where they are scarce.

Schools were the direct target of another federal law passed in 2010. The Healthy, Hunger-Free Kids Act requires the USDA to revise the nutrition standards for all foods sold in schools and is designed to improve the nutritional value of these foods in part by increasing the monies available for healthy school options. The law mandates a higher nutritional value for the meals provided to children who rely on the school breakfast and lunch programs, a larger number of children than ever before (Center for Science in the Public Interest 2010). Efforts such as these should be protected and enhanced.

First lady Michelle Obama's "Let's Move" campaign to fight childhood obesity included a proposal for $400 million annually to be devoted to making healthy foods available in the nation's food deserts. Those monies did not materialize, but what emerged instead were commitments from six grocery retailers to begin marketing healthy and affordable foods to almost 10 million people currently living in these underserved areas. The big commitments, which are pledged to be honored over five years, came from Supervalu (250 new stores) and Wal-Mart (300 new or expanded stores), while Walgreens agreed to sell whole vegetables and fruits at 1,000 of its stores (Office of the First Lady 2011). Obviously, this is a welcome development, and while time will tell if the commitments are fully implemented, any progress toward meeting the goals will be meaningful to the affected individuals.

Meanwhile, local governments need not sit idly by. Policy tools include zoning, land use planning, development and redevelopment efforts, and nutrition assistance. One such program, "Fresh" in New York City, uses financial incentives and zoning to boost the development, expansion, and upgrading of grocery stores in underserved areas. Other programs in New York City that are the product of various government groups are "Green Carts" to assist vendors in bringing produce to underserved areas, "Healthy Bodegas" to provide healthy foods in corner stores, and "Health Bucks" to encourage produce sales at farmers' markets (Treuhaft and Karpyn 2010). The growth of farmers' markets across the nation is itself phenomenal. From 1994 through 2011, the number grew more than fourfold to reach 7,175 (USDA Agricultural Marketing Service 2011). Policy support for farmers' markets is also an opportunity for government to encourage the sales of grass-fed animal products and local eggs. Community initiatives have also included the establishment of community gardens, zoning laws that allow urban chickens, and community space for aiding the deliveries of community-supported agriculture. Detroit has been noteworthy for establishing gardens on unused urban lots. These various activities often bring people with similar interests together, thereby building community and further enhancing the standard of living in dimensions well beyond the usual GDP measure.

CONCLUSION

A review of our industrial food system could focus on its achievement of the dramatic increase in yields per acre. Many others have done just that. But that emphasis can easily lead to complacency based on the expectation that those gains can be maintained and even expanded in the future, when in fact this expectation is unsustainable. The focus could also be on the ubiquity and cheap market price of unhealthy foods, but this emphasis is also misplaced. As I have outlined in this chapter, these foods are cheap only when externalities are ignored.

Making the transition to sustainable production and consumption across *all* sectors of the economy may be the most daunting challenge of our time. And it will occur only if we elevate the value we place on good health for people and the environment—both now and for many generations to come. It does not make sense to talk about a higher standard of living because food has become cheaper to purchase, when that food has also become less healthful and creates more negative effects in the world today and for future generations. As this chapter has outlined, many proven strategies are available to make the necessary transformational changes to improve the broader standard of living. It is vitally important that we accelerate our efforts.

BIBLIOGRAPHY

Ariely, D. 2008. *Predictably Irrational: The Hidden Forces That Shape Our Decisions*. New York: HarperCollins.

Badgley, C. 2002. "Can Agriculture and Biodiversity Coexist?" In *The Fatal Harvest Reader: The Tragedy of Industrial Agriculture*, ed. A. Kimbrell, 199–207. Washington, DC: Foundation for Deep Ecology/Island Press.

Bomford, M. 2010. "Getting Fossil Fuels Off the Plate." In *The Post Carbon Reader: Managing the 21st Century's Sustainability Crises*, ed. R. Heinberg and D. Lerch, 120. Healdsburg, CA: Watershed Media.

Breisinger, C., O. Ecker, P. Al-Riffai, and B. Yu. 2012. *Beyond the Arab Awakening: Policies and Investments for Poverty Reduction and Food Security*. Washington, DC: International Food Policy Research Institute.

Burkholder, J.A., et al. 2007. "Impacts of Waste from Concentrated Animal Feeding Operations on Water Quality." *Environmental Health Perspectives* 115, no. 2: 308–312.

Center for Biological Diversity. 2012. "Grazing." www.biologicaldiversity.org/programs/public_lands/grazing/index.html.

Center for Science in the Public Interest. 2010. "Landmark Child Nutrition Improvements to Become Law." News release, December 2. www.cspinet.org/new/201012021.html.

Centers for Disease Control and Prevention. 2004. *Obesity Costs States Billions in Medical Expenses.* CDC Office of Enterprise Communication press release, January 21. www.cdc.gov/media/pressrel/r040121.htm.

Chou, S.-Y., et al. 2004. "An Economic Analysis of Adult Obesity: Results from the Behavioral Risk Factor Surveillance System." *Journal of Health Economics* 23, no. 3: 565–587.

Congressional Budget Office. 2012. www.cbo.gov.

Dexter, J., and A. Ettinger. 2010. *Cultivating Clean Water: State-Based Regulation of Agricultural Runoff Pollution.* Chicago: Environmental Law and Policy Center. http://elpc.org/wp-content/uploads/2010/03/ELPC-Cultivating-Clean-Water-Report.pdf.

Drewnowski, A. 2004. "Obesity and the Food Environment: Dietary Energy Density and Diet Costs." *American Journal of Preventive Medicine* 27, no. 3 suppl.: 154–162.

Engelhard, C.L, A. Garson Jr., and S. Dorn. 2009. "Reducing Obesity: Policy Strategies from the Tobacco Wars." Urban Institute, July. www.urban.org/publications/411926.html.

Environmental Protection Agency. 2009. "Major Crops Grown in the United States." www.epa.gov/agriculture/ag101/cropmajor.html.

Environmental Working Group. http://www.ewg.org.

Eshel, G., and P.A. Martin. 2006. "Diet, Energy, and Global Warming." *Earth Interactions* 10, no. 9: 1–17.

Evans, A. 2009. *The Feeding of the Nine Billion: Global Food Security for the 21st Century.* London: Royal Institute of International Affairs.

Finkelstein, E.A., J.G. Trogdon, J.W. Cohen, and W. Dietz. 2009. "Annual Medical Spending Attributable to Obesity: Payer- and Service-Specific Estimates." *Health Affairs* 28, no. 5: w822–w831.

Flegal, K.M., M.D. Carroll, C.L. Ogden, and L.R. Curtin. 2010. "Prevalence and Trends in Obesity Among US Adults, 1999–2008." *JAMA: The Journal of the American Medical Association* 303, no. 3: 235–241.

Food and Agriculture Organization of the United Nations (FAO). 2009. *The State of Food and Agriculture.* Rome: FAO, 2009. www.fao.org/docrep/012/i0680e/i0680e.pdf.

———. 2010. *The State of Food Insecurity in the World: Addressing Food Insecurity in Protracted Crises.* Rome: FAO. www.fao.org.

———. 2014. FAO Food Price Index. www.fao.org./fileadmin/templates/worldfood/Reports and docs/Food price indices data.xls.

Food and Nutrition Service. US Department of Agriculture. www.fns.usda.gov.

Galbraith, J.K. 1971. *Economics, Peace, and Laughter.* Boston: Houghton Mifflin.

Gardner, G., and B. Halweil. 2000. "Escaping Hunger, Escaping Excess." *World Watch* 13, no. 4: 25.

Gliessman, S.R., and M. Rosemeyer, eds. 2010. *The Conversion to Sustainable Agriculture: Principles, Processes, and Practices.* Boca Raton, FL: CRC Press.

Goldman, D., D. Lakdawalla, and Y. Zheng. 2009. "Food Prices and the Dynamics of Body Weight." NBER Working Paper no. 15096. www.nber.org/papers/w15096.

Jackson, W. 2010. "Tackling the Oldest Environmental Problem: Agriculture and Its Impact on Soil." In *The Post Carbon Reader: Managing the 21st Century's Sustainability Crisises*, ed. R. Heinberg and D. Lerch, 128–139. Healdsburg, CA: Watershed Media.

Jacobson, M.F., et al. 2006. *Six Arguments for a Greener Diet: How a More Plant-Based Diet Could Save Your Health and the Environment.* Washington, DC: Center for Science in the Public Interest.

Jacobson, M.F., and K.D. Brownell. 2000. "Small Taxes on Soft Drinks and Snack Foods to Promote Health." *American Journal of Public Health* 90, no. 6: 854–857.

Kessler, D.A. 2009. *The End of Overeating: Taking Control of the Insatiable American Appetite.* Emmaus, PA: Rodale.

Lacey, M. 2008. "Across Globe, Hunger Brings Rising Anger." *New York Times*, April 18.

Mokdad, A.H, M.K. Serdula, W.H. Dietz, B.A. Bowman, J.S. Marks, and J.P. Koplan. 1999. "The Spread of the Obesity Epidemic in the United States, 1991–1998." *JAMA: The Journal of the American Medical Association* 282, no. 16: 1519–1522.

National Center on Addiction and Substance Abuse at Columbia University. 2011. "The Importance of Family Dinners." www.casacolumbia.org/templates/publications_reports.aspx.

National Institute for Food and Agriculture (NIFA). 2011. "NIFA Overview." www.nifa.usda.gov/about/background.html.

National Oceanic and Atmospheric Administration (NOAA). 2011. *Deep Oceans*. http://oceantoday.noaa.gov/happnowdeadzone/.

Nestle, M. 2002. *Food Politics: How the Food Industry Influences Nutrition and Health*. Berkeley: University of California Press.

———. 2010. "New York City Says No to Using Food Stamps for Sodas." *Food Politics*, October 7. www.foodpolitics.com/2010/10/new-york-city-says-no-to-using-food-stamps-for-sodas/.

Office of the First Lady. 2011. "First Lady Michelle Obama Announces Nationwide Commitments to Provide Millions of People Access to Healthy, Affordable Food in Underserved Communities." Press release, July 20. http://m.whitehouse.gov/the-press-office/2011/07/20/first-lady-michelle-obama-announces-nationwide-commitments-provide-milli.

Olshansky, S.J., D.J. Passaro, R.C. Hershow, J. Layden, B.A. Carnes, J. Brody, L. Hayflick, R.N. Butler, D.B. Allison, and D.S. Ludwig. 2005. "A Potential Decline in Life Expectancy in the United States in the 21st Century." *New England Journal of Medicine* 352, no. 11: 1138–1145.

Peeters, A., J.J. Barendregt, F. Willekens, J.P. Mackenbach, A. Al Mamun, and L. Bonneux. 2003. "Obesity in Adulthood and Its Consequences for Life Expectancy: A Life-Table Analysis." *Annals of Internal Medicine* 138, no. 1: 24–32.

Pimentel, D., B. Berger, D. Filiberto, M. Newton, B. Wolfe, E. Karabinakis, S. Clark, E. Poon, E. Abbett, and S. Nandagopal. 2004. "Water Resources: Agricultural and Environmental Issues." *BioScience* 54, no. 10: 909–918.

Pimentel, D., and N. Kounang. 1998. "Ecology of Soil Erosion in Ecosystems." *Ecosystems* 1: 416–426.

Pimentel, D., and M. Pimentel. 2008. *Food, Energy, and Society*. Boca Raton, FL: CRC Press.

Reganold, J.P., et al. 2011. "Transforming U.S. Agriculture." *Science* 332, no. 6030: 670–671.

Schor, J.B. 2010. *Plenitude: The New Economics of True Wealth*. New York: Penguin Press.

Shulman, S., et al. 2012. *Cooler Smarter: Practical Steps for Low-Carbon Living: Expert Advice from the Union of Concerned Scientists*. Washington, DC: Island Press.

Sturm, R. 2002. *The Effects of Obesity, Smoking, and Drinking on Medical Problems and Costs*. Santa Monica, CA: RAND.

Tilman, D., K.G. Cassman, P.A. Matson, R. Naylor, and S. Polasky. 2002. "Agricultural Sustainability and Intensive Production Practices." *Nature* 418, no. 8: 671–677.

Todd, J.E., L. Mancino, and B.H. Lin. 2010. *The Impact of Food Away From Home on Adult Diet Quality*. Washington, DC: US Department of Agriculture, Economic Research Service. http://purl.access.gpo.gov/GPO/LPS125443.

Trasande L., Y. Liu, G. Fryer, and M. Weitzman. 2009. "Effects of Childhood Obesity on Hospital Care and Costs, 1999–2005." *Health Affairs* 28, no. 4: w751–w760.

Treuhaft, S., and A. Karpyn. 2010. "The Grocery Gap: Who Has Access to Healthy Food and Why It Matters." PolicyLink. www.policylink.org/grocerygap.

US Food and Drug Administration (FDA). 2012. www.fda.gov/Food/LabelingNutrition/ucm248731.htm.

US Senate. 2012. S.2204. "Repeal Big Oil Tax Subsidies Act." 112th Congress, 2nd Session, Calendar No. 337.

USDA and US Department of Health and Human Services. 2010. *Dietary Guidelines for Americans, 2010*. 7th ed. Washington, DC: US Government Printing Office.

USDA Agricultural Marketing Service. 2011. "Farmers Markets and Local Food Marketing." www.ams.usda.gov/AMSv1.0/FARMERSMARKETS.

USDA Economic Research Service. ERS/USDA Briefing Room. 2011. "Food Security in the United States: Key Statistics and Graphics." September 7. www.ers.usda.gov/briefing/foodsecurity/stats_graphs.htm.

USDA Food and Nutrition Service. 2010. "Supplemental Nutrition Assistance Program: Putting Healthy Food Within Reach—State Outreach Toolkit." www.fns.usda.gov/snap/outreach/.

———. 2011a. *Supplemental Nutrition Analysis Program Monthly Data.* September 29. www.fns.usda.gov/pd/34SNAPmonthly.htm.

———. 2011b. "Eligible Food Items." August. www.fns.usda.gov/snap/retailers/eligible.htm.

USDA Natural Resources Conservation Service. 2007. "2007 National Resources Inventory." www.nrcs.usda.gov/wps/portal/nrcs/detail/national/technical/nra/nri/?&cid=stelprdb1041887.

———. 2010. "USDA Releases New Data on Soil Erosion and Development of Private Lands." News release no. 0211.10, April 27.

Warshall, P. 2002. "Tilth and Technology: The Industrial Design of Our Nation's Soils." In *The Fatal Harvest Reader: The Tragedy of Industrial Agriculture*, ed. A. Kimbrell, 167–180. Washington, DC: Foundation for Deep Ecology/Island Press.

Worldwatch Institute. 2011. *State of the World 2011: Innovations That Nourish the Planet.* New York: W.W. Norton.

11 Improving the Standard of Living Through Investments in Intangible Capital

JOHN TOMER

When mentioning the sources that improve productivity, economists typically list tangible capital and human capital. Rarely do they mention the more intangible forms of human capital. This chapter focuses on the importance of intangible capital not only for increasing productivity, but also for improving the overall quality of life and standard of living for individuals and society. The term *intangible capital* denotes all the human capacities embodied either in individuals or in human relationships. These individual capacities may be cognitive or noncognitive, and the relationships may be within organizations or outside organizations. The neglect of intangible capital by many economists who evaluate how to improve the standard of living limits our ability to understand why quality of life—in its many dimensions—is not what it could be. Important socioeconomic problems that limit both productivity and quality of life (and, therefore, our standard of living) require that investments be made in intangible capital as well as other kinds of capital.

I focus here on the intangible capacities that have tended to be neglected by economists, with the main body of the chapter explaining how low or poor intangible capital contributes to two socioeconomic problems that lower our standard of living: (1) chronic health issues, and (2) poverty in a rich society. If a country could make substantial progress on solving these socioeconomic concerns, this would greatly help to raise its standard of living. Unfortunately, a single-minded preoccupation with growth in material output seems to have led many economists and policy makers to neglect the intangible factors that also contribute importantly to our well-being. In fact, these factors may even be at the heart of these and other problems.[1] I begin by defining the broad category of intangible capital and some of its components.

DEFINING INTANGIBLE CAPITAL

Carefully defining intangible capital is particularly important because of the confusion associated with many different definitions and usages of the term *capital* in the social science literature. Intangible capital is consistent with economists' general understanding of the term *capital* as well as their recognition of its different forms (physical,

229

human, natural, and social), as outlined by Greenwood and Holt (Chapter 1 in this volume). However, intangible capital is much more than the standard definition of human capital that most economists use. Gary Becker (1964) defined human capital as the skill and knowledge that raise people's productive capacity. His definition is essentially the mainstream economic view. It involves a fairly limited view of human capital in that it refers largely to skills and knowledge acquired using cognitive mental capacities. This form of human capital is relatively tangible because the process of acquiring it is generally observable as it typically takes place in a classroom or on the factory floor.[2]

Intangible capital is much more and can be looked at as an overarching umbrella concept that includes all the elements of human capital in the broadest sense, including all the capacities or skills that are embodied in humans or their relationships. Thus, intangible capital includes standard human capital, social capital, and different aspects of human capital, such as personal capital, facets of intellectual capital, a number of overlapping categories, such as organizational capital, moral capital, ethnic capital, cultural capital, customer capital, and so on. Let us next look more carefully at these different components of intangible capital.

Social capital is an important component of intangible capital. It refers to features in the social landscape that provide productive capacity by enabling important recurring social activities. Social capital in its pure form is embodied in social relationships, but it may be at least partly embodied in individuals. It can exist within formal organizations, between or among organizations, or entirely outside organization boundaries. Every type of social capital has a specific form, an intermediate purpose, and an ultimate purpose.[3] The specific forms of social capital include obligations and expectations, information channels, social norms and effective sanctions, authority relations, family and friendship bonds, and intentional organization. Social capital's intermediate purposes include facilitating coordinated actions, gaining access to resources or opportunities, reducing transaction costs, making possible efficient organizations, and overcoming perverse, short-run temptations. The ultimate purposes of social capital include not only relatively tangible purposes like greater economic growth, making possible more effective public institutions, greater productivity, and greater wealth, but also relatively intangible purposes such as improving the standard of living and happiness. Depending on the historical time period, the type of economic system, and the particular institutions and enterprises involved, social capital can take on many different forms that serve many different purposes. Some social capital is relatively tangible; this is so when its form involves structure and networks that can be observed. Other social capital is relatively intangible insofar as its form involves different relationship dimensions such as trust, norms, obligations, and identification.

Another part of intangible capital is personal capital. Like standard human capital, it is a type of human capital that is embodied in individuals, but it is very different from standard human capital in that it consists of human capacities that are largely noncognitive and nonphysical. Personal capital relates to an individual's personal qualities and reflects the quality of an individual's psychological, physical, and spiritual functioning. One's stock of personal capital comes partly from one's genetic inheritance, partly from the life-shaping events that one has encountered, and partly from one's efforts to mature and grow in nonintellectual ways. In other words, it is in part produced intentionally (Tomer 2003, 456). A very important component of personal capital is emotional intelligence (see, e.g., Goleman 1994, 1998), which refers to a variety of personal and social competences. Different kinds of jobs, organizations, and industries require different kinds of emotional intelligence. Individuals who have the kinds of emotional competence demanded by their work situation can be expected to be successful in their job performance. On the other hand, people with emotional competence deficiencies may benefit substantially by making personal capital investments designed to correct these deficiencies.

Noncognitive human capital is quite similar to personal capital. Investments in noncognitive human capital are designed to raise noncognitive skills, enhancing personal qualities such as motivation, persistence, and self-esteem (see, e.g., Carneiro and Heckman 2003). Recent research by Heckman and various colleagues has demonstrated that noncognitive abilities (or what they call "socio-emotional skills") matter as much as or more than cognitive abilities for success both on the job and in school (Cunha and Heckman 2007; Heckman, Stixrud, and Urzua 2006, 27). The difference between personal capital and noncognitive human capital is that the latter is defined largely by what it is not—that is, it is not cognitive—whereas personal capital, although largely noncognitive, is defined in terms of the specific human qualities that it contains.

Figure 11.1 summarizes the essence of what intangible capital is. It includes (1) standard human capital, our knowledge and skills; (2) personal capital, the quality of our personal attributes; and (3) social capital, the quality of our relationships, in or outside organizations.

It also includes personal intellectual capital—the personal, informal, and informational aids to work performance that we possess. Essentially, intangible capital is all of what is embodied in or possessed by humans that make human effort more productive than it would be if the labor were totally unskilled. It is, thus, what would be lost if the existing labor force died and was replaced by totally unskilled and unaided laborers (using the word *skill* in the broadest possible sense). To the extent that intangible capital is an input into the production of private and public goods and services, the absence of intangible capital would mean much lower output and, correspondingly, lower provisioning and a lower standard of living.

It is important to note that Greenwood and Holt (Chapter 1 of this volume) define some of the intangible components of capital differently. First, my definition of intangible capital (with one small exception) only includes productive capacity that is embodied in humans. Thus, elements of the "social infrastructure"—such as nonmarket institutions, government policies, and laws or legal systems—which Greenwood and Holt include as social capital are not included in my definition of intangible capital even though these elements may have an intangible or qualitative nature. Also, innovations and technologies are included in the intangible capital category only to the extent that knowledge about these is embodied in humans. Moreover, no tangible capital (such as library or church buildings) is included in intangible capital. Thus, Greenwood and Holt's definition of human capital, depicted in Figure 1.2 in Chapter 1, is broader in some respects compared to the term *intangible capital* as used here. Greenwood and

Figure 11.1   **What Is Intangible Capital?**

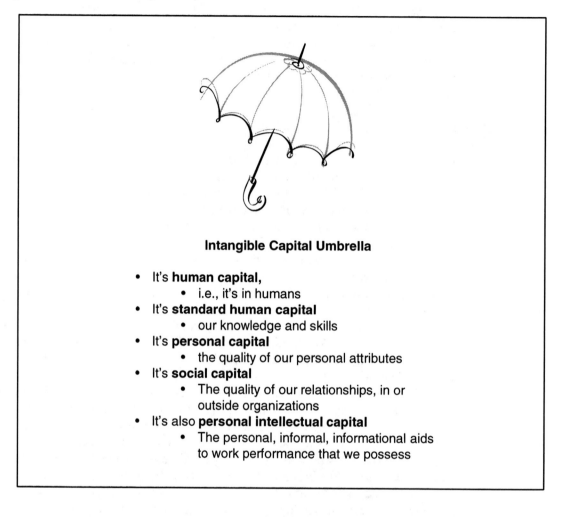

Intangible Capital Umbrella

- It's **human capital,**
  - i.e., it's in humans
- It's **standard human capital**
  - our knowledge and skills
- It's **personal capital**
  - the quality of our personal attributes
- It's **social capital**
  - The quality of our relationships, in or outside organizations
- It's also **personal intellectual capital**
  - The personal, informal, informational aids to work performance that we possess

Holt's Figure 1.2 is important insofar as it relates the different types of capital to the three different types of provisioning and ultimately to the standard of living.

However, there is another way to understand the importance of intangible capital, and that is with developing policies to deal with important socioeconomic problems. Intangible capital is not only an input to tangible production; it is also an important contributor to the nonmaterial aspect of the standard of living and overall well-being. To understand its importance, let us look at two socioeconomic problems: (1) chronic health problems, and (2) poverty and inequality. For each social problem, the cause or part of the cause is an important deficiency in some type of intangible capital. It follows that an important part of the remedy is to correct the deficiency through appropriate investment in the needed type of intangible capital. The standard of living would be expected to rise once the socioeconomic problems are resolved or substantially reduced.

A Socioeconomic Model of Chronic "Diseases of Affluence"

Chronic, degenerative diseases are distinctly different from acute, communicable diseases not only in their character but also in their incidence. Generally speaking, chronic diseases have been absent in nonmodern, less civilized populations or present only at low levels. It was only after these populations came into regular contact with modern, Western lifestyles and dietary practices and perhaps started on the road to greater economic prosperity that their incidence of chronic diseases rose dramatically (Taubes 2007, 89–99). Thus, these diseases have been variously referred to as the diseases of civilization, the diseases of affluence, or the "Western" diseases. Among the many diseases of civilization are obesity, diabetes, cardiovascular disease, hypertension and stroke, various forms of cancer, dental cavities, periodontal disease, appendicitis, peptic ulcers, diverticulitis, gallstones, hemorrhoids, varicose veins, and constipation (Taubes 2007, 90–91). Taubes notes, "When any diseases of civilization appeared, all of them would eventually appear" (91).

The model of the causes of chronic health problems described here closely resembles the socioeconomic model of obesity explained in Tomer (2011a). That model explained the socioeconomic factors, external and internal to the individual, which contribute to obesity by influencing individuals to make poor diet and behavior choices. It should be noted that the obesity model is an alternative to the mainstream economic model of obesity and that the health science part of the model is an alternative to the conventional wisdom on health science. The socioeconomic model developed here is an alternative to a mainstream-type model because there is no assumption of neoclassical economic rationality; instead, bounded rationality is assumed on the part of the relevant actors. Decision makers are bounded rationally in that their cognitive capacities are quite limited, especially in regard to dealing with complex, real-world situations.

The health science component of the model is based on the writings of Mark Hyman (2006) and Gary Taubes (2007). According to Hyman, many chronic health problems are caused by poor diet and poor behavioral patterns. A poor diet is (1) high in refined, processed carbohydrates, (2) high in bad fats, (3) low in fiber, (4) low in antioxidants, and (5) high in oxidants. The five poor behavioral patterns are (1) overly rapid eating, (2) eating when stressed, (3) sleep deprivation, (4) lack of exercise, and (5) high exposure to toxins. However, to understand the growth of chronic health ailments, it is necessary to consider much more than health science. Just as important are the many external and internal factors that influence an individual's choice of diet and behavioral patterns. Figure 11.2 depicts a worst-case scenario in which both internal and external factors make poor diet and behavioral pattern choices likely. The internal factors are the individual's endowment of (1) personal capital, (2) social capital, (3) health capital, and (4) genes that determine an individual's physical and psychological predispositions to chronic diseases.

The external factors are (1) technological change impacting on markets, causing changes in the prices of food and exercise, (2) the infrastructure of chronic ailments— that is, the socioeconomic structures that have a negative influence on the incidence

Figure 11.2   **Factors Causing an Increase in Chronic Health Problems**

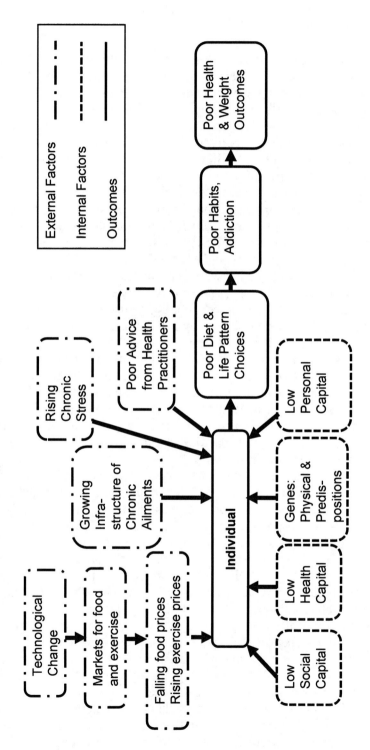

of chronic disease, especially the behaviors of various suppliers of processed food, (3) socioeconomic factors contributing to chronic stress in individuals, and (4) advice about eating and behavior from health professionals. The essence of the argument is that chronic health problems tend to occur when vulnerable individuals who have low personal capital, low social capital, low health capital, and genes predisposing them to particular chronic ailments encounter stressful situations, lower prices of unhealthy food and higher prices of exercise, poor advice from health practitioners, and the large and growing infrastructure of chronic ailments.

EXTERNAL FACTORS CONTRIBUTING TO CHRONIC HEALTH PROBLEMS

The first external factor is the infrastructure of chronic ailments. It refers particularly to the features of the socioeconomy that influence and contribute to a consumer's chronic poor health. One important part of this infrastructure is the changing behaviors of important actors in the food industry. Another part is changes in important socio-economic patterns that contribute to consumers' poor decision making with regard to food. To begin, consider the influences deriving from food suppliers, in particular the agricultural, food processing, food distribution, and food preparation industries, especially the food processors and food preparers. There is a great deal of evidence that they are increasingly selling unhealthy foods. What do we mean by unhealthy foods? Following Hyman (2006), unhealthy foods are foods high in (1) bad fats and (2) carbohydrates with a low phytonutrient index and high glycemic load, especially refined grains, sugar and sugary items, processed food, and junk food. Healthy foods, in contrast, are whole, unprocessed foods, full of fiber, antioxidants, vitamins, minerals, phytonutrients, and healthy fats (Hyman 2006, 52).

It is important to give a little background to the dietary changes related to growth in chronic diseases. It was during the second half of the nineteenth century in the United States that white flour and sugar became inexpensive enough for popular consumption, thus leading to a dramatic increase in their dietary consumption (Taubes 2007). This in turn, along with increased consumption of other refined, easily digestible carbohydrates, led to correlated increases in chronic diseases such as diabetes and various types of cancer. This pattern is part of a broader pattern known as the nutrition transition, which typically begins as countries start along the path to economic development (Caballero and Popkin 2002). In the United States, the food suppliers' role in the continuing nutrition transition has accelerated over the last thirty years. It is interesting to note that there are a few small places in the world where the outcome of the nutrition transition from traditional diets has been more favorable. Sally Beare (2006) has discovered five of these places in which the people are exceptionally long-lived owing to their exceptionally healthy diets and lifestyle habits. These five places—Okinawa, the Greek island of Symi, Campodimele in southern Italy, Hunza in northeast Pakistan, and Bama County in southwest China—have a remarkably low incidence of noncommunicable ailments such as heart disease, stroke, cancer, high blood pressure, ulcers, appendicitis, colitis, and osteoporosis. Essentially, these places retained the best of their traditional diets, keeping the whole foods and not transitioning to refined, processed foods.

Food suppliers today are not just supplying these unhealthy foods because consumers are demanding them. As Kessler (2009) explains, food suppliers are actively designing these foods to enhance their appeal. More specifically, they are creating foods with added sugar, fat, and salt to (1) make them hyperpalatable, (2) make them override the body's satiety signals, which indicate when a person is full, and (3) make them more habit-forming. In other words, these firms are optimizing every element in the hedonic equation (Kessler 2009, 127). The goal, according to an industry expert, "is to get you hooked" by creating foods with "craveability" (125). As Kessler sees it, the food suppliers are creating customers who are "conditioned hyper-eaters" (137–141). In a variety of ways, they have attempted to create a hyperstimulating environment conducive to triggering hypereating.

In addition to food suppliers' product design efforts, these companies have aggressively used advertising and other marketing strategies to persuade consumers to buy more of their products. In sum, food suppliers, processors, and preparers have created a toxic food environment. For more on the role of corporations in advertising and marketing unhealthy food and the societal costs involved, see Northrop (Chapter 10 in this volume). In the background are a number of important socioeconomic patterns that add to the potency of the food industry's efforts. Because of lifestyle and work changes, people are eating out more and shifting to foods requiring less preparation time at home. Typically, these are not fresh and whole foods.

Another factor (part of the infrastructure of chronic ailments) contributing to chronic health problems is the built or human-made environment, which often reflects our society's cultural values and priorities. What Richard Jackson in *Designing Healthy Communities* (2012, xi) understands well is that "urban design, especially the buildings and roads . . ., can give people access to the places that help them fill their life needs, including food, shelter, work, and health care—or take it away." Jackson clearly recognizes that community health depends not only on the "software" of human relations, but also on the "hardware" of homes, workplaces, roads, and other structures. In particular, the prevalence of chronic ailments is influenced by people's daily habits and regular exercise, and these in turn are influenced by the built environment. Too often, because of the priority on building roads through communities, neighborhoods lack places to walk, bicycle paths, access to health care, safe routes to school, and structures that encourage interaction. Thus, people are discouraged from needed physical and social activity. As a result, chronic disease will be much more likely to occur (Jackson 2012).

Another external factor is the impact of technological change on the markets for food and exercise. Technological change has led to lower food (or calorie consumption) prices and higher exercise (or calorie expenditure) prices. This factor requires some further explanation. First, the relative price changes differ for different types of food. Although the price of food relative to other goods has declined by 16 percent since 1960, the prices of fresh fruits and vegetables, fish, and dairy products have increased relatively since 1983 (Finkelstein and Zuckerman 2008). On the other hand, unhealthy foods—including fats and oils, sugars and sweets, and carbonated beverages—have become relatively less expensive. The evidence supports the view that it is the relative decline in price of unhealthy foods, not food in general, that has contributed to chronic health ailments. It should be noted that crop subsidies for crops such as wheat, soybeans, and especially corn have contributed to the decline in food prices (see Chapter 10 in this volume). While these subsidies may lead to greater food output, it is hard to call this "productivity" when it contributes so negatively to dietary health and the resulting chronic diseases of affluence.

The Internal Factors Contributing to Chronic Health Problems

Personal capital is one important internal factor in understanding the causes of chronic health problems, because people's accumulated personal capital largely determines how they respond to the influences deriving from the infrastructure of chronic ailments as well as to the economic incentives provided by the markets for food and exercise. With the price decreases of unhealthy foods along with the aggressive marketing and the appeal of fast, processed foods, it is not hard to understand why persons with small endowments of personal capital will to a great degree succumb to many of these external influences.

Other individuals who have acquired greater endowments of personal capital in the form of emotional competencies—that is, ingrained habits of thought, feeling, and behavior—will be in a much stronger position to resist these influences. Among the important personal capital qualities relevant here is the ability to be self-regulating or self-controlling—for example, the ability to control impulse, delay gratification, and keep distress from swamping the ability to think (explained more fully in Goleman 1998, 26–27, and Tomer 2008, 84–85). In general, people who have acquired a sufficient set of these basic competencies will have achieved a desired balance involving integration of emotions and thinking, more specifically an integration of the functioning of the amygdala and the prefrontal lobes of the brain.

People with a low endowment of the relevant personal capital are vulnerable to the infrastructure of chronic ailments and, accordingly, easily develop the attitudes, behaviors, and habits encouraged by the food suppliers (Kessler 2009). Another way of looking at this situation is that people with low personal capital are easily induced into habits (which could be termed investments in consumption capital) of using the various processed foods and the convenience of fast foods. These investments play an important role in keeping these people coming back as customers of the fast food and processed food suppliers.

As Hyman (2006) emphasizes, those with low personal capital typically experience chronic stress, eat rapidly, lack exercise, and are sleep-deprived—patterns frequently leading to obesity and other chronic health ailments. On the other hand, people with high personal capital have acquired an appreciation of the virtues and healthfulness of whole foods as well as an appreciation of the seductive, yet unhealthy, aspects of processed foods and fast foods. They have greater ability to choose wisely among healthful and unhealthful foods, resisting the attractions and incentives of what will not benefit them in the long run.

The second internal factor is the individual's endowment of what I call "health capital." Health capital is a stock consisting of the accumulated individual learning that contributes to a person's physical health and some aspects of mental health. These learned behaviors relate to our eating patterns, use of nutritional supplements, use of medicines, use of potentially toxic substances (alcohol, illicit drugs, and so on), exercise activity, recreational activity, and other lifestyle patterns. Certain kinds of health capital would be particularly important from the standpoint of avoiding chronic ailments. Following Hyman, it would be important to learn to eat slowly, understand the nutritional value of different foods, get sufficient sleep, and get sufficient exercise. In general, a person who has adopted a healthful, wholesome lifestyle and established many good habits would be high in health capital and less likely to suffer from chronic poor health. Note that the category of health capital overlaps with some aspects of consumption capital and personal capital.

The third internal factor is the individual's endowment of social capital. Social capital refers to the capacity that is embodied in an individual's social relationships or the bonds and connections between an individual and others. The strength and quality of an individual's social capital endowment arguably have a relationship to the person's likelihood of contracting chronic health problems. In the presence of strong, positive social relationships, people are less likely to be vulnerable to the enticements of low-quality food and behavior patterns. Conversely, when social capital is weak and negative, people are more likely to succumb to the enticements of the infrastructure of chronic ailments and the economic incentives offered by the markets for food and exercise.

INDIVIDUAL DECISION MAKING

As summarized in Figure 11.2 earlier, the socioeconomic model of chronic health problems includes four external factors that influence individual decision making: the infrastructure of chronic ailments, technological change and market prices, chronic stress levels, and advice from health practitioners. However, individual decisions regarding diet, exercise, and lifestyle depend very much on how different individuals respond to the external factors. Responses are determined to a great extent by individual endowments of personal capital, social capital, and health capital as well as a person's genes. Given strong, positive endowments of the three types of intangible capital, an individual is likely to choose a good diet and good behavioral patterns even if negative influences from the infrastructure of chronic ailments are strong and the prices of unhealthful food are falling. However, when the intangible capital of an individual is weak, the external factors are likely to produce an unfavorable outcome involving poor diet and poor behavioral patterns, the kind likely to cause chronic health problems. In general, the decision making outcome will be determined by the relative strength of the internal and external factors.

RELEVANCE OF THE MODEL

There is considerable evidence that in the United States the worst-case scenario represented in Figure 11.2 approximates the reality of the last thirty years or so. Processed food has become a larger and larger part of people's diets, and it has become cheaper in the sense of a lower price per calorie. Unfortunately, due to the lowered nutrition of processed food, it is at the same time becoming more expensive in the sense of a higher price for a given amount of nutritional value. As economic output (conventionally measured) grows, we are able to buy a greater volume of goods, including food, but it is making us less healthy as more and more of us suffer from debilitating chronic ailments. We seem to be on a nonsustainable path despite a generally growing economy. What is happening in the food arena is, if anything, reducing our standard of living. Also, arguably, it is contributing to greater inequality in the standard of living due to the unequal socioeconomic incidence of nutrition-related noncommunicable diseases. Therefore, if we are concerned about our standard of living, it is time to take the kind of policy actions necessary to prevent the growth of chronic diseases.

POLICY IMPLICATIONS: FOSTERING THE INVESTMENTS NEEDED TO OVERCOME THE CHRONIC DISEASES OF AFFLUENCE

The socioeconomic model of chronic ailments clearly points to low or poor endowments of personal capital, health capital, and social capital as an important cause of the high rates of chronic health problems. It follows that if people who are relatively poor in certain types of intangible capital could make investments to improve their intangible capital, they would be better off. As an example of this kind of investment, consider Kessler's discussion of obesity. Although Kessler does not explicitly use the language of intangible capital, his remarks on how to deal with the obesity problem recognize that people would need to make significant efforts to bring about lasting qualitative changes in their behaviors. In particular, Kessler specifies what conditioned hypereaters need to do in order to overcome their compulsive bad habits. "The cornerstone of treatment for conditioned hyper-eaters is developing the *capacity* to refuse the [food] cue's invitation to the brain in the first place. That refusal must come early, and it must be definitive" (Kessler 2009, 182).

According to Kessler, the ability to change entrenched habits involves five major components: (1) developing awareness of the food choice situations and the associated risks, (2) learning and developing alternative responses to these situations, (3) "formulating thoughts that compete with and serve to quiet the old [dysfunctional] ones," (4) developing relationships with people who can help the habit-plagued individual recognize and avoid tempting food cues and who will acknowledge the person's success, and (5) developing new emotional responses to food such as "changing one's emotional appraisal of salient food." Further, it is necessary for the afflicted individuals to develop a set of rules that provides needed structure in order to keep them from becoming aroused by unhealthy food. This step demands "attention, practice, and advance planning, motivated by the expectation" that the person will "ultimately derive emotional satisfaction in new ways." Essentially, the intangible investment necessary to overcome habitual hypereating of unhealthy foods involves making a "perceptual shift and learning new behavior that eventually becomes as rewarding as the old" (Kessler 2009, xx).

In essence, Kessler's recommendation is for consumers to make intangible capital investments in themselves (mostly personal capital investments) that will enable them to resist the influences of the infrastructure of chronic ailments and the incentives provided in food marketing and distribution that are pushing them toward poor diet and behavioral patterns. No doubt, some people will find the knowledge and motivation to make the kind of investments that Kessler suggests and realize the benefits. But, one suspects, many more will be too stuck in dysfunctional eating and lifestyle patterns to avail themselves of the wisdom of Kessler's recommendations. This raises a further issue. Perhaps many additional people could reduce or eliminate their chronic health problems (including obesity) with the help of programs designed to encourage them to make the needed intangible capital investments.

The needed personal capital investments can be viewed as radically rewiring the relationship between the brain's prefrontal lobes and its limbic system, which operates between the brain's thinking or executive part and its emotional part. If vulnerable people are to resist the negative influences from the infrastructure of chronic ailments, they need to develop more emotional intelligence and character, becoming more self-regulating, more able to think clearly in stressful situations, and generally more capable of integrating emotion and thinking. Such investments in personal capital may help many people overcome their poor personal qualities acquired as a result of adverse childhood experiences. Although this investment in personal capital must be carried out by an individual, sometimes with the aid of a therapist or counselor, there are likely to be many opportunities for communities, businesses, and governments to play significant roles in fostering or influencing the process. This is also true for important investments in health capital and social capital. The policy focus here is clearly on improving the internal factors.

Besides working to raise people's investment in intangible capital, another policy approach would be to improve the external factors. In particular, this approach would involve reducing or eliminating the negative effects of the infrastructure of chronic ailments as well as reducing the negative effects of food technological innovation and food price change. The essence of the problem arises because many food suppliers behave both innovatively and in a negative opportunistic fashion. These businesses, especially those in the United States, regularly take advantage of opportunities to develop new foods, develop new ways to process foods, and develop new food marketing strategies (Tomer 2013). The negative part is that many of these new foods are more highly processed and contain fewer nutrients and more calories than unprocessed foods. They are likely to be marketed more effectively, targeting the young and vulnerable segments of the population. However, while some companies are opportunistic in this negative sense, others are not. Some companies, instead, are motivated to be socially responsible. They implement strategies and behaviors that are simultaneously good for society, all their stakeholders, and themselves, and they avoid actions that impose costs on others.

Government policy could focus on encouraging these relatively responsible businesses to make intangible investments in their organization and management leading to even more responsible behavior. Optimistically, these food suppliers might be helped to learn how to better integrate their social responsibilities with their responsibilities for food production and marketing. Businesses whose leaders have become receptive to the idea that they have important social responsibilities can be expected to take cues from governments, communities, and society as a whole concerning the kind of behavior that is at once profitable, competitive, and responsible to all of the firm's stakeholders (Tomer 2013). With the encouragement of government and other stakeholders, these responsible food businesses can presumably learn how to produce food that is both demanded by its customers and, because of its nutritious qualities, good for them.

On the other hand, dealing with businesses that are not oriented to accepting their social responsibilities will inevitably require the use of economic policies on the part of government (Tomer 2013). Following standard economic theory, these policy measures could involve the use of financial incentives—in particular, taxation or subsidization. There are, however, some difficult challenges in attempting to apply standard microeconomics here. There is no single food or behavior that causes chronic health problems, nor is there a single problematic good or service that food businesses produce. Conventional economic policy thinking is not well geared to dealing with the behavior patterns of either businesses or consumers. Thus, it seems unlikely that externality-countering taxation could be used in the way that economists, following English economist A.C. Pigou, have envisioned. Nevertheless, there may be some role for taxes on egregiously unhealthy products such as sugary soft drinks. Although singling out these beverages for taxation while not taxing other foods that have equally bad health effects may seem unfair or inefficient, such taxation may have an overall beneficial effect by creating a stigma against a particularly unhealthy food or group of foods. The result is likely to be not only lower consumption of these taxed foods but improved public attitudes regarding healthy eating. Obviously, there is a need for empirical research on this issue.

Some useful broad policy observations can be made based on the general understanding that excessive consumption of refined carbohydrates plays a key causal role in the diseases of affluence. It should, of course, be noted that behavioral problems such as lack of physical exercise also play a very important role. As people in the public health field have recognized, dealing with the burden of nutrition-related, noncommunicable diseases by relying only on medical treatment would entail enormous health-care expenditures, not to mention the constraint on economic growth due to the reduced capacity of workers suffering for many years with chronic ailments. Thus, in the long-term, "prevention [not treatment] is the only feasible approach to these chronic diseases" (Caballero and Popkin 2002). To achieve the desired prevention will require a comprehensive effort to reverse the negative patterns arising from the nutrition transition.

Such a preventive effort will include the kinds of investment in intangible capital (mentioned above) that are necessary to help people deal with their personal, social, and health situations, thereby helping them discover and adopt satisfying and healthful eating, physical exercise, and other behavior patterns. In addition, the necessary effort will entail many changes in the food market and food businesses so that the negative socioeconomic influences and incentives from external factors will be reversed. Although taxes on unhealthy goods or activities, "nudges," education, and various therapies will presumably be part of the overall policy effort, many more elements will be required in a comprehensive program to make a major reduction in the patterns causing these chronic health problems. To bring about such a comprehensive effort will no doubt require a public that is aroused and actively engaged in countering these chronic health threats. In other words, there needs to be something tantamount to a broad social movement targeting the threats of the different chronic ailments.

THE SOCIOECONOMIC PROBLEM OF POVERTY IN RICH SOCIETIES

Following earlier arguments of the importance of intangible capital and social policy, this section deals with persistent poverty in rich societies. This kind of poverty contrasts with the poverty that results from economic downturns or from living in a poor society with limited opportunities for education and earnings. When overall economic performance is good and average incomes are high, poverty generally reflects substantial inequality in income and wealth. Although many factors might contribute to this inequality, differential investments in intangible capital are often ignored. That topic is our focus here.

Let us start with skill inequality. There is much evidence that "differences in levels of cognitive and noncognitive skills by family income and family background emerge early and persist. If anything, schooling widens these early differences." According to Carneiro and Heckman (2003, 92), these skills, when acquired early, make possible later learning, thereby raising the productivity of later human capital investment. Conversely, the rate of return on human capital investment on the part of people who have not acquired many of these early skills is low. With increased inequality, fewer people are likely to attain the highest ability level, in part because they did not acquire the needed skills early on. As a consequence, Heckman and Carneiro (2003) observe a shortfall in the labor supply of the highest skilled relative to the rapidly growing demand for their services. On the other hand, the supply of low-skill workers is more than meeting the demand. Not surprisingly, this discrepancy contributes to increased wage and income inequality by raising returns to the group with the highest skills relative to the lower-skilled group.

One reason hypothesized for low earnings is the existence of credit constraints for children of low-income parents. Certainly, if members of this group are unable to obtain educational loans, they are less likely to attend college. Heckman and Carneiro (2003) indicate, however, that there is not much evidence supporting the view that credit constraints are an important cause of low income. They argue instead that long-run "family influence" factors (such as parental education, family structure, and place of residence) rather than credit constraints are the key to producing the cognitive and noncognitive skills that raise the return to future schooling. Early development of noncognitive abilities is particularly important for attaining success in schooling and in the labor market. However, "current analyses of skill formation focus too much on cognitive ability and too little on noncognitive ability" (Carneiro and Heckman 2003, 93). The studies of Carneiro and Heckman strongly suggest that early childhood interventions primarily improve noncognitive skills and that raising these for poor youth is much more feasible (i.e., less costly) than attempting to raise IQ. Whereas IQ is fairly set by age eight, personal qualities such as self-discipline and motivation are much more malleable at later ages. And it is these "noncognitive skills [that] substantially determine socio-economic success later in life" (Carneiro and Heckman 2003,

148). Hence, the authors recommend early investments in personal capital to improve personal qualities such as self-discipline, persistence, dependability, perseverance, consistency, self-esteem, optimism, and future orientation among youth.

THE INVESTMENTS NEEDED TO REDUCE POVERTY

Clearly, long-run family influence factors are crucial for the development of important skills in early childhood, especially the noncognitive ones that are the basis for later learning. Carneiro and Heckman suggest an interesting hypothesis for problems with the quality of US high school graduates and the US workforce: "an increasing fraction of all US children are growing up in adverse environments" (2003, 207). This suggests a need for devising family policies that emphasize investments in personal capital, especially investments in noncognitive skills in early childhood.

It follows that in order to raise the incomes of the poor, it is necessary to make efforts to improve long-run family factors and the skills of disadvantaged youth at an early age. Carneiro and Heckman state, "the relevant policy issue is to determine what interventions in bad families are successful" (2003, 135). Because parental inputs have so much to do with the development of the important noncognitive skills, it can be argued that society should be involved with the life of families whose children's noncognitive skills are very low. Although this position is controversial, it is based on extensive empirical work showing the remarkable success of investments in high-quality preschool for children from severely disadvantaged backgrounds (Carneiro and Heckman 2003; Cunha and Heckman 2007; Duncan and Magnuson 2004; Heckman et al. 2010). The benefit from such investments is found not only in school and workplace performance, but in the development of increased personal capital which appears to lead to less criminal activity and better integration into the societal mainstream for these children (171). Most federal and state subsidies for child care are targeted to the needs of working parents, not to early childhood development. While these subsidies undoubtedly raise the number of children (of all ages) in child-care programs, it is uncertain how much effect they have on enrollment in the high-quality preschool programs that have been successful in altering the life paths of many children.

A somewhat different line of research by Timothy Bartik (2011) has demonstrated that governmental investments in high-quality early childhood programs also make sense purely as an economic development strategy. Bartik has estimated the economic development effects of three different early childhood programs: (1) universal prekindergarten education, (2) the Abecedarian program involving free child care and early education for disadvantaged families, and (3) the Nurse-Family Partnership program involving thirty home visits by nurses to first-time mothers (from prenatal care until the child is two) from disadvantaged backgrounds. These programs provide substantial benefits to parents and to the child participant, notably future increases in education and employment as well as greater occupational attainment. Not surprisingly, the benefits to children largely come in the long term after they reach age twenty or so.

Despite this, Bartik's careful, conservative estimates indicate that the present value of the economic development benefits of these programs substantially exceeds the present value of the costs. Further, the resulting improvement in state and local employment and earnings from these childhood programs compares favorably with those of more traditional economic development programs, which involve business incentives. The business incentives approach pays off more quickly than early childhood programs and tends to be better at raising *average* earnings, but it is *less* effective at raising earnings of the lowest income groups. The early childhood programs tend to be better for creating employment.

For both types of programs, the present value of the economic development benefits is estimated to be two to three times their costs. These benefits are due not solely to higher academic performance or graduation rates (where the evidence is mixed) but to better health outcomes, improved socialization and behavior, and so on. Thus, much of the evidence indicates that expenditures on early childhood programs are worthwhile investments because of their effects on intangible capital. As a result, there are a few signs that state and local governments are starting to recognize investments in early childhood programs as part of their economic development efforts.

The growing recognition of the importance of early childhood programs was underscored by President Obama's remarks during his State of the Union message on February 12, 2013. He proposed to "make high-quality preschool available to every single child in America" (Motoko 2013) through federal dollars supporting universal preschool for three- and four-year-old children. Families of low and moderate income would not have to pay for the preschool, and higher income families would pay on a sliding scale. Also, under the Obama plan, the federal government would give states wide latitude in developing their preschool programs in a way that meets local needs. It is anticipated that the emphasis in these preschools would be not on academic preparation but on providing a nurturing environment where children can develop in a way that improves their school readiness.

Another approach for improving children's intangible capital endowments is recommended by Pressman and Scott (Chapter 8 in this volume). They argue that the United States has been remiss in not adopting a paid parental leave policy, which typically involves paying parents a share of their lost income if they stay at home for some defined period of time before and/or after the birth of their child. A key to the case for paid parental leave is the understanding that in the absence of paid parental leave, many young families fall into poverty. As a consequence, the children of these poor families suffer a variety of physical health problems "due to poor nutrition, lack of a decent living environment, and lack of immunizations and proper infant care" (168). Children in poverty also suffer from poor social and emotional development. Thus, they experience "greater moodiness, more tantrums, greater anxiety, and increased aggression" (169).

It follows, as Pressman and Scott point out, that paid parental leave can be viewed as an investment in the future of a family's children. It is an investment in personal capital because the time that parents spend with their young children has been shown to develop the emotional intelligence and other noncognitive capacities (not to mention other types of human capital) of the child. Thus, while paid parental leave is not itself an investment in intangible capital, when it is made available to parents who otherwise could not afford to take time away from work, along with programs that support such investments, it allows those families to build a variety of types of intangible capital. And this intangible capital enables these children to do better in all phases of their life, not just work and education.

Economic growth in the usual material sense by itself is clearly no guarantee that poverty will be reduced. The last fifty years of American history document that. A result is that children whose families are unable to provide needed care during the crucial early years are liable to grow up without the noncognitive abilities that make possible productive work lives and positive adult relationships. Children without these critical personal and health capital endowments are, thus, unlikely to escape poverty and low socioeconomic circumstances even in the presence of economic growth.

CONCLUSIONS

This chapter has examined in detail the effects of intangible capital on two major socioeconomic problems: the chronic health problems often called diseases of affluence and the persistence of poverty in affluent societies. The analysis has focused on how investment in particular kinds of intangible capital can be a key to resolving these problems, thereby raising the standard of living. For instance, with respect to chronic health problems, the analysis indicates how investments in personal capital (especially personal competences related to self-regulation and self-control) and health capital (especially learned behaviors related to eating and exercise) raise the personal capacities that are important for lowering the likelihood of chronic disease. In the case of poverty and inequality due to skill disparity, greater investment in personal capital, notably the noncognitive capacities of very young children, raises the rates of return on later human capital investment and ultimately leads to more skilled and higher-paid workers. In the absence of these investments, poverty and chronic poor health are likely to persist even as material economic growth continues.

In light of these effects, it makes sense for both individuals and society to make investments in the types of intangible capital needed to lower the incidence of these problems. If successful, these investments will raise the productive capacity of workers, raise the performance of students, and improve overall family relationships, thereby raising the standard of living. Developing effective policies to resolve these socioeconomic problems is, however, difficult to do, particularly because the difficulties are caused by problematic socioeconomic patterns of consumption (and production) involving many goods, not just a single one.

Counteracting deep-rooted socioeconomic problems such as chronic diseases will require comprehensive societal efforts. The usual economic prescriptions are often no more than a change in the economic incentives. Because of the high and worrisome growth rate of these problems, in developing as well as affluent nations, and because of their implications for the standard of living, economists have an obligation to lead the way in conducting research about the importance of human intangible capacities for the growth and maintenance of satisfactory standards of living.

Targeted investments in intangible capital should become a high priority, not just for combating socioeconomic problems like chronic health ailments and poverty, but also for dealing with other societal issues such as lower-than-expected work productivity and general happiness. Ultimately, to achieve the kind of economic development that raises the standard of living for all, society must make the key investments in people that enable everyone to enjoy health, productivity, and well-being. These investments involve, among other things, changes in the care and education of very young children. In times of low economic growth when many governments are experiencing budgetary deficits, we can urge government leaders not to cut expenditures on important programs related to investment in intangible capital. These programs do not have a strong constituency, but they yield great benefits in the long term.

NOTES

1. This chapter develops the view that the standard of living is negatively impacted when new external factors appear in the social and economic environment that requires skillful coping responses. Less skillful responses may come from a lack of adequate investment in intangible capital. Since it may take time to understand the interaction of these external factors and make the needed investments in intangible capital, these socioeconomic problems may, unfortunately, persist for very long periods of time.

2. Quite a few well-known economists, including Adam Smith, Walras, and Irving Fisher, have recognized the capital nature of people skills (Kiker 1966, 481). More recently, in addition to Becker (1964), the research contributions of T.W. Schultz and Jacob Mincer have been important.

3. Among the important contributions to the social capital literature are Bourdieu (1986), Coleman (1988, 1990), Putnam (1993), Fukuyama (1995), and Ostrom (2000).

BIBLIOGRAPHY

Bartik, T. 2011. *Investing in Kids: Early Childhood Programs and Local Economic Development.* Kalamazoo, MI: Upjohn.

Beare, S. 2006. *50 Secrets of the World's Longest Living People.* New York: Marlowe.

Becker, G.S. 1964. *Human Capital: A Theoretical and Empirical Analysis with Special Reference to Education.* New York: National Bureau of Economic Research.

Bourdieu, P. 1986. "The Forms of Capital." In *Handbook of Theory and Research for the Sociology of Education*, ed. J.G. Richardson, 241–258. New York: Greenwood Press.

Caballero, B., and B.M. Popkin. 2002. *The Nutrition Transition: Diet and Disease in the Developing World.* Amsterdam: Academic Press.

Carneiro, P., and J.J. Heckman. 2003. "Human Capital Policy." In *Inequality in America: What Role for Human Capital Policies?* ed. J.J. Heckman and A.B. Krueger, 77–239. Cambridge, MA: MIT Press.

Coleman, J.S. 1988. "Social Capital in the Creation of Human Capital." *American Journal of Sociology* 94: S95–S120.

———. 1990. *Foundations of Social Theory.* Cambridge, MA: Belknap Press.

Cunha, F., and J.J. Heckman. 2007. "The Technology of Skill Formation." *American Economic Review* 97(2): 31–47.

Duncan, G.J., and K. Magnuson. 2004. "Individual and Parent-Based Intervention Strategies for Promoting Human Capital and Positive Behavior." In *Human Development Across Lives and Generations*, ed. P.L. Chase-Landsdale, K. Kiernan, and R.J. Friedman, 93–135. Cambridge: Cambridge University Press.

Finkelstein, E.A., and L. Zuckerman. 2008. *The Fattening of America: How the Economy Makes Us Fat, If It Matters, and What to Do About It.* New York: John Wiley.

Fukuyama, F. 1995. "Social Capital and the Global Economy." *Foreign Affairs* 74, no. 5: 89–103.

Goleman, D. 1994. *Emotional Intelligence.* New York: Bantam Books.

————. 1998. *Working with Emotional Intelligence*. New York: Bantam Books.

Heckman, J.J., et al. 2010. "The Rate of Return to the High Scope Perry Preschool Program." *Journal of Public Economics* 94: 114–128.

Heckman, J.J., J. Stixrud, and S. Urzua. 2006. "The Effects of Cognitive and Noncognitive Abilities on Labor Market Outcomes and Social Behavior." NBER Working Paper 1, January. Cambridge, MA: National Bureau of Economic Research.

Hyman, M. 2006. *UltraMetabolism: The Simple Plan for Automatic Weight Loss*. New York: Atria Books.

Jackson, R.J. 2012. *Designing Healthy Communities*. San Francisco: Jossey-Bass.

Kessler, D.A. 2009. *The End of Overeating: Taking Control of the Insatiable American Appetite*. New York: Rodale.

Kiker, B.F. 1966. "The Historical Roots of the Concept of Human Capital." *Journal of Political Economy* 74, no. 5: 481–499.

Leibenstein, H. 1976. *Beyond Economic Man: A New Foundation for Microeconomics*. Cambridge, MA: Harvard University Press.

Motoko, Rich. 2013. "In Alabama, A Model for Obama's Push to Expand Preschool." *New York Times*, February 14.

Ostrom, E. 2000. "Social Capital: A Fad or a Fundamental Concept?" In *Social Capital: A Multifaceted Perspective*, ed. P. Dasgupta and I. Serageldin, 172–214. Washington, DC: World Bank.

Putnam, R.D. 1993. *Making Democracy Work: Civic Traditions in Modern Italy*. Princeton, NJ: Princeton University Press.

Taubes, Gary. 2007. *Good Calories, Bad Calories: Challenging the Conventional Wisdom on Diet, Weight Control, and Disease*. New York: Alfred A. Knopf.

Tomer, J.F. 2003. "Personal Capital and Emotional Intelligence: An Increasingly Important Intangible Source of Economic Growth." *Eastern Economic Journal* 29, no. 3: 453–470.

————. 2006. "Organizational Capital and Personal Capital: The Role of Intangible Capital Formation in the Economy." In *Handbook of Contemporary Behavioral Economics: Foundations and Developments*, ed. M. Altman, 257–274. Armonk, NY: M.E. Sharpe.

————. 2008. *Intangible Capital: Its Contribution to Economic Growth, Well-Being and Rationality*. Cheltenham, UK: Edward Elgar.

————. 2011a. "Enduring Happiness: Integrating the Hedonic and Eudaimonic Approaches." *Journal of Socio-Economics* 40, 530–537.

————. 2011b. "What Causes Obesity? And Why Has It Grown So Much?" *Challenge* 54, no. 4: 22–49.

————. 2013. "Stemming the Tide of Obesity: What Needs to Happen." *Journal of Socio-Economics* 42: 88–98.

About the Editors and Contributors

Richard P.F. Holt is a professor of economics at Southern Oregon University. He has authored, coauthored, and edited a number of books, two of which were named a *Choice* Outstanding Academic Book Title for the years 2005 and 2010. He has also published more than sixty articles and book reviews in a variety of academic journals, along with serving on different editorial boards. He is presently editing a volume of letters by John Kenneth Galbraith for Cambridge University Press and writing a book on the political times and friendship of William F. Buckley, Jr. and John Kenneth Galbraith.

Daphne T. Greenwood is a professor of economics and director of the Colorado Center for Policy Studies at the University of Colorado, Colorado Springs. She has written numerous book chapters, journal articles, and policy papers, as well as coauthored *Local Economic Development for the 21st Century*—a *Choice* Outstanding Academic Book Title. She has been a visiting scholar at the Institute for Research of Poverty at the University of Wisconsin in Madison and the Office of Tax Analysis in the US Department of the Treasury, Honors Professor at the US Naval Academy, and an economist with Esmark Inc. She also served on the editorial board of the *Journal of Economic Issues* and the *Review of Income and Wealth* and was elected twice to the Colorado House of Representatives.

Bert M. Azizoglu is a doctoral student in public and urban policy at The New School in New York City. His dissertation focuses on the interaction between financial and labor markets, in particular corporate governance, household debt, and income distribution.

David Colander is College Professor at Middlebury College. In 2001–2002 he was the Kelly Professor of Distinguished Teaching at Princeton University. He has authored, coauthored, or edited more than 40 books and 150 articles on a wide range of topics. His books have been translated into a number of different languages. He has been president of both the Eastern Economic Association and the History of Economic Thought Society and is, or has been, on the editorial boards of numerous journals, including *Journal of Economic Perspectives* and *Journal of Economic Education.*

Selçuk Eren is a research scholar working on the Levy Institute Measure of Economic Well-Being within the Distribution of Income and Wealth program at Levy Economics Institute of Bard College. He received his PhD in economics from Stony Brook University in 2006.

Robert H. Frank is the Henrietta Johnson Louis Professor of Management and Professor of Economics at Cornell's Johnson Graduate School of Management and the codirector of the Paduano Seminar in business ethics at NYU's Stern School of Business. His "Economic View" column appears monthly in the *New York Times.* He is a Distinguished Senior Fellow at Demos. His papers have appeared in the *American Economic Review, Econometrica, Journal of Political Economy,* and other leading professional journals. His books include *Choosing the Right Pond, Passions Within Reason, Microeconomics and Behavior, Principles of Economics* (with Ben Bernanke), *Luxury Fever, Falling Behind, The Economic Naturalist,* and *The Darwin Economy.*

David R. Howell is a professor and director of the doctoral program in public and urban policy at The New School in New York City. His recent publications have examined the effects of labor market institutions and social policy on patterns of unemployment in Europe and the United States, the employment effects of unemployment benefits, evidence for tradeoffs between inequality and unemployment, and the measurement of unemployment and underemployment.

Paul J. Kozlowski is professor emeritus of business economics and finance and a former research associate at the Urban Affairs Center, the University of Toledo. He was a senior economist at the W.E. Upjohn Institute for Employment Research and past president of the Mid-Continent Regional Science Association. He has served on the editorial boards of the *Journal of Regional Analysis and Policy* and the *Mid-American Journal of Business.* In addition to being published in a number of economics journals, his research has been published by the National Governors' Association, the Decision Sciences Institute, and the Association for University Business and Economic Research.

Thomas Masterson is director of applied micromodeling and a research scholar working on the Levy Institute Measure of Economic Well-Being; the Levy Institute Measure of Time and Income Poverty; and the Inequality Impact Assessment model in the Distribution of Income and Wealth program at Levy Economics Institute of Bard College. He received his PhD from the University of Massachusetts Amherst in 2005.

Emily Northrop is an associate professor of economics at Southwestern University in Georgetown, Texas. Her current research includes critiques of the conventional introductory economics course.

Anna Okatenko is a research associate at the Centre for Research and Analysis of Migration located in the Department of Economics at University College London. Her main research interests are labor economics, migration studies, and applied econometrics. Her most recent work, coauthored with Christian Dustmann, is "Out-migration, Wealth Constraints, and the Quality of Local Amenities" (CReAM Discussion Paper 13/13).

Robert Pollin is a professor of economics at the University of Massachusetts Amherst and founding codirector of its Political Economy Research Institute.

Thomas Michael Power is a research professor and professor emeritus in the Economics Department of the University of Montana, with which he has been associated since 1968. He served as chair of the economics department for thirty of those years. He received his PhD from Princeton University. He is the author of six books, two dozen book chapters, and more than 100 articles and reports in the fields of natural resource and regional economics.

Steven Pressman is a professor of economics and finance at Monmouth University in West Long Branch, New Jersey. He is North American editor of the *Review of Political Economy*, associate editor and book review editor of the *Eastern Economic Journal*, and treasurer of the Eastern Economic Association. He has published more than 150 articles in refereed journals and as book chapters and has authored or edited sixteen books, including *A New Guide to Post-Keynesian Economics*, *Alternative Theories of the State*, and *50 Major Economists*, third edition, which has been translated into five languages.

Robert H. Scott III is an associate professor of economics at Monmouth University in West Long Branch, New Jersey. His research interests include credit cards, consumer debt, financial literacy, and Kenneth Boulding.

Steven Spirn holds a PhD from the University of Illinois–School of Labor and Employment Relations. He has a JD degree with a labor law concentration from the University of Toledo Law School and served thirty-five years as labor relations consultant to public jurisdictions. He is a retired professor of labor relations, College of Business, University of Toledo.

John Tomer is an emeritus professor of economics at Manhattan College in Riverdale, New York. He is a founding member and past president of the Society for the Advancement of Behavioral Economics. From 2001 to 2012, he was coeditor of the *Journal of Socio-Economics*.

Edward N. Wolff is professor of economics at New York University. He is also a research associate at the National Bureau of Economic Research and is on the editorial board of *Economic Systems Research, Journal of Economic Inequality, Journal of Socio-Economics,* and *Review of Income and Wealth.* He served as managing editor of the *Review of Income and Wealth* from 1987 to 2004 and was a senior scholar at the Levy Economics Institute of Bard College (1999–2011); a visiting scholar at the Russell Sage Foundation (2003–2004); president of the Eastern Economics Association (2002–2003); a council member of the International Input-Output Association (1995–2003); and a council member of the International Association for Research in Income and Wealth (1987–2012).

Ajit Zacharias is director of the research program on Distribution of Income and Wealth at the Levy Economics Institute of Bard College. His research focuses mainly on economic measurement and political economy of inequality and deprivation. He holds an MA from the University of Bombay and a PhD from the New School for Social Research.

Index